Raising Your Child in Washington

A Guide for the Growing Years

What Parents are Saying about:
Raising Your Child in Washington

"I'll put this book right next to my Dr. Spock and Penelope Leach. What a terrific local reference book."
—Stephanie W. Havenstein

"As the mother of three active sons, two of whom need specialized medical care, I found this book to be an excellent guide in leading me to the experts."   —Jan Simmons Smith

"This book makes a perfect shower gift. First-time mothers as well as those having a second or third child will find this book helpful. The shopping tips are fantastic."   —Robin Pollock

"The information contained in Raising Your Child in Washington is presented in a format that is easy to read and understand. It is a great resource for parents in the Washington area."
—Ann Metz

What the Experts are Saying about:
Raising Your Child in Washington

"With contributions from leading authorities like Dr. Larry Silver, an acknowledged expert in Attention Deficit Disorder, this book fills a longstanding gap for area parents."
—Joseph R. Novello, M.D.,
Professor of Psychiatry and Pediatrics,
Georgetown University School of Medicine

"A wonderful resource for Washington parents. The book is full of good advice on serious subjects and offers great ideas on having fun with your family."
—Doreen Gentzler, WRC-TV News Anchor
and mother of two

"Prerequisite reading for anyone dealing with children in the Washington area."
—Paul E. Herman, Head
St. Albans Lower School

Raising Your Child in Washington

A Guide for the Growing Years

Roberta Gottesman, Editor
Deborah Benke, Associate Editor
Roberta Masters, Assistant Editor

ACKNOWLEDGMENTS

We would like to thank the following people for their invaluable contributions to this book:

Susan Douglas
Dunya Hecht
Marylou Hoeman
Jennifer Bryant
Jennafer D'Alvia
Judi Sweeney
Jerilyn Watson
and
Alane K. Ludin, the very best layout artist in town

To order this book, call or write:
Piccolo Press, 901 King Street, Suite 102
Alexandria, VA 22314
Telephone: 703-519-0376 Fax 703-836-2349

ISBN 0-9631756-2-9
Raising Your Child in Washington: a Guide for the Growing Years/ Roberta Gottesman, editor, Deborah Benke, associate editor

Printed and bound by Bookcrafters
Design and layout by Kodiak Design
Cover design by Kodiak Design

Please be advised:

Although every effort has been made to research all sources to ensure accuracy and completeness of the information contained in this book, programs and telephone numbers change, people move and the unexpected happens. Therefore Piccolo Press assumes no responsibility for errors, inaccuracies, omissions or any other inconsistency herein. The opinions expressed in this book are solely those of the authors. The resources listed in this book are informational and not to be taken as an endorsement by the publisher.

Table of Contents

Chapter 3   Child Care
by Ann Byrne, M.Ed. **131**
and Celia Boykin, M.A.

Chapter 4   Education
159

Chapter 5   Summertime
219

Chapter 6   Creative Arts
239

Chapter 7 Savvy Shopping by Mindy Bailin **289**

Chapter 8 Family Togetherness **311**

Appendices 363

Index 387

Foreward

I have been the editor of *Washington Parent* for the last seven years. During that time, I have been privileged to work with Washington's leading experts in the fields of health, education, psychiatry, psychology, social work, childcare, family development and many other areas. I also have come in contact with some of the finest local writers and editors. Issue after issue, these distinguished women and men share their wisdom in *Washington Parent*.

Many times I have dreamed of publishing a book which would be a resource for parents in our metropolitan area. However, I considered this a pipe dream, because I am all too aware what a job it would be to undertake such a project. When Roberta Gottesman called me and said she would like to discuss the possibility of collaborating on a book, I needed no arm twisting.

From the start, it was an easy relationship with mutual respect for one another's role. Throughout the months of calls, faxes and meetings, a spirit of friendship and cooperation prevailed. Consequently, the book came together beautifully and quickly. It is a product of which we both are extremely proud. I am grateful to Roberta and Piccolo Press for the vote of confidence in *Washington Parent*.

To parents in the Washington area, I hope that this joint effort will be a valuable resource and guide through the "growing years." Read, use and enjoy!

Deborah Benke
Editor, *Washington Parent*

Preface

Many young parents come to the Washington metropolitan area to further their careers, only to find that this means raising their children away from extended family and friends, establishing traditions, finding ways of bonding as a family and providing the *best* upbringing for their children all without help from those they trust most! Doing this while trying to stay on the frantic merry-go-round that we call Washington is no easy task.

Every day questions come to mind about child-rearing that need immediate answers—and there is often no close friend or relative to ask. This can be frustrating at best and often terrifying, especially to first-time parents. The issues that most concern area parents run the gamut from serious topics like how to find the best medical care or private schools, to the sublime like how to locate the best performances for children or how to develop a child's special creativity. Parents are also concerned with practical issues like where to find the best bargains in clothing and toys.

To help new parents, as well as the rest of us who are struggling to provide the best for our children, we contacted 45 of the area's leading experts. We asked them for the information and resources we would need to answer questions as would an expert. For example, how would a well-known pedodontist go about selecting a good dentist, or how would a leading educational consultant go about choosing a private school? We have tried to capture their expertise and recommendations just as if we were chatting with them to seek their advice.

You will find two sets of questions after each article. The first appears under an icon depicting Rodin's Thinker. These are questions to ask yourself about your child and the issue at hand. They will help you assess your child's personality, situation and needs, as well as those of the rest of family.

The other set, which appears under a question mark icon, are questions to use when interviewing professionals: doctors, childcare providers, school administrators, music teachers, etc. This section is designed to elicit important information from the person or entity whose services you are seeking so that you can determine whether your needs will be met.

Following each article you will find a treasure chest icon, our symbol for an extensive listing of resources around the Beltway. A star icon is used for resources we have found for children with special needs.

We were fortunate to collaborate on this project with the 13-year-old *Washington Parent*, the metropolitan area's leading paper for parents. With the assistance of Editor Deborah Benke, we were able to determine the most perplexing questions facing today's parents and secure the most respected leaders in their fields to provide the answers.

We hope this book, with its expert advice and extensive local resources, will make life a little easier and a lot more fun for parents in the metropolitan area.

Roberta Gottesman
Editor

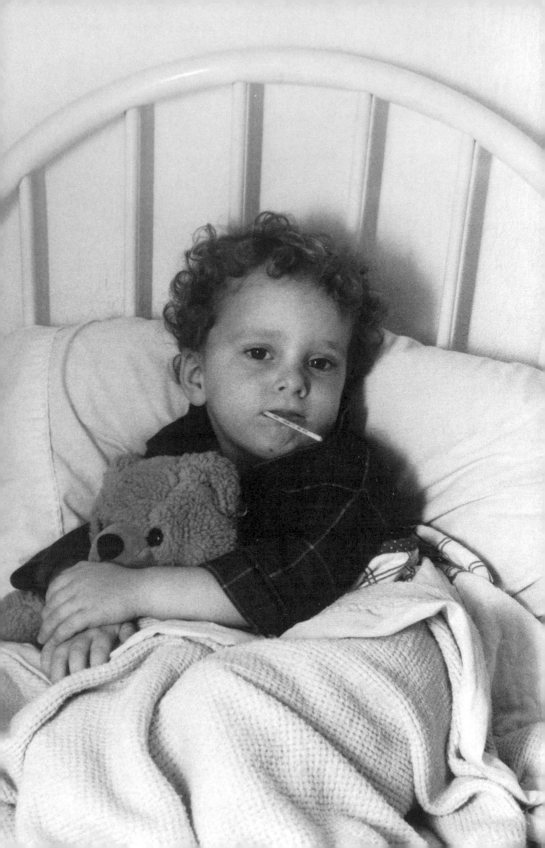

Medical Care

One of the most important decisions parents face is how to best provide for their children's health. And, as if this were not difficult enough, those of us who live in the Washington area often face an even greater challenge: grandma and other extended family members live hundreds of miles away and are not around to offer advice and answer our questions.

Corrine and David, newlyweds who come from different parts of the country, are typical. They just discovered that Corrine is expecting and are ecstatic, but a bit overwhelmed. Corrine has said, "We had no idea it was so complicated to have a baby. For one thing, we're trying to find the best obstetrical and pediatric care, but first we've got to determine the difference between HMOs and PPOs and fee-for-service care to figure out which would be best."

"It reminds me of the old riddle of which comes first, the chicken or the egg?" adds Corrine. "I think we have to select a health plan before we can decide if we want a traditional hospital delivery or a birthing center. And we need to select an obstetrician, make up our minds about whether we want to take childbirth classes, how to nurse the baby, and . . ."

Once their child has arrived, their health concerns will broaden. What can be done to identify and deal with physical, emotional and developmental problems as a baby becomes a full-fledged child? Can a child's dental development be improved? Can a child be protected from lasting trauma if she or he has to go to the hospital?

How can you choose the right orthodontist, ophthalmologist and other specialists? What is the right way to raise a healthy, happy eater?

Answers to these questions, and many others, can be found in the following pages.

Photo by Kids by Kim - Kim Nye Zeiss

How to Find the Right Health Plan for Your Family

by John Boyer, Ph.D.

There is no question that without health insurance, a single, serious medical illness or injury can result in a family's financial ruin. Thus, most people today maintain some kind of health coverage. But choosing the "right" type and extent of protection can be a daunting task, and for families which include members with special health care needs, the problem can be even more difficult. Of major importance to most of us is the cost of health care, but serious consideration must also be given to a host of other factors, such as the comprehensiveness and limits of the benefits offered, the freedom with which providers of health services can be chosen, and where care can be obtained. The following is a discussion of the most important considerations in choosing health coverage, and some basic guidelines to help you become a better informed consumer.

Types of Coverage

The way health care is delivered and financed in the U.S. has changed dramatically during the 20th century. There has been significant growth in the number of medical specialists, physicians practicing in groups and corporations engaged in the delivery of health services, as well as in the proliferation of public programs, laws and regulations affecting how people obtain and pay for care. Many of these changes can be attributed to consumer demand for more and better care, and to efforts on the part of payers to curb the spiraling costs. We know that health care reform has been the subject of great national debate and that further change in our health care system can be expected.

Today there are many options available for health coverage ranging from traditional indemnity, fee-for-service plans to a variety of managed health care alternatives. Two of the most common managed care plans are the Health Maintenance Organization (HMO) and the Preferred Provider Organization (PPO). The most important consideration when choosing among the various types of coverage is, all else being equal, the extent to which you are willing to relinquish some control over choosing a provider to obtain lower out-of-pocket costs.

John F. Boyer, Ph.D., is a Captain in the U.S. Navy Nurse Corps, now assigned as Director, Health Services Financing Policy, in the Office of the Assistant Secretary of Defense (Health Affairs).

Traditional fee-for-service plans generally allow the greatest freedom in choosing physicians and hospitals. But usually, in addition to requiring participants in the plan to find their own providers, they involve additional paperwork and higher costs. If you enroll in an HMO, you agree to receive all of your care from a specified set of providers, and at specified locations, in return for substantially reduced costs and usually no paperwork. PPOs are considered to be in between fee-for-service plans and HMOs, in that most PPOs allow greater flexibility in obtaining care than is allowed by HMOs, and they also offer reduced costs if care is obtained from a specified group of providers. Cost reductions, however, usually are not as substantial as in HMOs.

Many HMOs rely heavily on non-physician providers such as nurse practitioners and physician's assistants to provide routine outpatient care. Typically, in HMOs, patients are admitted to hospitals less frequently than those in fee-for-service plans and, when they are, they stay there for a shorter period of time. Again, it's important to remember that in an HMO you are limited in your choice of doctor. If you already have a private physician, you may have to change if you join an HMO, and if you become seriously ill and want to go to a nationally recognized center for specialty care, you may not be able to do so.

On the positive side, HMOs generally tend to stress preventive treatment and health education; they assure timely access to health care providers for all types of care; and they eliminate the possibility that a physician will charge more than the plan will reimburse for a particular procedure.

Since studies have shown no difference in medical outcomes among managed care delivery systems and traditional practice plans, the decision among types of health coverage becomes one of personal choice. Your decision probably will be based on personal experience, cost, convenience and the extent to which you desire freedom of choice.

Cost

Since most of us do not know in advance what medical expenses we will incur during any given time, there is no way we can be certain that the plan we choose will result in the lowest possible cost. Therefore, in choosing health coverage we must gamble to some extent—just as we do with most other types of insurance. Of course, there are a number of features in many plans that are obvious cost concerns such as premiums, deductibles and co-payments. Consideration of certain other known circumstances, however, also can lead to a better decision relative to cost.

First of all, you should take stock of your family's general health status. If a family member has a known condition such as diabetes or cystic fibrosis, for example, you can expect to use certain types of care more extensively than others. A couple planning to have a baby can expect a significant medical expense, and families with histories of cancer or heart disease, or in which there are heavy smokers or drinkers, may also require more health care than others.

After evaluating the general health status of your family, you should decide on the amount of risk you are willing (and able) to assume. If you want to be certain that your out-of-pocket expenditures are kept to a minimum, you may want to select a plan that is designed for families with higher than average medical bills. Such plans offer somewhat reduced risk, but usually cost a little more. On the other hand, if your family is reasonably healthy, and you do not anticipate using many medical services, your primary reason for obtaining coverage may be solely to protect against major financial catastrophe. In that case, you may wish to look for a plan that covers only the most expensive procedures or situations. That is, you would approach coverage selection by comparing plans on the basis of total potential financial risk, rather than on average cost.

Another important cost consideration in choosing a health plan is the maximum dollar amount for which you will be held responsible before the plan begins to cover all of the cost of care. Most plans today have dollar limits on the hospital, physician and other related expenses you must pay each year. Usually, less expensive plans have higher limits. There is wide variation among plans in these "caps," and hence, differences in comparative costs can be very dramatic. One concern of particular importance for many families is the limit on prescription drug costs. Because pharmaceuticals required in the treatment of many disorders can cost as much as $10,000 or more per year, plans which do not limit the amount families must pay for prescription drugs can leave families vulnerable to high out-of-pocket expenses. Other costs not capped in many plans are those incurred for dental care and mental health treatment. While many plans offer coverage in these areas, benefits and patient cost-shares vary dramatically. Families that expect to require such services should examine carefully the relevant provisions of any plan before a final choice is made.

If you have health coverage from two or more sources, you should also pay special attention to selecting the best combination for your family. Thought must be given to such factors as the extent to which the coverages are complementary rather than duplicative, as well as the implications for medical expense deductions on tax returns. If yours is a family with two wage earners, you may wish to explore with an employer the possibility of exchanging health coverage for other benefits or a higher salary.

Benefit Coverage and Limitations

Comparing various plans on the basis of average costs can be quite informative, but for most families, cost is only one consideration in choosing health coverage. Particularly for those families with special medical needs, or those who anticipate extensive use of a certain type of services, careful examination of specific benefits and limitations should be undertaken. For example, a couple planning to have a baby should check the extent to which prenatal, delivery and postpartum services are covered and are readily accessible. How many board-certified obstetricians are employed by the plan? What facilities are available, such as specific hospitals or birthing centers? What capabilities does the plan offer relative to high-risk cases? What provisions are established for emergencies? What followup services are offered?

For families that anticipate the need for psychiatric care, an examination of benefits and limitations is especially important. Almost all plans have a stringent limit on visits to psychiatrists, psychologists and other mental health professionals such as clinical social workers. Most plans cover a number of outpatient visits (usually 10 to 20), but often, there may be a separate deductible for mental health care. Additionally, the co-payment on mental health visits is often higher than that for other types of care. Most plans also treat inpatient mental health treatment somewhat differently than medical-surgical care, and almost always, there are special provisions for treatment of alcoholism and drug abuse. Because mental health services are often comparatively longer term, and hence, more expensive, many plans have sharply reduced mental health coverage. So again, a careful assessment of the benefit and limitations in this area is advisable for any family that anticipates requiring such services.

Another benefit to check when comparing plans is coverage for routine physical exams. Although most plans provide some coverage in this regard (especially well-baby checkups, childhood examinations and immunizations), there is growing variability in the extent to which plans pay for routine exams. Some pay for such examinations in full; many pay for adult exams only when you are ill. Also, of importance to women, is the degree to which a plan covers screening exams such as mammograms and Pap smears.

Other benefit areas of common concern are the extent to which a plan covers services of non-physician providers such as chiropractors, certain types of supplies such as those needed by diabetics, dental care, prescription drugs and blood transfusions. For any plan you are considering, take special note of provisions for "preexisting conditions." Some plans do not provide (or significantly limit) coverage for services or treatment of medical problems identified prior to joining the plan, regardless of their medical necessity.

While only a few benefit areas have been highlighted, there may be many others that are important for you to consider when choosing a health plan. The best advice is that when looking at plan costs and benefits, families should first carefully assess their own needs and circumstances, consider past medical experience and expense and thoughtfully evaluate possible future medical care requirements.

Comparing Quality of Care Among Plans

Although most of us are not able to fully evaluate the technical expertise of the medical and support staff in a health plan, there is usually information available to make some determination of the general quality of care you can expect. Since that quality is largely dependent on your primary care physician, a review of the general training and experience of a plan's staff can be useful. For example, one question to ask is the percentage of the plan's physicians that are board certified in their specialties. Board certification is not a guarantee, but it can be an important indicator of quality.

Other indicators of plan performance and quality include physician turnover rate (how frequently physicians terminate their affiliation with a plan), the ratio of primary care physicians to specialists and the number of plan members per physician. These latter factors are important because they relate to how easily you might be able to secure appointments on a routine basis and for specialty care.

As many patient-doctor relationships have become less personal, more people are questioning the economic incentives physicians may have in making medical decisions. Compensation systems in HMOs vary a great deal, and some argue that the way physicians are paid affects the style in which they deliver care. Some plans pay primary care physicians a salary; some pay on a "capitation" basis (i.e., a certain dollar amount per month per patient regardless of how much care each patient receives); some pay on a fee-for-service basis; and others use a combination of approaches which create a variety of incentives. A brief conversation with a few plan physicians to determine their perceptions of pressures generated by their compensation system can provide important information about the quality of care you can expect to receive.

In terms of hospitals, you should look at the general reputation of the facility in the community. Is the institution recognized as a "center of excellence" for certain types of care? Do they have state-of-the-art equipment? Is the facility adequately staffed with qualified nursing personnel? What are typical waiting times in the emergency room? In clinics? What are the mortality rates for various procedures and how many operations and procedures are performed each month or year? How comprehensive are the services offered? What accommodations do they offer parents when a child must be hospitalized? Pursuing answers to questions such as these from neighbors, friends and the institutions themselves can be very useful in reaching a decision about a health plan.

Making a Choice

As the time approaches when you must reach a decision about health coverage, you may be overwhelmed with details and confused by the many factors you must consider. But don't despair. Using the information discussed above regarding costs, benefits and quality, should enable you to narrow your choices to two or three plans. Carefully read the brochure describing each plan and focus on the differences between them—then prioritize them. As you sort out the features of the plans that are most important to you and your family, you probably will begin with some of the fundamental questions already mentioned. To help reduce expenses, are you willing to give up your family doctor (if necessary) and join an HMO? Will anyone in your family be needing surgery during the next year, or are you planning on having a baby? Are there any particular benefits you especially need or expect to be using a lot? Can you afford to pay a higher premium to avoid more risk? With which of the hospitals in your local area are you most familiar, and what exactly do you know about them?

Gathering sufficient information about various health plans to make an informed decision can, itself, be a difficult task. Help is available, however, from a number of sources. Many employers have health benefits advisors who can guide you through the maze of available plans, and there are many professional organizations and consumer advocacy groups ready and willing to help you with these decisions. Just remember, the time and thought invested in finding out all you can about various plans can help you avoid the substantial financial burden and mental anguish commonly experienced by those consumers who choose poorly because they are uninformed.

Questions to ask yourself

1. Do we need coverage for special health care needs? Will we have higher than average medical bills based on our family history?
2. Do we need to find a plan with special benefits, with no caps on prescription drugs, or one with mental health or dental care coverage?
3. Is it most important for us to have freedom to choose our health care provider, or will we be comfortable seeing doctors provided by a health plan? How important is it to have a health provider close to our home?
4. Is it important to us to have comprehensive benefits, or is it of greater importance to limit our benefits to save money on our insurance plan?
5. Would we be more comfortable with an HMO, a PPO or a traditional fee for service plan, weighing the extent to which we are willing to relinquish some control over choosing a provider in exchange for lower out-of-pocket costs?
6. Do we have health coverage from two sources? Do they complement and not duplicate each other?
7. What is the reputation in the community of the hospital used by the health plan we are considering? Does it offer state-of-the-art care and facilities?

? Questions to ask the administrators

1. Which board-certified hospitals and doctors are in the plan? What percentage of physicians are board certified? What is the turnover rate for physicians and specialists?
2. What are dollar limits on hospital coverage and doctors? What are the maximum dollar amounts for which we will be held responsible before the plan begins to cover all of the costs of care?
3. What are the "caps" (limitations) on prescription drugs and other non-physician services and providers?
4. What are the provisions concerning pre-existing conditions?
5. What is the plan's ratio of patients to doctors? Can I make an appointment and see a doctor on the same day?
6. Are physicians on salary, or are they paid a certain amount based on the number of patients they see?
7. What specific benefits and limitations are there on services we need: prenatal, delivery, postpartum?
8. What provisions are there for local or out-of-town emergencies?
9. What coverage is available for routine physical exams, and well-baby checkups? Are they paid for in full or in part?

Resource

CHECKBOOK'S Guide to Health Insurance Plans for Federal Employees, 16th Edition. Washington, DC: The Center for the Study of Services, 1994. This booklet rates every health insurance plan available to Federal employees in the United States, both fee-for-service plans and nearly 400 HMOs.

★ Special Needs

Health Insurance Association of America
1025 Connecticut Ave. NW
Washington, DC 20036-3998
202 223 7796
Provides informational publications on health insurance.

Medicaid Source Book/Stock # 052-070-06848-5
Superintendent of Documents
US Printing Office
Washington, DC 20402
202-783-3238
Medicaid often serves as the primary health insurer for children with disabilities. The Source Book, a major key to obtaining services for children with disabilities, addresses early periodic screening, diagnosis and treatment programs. Identifies medical

needs which qualify for Medicaid coverage. Also available in
public and university libraries.

Richard Epstein c/o
Exceptional Parent Magazine
209 Harvard Street, Suite 303
Brookline, MA 02146
FAX: 617-730-8742
Health insurance expert and columnist who answers health coverage
questions.

How To Choose An Obstetrician

by Charles Greenhouse, M.D., F. A.C.O.G.

Congratulations, you're pregnant! You're excited, nervous—and in need of an obstetrician. You know this is a very important medical decision, but how do you choose the right doctor? Before you start looking at the many issues that will help you decide on your physician, think about who you are. Be certain you understand your own temperament and expectations.

Examine Your Needs

Do you have high blood pressure, medical concerns or a family history of difficult pregnancies or genetic problems? Are you over 35? Women in these groups must be monitored more closely throughout their pregnancies. Do you work full time and plan to continue as long as possible into your pregnancy? Do you have other children? The location of your obstetrician's office and flexibility of office hours may be very important to you. How do you communicate with doctors? Are you a passive patient who prefers that your physician make the decisions? Or do you ask questions, want detailed answers and expect to be thoroughly involved in the management of your health?

Do you have definite ideas about childbirth? Would you prefer a practice that includes the father-to-be? Whether you are changing doctors or looking for your first obstetrician, it is important to understand any circumstances that make your needs and pregnancies unique.

In looking for an ob-gyn, ask what other services they offer. A number of doctors now provide testing as well as other services within their own practice. Do they offer childbirth education classes? Is there someone to answer questions that may arise between visits? Finding a practice that offers a broad range of services may be the best way for you to address current issues as well as those that will arise during your pregnancy.

Finding a Doctor

In looking for an ob-gyn, it is most important to find someone with whom you feel comfortable. Is the doctor warm and empathic? Does he or

Dr. Greenhouse is presently President and Chairman of the Maryland Ob-Gyn I.P.O. and was recently Chairman of the Peer Review Committee of the Maryland Ob-Gyn Society. An experienced, board-certified obstetrician-gynecologist who is extremely interested in communicating with his patients, he is currently in a group private practice in Silver Spring, Maryland.

she listen to your questions without interrupting and answer them infor-
matively and patiently?

If you already have a good relationship with a gynecologist who is an
ob-gyn, schedule an appointment to discuss any issues specifically related to your expectations of an obstetrician. If your gynecologist does not
practice obstetrics, ask for a recommendation. Your doctor may be able
to direct you to someone with a similar approach, with whom you are
likely to establish good rapport.

Ask the doctor to describe a normal pregnancy, labor and delivery.
What is his or her opinion on prenatal testing, childbirth education classes,
pain relief, episiotomies, the use of birthing rooms, breastfeeding? Is the
father welcome at office visits, in the labor room and during delivery?

Questions may arise that are not directly related to your pregnancy.
One patient who always took aspirin for a sinus headache wondered what
to do now that she was pregnant. Her best friend said to take only ac-
etaminophen, her mother said to take nothing. Someone in your ob-gyn's
practice should be available to respond quickly and knowledgeably to
this type of question and to any other concerns you may have.

Did you have a previous delivery by Cesarean section? Ask the doctor whether you could be a candidate for a vaginal delivery this time. If
you do need a Cesarean, what kind of anesthesia might be used? What
type of incision will be done? What will be your limitations after the delivery? Having a Cesarean should not preclude your partner from being
present during the birth, the baby staying in your room or siblings coming for visits. What are the ob-gyn's feelings about this? Ask the doctor
about the rate of Cesareans both in his or her practice and at the hospital.
Discuss situations in which your physician would do a C-section, as well
as anything he or she does to avoid them if possible.

Word-of-mouth is the most common means of finding a new physician. Ask for recommendations from family and friends who share your
perspectives on pregnancy and childbirth. Were they satisfied with the
relationship throughout the entire time? Was a doctor or nurse available
to answer questions between visits? Were they seen promptly for scheduled appointments? Were there things their doctors did not discuss that
came as a surprise during labor or delivery?

Prologue-Dial Doctors is a doctor referral service in the Washington
area which helps a consumer choose a provider based on her particular
needs. A computerized data base includes such information as geographic
location, office hours, doctors' credentials, specialties, philosophy of practice and languages spoken. Many hospitals in the area have a referral
service for physicians on their staff. This is especially helpful if you are
aware of a convenient hospital but do not know which doctors are practicing there.

Other resource lists of obstetricians in your community may be obtained by contacting state and county medical societies, local La Leche
League Chapters, the International Childbirth Education Association and
the American Society for Psychoprophylaxis in Obstetrics/Lamaze.

Is the Obstetrician Board Certified?

Inquire about the ob-gyn's professional background and training. While licensed physicians may call themselves specialists, the obstetrician you choose should be certified by the American College of Obstetricians and Gynecologists (ACOG). This indicates that the doctor has completed three to four years of specialized training (a residency) in obstetrics and gynecology after graduating from medical school and has passed a written and oral exam. The initials FACOG signify that the doctor is a Fellow of the American College of Obstetricians and Gynecologists. This association represents the profession and keeps its membership aware of the latest medical advances through periodicals, workshops and continuing education.

To learn more about the background of any obstetricians you are considering, look for the Directory of Medical Specialists, published by the American Board of Medical Specialties, which is available in most library reference sections. Or, contact the American Medical Association Department of Physician Data Services.

Whether you use a referral service or word-of-mouth recommendations, if you have a particular interest in subspecialties such as infertility workups or high-risk pregnancies, be sure to discuss these issues up front so that the doctor you select will most likely have the background to meet your needs or will be prepared to make appropriate referrals.

A Group Practice Can Offer An Umbrella of Services

There is much to be said for the rapport that can be established with your physician when you choose an ob-gyn in a solo practice. But it is also important to examine the umbrella of services that can be provided by a group practice. It is always possible that your own doctor will be unavailable at the time you go into labor. In a solo practice, there will be a covering physician, who you may or may not know, to answer your call. If you have chosen a group practice, you will at some point during your pregnancy meet all the partners.

A group practice is able to offer an umbrella of services which can help see a woman through all aspects of her pregnancy. The doctors often work as a team with their nurses and other members of their staff to provide childbirth preparation classes, fast response to patient phone calls, educational materials, in-office tests and liaison between the practice and community services. Having an early-pregnancy educational program enables the practice to set a tone of openness and communication by outlining a philosophy of care, mapping out the course of normal visits and lab studies, and discussing the discomforts of pregnancy, expected weight gain and the benefits of good nutrition. Focusing on the whole woman and trying to anticipate her needs during the pregnancy can be a convenience and a comfort.

Recent changes in insurance coverage, often allowing no more than two hospital overnights for a vaginal delivery or four for a cesarean section, have forced obstetricians to examine the additional assistance their practices might offer. The nurse/educator on an office staff who makes hospital rounds after babies are delivered is met with enthusiasm and appreciation by patients. She can do some teaching, answer questions and provide emotional support.

Ask the doctor about fees for prenatal care, labor and delivery and lab tests. Be sure to check with your insurance provider about any restrictions in your coverage, especially if you are limited to specific ob-gyn practices. Many offices have a business manager who can help with your paper work and answer insurance questions.

What About the Hospital?

All ob-gyns are associated with specific hospitals. In exploring your choice of doctors, you may have questions about the hospital where you will deliver. What is the setting for labor and delivery? Many hospitals have comfortable birthing rooms where members of the family can be present. What is the level of nursery care? How do they handle premature or multiple births? Does the hospital have a Neonatal Intensive Care Unit in case your baby should need more than regular newborn care? If they are not equipped to handle special circumstances your infant might need to be treated at a different facility.

Is the hospital an educationally oriented institution? Do they offer classes for both the mother and father? Ask about programs for the family, which would include your other children who will soon be big brothers or sisters. Does the hospital have rooming-in?

This can be an advantage not only for early bonding between you and your baby, but also as a means of early intervention in both medical and educational issues. When you and your newborn are together all day and night there is more opportunity for questions that arise about feeding, holding and diapering, to be addressed before you go home. If you do plan to have your baby in your room overnight, ask about security and whether the rooms have doors that you can lock.

Many of your questions about the hospital can be answered in your physician's office, either by your doctor or a member of the staff. Choose your doctor first. A doctor in a progressive practice will most likely be affiliated with a hospital that will meet your particular needs.

Discuss Prenatal Testing

During a normal pregnancy you will see your doctor once a month for the first 28 weeks, every 2 weeks until the 36th week and every week thereafter. You can expect to have routine glucose testing, blood testing and typing and urinalysis. But, if your pregnancy is considered high risk or if there is some indication of a problem, your doctor may recommend other tests to help determine the health of the fetus.

Chorionic villus sampling (CVS) is usually done between the 9th and 12th week of pregnancy and is an early indicator of genetic abnormalities.

Maternal-serum alpha-fetoprotein (MSAFP) screening, performed at about 16 weeks, is a blood test that looks at the level of alpha-fetoprotein, a substance produced by the fetus. Elevated levels may indicate spinal or neural tube defects and further testing will always be recommended.

Amniocentesis is recommended for women over 35, when there is a family history of genetic problems or in situations where other tests indicate an abnormality. This second trimester testing for genetic disorders is done between the 14th and 18th weeks. During the last trimester, amniocentesis may be performed to determine the maturity of the fetus.

Ultrasound (sonogram) is used for different reasons throughout a pregnancy to provide information about fetal size, development, position and movement as well as to locate the placenta, diagnose multiple fetuses and verify the due date.

Nonstress testing is used to evaluate the well-being of the fetus by focusing on fetal heartbeat relative to fetal movement.

Discuss prenatal testing with the obstetricians you are considering. Since some risks have been associated with a few of these tests, you should be prepared to ask your ob-gyn about when and where he or she recommends they be performed. Do you feel that your doctor will help you in weighing risks and benefits if a decision about testing must be made during your pregnancy?

Ask what testing is offered within the ob-gyn practice. Toward the end of their pregnancies some women may need frequent sonograms and nonstress testing. When you are nine months pregnant and wondering if your baby will ever come, traveling back and forth to work and/or managing other children and a household, it could be very comforting to know that your testing can be accomplished with one appointment, one trip. The convenience of this service may also foster a greater sense of communication with your physician, since the follow-through is all within one office.

In looking for your ob-gyn, try to be realistic about your own questions and expectations of the doctors you interview. Have a variety of issues that you ask the ob/gyn to address. A doctor who responds to your initial visit in a pleasant, straightforward manner, who willingly and patiently answers any questions you present and who is aware of and provides for a range of related services, will most likely be professionally and personally responsive to your needs in all the months to come.

 # Questions to ask yourself

1. What kind of patient am I?
2. Do I have any medical conditions which would affect my pregnancy?
3. Do I want my partner included as much as possible during the pregnancy, labor and delivery?
4. Do I want to take childbirth education classes?
5. Would I prefer a solo or a group practice? (This may be dictated by insurance coverage.)

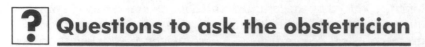

Questions to ask the obstetrician

1. Is he or she board certified as an obstetrician-gynecologist?
2. Does the practice include the father?
3. Does the practice offer other services such as testing and classes?
4. If a group practice, what, if any, subspecialties do the doctors have?
5. With what hospitals is the doctor affiliated?
6. What medical level nursery do the hospitals have?

Resources

Alexandria Medical Society
Physicians Referral Service
101 South Whiting Street, Suite 210; Alexandria, VA 22304
703-341-7758

American Academy of Husband-Coached Childbirth
P.O. Box 5224
Sherman Oaks, CA 91413   818-788-6662

American College of Obstetricians and Gynecologists
409 12th Street SW
Washington, DC 20024-2188 202-638-5577

American Medical Assoc. Dept. of Physician Data Services
515 North State Street
Chicago, IL 60610

American Society for Psychoprophylaxis in Obstetrics/Lamaze
1101 Connecticut Avenue NW, Suite 300
Washington, DC 20036   202-857-1128

Cesarean Prevention Movement
P.O. Box 152 University Station
Syracuse, NY 13210   315-424-1942

Cesarean/Support, Education and Concern, Inc. (C/SEC, Inc.)
10 Speen Street
Framingham, MA 01701   508-820-2760

Holy Cross Hospital
Cross Connect Physicians Referral Service
1500 Forest Glen Road
Silver Spring, MD 20910   301-905-1214

International Childbirth Education Assoc.
P.O. Box 20048
Minneapolis, MN 55420 612-854-8660

Montgomery County Medical Society
Patient Advocacy Referral Service
P.O. Box 5689
Rockville, MD 20855 301-963-3100

Prince George's County Medical Society
Physician Referral Service
6307 Landover Road
Cheverly, MD 20785   301-341-7758

Prologue-Dial Doctors
901 N. Washington Street, Suite 500
Alexandria, VA 22314   1-800-PROLOGU

Get Ready, Get Set, Deliver
What Area Hospitals Offer Expectant Parents

by Michele M. Newman

When many of our mothers were pregnant, 30 and 40 years ago, women learned about childbirth by word of mouth—stories from their mothers, aunts and friends about delivery. Often they checked into the hospital, were sedated and woke up to find themselves with a newborn. Advice on feeding, bathing and caring for their infants was dispensed by relatives and friends.

Hospitals have changed for the better since then. Now they offer childbirth education classes, exercise programs, tours of the hospital's maternity facilities and even help for siblings in dealing with the newcomer to the family. As you get ready for this important time, there are a number of things to consider when you look at the hospital you will use. While hospital policies vary, keep in mind that nothing is absolute. Your doctor's decisions will supersede hospital policy, and your individual labor and delivery will govern what your doctor will—and will not—allow.

Staff

You want to be sure that the hospital has the trained professionals you may need for your delivery. While you may not be able to anticipate the need for an anesthesiologist or a neonatologist, most but not all Washington area hospitals have them on staff. If you think you may need a perinatologist (an obstetrician who specializes in high risk pregnancy), check with the hospital you are considering since few hospitals in this area have them on staff.

The nurse-patient ratio is about 1:2 in most area hospitals for labor and delivery and from 1:4 to 1:6 during the postpartum phase. Some hospitals have the same nurse care for the mother and the baby. Twelve of the area hospitals now offer privileges to midwives.

Your Hospital Experience

One of the most significant changes in hospitals over the past 10 years has been the move to Labor Delivery Recovery rooms (LDRs) or

Michele Newman has written extensively on issues of raising children in today's society. Her work has appeared in most of the Washington area publications for parents and expectant parents. When not otherwise occupied raising her two sons and researching her next article, Ms. Newman researches, writes and edits for Washington Researchers Ltd.

birthing rooms. The majority of Washington area hospitals now use LDRs, where you labor, give birth and then recover, all in one room. Some hospitals also use the traditional, separate labor and delivery rooms but will allow the mother to deliver in the labor room if a birthing room or LDR is not available.

All hospitals allow fathers to be present for the delivery, assuming there are no complications. Many also allow siblings or anyone else the mother wants present if prior arrangements are made but limit the number of people allowed. Some hospitals allow siblings in as long as they have their own care givers or someone other than the father/coach to care for them. If having siblings or others at your delivery is important to you, be sure to talk with your health care provider and ask about hospital policy.

All hospitals have either a regular or intermediate nursery to care for newborns. Only eight have intensive care nurseries. Check with your health care provider to see whether your pregnancy warrants more than a regular nursery.

With shorter hospital stays, whether you have a private or semiprivate room becomes less important. However, if having a private room is important to you, make sure the hospital has an adequate number. Women experiencing complicated births usually have priority for the few private rooms in the maternity wings. While visiting hours for nonfamily members are still restricted at most hospitals, fathers, siblings and grandparents generally have liberal visiting hours.

Be aware that the days of a long hospital stay are over and plan accordingly. The move in the past five years has been to discharge mother and baby as soon as possible after the delivery—sometimes in four to six hours. Depending on what time of day you deliver, you may be allowed to stay one night. This is a matter you should check into carefully—both with the hospital and your insurance provider.

Childbirth Education

Hospitals have an array of both pre- and postnatal classes for expectant parents. Many have brochures detailing their offerings, which include childbirth preparation, sibling classes, exercises classes, infant care and breastfeeding. Some hospitals offer classes for grandparents to assist them in their new roles.

Childbirth education classes typically meet for six to eight weeks. You'll learn about the changes in your body during pregnancy, labor and delivery, fetal development, breathing and relaxation techniques, medications you may want to consider, types of delivery, hospital procedures and postnatal changes. While newborn care and changes in family relationships may be touched upon, most classes emphasize getting you ready for labor and delivery.

You don't have to take childbirth education classes at the hospital where you will deliver. Since the hospital classes usually include a tour of the labor and delivery facilities, if you are taking classes somewhere else, contact your hospital for their tour. (See page 40 for discussion of area childbirth classes.)

Most hospitals have some type of breastfeeding class or support mechanism. While breastfeeding is covered in childbirth education, the one-day hospital seminars go into more detail, discussing the advantages of breastfeeding, providing advice on getting off to a good start, and exploring common problems and concerns for the working mother. Many hospitals now have lactation specialists on staff to support you prior to birth and while you are in the hospital. Some will continue to help after you have been discharged from the hospital.

Many of the hospitals offer a refresher course for women who have previously been through childbirth. These classes are usually of shorter duration and focus on the physical and emotional differences in a second pregnancy. They also cover introducing your first born to the new baby.

Years ago expectant mothers were told not to exert themselves. Now doctors know the importance of good muscle tone for labor and delivery. This has resulted in many hospitals offering prenatal exercise classes. Participation will require your doctor's permission and will focus on stretching and toning. You will also find postnatal classes, designed to help you get back in shape after the baby is born.

 Resources

For further information on the types of resources area hospitals provide, call the following obstetric departments:

Alexandria Hospital	703-504-3000
Arlington Hospital	703-558-5000
DC General Hospital	202-675-5288
Fair Oaks Hospital	703-698-3106
Fairfax Hospital	703-204-6000
George Washington Univ. Hospital	202-994-4357
Georgetown University Hospital	202-687-8531
Greater Laurel-Beltsville Hospital	301-725-4300
Greater SE Community Hospital	202-574-6591
Holy Cross Hospital	301-905-1201
Howard University Hospital	202-865-1161
Loudoun Memorial Hospital	703-771-2862
Montgomery General Hospital	301-774-8700
Mount Vernon Hospital	703-664-7000
Potomac Hospital	703-670-1593
Prince George's Hospital Center	301-618-3540
Prince William Hospital	703-369-8000
Providence Hospital	202-269-7275
Reston Hospital Center	703-689-9000
Shady Grove Adventist Hospital	301-279-6386
Sibley Memorial Hospital	202-537-4370
Southern Maryland Hospital	301-899-4150
Washington Adventist Hospital	301-891-5400
Washington Hospital Center	202-877-6037

★ Special Needs

Center for Study of Multiple Births
333 E. Superior St., Suite 464
Chicago, IL 60611
312-266-9093
Disseminates information on the medical risks of multiple births

Confinement Line
Childbirth Education Association, Inc.
P.O. Box 1609
Springfield, VA 22151
703-941-7183
Offers information and telephone support for women confined to bed because of pregnancy complications

Healthy Mothers, Healthy Babies
409 12th St., SW
Washington, DC 20024-2188
202-863-2458
Publishes resource material relating to healthy prenatal development and prevention of birth defects

High-Risk Pregnancy Support Group
Georgetown University Hospital
3700 Reservoir Rd., NW
Washington, DC 20007-2197
202-784-3750
For Georgetown University high-risk inpatients and outpatients, this group offers peer support to help reduce stress and the sense of isolation

Office of Research Reporting
National Institute of Child Health and Human Development at NIH
9000 Rockville Pike, Bldg 31, Rm. 2A-32
Bethesda, MD 20892
301-496-5133
Free government publications on topics such as Downs Syndrome, infertility, genetics, developmental biology and nutrition, and developmental disabilities

The Childbirth Class
Your First Step Toward Becoming a Family

by Judy A. Brady, R.N., A.C.C.E.

Having a baby is one of life's greatest joys and represents a time of hallmark transition. Special attention, preparation, and goal setting are important for this new beginning. Attending a childbirth course can provide the foundation on which to help build positive lifestyle skills, not only for the actual pregnancy, labor and birth, but after the baby is born when families must work on issues of self-awareness, couple dynamics, parenting skills and becoming a family. Participation in a childbirth program allows that "special time" during your busy week to focus on the task at hand: the changing self, the birth of a baby, the birth of a family. Participants in the course often become an extended family, all sharing common concerns. Fears are expressed, excitement is shared and goals are identified. This sharing of feelings and experiences can provide a source of strength and support, especially important in the transient Washington area where new parents often find themselves alone, hundreds of miles from their families.

The Differences in Birthing Methods

Historically, there have been three main philosophies or methods that have impacted childbirth education. In 1944, Dr. Grantly Dick-Read (Dick-Read Method) promoted the advantages of natural childbirth. He published the book *Childbirth Without Fear* suggesting that a cycle of fear-tension-pain resulted from women's lack of knowledge and preparation about childbirth and that much of the pain would be alleviated through relaxation and breathing techniques.

In the 1940s and 1950s, Dr. Fernand Lamaze developed quite a different approach to childbirth preparation. His was the Psychoprophylaxis Method based on the belief that the perception of pain could be greatly reduced or eliminated through conditioned responses to uterine contractions. By the use of focusing techniques, pain of childbirth could be decreased.

The third major theory in childbirth education was that of an American obstetrician Robert Bradley. His 1965 book *Husband Coached Child-*

Judy A. Brady, RN, BSN, ACCE is currently employed at OB/GYN Associates in Silver Spring, Maryland. She is a Nurse Educator/Clinician who is the patent and trademark owner of several products in the obstetrical field. She is the author of Lower Back Pain in Pregnancy.

birth promoted the role of the spouse as the most effective person for supporting the woman during childbirth. Childbirth education today is moving away from a concentration on any specific theory or method toward an eclectic approach or a blending of theories.

Drawing from these three methods a framework of relaxation techniques, patterned breathing, massage, visualization, music and other pain reduction techniques are provided, along with guidelines for personalization to suit the individual.

Credentials & Affiliations

A childbirth program becomes a unique combination of course content and discussion based on the background and characteristics of the instructor, the resource and knowledge availability, the setting or community in which the classes are taught and, of course, the expectant parents attending the class.

Childbirth classes are taught in a variety of settings: hospitals, private physician offices, home-based programs, and weekend getaways. When deciding to choose a program that best suits your needs, begin discussions with your physician, with friends who have babies and with the hospital in which your delivery will take place. Call and ask childbirth education program directors to describe their classes and philosophy. You can gain a wealth of information during a phone conversation, and through any literature which describes their services. Find out who the teachers are and ask to interview them before registering for a class. There are many different styles of teaching and presentation; some may encourage more group discussion, role playing, more time allowed for practicing breathing and relaxation techniques. Others may be more lecture oriented with less emphasis on practicing, group dynamics and interaction.

Plan to start your childbirth class in your seventh month and allow ample time for your "shopping around." Be sure to inquire about the instructor's qualifications. Does she have a medical background? Is she a nurse? Is the instructor an independent certified childbirth educator who subcontracts her services? Is she an employee of a hospital or group? Does she belong to one or more of the local and national organizations of childbirth educators? Has she had a baby? Is there any particular childbirth method taught, for example Dick-Read, Lamaze or Bradley or a combination of methods?

Class Structure and Content

The ideal class size should range from about 5 to 10 couples, large enough to promote group interaction, but yet small enough so that each participant can receive support and attention from the instructor.

Typically childbirth classes meet once a week for two hours over a six-week period. Some programs offer a concentrated weekend session. A refresher course, which is designed to meet the special needs and concerns of parents who already have a child, is generally shorter in length.

The cost of a six-week class ranges from $75 to $105, a concentrated weekend class from $90 to $140 and a refresher class from $25 - $65.

Class content is designed to familiarize you with childbirth and parenting issues. Programs include discussion of the physical and emotional changes that occur during the third trimester of pregnancy; how the body begins preparation for the labor process; the stages of labor and birth including female anatomy and physiology; relaxation techniques; the use of massage, visualization and breathing exercises; and the role of the support person. Family roles and adjustments throughout the postpartum period are also explored as are newborn appearance and breastfeeding/bottlefeeding issues. A hospital tour may be incorporated into the program, as well as labor/birth movies. Course content should provide couples with realistic, but flexible birth plans, and encourage expectant couples to check their hospitals regarding policies and procedures for their labor and delivery experience.

Some programs offer special services. One such service that is becoming quite popular is that of a professional labor support person (LSP). Today, women who offer postpartum home-care services and women who provide labor support are called "doulas." The term "doula" is a Greek word meaning "woman care giver." They are knowledgeable about childbirth practices and can provide support and encouragement. They can be utilized in addition to the support person, or they can be the sole support person for the woman in labor.

Expectant parents will find that there is a wealth of information, education and training available to them to make their childbirth experience positive and rewarding. Childbirth education can make this very special journey exciting and fulfilling for couples on their way to becoming parents.

 ## Questions to ask yourself

1. How do we feel about the birthing process? Do we want a natural delivery, or a delivery under medication?
2. Do I want my husband or support person involved during the delivery?
3. What is our plan for postpartum care?
4. How much do we want to spend on a course?
5. Does my obstetrician offer or recommend a specific course?
6. Does the hospital where I am to give birth offer classes?

 ## Questions to ask class administrators

1. What are the credentials and background of the instructor?
2. Is the course content realistic and appropriate for the type of maternity care available in the community?
3. Are the classes offered at a convenient location and time?

4. How many couples per class?
5. How much does the course cost? What is the method of payment?
6. Is the setting in which the classes are to be offered appropriate? Is the room well ventilated? Is it heated and cooled according to the seasons?
7. Is childcare available for siblings?
8. Is the childbirth educator also available as a labor support person if desired?
9. Is a tour of the community hospital where the birth will occur incorporated into the childbirth course?
10. Is there a lending library to check out books and videos during the course?

? Questions to ask in class

1. What different labor/birth options are available?
2. What are the potential obstetrical interventions that may occur during the labor/birth process?
3. What is the hospital's policy: rules and regulations during the birthing process and philosophy of postpartum care? How many support people may be present during the labor process?
4. What is consumer advocacy? How may it best be utilized during the labor/birth process?
5. If a private physician teaches the course in his/her office, ask about his/her feelings concerning natural delivery, medications, the presence of a support person, and philosophy of birthing and postpartum care.

Resources

Childbirth classes for the Washington Metropolitan Area

Childbirth Education Association (CEA)
P.O. Box 1609
Springfield, VA 22151
703-941-7183
Resource listing of childbirth educators in the Maryland, Washington and Virginia area. All instructors are R.N.s who utilize the Lamaze method and have had at least one Lamaze delivery of their own. A 6-week childbirth refresher class; intensive weekend class, food provided; private lessons offered if desired; scholarships provided for educational classes if in need. Confinement line for bedrest moms during the pregnancy; call 703-941-7183.

Columbia Hospital for Women
2425 L Street, NW
Washington, DC 20037
202-293-3239
Childbirth preparation series (4 weeks of 2½-hour sessions); a
childbirth review class; sibling class and tour; an obstetrical tour (free
of charge); a breastfeeding class (1½-hour session); a babycare class
(2½ hours of instruction); an infant safety and CPR class, and a pain
relief/labor and delivery class (free one-time class)

FLAME "Family Life and Maternity Education, Inc."
P.O. Box 379
Dunn Loring, VA 22027
703-276-9248 or 800-776-9248
A nonprofit organization that has provided childbirth education since
1971. All instructors are certified in the Lamaze method, and have
had personal experience with the Lamaze method. A 6-week Lamaze
childbirth educational course is offered; a 4-week childbirth refresher
course is offered for repeat parents; private instruction offered if
desired; financial assistance available if needed.

Georgetown University Hospital
3800 Reservoir Road, NW
Washington, DC 20007
202-342-2400
A childbirth education class is offered on weekday evenings; a
weekend alternative class-6 hours of instruction on Saturday and
Sunday; a childbirth refresher class all day on a Saturday; a sibling
class on Saturday mornings featuring a puppet show, singing, and
hospital tour for children; a hospital tour every Sunday at 4 p.m. (free
of charge); and a Breastfeeding Your Baby class, a one-time class for 2
hours.

Holy Cross Hospital
1500 Forest Glen Road
Silver Spring, Maryland 20910
301-905-BABY
A 6 week prepared childbirth class called "Make Way For Baby" is
offered once a week on weekday evenings; Saturday sessions also
available; a 3-week childbirth refresher class called "Childbirth
Revisited" weekday evenings, Sat. sessions are also available; a 45-
minute free tour of the birthing facility; a sibling class and tour called
"What About Me?" on Saturdays helps siblings take the first step
toward becoming big sisters or brothers, a prenatal exercise class that
focuses on increasing flexibility and muscle tone for labor and delivery
(doctor's permission is required); and a 2-hour breastfeeding class.

Greater Laurel-Beltsville Hospital
7100 Contee Road
Laurel, Maryland 20707
301-497-7977
A 6-week Lamaze educational class weekday evenings; a 3 week
childbirth refresher class; and a monthly sibling class (1 hour tour
and movie) for children.

Inova HealthSource of Fairfax Hospital
8110 Gatehouse Road
Falls Church, Virginia 22042
703-204-3366
A 6-week ASPO Lamaze class weekday evenings/weekends; a monthly ASPO Lamaze "Weekend Getaway"—taught in a luxury hotel—includes Sat. night accommodations, some meals, use of hotel facilities and a gift package for the new family. A 6-hour refresher class for expectant parents who have taken a Lamaze class in the past five years; a new brother/new sister class to help older children learn what to expect when the new baby arrives; a two-session Cesarean Childbirth Class; a four-session Vaginal Birth After Cesarean Class, a Breastfeeding Class featuring a video presentation and lecture by a certified lactation consultant; a two-session baby care class for parents who are expecting/adopting their first child; and a 1-hour tour of the Labor-Delivery-Recovery and Family-Centered Care units (most Sundays).

Montgomery General Hospital
18101 Prince Phillip Drive
Olney, MD 20832
301-598-9815
A 6-week Childbirth-Lamaze Class weekday evenings with a reduced fee if delivering at Montgomery General Hospital; a bimonthly two-session Refresher Prepared Lamaze Class; 3-hour Breastfeeding class is offered once a month; Our First (designed for first-time parents) providing a monthly newsletter and a 24 hour telephone line to the OB-GYN nurses at Montgomery General Hospital for questions during pregnancy and after the baby is born; a Sibling Class and tour; and a general tour and orientation of the Maternal Newborn Center; a Fitness for Two prenatal exercise program once a week for 6 weeks; and a monthly 3-hour Infant Care Class.

OB/GYN Associates Judy A. Brady, R.N./Childbirth Educator
2101 Medical Park Dr./#307
Silver Spring, Maryland 20902
301-681-6772
A Prenatal Orientation Class once a month for 2 hours covering physical/emotional changes during pregnancy, nutrition and weight gain, exercise and appropriate posture and body mechanics for daily activities, and common laboratory tests/procedures done during a pregnancy; a 7-week Prepared Childbirth Educational Class, a 4-week Childbirth Refresher Class, Sibling Movie and Tour night. Private instruction available.

Shady Grove Adventist Hospital
9901 Medical Center Drive
Rockville, Maryland 20850
301-279-6529
A 6-week Childbirth Preparation Class is offered on weekday evenings, Sat. or Sun.; Childbirth Refresher Class on two Sundays 3-6p.m.; and a one day seminar on breastfeeding is offered on Sun. 1-4p.m. with a reduced fee if also enrolled in Shady Grove Adventist Hospital's Childbirth Classes.

Sibley Hospital
5255 Loughboro Road NW
Washington, DC 20016
202-537-4000
A free quarterly 2-hour seminar "Planning for Pregnancy"; 7-week
Preparation for Birth and Parenthood Class incorporating relaxation
and breathing as well as parenting issues on weekday evenings, Sat.
and Sun.; a Weekend Intensive Program Sat. and Sun. 9-4p.m.; a one-
night 3-hour Comfort Refresher Class; a free Maternity Tour; and a
Preparing to Breastfeed Class on the first Monday night of the month.

Washington Adventist Hospital
7600 Carroll Avenue
Takoma Park, Maryland 20912
301-891-5305
A 6-week Prepared Childbirth Class; a Childbirth Refresher Class
(three-session course providing experienced parents a review of
Lamaze techniques); a free tour of the Special Additions Maternity
Center; a Cesarean Preparation Class; a Preparation for Vaginal Birth
After Cesarean Class; a Sibling Preparation Class for 3-9 year olds;
and a Adoption Preparation Class consisting of four 2-hour classes, a
Siblings At Birth class for parents who want to have other children
attend the birth.

Associations

American Society for Psychoprophylaxis in Obstetrics, Inc.
(ASPO Lamaze)
1200 19th Street, NW Suite 300
Washington, DC 20036-2401
202-857-1128/ 1 800 368 4104

American Academy of Husband Coached Childbirth
(The Bradley Method)
P.O. Box 5224
Sherman Oaks, CA 91413
818-788-6662/ 1-800-423-2397

American College of Obstetricians and Gynecologists (ACOG)
409 12th Street, SW
Washington, DC 20024
202-638-5577

American College of Nurse-Midwives
818 Connecticut Avenue, NW Suite 900
Washington, DC 20006
202-728-9860

Association of Women's Health-Obstetrics and Neo-Natal Nurses
700 14th Street, NW Suite 600
Washington, DC 20005
202-662-1600

Cesarean/Support, Education, and Concern (C/SEC)
22 Forest Road
Framingham, MA 01701
508-877-8266

Doulas of North America (DONA)
1100 23rd Avenue
Seattle, WA 98112

Healthy Mothers, Healthy Babies National Office
409 12th Street, SW
Washington, DC 20024
202-863-2458

International Childbirth Education Association (ICEA)
P.O. Box 20048
Minneapolis, MN 55420
612-854-8660

Maternity Center Association
48 East 92nd Street
New York, NY 10128
212-369-7300

National Association of Childbirth Assistants (NACA)
205 Copco Lane
San Jose, CA 95123
408-225-9167

Read Natural Childbirth Foundation
P.O. Box 956
San Rafael, CA 94915
415-456-8462

Further Reading

The American College of Obstetricians and Gynecologists. *Planning For Pregnancy, Birth, and Beyond*. 1990.

Bing, E. *Six Practical Lessons For An Easier Childbirth*. Bantam Books, 1994.

Eisenberg, A., Murkoff, H.E., and Hathaway, S.E. *What To Expect When You're Expecting*. New York: Workman Publishing, 1991.

Kitzinger, S. *The Complete Book of Pregnancy and Childbirth*. New York: Alfred A. Knopf, 1993.

Marshall, C. *The Expectant Father*. Conmar Publishing, Inc., 1992.

Nilsson, L., and Hamberger, L. *A Child Is Born*. Delacorte Press/ Seymour Lawrence, 1993.

Ostermann, R., Spurrell, C., and Chubet C. *Fathering--Playing Your Part in Pregnancy, Birth and Beyond*. Longmeadow Press, 1988.

Simkin, P., Whalley, J., and Keppler, A. *Pregnancy, Childbirth and The Newborn*. Meadowbrook Press, 1991.

Nurse-Midwifery
A Satisfying Alternative

by Rebecca L. Skovgaard, M.S., C.N.M.

Nurse-midwifery began as a profession in the 1920s at the frontier Nursing Service, where nurse-midwives on horseback in the remote mountains of Kentucky developed a remarkable record of safety. Today, it is practiced in every state. Though currently only about 3 percent of U.S. births are attended by Certified Nurse Midwives (CNM), the numbers are increasing rapidly. In Washington, D.C., Maryland and 10 other states, midwives participate in at least 5 percent of all births.

Qualifications of Nurse-Midwives

Certified nurse-midwives are women (or, in a few cases, men) who, having become registered nurses and obtained experience in obstetrical or maternity nursing, have completed advanced education in midwifery. There are currently 30 nurse-midwifery programs in the country, most of which are masters programs. They are accredited by the American College of Nurse-Midwives. Graduates of these programs become CNMs after passing a national certifying examination.

Nurse-midwives' education and experience are focused on the care of normal women and infants. Their practice may include care of women during pregnancy, labor and delivery, postpartum care of women and newborns, and gynecological care of women of all ages. Well-woman care may include annual examinations, contraception, pre-pregnancy counseling and fertility awareness.

All nurse-midwives work in some formal relationship with an obstetrician. If a woman's condition varies significantly from normal, then consultation with, or occasionally referral to, a physician is arranged.

CNMs work in a variety of settings. In the Washington D.C. area where there are over 200 nurse-midwives, virtually all types of practice are represented. There are nurse-midwives in private practice whose patients deliver in a hospital and others who attend birth center or home deliveries. There are nurse-midwives working in public clinics and at hospital clinics. Some are at military bases. And there are a large number working in health maintenance organizations.

Rebecca L. Skovgaard, MS, CNM, is a certified nurse-midwife who was on the faculty of the Georgetown University School of Nursing and a member of Georgetown Midwifery Associates before leaving the Washington area.

The Nurse-Midwife Philosophy

One of the most basic tenets of the nurse-midwifery philosophy is that birth is a normal process which in most cases works well without extensive interference. Nurse-midwives' efforts, therefore, are directed toward support of the process and toward promoting the woman's ability to cope.

This approach encourages individualized care and the greatest freedom of choice. It also reduces reliance on technology, resulting in equally good outcomes with less interference and decreased costs. However, CMNs are also skilled in the use of fetal monitoring and use pain relievers and anesthesia such as epidurals when they are indicated.

The belief in childbirth as a natural process does not, however, mean that nurse-midwives assume that all is normal. Indeed, because the scope of practice is limited to pregnancies which are basically normal, a meticulous screening is an inherent part of the practice. Any suggestion of a complication is carefully scrutinized.

A Satisfying Alternative

Trust in the process and careful monitoring have important benefits. First, thorough screening facilitates early intervention and even prevention of complications. Pre-term labor problems, for example, may be avoided by identifying women at risk and taking preventive steps.

Second, a woman's sense of security and safety are fostered. Careful evaluation at every visit and throughout labor provides assurance that all is well and greatly eases a mother's fears and anxieties, a critical advantage during labor when apprehension can interrupt the process and inhibit progress.

Finally, a woman gains confidence in her body. She learns from the nurse-midwife's respect for her ability to successfully negotiate the challenges of pregnancy and childbirth that she herself has accomplished the amazing feat of birth.

Questions to ask yourself

1. Do I want a hospital/midwife experience if possible?
2. Am I a good candidate, young and healthy enough for this type of delivery?
3. Will my partner be supportive of a nurse-midwife delivery?
4. What is the difference in cost between using a doctor or midwife for the delivery?
5. Is the midwife practice convenient to my home/workplace?

? Questions to ask the midwife

1. What is the experience of this midwifery practice? How many successful births has this practice delivered?
2. Which doctor and hospital is the practice affiliated with?
3. Can I have a hospital/midwife delivery?
4. What is the procedure if there is trouble during the delivery?
5. Are there options for pain relief if the labor is long and difficult?

Resources

Georgetown Midwifery Associates
3700 Reservoir Road, NW
Washington, DC   20007
202-687-4772
Private nurse/midwife practice attending deliveries at Georgetown University Hospital.

Donna Chuzi, CNM & Janey Roth, CNM
19537 Doctors Drive
Germantown, MD 20874
301-540-8800

15225 Shady Grove Road #204
Rockville, MD 20850
301-216-2400
At the offices of Drs. Lakner, Gerber & Furlong.
Midwifery births at Shady Grove Hospital

Maternity Center
6506 Bells Mill Road
Bethesda, MD
301-530-3300
Free-standing birth center with a backup doctor, offering well-woman and prenatal care, annual gynecological exams, contraceptive management. Classes: infant & child CPR, breastfeeding, nutrition, infant message, postpartum support group, pre- and postnatal exercise class, sibling class.

Takoma Women's Health Center
7005 Carroll Avenue
Takoma Park, MD
301-270-8880
Three certified Nurse/Midwives who work in association with five Ob-Gyns. Do deliveries at Columbia Hospital for Women and offer gynecological visits, over the phone advice and visits for breastfeeding guidance.

BirthCare & Women's Health
1501 King Street
Alexandria, VA 22314
703-549-5070
Four certified nurse midwives work with various consulting
physicians.
Provide well-woman care, family planning services, and pre-natal care.
Offers the only home birth service in the metro area; also births in a
freestanding birth center in Alexandria.

**David Giammittorio, M.D., Beverly Johnson CNM, Karen Gonzales
CNM**
5249 Duke Street, Suite 410
Alexandria, VA 22304
703-370-0223
Two certified nurse midwives working with one Ob-Gyn. Care for
women throughout the reproductive cycle and deliver at Alexandria
Hospital. Classes in early pregnancy and relaxation, as well as
childbirth classes.

Breastfeeding

Making Nature's Perfect System Work for You

by Edie Armstrong, R.N., I.B.C.L.C.
and Janet Montrie R.N., I.B.C.L.C.

Breastfeeding is one of nature's perfect systems. Just as a mother is capable of nourishing her baby for months in the womb, she is also capable of completely nourishing her infant at the breast. Each species of mammal makes the type of milk that is especially suited to help its young survive and develop to maximum potential. Human breastmilk contains special proteins and fats which promote the growth of the brain, the organ that ensures the survival of our species. Each mother's breastmilk is genetically unique, and is therefore tailored to meet her infant's specific needs.

Benefits of Breastfeeding

The benefits of breastfeeding begin immediately after the birth of the baby. Fresh from the trauma of being born, a baby that is put to his mother's breast is near the enveloping warmth and touch of her body. He can hear the familiar sounds of her voice and heartbeat, finding a place to suck that will help his tension subside and make him feel secure. Breastfeeding helps to ease his transition from the womb to the world outside. Breastfeeding enables a woman to establish a physical and psychological bond with her child that occurs naturally during the intimacy of breastfeeding.

Breastmilk contains all the nutrients babies need in exactly the right proportions. It changes from hour to hour and day to day to meet an infant's needs. For example, colostrum (the milk first present in the breasts after delivery) is very high in special disease-fighting cells to protect the baby right from the start. It also contains a laxative to help the baby pass his first stools, called meconium. It is thick and in small quantities at

Edie Armstrong is currently the Lactation Consultant for Inpatient Services at Holy Cross Hospital in Silver Spring, Maryland. Holy Cross has a delivery rate of approximately 7000 babies per year. She has been an Internationally Board-Certified Lactation Consultant since 1990. Edie lives in Fairfax with her husband and two children.

Janet Montrie is a Registered Nurse and an Internationally Board- Certified Lactation Consultant. She is employed full-time by Holy Cross Hospital as the Coordinator of the Holy Cross Hospital Lactation Center. She is a native Washingtonian who currently resides in Bethesda with her husband and three sons.

first so the newborn baby can learn to coordinate his sucking and swallowing before being asked to cope with larger volumes of liquid. By the time the baby has mastered the rhythm of eating, his mother's milk will be in. Breastmilk is generally higher in fat in the morning, when most babies are hungriest and decreases in fat content as the baby gets older and requires fewer calories.

Besides being more easily digestible than formula, a mother's milk contains immune-boosting elements that prevent infection in the baby for as long as he nurses. These elements may also prevent certain childhood diseases. Breastfeeding babies are known to have fewer gastrointestinal infections, ear infections, allergic disorders and respiratory illnesses than those who are fed formula. Studies show that breastfed infants are eight times less likely than formula fed babies to be hospitalized for an illness during the first year of their lives. Recent evidence also suggests that breastfed infants have a lower incidence of Sudden Infant Death Syndrome (SIDS) and juvenile diabetes. Extensive studies by experts such as Dr. Alan Lucas in Great Britain have found evidence that breastfed infants have higher levels of intelligence and are less apt to develop learning disorders than those who are bottlefed. The American Academy of Pediatrics recommends that all infants be breastfed during their first year of life. However, breastfeeding for any length of time can benefit infants for up to a year after nursing has stopped. We know, for instance, that even one dose of colostrum can reduce a premature baby's risk of disease.

Research on infant development shows that a mother's responsiveness is one of the biggest influences on a baby's behavior and developmental skills. When a baby gives a cue that signals hunger or distress, and his mother responds quickly to that cue by offering the breast, the baby learns to trust that his needs will be met. Breastfeeding mothers respond intuitively and promptly to their babies' signals. There is no need to turn attention away from the baby to prepare a bottle. Breastmilk is also less expensive than bottles and store-bought formulas and is considerably more convenient, requiring no equipment or mixing.

There are some advantages to breastfeeding for the mothers as well as their infants. Women say that breastfeeding makes them feel at peace with the world. This is because nursing mothers secrete significantly more betaendorphins, the body's natural tranquilizer, making them feel relaxed and content. Also, because calcium is better metabolized, women who have breastfed have less osteoporosis when they are older and seem to have some protection against breast and ovarian cancer.

Getting Started

It has been well documented that the information and support a family receives before, during and after delivery can have a tremendous impact on how long breastfeeding continues. Breastfeeding is indeed a "natural" process but must be learned by both mother and baby. There are some ways in which you can ensure that your breastfeeding experience is a positive one.

Before delivery: The best preparation for any mother is to learn as much as possible about breastfeeding before she begins to nurse. You can take prenatal breastfeeding classes, join a community-based breastfeeding support group (such as La Leche League) and attend meetings. You can also read up on the subject. However, be aware that reading materials or films prepared by formula companies or companies that make infant feeding equipment often leave the impression that breastfeeding is difficult and requires the use of supplements. A good source of information and support may be neighbors or friends who have successfully breastfed.

While talking and reading about breastfeeding ahead of time is important, physical preparation may be another concern. The shape of your nipples can have an impact on how easy it is for your baby to attach to the breast. You can check your nipples by doing a simple test called "the pinch test." Place your thumb and forefinger on the top and bottom of your nipple skin, about one inch or so behind the nipple, and gently pinch. What happens to your nipples? If they stick out farther it should be easy for your baby to latch on. Nipples that flatten or go inward when pinched may present the baby with more of a challenge. You may benefit from wearing breast shells inside your bra before delivery to encourage your nipples to protrude farther. A breastfeeding expert can help you obtain these. Aside from this, the only preparation necessary is to avoid using soap on your nipples at the end of pregnancy as soap washes off the natural lubricants.

During delivery: Keep medications to a minimum whenever possible. Babies born with medication in their systems may be hesitant to suck for hours or even days.

After your baby is born: Keep her with you as much as possible, starting right after birth. There is usually no good reason for healthy mothers and babies to be separated right after delivery. Putting your baby skin-to-skin, clad only in a diaper (and maybe a hat), against your chest (with a blanket over both) immediately after delivery, can encourage her to get to the breast sooner. Research has shown that babies stabilize faster held skin-to-skin and that they are much more likely to be able to find the breast. Skin-to-skin contact can be a good way to wake a baby to feed hours or even days after birth as well. We know that it is normal for newborns to be wide awake for one to two hours after being born. This is a special opportunity to try breastfeeding. In fact, studies show it may boost your confidence in your ability to breastfeed your baby if you can make an attempt during this time. Once past, it may be unusual for your baby to wake often on his own to feed for the next few days. If you are together, you will be able to read his cues and learn how to respond. When he stirs in his sleep, bringing his hand to his mouth, and moves his head around as if looking for something (rooting), it is time to breastfeed.

When you breastfeed watch your baby, not the clock. Your baby needs to nurse from one breast until she is finished. Babies take just what they need from the breast and, when they have gotten enough to eat, will generally come off the breast by themselves. If you take your baby off the breast at a prescribed time, she may not have gotten to the high fat milk that comes at the end of a feeding and tells her the feeding is over.

After the feeding is finished, it is recommended that you express some colostrum or milk onto your nipples and air dry your skin. Nothing more than daily washing with water is needed to care for your breasts.

Common Breastfeeding Challenges—The First Weeks

Most people don't realize that for both mother and baby breastfeeding is a learned response. It often takes some time for this learning to take place and some mistakes may be made along the way. However, with good preparation and support most problems are not insurmountable. The following is a brief discussion of the most common breastfeeding challenges, the usual causes and some solutions. If you need more help with breastfeeding, contact a lactation consultant, La Leche League leader, physician or midwife. See page 54.

Sore Nipples: You may be given the well-intentioned advice that, if you feed for longer than 10-15 minutes per side, you will get sore nipples. Actually, it is not the length of time but the incorrect positioning of the baby's mouth on your breast that is the most likely cause of sore nipples. Nipple soreness during the first weeks is very common but should never last past the first 10-20 seconds of latch-on. Check to make sure that you are positioning the baby correctly at your breast. Start by supporting your breast with your hand in a "C" position (with your fingers well behind the nipple). Position the baby so that he is well supported in your arms and his body is in a straight line, with his trunk turned in toward you. Stroke his lower lip with your nipple until he opens as wide as if he were yawning. Pull him quickly onto the breast. Avoid pressing down on the top of your breast to make an airway as this may pull your nipple partway out of the baby's mouth, causing sore nipples. If the baby is unable to breathe, he will pull himself off the breast. If you are not able to correct the situation and continue to have more pain than during the initial latch-on, it may be wise to have an expert check your technique.

Engorgement: Engorgement is an overfullness of the breast that may occur when your milk comes in, two to five days following the birth of your baby. There is some swelling of the breasts due to the increased blood supply associated with milk production. This may cause the breasts to feel heavy, full and sensitive to the touch. You may even run a low-grade fever (99 - 100 degrees F). It is important to nurse frequently during this time but not uncommon for the baby to have some trouble latching on due to the increased fullness of your breasts from the swelling. It may help to put warm, moist compresses on your breasts for just long enough to open up the milk ducts (about three to five minutes), followed by hand expression or pumping of enough milk to enable your baby to latch on. If you have been nursing your baby around the clock at least 8 times in every 24 hours, starting soon after delivery, you will be less likely to become engorged. It is also important not to skip night feedings or limit the baby's sucking time at the breast. Avoid supplements of any kind unless they are medically necessary. Remember, engorgement is a temporary condition! If it does not seem to be resolving in a day or so, it might be a good idea to consult a breastfeeding expert.

Adequate Milk Supply: Many new mothers express concern about whether or not the baby is getting enough to eat from the breast. If you are feeding your newborn 8-12 times in every 24 hour period, he should get plenty to eat. Breastmilk is produced constantly in direct relation to your baby's needs. Your breasts will supply what your infant demands. The more the baby sucks, the more milk you will produce. One helpful guide may be to look at your baby's diapers. Some signs that your infant is getting enough include: six to eight wet diapers and several stools per day (after your milk is in), contentment between feedings and weight gain as determined by your doctor at your well-baby visits. Be sure to take care of your needs too. A nutritious diet, plenty of fluids and adequate rest and relaxation will help ensure a good milk supply.

Breastfeeding and Working

It has been estimated that 80 percent of the 34 million working women in the United States will have children during their working years. When a woman chooses to combine motherhood with a career or school, breastfeeding need not be sacrificed. With a little planning she can continue to breastfeed. In fact, continuing to breastfeed may be of great benefit to her employer, too. Breastfeeding mothers have less absenteeism due to baby illnesses.

If possible take at least the first six weeks to learn about your baby and breastfeeding. If you will be missing one or more feedings while you are away at work or school, you must plan to express your breastmilk to prevent engorgement and maintain your milk supply. Two to four weeks before you plan to return to work or school it is a good idea to begin expression and storage of breastmilk. This way, by the time you must be away from your baby, you will be familiar with how to express and store milk and you will have built up a stockpile of milk in your freezer. There are several ways to express your breastmilk. Talk to your nursing friends or a breastfeeding expert for suggestions and decide on a method that fits your needs. Double pumping with a high-quality electric breastpump is an easy, efficient way to maintain your milk supply while you and the baby are separated. Both breasts can be emptied simultaneously in about 10-15 minutes. The milk can be stored and given to the baby another day. The cost of the rental of the breastpump is about one third the cost of formula. Choose a caregiver who is supportive of your commitment to breastfeeding. Plan to breastfeed the baby before work, as soon as you return from work (if possible the baby should not be fed for two hours prior to your arrival) and breastfeed frequently during the evening and on weekends. Give your caregiver written instructions on how to store breastmilk. Human milk can be stored in the refrigerator for up to 72 hours. It can be frozen for three to six months. Thaw or heat frozen breastmilk in warm water. Never boil it or place it in the microwave. Introduce a bottle to your baby after breastfeeding is well established. Some babies refuse to take a bottle from mom so it may be helpful for dad or the sitter to try. Avoid bottles, if possible, for the first three to four weeks of life as nipple confusion may occur.

Today a growing number of women returning to the work force are continuing to breastfeed their infants. With a minimum effort and a little planning the benefits of breastfeeding can continue while you continue your career.

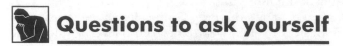

Questions to ask yourself

1. Will I find the help I need to continue breastfeeding from our health care professionals, family and friends so that I can continue breastfeeding?
2. How can I combine breastfeeding with working or school?
3. If I have questions or problems where can I turn for help?

? Questions to ask the professionals

1. Pediatrician: If I have trouble with breastfeeding what would you do? (i.e., would you refer to a Lactation Consultant?)
2. Hospital: Do you have a Lactation Consultant(s) on staff to help me if problems arise?
3. Obstetricians (prenatally): How can I tell whether I will be able to breastfeed?
4. Lactation Consultant: How can I tell if my baby is getting enough to eat?
5. Hospital: When or for what reason are mothers and babies separated? Can I be with my baby around the clock?

Resources

Lactation Consultants - Available for consultation pre- and postnatally in your home or in their offices. Often do telephone consultations as well. IBCLC means a consultant is an Internationally Board-Certified Lactation Consultant.

Associations and Centers

La Leche League International
P.O. Box 4079
Schaumberg, IL 60168-4079
1-800-LA-LECHE/ in Washington 202-269-4444
A mother-to-mother support network for breastfeeding mothers.

Georgetown Lactation Center and Milk Bank - 202-784-6455
Holy Cross Hospital Lactation Center - 301-905-1036

Breastfeeding Supplies

Birth and Beginnings
6832 Rt. 108
Gaithersburg, MD 20882 301-990-7975
(ships supplies to VA, DC, MD and nationwide)
Rents and sells Medela breast pumps and products. Provides personal support and breastfeeding counseling as part of the rental.

Center Pharmacy
4900 Massachusetts Avenue, NW
Washington, DC 20016 202-363-9240
Entire Medela line of breast pumps and accessories for rent or for sale. Special rates if you rent for three months or more.

Foer's Pharmacy
8218 Wisconsin Avenue
Bethesda, MD 301-657-3500
Rents Medela Lactina breast pumps and all accessories.

Foer's Pharmacy
2440 M Street, NW
Washington, DC 202-775-4400

Holy Cross Hospital Lactation Center
9805 Dameron Drive
Silver Spring, MD 301-905-1036
Carries all Medela breast pumps and products as well as breastfeeding accessories. Support and instruction included with all rentals.

Medela Breastpump Rentals
4604 Chase Avenue
Bethesda, MD 20814 301 654 0934
Rental station for Medela.

Medela, Inc.
P.O. Box 600
McHenry, IL 60051
They have a help line, Breastfeeding Nat'l. Network 1-800-TELL-YOU.

Mother's Matters
11800 Sunrise Valley Drive, Suite 305
Reston, VA 22091 703-620-3323.
Medela pump rental station, and breastfeeding supplies. Maternal infant "Doula" service. Support mothers during labor as well as postpartum. Childbirth assistants, trained to assist mother and father through labor with visualization, relaxation techniques. Breastfeeding support, sibling care and support, postpartum depression. Board-certified lactation consultants. Childbirth classes in home and community. Skilled care for home phototherapy and high-risk care.

Consultants

Breastfeeding Consultants of Northern Virginia
703-207-9091
Specifically tailored to the needs of breastfeeding women including consultation work, and hands-on assistance for unusual and difficult nursing problems. Board Certified.

Holy Cross Lactation Center
9805 Dameron Drive
Silver Spring, MD 20902 301-905-1036
Comprehensive breastfeeding support and consultation by trained Lactation Specialists who are Registered Nurses. Both home and office visits available.

International Lactation Consultant Association
1-708-260-8874
Information on how to find board certified lactation consultants in your area.

National Capital Lactation Center
Community Human Milk Bank
Georgetown University Hospital, DC; Rockville, MD; Annandale, VA
202-784-MILK
Staff of registered nurses, who are certified lactation consultants. Attend all breastfeeding mothers at Georgetown University Hospital and do outpatient consultations for any woman having a breastfeeding difficulty. Supplies available including breastpumps for sale or rent. Human Milk Bank for babies who need the advantage of human milk, available on doctor's prescription. Internationally known training center for professionals in lactation management.

Further Reading

La Leche League International. *The Womanly Art of Breastfeeding*. 4th Edition. Franklin Park, Ill. 1987.

Mason, D. and D. Ingersoll. *Breastfeeding and the Working Mother*. New York: St. Martin's Press, 1986.

Pryor, Karen. *Nursing Your Baby*. P.B. Publishing, 1991.

Finding A Great Pediatrician

by Michele R. Berman, M.D.

One of the most important tasks parents must undertake is the selection of a pediatrician. Besides being a place to take a sick child, or a place to get "baby shots," a pediatrician's office is an important resource for both new and experienced parents. Today, many families find themselves without the traditional support systems their own parents had available to them. Family members are often separated by many miles. For these families, the pediatrician provides advice and encouragement, as well as basic childcare knowledge. Many pediatricians see patients from birth through adolescence, so picking the right pediatrician may well be the beginning of a "long-term relationship."

Pediatrics, in general, is a *preventive* health care specialty. Well-care visits provide the framework of information to keep your child happy and healthy. A typical well-care visit starts with weighing and measuring the child and plotting those measurements on a growth chart to follow his or her progress. The pediatrician will then ask several questions about your child's eating, sleeping and bowel habits, and about what new developmental milestones have been reached. Then it's your turn to ask the doctor any questions or discuss concerns you may have. Write them down as you think of them at home, and bring the list with you. After examining the child, the pediatrician may discuss a variety of topics, such as immunizations, safety issues or behavioral stages of development. Some will also have handouts to supplement the discussion. On average, pediatricians should provide seven well visits in the first year of a child's life, three in the second year, and one every one to two years thereafter.

Pediatric Training

Pediatricians attend four years of medical school, followed by three years of a pediatric residency. During this time, they learn, under supervised conditions, how to care for a broad range of conditions from the mildest childhood illnesses to the most serious diseases. To become board certified in pediatrics, a doctor must pass a rigorous written examination given by the American Board of Pediatrics. In addition, to renew his or her medical license, a physician must keep up to date in the

Michele R. Berman, M.D., attended medical school at Washington University in St. Louis, Missouri and did her Pediatrics training at St. Louis Children's Hospital. She was board certified in 1985. Currently she has a private practice at The Pediatric Center, with offices in Bethesda and on Capitol Hill.

field by taking a certain number of continuing medical education courses each year. Some pediatricians receive subspecialty training for one to three years after their residency, adding additional knowledge in areas dealing with diseases of the heart, lungs, kidneys, allergies, etc. These physicians may also be board certified in these subspecialities. In general, your pediatrician will ask a subspecialist to consult on a patient whose medical problems may require additional expertise.

The Prenatal Appointment

If this is your first child, the decision as to who the baby's pediatrician will be should be made well in advance of your due date. (Remember—babies often come earlier than expected!) This allows the pediatrician you choose to give your newborn its very first exam in the hospital, and to support you during those joyful, yet overwhelming first days. Although all pediatricians are dedicated to helping you raise healthy, happy children, each has his or her own approach. You will, therefore, want to meet with several pediatricians so that you can pick the one with whom you feel most comfortable and whose approach is most consistent with your own ideas about child raising.

Most pediatricians encourage parents to come for a prenatal appointment. This is your opportunity not only to meet the pediatrician but look at the office itself. If possible, both parents should be present, so the two of you will agree on your choice. If the new mom is unexpectedly put under strict bedrest for complications during pregnancy, it may be possible for the pediatrician to talk to her on the phone. However, it might still be nice to send dad over to the office to look around. When you set up the visit, find out who you will be seeing (one or more doctors? office staff?), about how long it will last and if there is a charge for the visit. If the visit consists of a quick hello by the pediatrician while the office staff shows you around, there may not be a fee. However, there may be a charge if the pediatrician sets aside a block of time specifically to talk with you and answer any questions you have. Many insurance companies will pay for this, but check with your plan first.

During the interview you should first find out how the practice works. What are the office hours? Do they include evening or weekend hours? How are "after-hours" calls handled? Who are the doctors in the practice and what are their qualifications? Can you see any of the doctors in the group, or are you assigned to one doctor? How far in advance do you have to call to get a well-child appointment? A sick-child appointment? To what hospitals do the doctors admit their patients? Do the doctors come to the hospital where you are delivering? Who handles phone calls during the day and after hours? What is the schedule of visits and immunizations? Most pediatricians follow the guidelines of the American Academy of Pediatrics for these.

NOTE: Although the title of this section is The Prenatal Appointment, most of what follows also holds for parents adopting babies or parents of older children.

After determining how the practice works, try to get a feel for the pediatrician's personality. How does the doctor respond to your questions? Does he or she seem open to your concerns or seem to shrug them off? Is the doctor stiff or relaxed? Distracted? Does he or she have a good sense of humor? Observe how the doctor interacts with the patients that may be in the office at the time of your visit. The feelings you get during your visit will set the tone for the relationship you will develop with the pediatrician you choose. You want to feel comfortable and confident about someone who is going to help you take care of that special baby of yours.

Ask the pediatrician her opinions about circumcision, breastfeeding or the use of antibiotics or other medications. If you are going to breastfeed, what kind of support can she give you? What is her philosophy about the role of a pediatrician? If you know there may be problems with the new baby, ask if she has any experience in that area or who may be used as a subspecialist to help manage the problem.

Lastly, look around the office. Does it seem inviting to children? Are there things for the children to do if they have to wait to see the doctor? Will older children and adolescents also feel comfortable here? Are there ways to separate sick from well children? What kind of feelings do you get about the office staff? The nursing staff and front desk personnel are also important in making a trip to the doctor a pleasant experience.

Looking for Dr. Right

So, how do you find your dream pediatrician? There are several ways. First, ask your friends and neighbors who they use. Are they happy there? What do they like about the office? Is there anything they don't like? Next, ask your obstetrician for a list of recommended pediatricians. Your internist, family practitioner and other medical professionals can also be good resources. Also helpful are several telephone based physician referral services that are available in the Washington metropolitan area. Most of these are associated with local hospitals and include First Call, Prologue, Physician Preference, Cross Connect, etc.

Increasingly, families are covered by health plans that limit their choices to physicians who are members of the plan. In this instance, start with the list of pediatricians provided by the health plan and see which ones are available in your area. Then ask your friends and other doctors what they know about those physicians. Make an appointment with the pediatricians you'd like to know more about. Remember to check with your health plan to determine whether it will cover prenatal visits, and whether a referral form is necessary.

Parents of older children may need to find a new pediatrician for a variety of reasons. They may be unhappy with their present pediatrician. Or they may be new to town or may have moved to a new neighborhood within the metropolitan area. Many times, their health insurance may have changed, and they can no longer see their present pediatrician without incurring large out-of-pocket expenses. For the most part, these parents should be asking the same questions as those asked at a prenatal visit. But there may be some different issues as well. An older child may have some preexisting medical problems. Is the pediatrician familiar with these kinds of problems, and what is his/her approach to them? What resources does the office have for children with special needs? Do any of the physicians in the office have subspecialty training, or are there other health professionals, such as dieticians, clinical psychologists, etc. associated with the practice? What resources does the practice have to deal with school problems? If the child is an adolescent, are there male and female physicians available to them if they have a preference?

Pediatrician's fees may vary widely. Don't be afraid to ask about fees before you go to the office. Ask if you will have to pay for services at the time of the visit, or whether they will bill you or submit the insurance claim for you. If you are a member of a health plan, and the pediatrician is a provider for that plan, the office will file for you, but you must usually pay a small co-payment at each visit. Look at your health plan or insurance coverage carefully. Not all insurance plans cover well-child care, or you may have to meet a deductible, or they may cover only a certain number of well visits. For these financial matters, it's best to know what the office policies are before you get there. If you anticipate a problem with payments, many offices will work with you, as long as you talk to them up front.

As mentioned earlier, many families find themselves using the same pediatrician for many years, so you want to choose one with whom you feel comfortable, and in whom you have confidence. Shop around. Ask questions. Use your instincts. Remember, your decision does not have to be a final one. If you are unhappy with your choice, there are many other fine physicians in the area.

Questions to ask yourself

1. Do I (or my children) prefer a male or female physician? An older, more experienced physician, or a more recently trained physician?
2. Would it be more convenient to have the office close to work, home or childcare?
3. Are the office hours flexible enough for my needs?
4. What does my insurance cover, and is the doctor a provider for that plan? Do I have the option to go "out of plan"? If so, how much will it cost to do so?
5. Do I prefer a group practice where there are several physicians to see my child or do I prefer a solo practitioner?
6. What feelings did I get about the pediatrician from our initial visit?
7. Did the office surroundings and staff make me (and my child) feel comfortable?

? Questions to ask the pediatrician

1. Who are the physicians in the practice and what are their qualifications?
2. At which hospitals do the physicians have admitting privileges?
3. Are patients assigned to one physician in the practice or are they free to see anyone?
4. How are phone calls handled? Is there a special call-in time?
5. Who covers the office after hours?
6. How are emergency calls handled?
7. How quickly can you get a well-child or sick visit appointment?
8. How long are typical visits, and what is the well-child schedule of visits?
9. Are there any subspecialists in the practice, or any allied health professionals associated with the group?

 # Resources

National Directories, Inc. *The Washington Physicians Directory*. Washington, D.C., 1994.

See page 30 for a list of local referral services.

Food Guide Pyramid
A Guide to Daily Food Choices

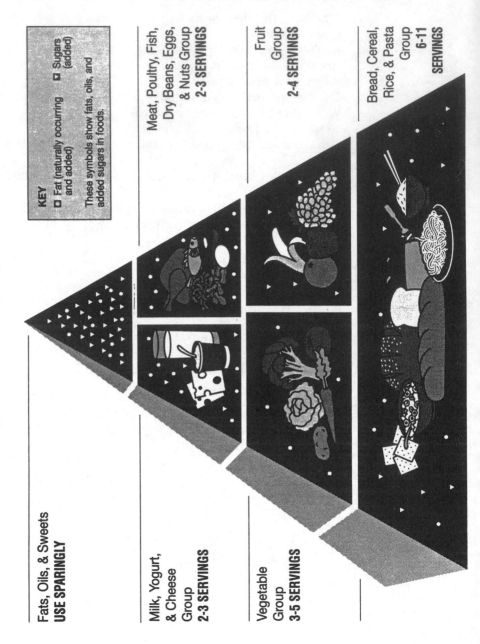

Fats, Oils, & Sweets
USE SPARINGLY

KEY
□ Fat (naturally occurring and added)
□ Sugars (added)

These symbols show fats, oils, and added sugars in foods.

Milk, Yogurt, & Cheese Group
2-3 SERVINGS

Meat, Poultry, Fish, Dry Beans, Eggs, & Nuts Group
2-3 SERVINGS

Vegetable Group
3-5 SERVINGS

Fruit Group
2-4 SERVINGS

Bread, Cereal, Rice, & Pasta Group
6-11 SERVINGS

Raising a Healthy Eater

by Ann Selkowitz Litt, M.S., R.D., L.D.

Feeding your family the right way teaches your children to respect their bodies and sets the stage for lifelong healthy eating habits. The science of nutrition, or what we need to eat to be healthy, is always evolving, but general requirements are well accepted. Getting kids to eat that healthy diet—the art of delivering nutritious foods in an acceptable way—is often the challenge for many parents. With a basic understanding of children's physical growth and development, an acceptance of your responsibility as a parent in the feeding relationship, and a blend of the science and art of nutrition, feeding your child can be an enjoyable aspect of parenting.

Developmental Readiness

During the first year of life, developmental readiness determines which foods should be introduced. From birth through 6 months, nutritional and developmental needs are easily met by breastmilk or formula. Before solid foods are offered, babies should be able to sit with support and close their lips around a spoon. This usually happens between 4 to 6 months, the time most babies will be ready to eat cereal from a spoon.

Around 6 to 7 months, babies start grasping for food. This is the time to offer finger foods such as soft toast and crackers. Rotary chewing begins at about 8 or 9 months. Foods that require some chewing, such as mashed vegetables and soft mashed fruits, can be added. A baby's lips can close around a cup at this age. A cup can be used for practice, but babies will still need to suck most of their liquids. Between 10 to 12 months, the transition to table foods is made. Babies now become interested in self feeding, although they lack the skills to manage the entire meal. Self-feeding is a wonderful way for babies to show their independence, and it should be encouraged in spite of the tremendous mess that it makes.

Throughout the first year, solids are added merely to introduce new flavors and textures. Provide your baby with opportunities to explore foods for that purpose. Some babies show no interest in food at first. Since feeding should be pleasurable, take the cue from your baby and don't pressure him to eat. It may be necessary to hold off on feeding for a few

Ann Selkowitz Litt, M.S., R.D., L.D. has been in private practice since 1980. Ann has counseled hundreds of families on how to feed children healthfully. She has acted as a consultant for the ABC affiliate in Washington, is often quoted in The Washington Post *and is a columnist for* Washington Parent.

days, if the baby was particularly upset. Be relaxed during the feeding, and don't push foods that seem to be rejected.

After the first year, many feeding issues emerge. They often parallel developmental stages. Being aware of these stages is important so you are prepared for what to expect. For instance, a 2-year-old refusing broccoli is most likely using the powers she has discovered with her favorite word, "No," and not really refusing the much maligned vegetable. "No" should not be seen as a rejection of food, but only as vocalizing a favorite word. Continue feeding small amounts of the food without any discussion.

How to Avoid Raising a Picky Eater

It is our overreaction to what is really normal development that creates the picky eater. For example a food jag, a request for the same food all the time, is a common developmental pattern that concerns many parents. Jags are a normal phase of development, usually occurring when a child is struggling for autonomy. Repeated requests for a familiar food assures your child he can control something within his environment. Your reaction dictates how long and how problematic these normal stages are. Acknowledging the pattern, but not making a big deal about it, will help to end the stage quickly.

From the first feeding, there is a clear-cut division of responsibility between parent and child. Parents are in charge of providing foods and setting limits about the mealtime environment, and children are responsible for eating or not eating, and deciding how much is needed. This approach requires parents to trust their children, and it also forces parents to set limits and live within those limits.

Most parents are unsure of how much to feed a child. Remember your responsibility is to provide the food, not to eat it. Trying to control this part of the feeding relationship sets you up for unending food battles. Since babies are born with the natural ability to eat when they are hungry and stop when they are full, they are capable of adjusting their intake based on what they need. During periods of rapid growth, they eat a lot. It often seems like too much food for such a small child. As growth slows down, intake will slow down also. The rapidly growing 15-month-old becomes an active, albeit slower growing, 2-year-old. With many developmental changes during this phase, coupled with a diminished growth rate, the 2-year-old seems to exist on air for days. When we interfere by pushing her to eat more or withholding foods because we think she's had enough, the natural mechanisms satisfying hunger and fullness become damaged.

Parents are in charge of establishing an age appropriate feeding schedule and setting limits about the eating environment. Avoid constantly doling food out on demand, but rather set up meal and snack times. Regular mealtimes provide a reliable and predictable pattern that eliminates continuous grazing and lets children sit down to meals ready to eat.

You are also responsible for creating an acceptable eating environment. Some ground rules work well, too many backfire. Simple rules such as eating only in the kitchen and no television during meals should hold regardless of age. Expectations for manners and length of time you expect your child to stay at the table need to be flexible and assessed often. As in all parenting, we need to evaluate and change as our children change.

You choose and prepare the foods that you consider healthy. If you don't want hot dogs in your house, don't buy them! Children are entitled to like and dislike foods, but we should not be slaves to their tastes. When preparing a meal, have at least one nutritious food you know your child will eat, even if it is always bread. After you serve the meal, your job is done. You are not responsible for preparing separate meals for "picky eaters." Short order cooking has no place in the busy lives most of us lead. Constantly catering to your child's requests for "chicken nuggets" will not provide him with the opportunity necessary to broaden his food repertoire.

Children older than 3 should be asked to taste new foods, but should never be forced to eat foods they don't like. Since it does take repeated exposure to a new food to get to the acceptance stage, continue to place it on your child's plate regardless of previous rejections. Simply tasting is all you should require. There is no benefit to bribing, forcing or cajoling. If you bargain with your child to eat "something green," he will not go back to that food on his own. He will continue to expect a reward for trying the "yucky" healthy foods.

Encouraging your child to "clean his plate" oversteps your boundaries. By doing this, your are ignoring her internal control for hunger and fullness. You are encouraging overeating, a practice many adults have tried to break their whole lives. If a meal is left uneaten, however, it is not your job to fix something an hour later.

Dessert battles tend to dominate feeding discussions. If dessert is an issue, serve it with the meal. By making children eat an arbitrary amount of food to receive dessert, you encourage overeating and also elevate the least nutritious part of the meal to the most important one. Dessert should usually be simple foods such as plain cookies, frozen pops or small scoops of ice cream or frozen yogurt.

What Is a Healthy Diet?

The development of the new food pyramid illustrates our current emphasis on providing a diet that promotes lifelong good health. The pyramid is a guideline for healthy eating at any age, encouraging a low fat, high carbohydrate diet. The types of food we should eat remain the same, only the amount needed changes.

Grain foods form the base of the pyramid. Getting enough from this group has never been a challenge when feeding children. Whole grain breads, cereals, rice and pasta are important sources of complex carbohydrate and fiber, nutrients essential for good health. Not all choices need to be whole grain, but since they do contribute more nutrients than refined breads and cereals, try to introduce your child to whole wheat bread, brown rice or whole grain cereal.

Fruits and vegetables are important sources of many nutrients and may be helpful in preventing certain types of cancers. Of course, kids have never eaten foods just because they are healthy, and it is unwise to coax them into eating more because of nutritional value. Offer fruits and vegetables in an "eater friendly" way: peel, cut, seed or steam them until you hit upon one that is acceptable. If your child prefers fruit over vegetables, try using a variety of fruits and don't push the veggies. Children tend to devalue those foods we push, and are less likely to try them on their own.

Milk and dairy products, now towards the top of the pyramid, show our newer thinking about the nutritional role they play. Although they are an important part of a growing child's diet, they are no longer considered the backbone of a diet. Because of our increased understanding of the dangers of a high fat content, leaner foods are emphasized. However, for children under 2, whole milk and whole milk products are recommended, because toddlers require a higher fat intake to meet the demands of growth and brain development. After the age of 2, most children can use the same lower fat milk products eaten by the rest of the family.

Protein foods typically eaten by the whole family can be fed to children, although some object to stringy or chewier types of meats. Mashed legumes, eggs, cottage cheese and peanut butter are excellent protein sources if meat is rejected.

At the top of the pyramid are foods that contribute fewer important nutrients, commonly referred to as "junk food." It is important to include some foods that are just plain fun. If a house is too pure, and there isn't "junk" around, your child will become very resourceful in finding it. While junk food isn't advocated, every healthy child should be allowed to enjoy cookies, chips and candy in a limited amount. Totally restricting sweets creates an aura that they are special. Including them in a reasonable amount helps children keep them in perspective and not crave them or sneak eat them. Using sweets and "junk foods" to bribe children, is an inappropriate use of foods. It sends children the wrong message, teaching that good behavior is rewarded with food. Since most kids are not bribed with carrots, more nutritious foods become regarded as foods to endure, while junk food should be devoured with enthusiasm.

Family Dinner Time

In our busy lives, the family dinner often does not exist. This is a big mistake as dinner can be a wonderful time to share ideas and interests. All efforts should be made to have some family meal regularly. Children need and like the structure and discipline of family mealtime to feel secure. The food served is often the least important aspect of a family meal. Make every effort not to nag or use the dinner table as a battleground over food.

Including your children in different parts of meal planning is helpful. If you have problem eaters, let them choose some part of the meal occasionally. Even young children can be responsible for preparing some parts of the dinner. Including them in simple preparations, encourages them to eat a wider variety of foods. (See page 325.)

Specific eating problems can cause tension around meals. If you have an overweight or underweight child, or a picky eater, the division of responsibility between you and your child must be clearly understood and accepted. You decide what and when, he is in charge of how much. This requires a great deal of trust in your child. You may require professional assistance to feel comfortable with a new approach. There are many reasons why eating problems occur. Improving the diet is only the beginning. Evaluating parenting skills, looking at your child's self-esteem and accepting your child's genetic composition are all necessary for resolving eating issues.

As in all other aspects of parenting, your children look to you to set limits and develop structure for them. They also see you as a role model. While we don't need to have perfect bodies or have to eat only nutritious foods, feeding children may mean improving our own habits. Providing your children with nutritious foods in a pleasant environment is critical for their growth and development. Accepting your responsibility as a parent in the feeding relationship, and letting your children assume what is their job, helps them become independent and secure, and avoids many eating issues. Helping your son or daughter learn to eat a great variety of foods in an enjoyable way is one of the best lessons you can teach them.

Questions to ask yourself

1. My child will not eat any vegetables. Has he observed me eating vegetables?
2. Do I push my child to eat more than he seems to want?
3. Am I comfortable with my child's body, or do I have an unrealistic idea of how he/she should look?
4. Do I use desserts and other sweets as rewards?
5. Have I set up an age appropriate meal pattern for my child?
6. Do I know what a healthy diet is? Am I familiar with the food pyramid?
7. Do we have a family mealtime?

? Questions to ask a nutritionist or doctor

1. At what age should I introduce solids in my baby's diet?
2. When should I wean my baby from breastmilk or formula to whole milk?
3. Do you recommend vitamin supplements for babies? For children?
4. How do I know if my child is growing and developing appropriately?

 # Resources

Associations

Consulting Nutritionists of the Chesapeake Bay Area and District of Columbia Metropolitan Area Dietetic Association: Consulting Nutritionists provide counseling for individuals or groups and can assist with family nutrition planning, special diets, weight management. 202-289-4215

Kids Against Junk Food: An organized campaign to get kids involved in improving the foods marketed and sold to children, and in improving eating habits. Contact the Center for Science in the Public Interest: 202-332-9110

Consumer Hotlines on Nutrition Issues

American Dietetic Association Consumer Hotline (operates 9 a.m.-4 p.m. Central Time) 1-800-366-1655
American Institute for Cancer Research 1-800-843-8114
USDA Meat and Poultry Hotline 202-720-3333

Nutrition literature/guides for Washington Metropolitan Area

Giant Food, Incorporated: 301-341-4366
Provides free literature, handouts, recipe guides for consumers.

Safeway Stores, Incorporated: 301-386-6803
Provides free literature, handouts, recipe guides for consumers.

Further Reading

Satter, Ellyn, M.S., R.D. *Child of Mine: Feeding With Love and Good Sense.* Palo Alto, Ca.: Bull Publishing Company, 1986.

Satter, Ellyn, M.S., R.D. *How to Get Your Kid to Eat...But Not Too Much.* Palo Alto, CA.: Bull Publishing Company, 1986.

Starke, Rodman D. and Mary Winston, eds. *The American Heart Association Cookbook, Fifth Edition.* New York: Times Books/Random House, 1984.

Ponichtera, Brenda, R.D. *Quick and Healthy Recipes and Ideas: For People Who Say They Don't Have Time to Cook Healthy Meals.* The Dalles, Oregon: Brenda Ponichtera, 1991.

Winston, Mary, ed. *American Heart Association Kid's Cookbook.* New York: Times Books, 1993.

★ Special Needs

Educational Video:
"Near Normal Feeding for Infants with
Oral-Facial Anomalies" ($39.95 + $3.50 shipping & handling)
Exceptional Parent, Dept EP9409
P.O. Box 8045
Brick, NJ 08723
1-800-535-1910
Feeding for infants born with cleft lip and/or palate. Video outlines common variations of oral defects, feeding concerns and strategies parents can follow.

Feingold Association of the US
P.O. Box 6550
Alexandria, VA 22306
703 768-FAUS
Provides information on food additives and possible effects on child behavior, such as overactivity, attention deficit, anxiety, aggression, sleep disturbances and learning disabilities.

Food Research and Action Center/National Anti-Hunger Coalition
1875 Connecticut Ave., NW, Suite 540
Washington, DC 20009
202-986-2200
Disseminates information on federal programs available to help low-income families purchase food. Also provides nutrition counseling for parents.

Your Child's Mental Health

Finding Help for Emotional and Behavorial Problems

by David Mrazek, M.D.

Being a parent is a special privilege and a daunting challenge. While much of behavior and personality has an inherited basis, early experience still has an important impact on the emotional well-being and ultimate personality development of children. All families experience periods of intense stress during the years that their children are growing up. Being able to support your child through these stressful times, particularly if you, too, are under pressure, is one of the most important and most difficult aspects of being a parent.

To be able to raise a child effectively, parents must have a sense of what the timetable of normal child development is likely to be. It makes good sense to know what developmental milestones to look for and take the time to make sure your child is on track. It helps to adopt a child-centered philosophy and to be prepared to make family changes if problems occur. While it is easy to adopt this perspective when things are progressing smoothly, difficult decisions must be faced when the needs of parents compete with the needs of their child.

What Are the Early Warning Signs?

There are many signs and signals to alert parents that their child is having difficulties in adapting to problems at home or at school. These include minor problems that simply represent a slower unfolding of developmental achievements as well as more serious symptoms such as the expression of bizarre ideas or aggressive behaviors. For developmental problems, the "wait and see" strategy is appealing and is probably the correct course to take for reasonably minor delays. If your child is three or four months behind on either her emotional or physical accomplishments, she may be simply growing up at her own pace. However, when delays stretch out to more than six months, it is prudent to take some action. Perhaps the most straightforward example is observing how young

David A. Mrazek, M.D., is the Chairman of Psychiatry at the Children's National Medical Center in Washington, D.C. He earned his undergraduate degree from Cornell University, his medical degree from Wake Forest University, and received postdoctoral training at the University of Cincinnati and the University of Colorado. Formerly on the faculty of the University of London and the University of Colorado, he is currently a professor of Psychiatry, Behavioral Sciences and Pediatrics at the George Washington University School of Medicine.

children begin to talk. If a child is slow to produce single words but then begins to speak in short sentences, there is little to worry about as the sequence of skill acquisition is normal. However, if there is a sudden loss of language or the sudden production of unusual, bizarre phrases, this is a sufficient indication to pursue an early mental health evaluation. Similarly, hyperactive behavior and difficulty in maintaining attention may be present with a range of severity varying from mild symptoms that can be easily resolved using behavioral modification techniques to severe and persistent disturbances that require a thorough child psychiatric diagnostic evaluation and judicious use of medications. Yet another example is the expression of early moodiness and sadness. All children experience moments of grief in times of loss and disappointment, but persistent or intense depressive symptoms are strong indications of the need for a prompt evaluation.

Who Can Help?

There are a number of professionals who have specific training that allows them to both identify and treat children who have emotional and behavioral disturbances. There are three general pathways to becoming a "clinician." The shortest training period is required in order to become a clinical social worker. Such individuals can usually receive a master's degree in social work in two years. Then they are eligible for licensure in Washington, Virginia and Maryland. However, they may pursue additional training in working with children and families or further graduate training leading to a doctorate in social work or a related field. These individuals are well prepared to understand deviations from normal development. Many are specifically trained to work with families to help them cope with stresses that arise at school or as a result of family conflicts.

Clinical child psychologists have more extensive academic training which requires four to five years of graduate training in clinical psychology. This includes a one year clinical internship at an approved training site and the completion of a doctoral thesis prior to receiving a Ph.D. Following graduation candidates must undergo supervised clinical work for an additional one to two years and successfully pass a national examination in order to obtain a license. It is prudent for parents to inquire directly about whether a clinical psychologist is fully licensed prior to pursuing services.

A child and adolescent psychiatrist is the most extensively trained child mental health clinician. Child psychiatrists require four years of graduate training in medical school prior to beginning their formal psychiatric training. They then serve as an intern for one year during which time they often receive direct training in pediatrics and have the opportunity to care for children who have severe medical and emotional disturbances.

The first year is followed by a residency that requires working with adult patients for two years and then two additional years working under close supervision, exclusively with children and adolescents who exhibit a wide range of clinical problems. On completing adult training, a psychiatrist must take and successfully pass an intensive examination conducted by the American Board of Psychiatry and Neurology, that involves direct clinical assessment of a specific patient. After becoming board certified in general psychiatry and completing child and adolescent training, the child and adolescent psychiatrist is eligible to take the board examination designed to establish clinical competence in working with children and adolescents. While medical licensure is a requirement to practice medicine in the District of Columbia, Maryland and Virginia, it does not address issues of competence in the specialty. In contrast, board certification in child and adolescent psychiatry is a very strong indication of competence and parents should inquire about whether the doctor has obtained this credential.

It is important to be assertive in determining the competence of a prospective mental health provider. In addition to assuring that the clinician has the basic credentials just described, parents should establish that the individual has either sufficient experience with the problems that their child is having, or, at the very least, has access to appropriate supervision from more senior clinicians. Certainly, one safeguard is to seek treatment from a well-established clinical group practice specializing in child psychiatric or psychological problems. A clear local example is the Children's National Medical Center that has established clinical practice standards for all child mental health professionals who practice within the system and has organized four suburban multidisciplinary teams as well as an extensive outpatient department at the primary center site in northwest Washington.

Another effective method of assuring clinical competence is to confer with other professionals who care for children. These include the child's pediatrician or the family physician as well as school counselors and religious leaders. Often these individuals can provide important preliminary suggestions about how to handle more circumscribed problems. If these problems persist or are more serious and require immediate assessment, these professionals can often direct parents to well-respected local mental health clinicians.

How Much Does It Cost?

Clinical fees vary dramatically, and it is important to establish the expected cost of both evaluation and treatment early on in the process. For more minor problems, a single evaluation session may be sufficient to provide a family with some guidance on how to handle a straightforward problem. Depending on the type of clinician and his training and experience, the cost of such an initial session may vary from $60 to $250. For more complex problems, a series of diagnostic evaluations are usually necessary that involve both individual sessions and family meetings. If psychological testing is required, the cost will vary from a few hundred dollars for one or two specific tests, to well over $1,000 for more complicated test batteries. The cost of ongoing treatment sessions can also vary widely, but generally cost less and are scheduled for shorter intervals of time than the initial diagnostic evaluation sessions. Group psychotherapy sessions can be very effective for some problems and are generally the most economical form of treatment.

Questions to ask yourself

1. Does my child seem happy most of the time?
2. Does my child have friends?
3. Is my child doing OK in school?
4. Is my child sleeping well and eating normally?
5. Is my child cooperative?
6. Are my child's problems primarily related to tensions in the family?
7. Are my child's problems primarily related to behavior that I can learn to control?
8. Does my child seem to have problems with sadness, anxiety, attention or hyperactivity that may require the use of medication?
9. Are my child's problems associated with a pediatric problem?

*The general rule is that the more serious the problem or the more it involves medical consideration, the more important it is to seek out a professional with more extensive training.

Questions to ask the professional

1. Is my child's behavior a sign of immaturity or an early symptom of an emotional or behavioral problem?
2. How will you establish whether my child has a problem?
3. What kind of training experience have you had with these kinds of difficulties?
4. If there is a problem, how would you treat it?
5. Are there alternative ways to approach this problem?
6. Could this problem be associated with a medical problem?

Resources

Area Mental Health Hotlines for Parents and Children

Montgomery County Crisis Center: 301-656-9161
Northern Virginia Hotline: 703-527-4077
Washington, DC Hotline: 202-574-5442

Consultative Centers

Children's Hospital Consultative Centers

Laurel Lakes
13922 Baltimore Avenue/Unit 4A
Laurel, MD 20707
301-369-4100   1-800-787-0006

Montgomery County
14804 Physician's Lane/Suite 122
Rockville, MD 20850
301-424-1755   1-800-787-0243

Northern Virginia
3022 Williams Drive/Suite 100
Fairfax, VA 22031
703-573-9383 1-800-787-0467

Spring Valley
4900 Massachusetts Avenue NW/Suite 320
Washington, DC 20016
202-745-8860

University of Maryland Parent Consultation & Child Evaluation Program
301-314-7673
Offers residents of the metro area: psychiatric evaluation and diagnostic testing, individual and group therapy, parent counseling, family counseling.

Further Reading

Brazelton, T. Berry. *Families: Crisis and Caring*. New York: Balantine Books, 1989

Brazelton, T. Berry. *Listen to a Child*. New York: Addison-Wesley, 1984.

Brazelton, T. Berry. *The Earliest Relationship*. New York: Addison-Wesley Publishing, 1990

Brazelton, T. Berry. *Toddlers and Parents, A Declaration of Independence*. New York: Dell Publishing, revised 1989.

Fraiberg, Selma. *Understanding and Handling the Problems of Early Childhood*. New York: Charles Scribner's Sons, 1959

Greenspan, Stanley. *First Feelings: Milestones in the Emotional Development of Your Infant and Child from Birth to Age 4*. New York: Viking Press, 1985.

Greenspan, Stanley. *Playground Politics: The Emotional Life of the School Age Child*. Reading, Massachusetts: Addison Wesley, 1993.

Mrazek, David and Bill Garrison. *The Children's National Medical Center A to Z Guide to Your Child's Behavior*. New York: Perigee Books, Bantam Publishing Company, 1993.

★ Special Needs

American Association of Children's Residential Centers
1021 Prince Street
Alexandria, VA 22314
703-838-7522
Maintains a national directory of residential treatment facilities for severely emotionally disturbed children and adolescents.

Center for Infant Study
University of Maryland School of Medicine
Dept. of Psychiatry/Howard Hall, Room 132
660 W. Redwood Street
Baltimore, MD 21201
301 328-2485 or 2486
Studies infant mental health, and will make referrals to parents with children under the age of three who are at risk for illness.

Children's National Medical Center
111 Michigan Avenue, NW
Washington, DC 20010
202-884-5386

What to Look for in a Family Dentist

by Ronald M. Starr, F. A.A.P. D.

Good dental care begins before birth and can continue for a life time. Long before they can be seen or felt, a child's teeth have started to develop. An expectant mother who gets enough fluoride helps the in-utero formation of her child's front teeth. Permanent front teeth and first molars begin to form beneath the gums when a baby is only 6-months old, and by age 9 a child's wisdom teeth have already started to develop, although they may not emerge for 10 more years.

Even during your child's infancy, you can be instrumental in helping to minimize future tooth decay. Many parents may not realize that milk remaining in the mouth will start to ferment and increase the bacteria count. Children should therefore never be put to bed with a bottle. Gums should be wiped clean of milk from either bottle or breastfeeding to prevent bacteria from filtering through the tissue during the night and beginning the formation of plaque. It is not impossible for 1- or 2- year-olds to develop cavities, which can penetrate very quickly into the nerves of the teeth and create abscesses.

While teeth should be cleaned from their onset, children between ages 3 and 6 should learn the proper way to brush. It is wise for parents to monitor their children's technique. Using some of the staining dyes, which color just the plaque, and brushing a child's teeth for him during the day will help teach good dental habits.

Fluoride is essential to the development of healthy teeth, strengthening the enamel to build resistance to acid penetration and decay. In the Washington area, children get adequate fluoride in their drinking water and in foods cooked in tap water. In areas without fluoridation or for families using well-water or only bottled water, children should receive fluoride supplements until they are 8 years old. Toothpastes with fluoride provide only topical protection.

Parents should set an example for their children by maintaining good dental habits themselves. You should be aware that your own oral bacteria is transmissible to your children through kissing and food sharing. A

Dr. Ronald M. Starr has been a practicing pedodontist in Bethesda, MD for 35 years. He taught pedodontics at the University of Maryland and Howard University as associate professor and was Acting Chairman at Howard University in 1971. Graduating the University of Maryland School of Dentistry in 1958 and the University of Illinois Pedodontic program in 1959, he has been a fellow of the American Academy of Pediatric Dentistry since 1968.

positive attitude toward dental visits can also have a direct effect on your child's health. Tell your child how much you enjoy having your teeth cleaned and try to avoid communicating your own negative feelings or fears of the dentist.

The best approach to good care is a comprehensive *preventive* program involving you, your child and your dental professionals. Following a course of "anticipatory guidance" your dentist can give you information about what to expect in your child's dental growth and development. Knowledgeable parents can be prepared to deal with each stage and be more alert to any problems. A dental practice that emphasizes communication both with parents and the young patients will follow your family through many years of good dental health.

The Right Dentist

When choosing a dentist for your child the best sources of information are the people who are closest to you and professionals whose opinions you would trust on other medical matters. Check with your friends and relatives. Ask your child's physician for a recommendation of a dentist with whom he or she has had good communication or who may happen to have been the choice of a number of the families in the pediatric practice. One new patient recently checked references by standing up and asking for a dental recommendation at a PTA meeting. Don't be afraid to ask around. In looking for a dentist, a group practice may be able to offer a range of comprehensive care, including orthodontics, specifically directed to a younger population.

Regional dental societies are listed in the phone books and can send you names of pediatric dentists in your area. Individual dentists are also listed in the yellow pages by specialty and geographic location. Dental referral services may also provide useful information, but be aware that participating dentists pay to advertise through these organizations.

Be sure the dentist has a degree from a qualified dental school and be sure s/he is certified in the area of specialty in which you're interested. All dentists must have completed four years of college, four years of dental school and two years of graduate work in an area of specialization, three if that area is surgery. This extra training, in addition to five years of active practice, qualifies the graduate to sit for his or her boards in that specialty. A specialty in pedodontics focuses on general dentistry for children, including problems of their growth and development. Dentists receive either a DMD or the equivalent DDS certificate, depending on the school attended.

Every state has continuing education requirements for a dentist to renew his license. Locally this consists of about 25 hours of course work every year. As new materials such as polyurethane and plastics are introduced, techniques also change. This ongoing education process allows a dentist to keep up with new developments, maintain a fresh outlook and be a state-of-the-art practitioner.

The First Visit

By the time your child is about 3 years old she should have all her baby teeth. This is a good time to schedule the first visit to the dentist. This visit should be a gentle introduction to the office procedures. Your child can be shown how to use a toothbrush and may allow the hygienist to clean off some accumulated tartar. It will not be painful, but it will feel different. Try to make the appointment early in the day, when your child is fresh and better able to cope with any new situations that may seem stressful.

When calling the dental office for an appointment be sure to ask the receptionist any questions you feel are important about the nature of the visit and the costs. If you have chosen to go to a general dentist, rather than a pedodontist, you may want to inquire about the number and age of children seen in the practice. Feel free to interview the dentist and anyone in the office who will be seeing you and your child.

Use common sense. Do you feel comfortable with the people in the practice? Does the receptionist respond courteously and competently to your initial phone calls? Is the hygienist friendly? Since a doctor chooses his or her staff, you can assume that a staffers' communication with the patients is usually a direct reflection of the dentist's approach and philosophy.

Check out the facility. Are the surroundings pleasant? Is there child-sized furniture in the waiting area? Are there books or toys to interest your son or daughter if you have a short wait for your appointment?

The dentist should try to create a comfortable environment for your child. Asking some friendly questions and talking informally with you can decrease some first-visit anxiety. Distractions such as a TV or a Walkman may be useful with older children, but are not advisable with a 3-year-old. You want your son or daughter to pay attention and be involved in what is going on. Of course, if your dentist is fortunate enough to have a name like Starr, he or she has a built-in icebreaker. Many children have giggled through my introduction as Dr. Moon or Dr. Sun.

A very upset child may be difficult to calm during the first visit, but with good communication each successive visit should begin to build a comfortable relationship and there should be less and less nervousness. One patient, now 18 years old, insists he looked forward to his childhood checkups only because of his end-of-visit selection from the office Toy Chest. While this was filled only with very inexpensive novelties, an attempt to eliminate it provoked an outcry from parents and children alike. If children are treated with respect and told what is going on, they will have fewer unpleasant experiences and look forward to coming back.

What Happens Now?

Once you are satisfied with the initial relationship established between your child and a dentist, you should plan to return for checkups every six months. Each recall visit should include a cleaning, usually by the dental hygienist, as well as an examination of the soft tissues for any infections or abnormalities.

Teeth should be counted and checked for any defects. Instruction in the proper method for cleaning and removing the daily plaque formations should be given to both you and your child. A discussion of diet and its effect on the teeth, including a recommendation to limit sugar and fermentable carbohydrates would also be appropriate at this time. There is little need to worry about children who do not drink milk, since the body will take calcium from other food sources.

Your dentist may recommend that preventive sealants be applied to the biting surfaces of the permanent teeth whenever these new teeth erupt. Over the past 20 years, this preventive technique has proven to be better than 80 percent effective in preventing the penetration of bacteria.

Early Intervention Helps Straighten Teeth

"Early intervention" is an approach used by many pedodontists to help the growth and development of your child's teeth by recognizing and treating problems before all the permanent teeth have come in. There are many things that can be done to make way for permanent teeth to emerge in a better position. Headgear, one of the more common of these treatments, controls the upper jaw movement. It allows for more lower jaw development using the natural growth force in a younger child rather than pushing against already established dentition.

Some of the most recent advances in the field of growth and development are seen in the early diagnosis and treatment of upper- and lower-arch size discrepancies. If baby teeth are crowded, an early-treatment orthodontic appliance can help increase the upper arch of the mouth to create space for the permanent teeth.

During the transition stage, when teeth are changing from primary to permanent, most growth differences have an excellent chance of being resolved. This can modify dentition to create normal facial contours and profiles, or, if braces are needed later on, may shorten their active phase by as much as one half. Don't worry about spaces. Spaces in primary teeth are wonderful. It means more room will be available for the larger, permanent teeth when they are ready to come in.

As your child matures, your dentist should be able to inform you of any growth or development problems that appear to need closer examination. Your child should be encouraged to ask questions about his or her treatment and should be given considerate and thoughtful answers. If the dentist has *not* had extensive training in a field, he or she should be comfortable making a referral to a specialist.

If the decision is made to address a problem by introducing a dental appliance, you should attempt to get maximum cooperation from your child. Children themselves will choose whether or not they want to make something work. Get clear information about how often an appliance must be worn, how to properly care for it and what, if any, foods are restricted. If your child shows a lot of resistance, it may be better to avoid removable types of retainers when possible, since these items can easily be "lost." If this is not possible, you might try what some parents have found effective: a line-item in the child's allowance for replacement of frequently lost dental appliances.

This early preventive first stage approach has many appealing aspects. Children tend to be much more cooperative in the preteen years and may willingly use an appliance properly. In addition, the natural growth of the child can often be utilized to develop corrective measures. You and your child should feel comfortable discussing all options with the dentist.

How Quickly Should I See the Dentist?

As with your pediatrician, find out how to reach your dentist in case of emergencies, and who covers the office when the dentist is away. Most practitioners will have their home phone, a beeper number or an answering service available for easy access. Ask for a list of those dental emergencies that need care and how to handle them efficiently.

Children fall down all the time and bump their teeth. But not everything is an emergency. Immediate attention is needed if there is bleeding, a possible jaw fracture, a broken tooth or a knocked out permanent tooth. (See chart of First Aid for Dental Emergencies p. 83.) If the baby teeth have been displaced, responding quickly and moving them back in place can avoid problems. A 3-year-old who receives a bump around the gums but still has the teeth in the original position may require only an x-ray and careful watching.

The younger the child, the better the chance of saving a tooth because the root has not yet closed and is therefore still being supplied with blood. Some grayness in the tooth, which is like a bruise on the arm, may go away when blood is still being furnished.

If there is any indication of infection, however, this must be treated immediately. If necessary, a damaged baby tooth may even be removed without causing future problems. A space left by removing more than one tooth, however, should be temporarily filled in to prevent excessive movement of the remaining teeth.

Although these situations are commonplace occurrences and healthy children heal fast, you should call the dentist, who should help evaluate the seriousness of your child's condition.

In choosing the right dentist for your child, be a smart consumer. Collect information, investigate claims of quality and savings, rely on an honest and clear approach. Look for a professional who makes you feel comfortable, communicates well, is willing to answer questions and wants to educate you and your child. If you shop wisely, the dentist who gives your child his first exam will be the same dentist who 15 years later wishes him good luck on the way to college.

Questions to ask yourself

1. Is the dentist's location convenient?
2. Are the office hours flexible to fit my needs?
3. Does the office generally run on time and stick to its schedule?
4. How are emergencies handled?
5. What was the feeling of my first contact with the office staff on the phone?
6. What, if any, dental insurance coverage do I have?

 # Questions to ask the dentist

1. Who will be seeing my child and how long is the appointment? (If the hygienist does the cleaning and instruction, will the doctor spend time answering questions?)
2. Do you see my child on each visit? What do you look for?
3. If not a pediatric office, how many children do you see?
4. Are there any special dental problems that may come up before our next appointment?
5. What is the cost of each visit and what is included?
6. Does the office accept insurance? Will they file?
7. If there will be extensive work needed, is a payment schedule available?

Resources

District of Columbia Dental Society
502 C Street, NE
Washington, DC 20002
202-547-7613

Northern Virginia Dental Society
4201 John Marr Dr.
Annandale, VA
703-642-5297

Southern Maryland Dental Society
4920 Niagra Road
College Park, MD
301-345-4196

★ Special Needs

Academy of Dentistry for Persons with Disabilities
611 E. Chicago Ave.
Chicago, IL 60611
312-440-2660

Dental Guidance Council for Cerebral Palsy
UCP Association - Professional Services Program Dept.
66 E. 34th St.
New York, NY 10016

National Foundation of Dentistry for the Handicapped (NFDH)
1600 Stout St., Suite 1420
Denver, CO 80202
303-573-0264

National Institute of Dental Research (NIDR)
National Institutes of Health Bldg. 31, Rm 2C35
31 Center Dr., NSC 229
Bethesda, MD 20892-2290
301-496-4261
Research and treatment of dental diseases and craniofacial
disorders, including cleft lip and palate.

Orthodontia

Brace Yourself for a Positive Experience

by Jeremy D. Orchin, D.D.S.

Orthodontics is the branch of dentistry that specializes in the diagnosis, prevention and treatment of dental and facial irregularities. These problems are technically called malocclusions, meaning bad bites, and can be caused by inherited factors such as crowded or widely spaced teeth, extra or missing teeth, receding or protrusion of the lower or upper jaw, or a cleft palate. Malocclusions can also be acquired from thumb or finger sucking, mouth breathing related to enlarged tonsils or adenoids and premature loss of primary teeth. Whether inherited or acquired, malocclusions can affect your child's dental structure as well as overall appearance, and should be treated.

Although there is no ideal time to first see an orthodontist, the American Association of Orthodontists (AAO) recommends that every child make a first visit at about age 7. This early examination allows the orthodontist to identify problems which may escape the attention of a general dentist or pediatrician and decide when, if and how a particular malocclusion can best be treated.

Early treatment can achieve results that are often unattainable once growth is completed. Skeletal discrepancies that result in an overbite, underbite, open bite or irregularities of the jaws are problems that are best treated when a child is still growing. A good age to begin is when a child is about 8 years old. At that point the permanent 6-year molars have fully erupted and a child is usually amenable to treatment. In other cases, if there is a minor amount of irregularity such as mild crowding in front but a good bite in back, waiting until all permanent teeth have erupted prior to starting treatment may be best.

To choose an orthodontist, ask for referrals from your family dentist as well as friends and neighbors who have had positive experiences with their orthodontists. Talk to your children's friends who are already in active treatment for first-hand information. If you are new to the area, the local dental societies or the AAO can send you a list of qualified orthodon-

Jeremy D. Orchin, D.D.S., has been in private practice in Washington, D.C. for 25 years. He received his D.D.S. from Western Reserve University, in Cleveland, Ohio, and Certificate in Orthodontics from Columbia University, New York, NY. Presently he is on the Senior Attending Staff of Children's Hospital Medical Center, Washington, DC. He is also on the Clinical Faculty, Department of Otolarygology-Head and Neck Surgery, at Georgetown University.

tists in your community. Phone book listings (not advertisements) must be done through the Association, so you can use this as a source of information. But keep in mind that the list will not be complete since not all orthodontists choose to be included. Ask questions of as many people as possible so you can determine the orthodontist with the best professional reputation who fits your family's medical and scheduling needs.

Board Certification Is Important

Although any licensed dentists can provide orthodontic services they cannot claim to be "orthodontic specialists" unless they have completed a minimum of two years postgraduate work at a recognized dental school. If your orthodontist is a member of the American Association of Orthodontists he or she must have met exacting standards of both the AAO and the American Dental Association.

Ask the doctor you intend to use if he or she is a Diplomate of The American Board of Orthodontics. Only about 35 percent of orthodontists have achieved certification by the American Board of Orthodontics. This recognition requires an extensive written examination and proof of clinical expertise by presenting and defending to the Board 10 ideally finished orthodontic cases, a process which takes at least four to five years after graduation from orthodontic school. Ongoing licensing in most states and the District of Columbia requires about 25 hours of continuing education per year.

The exacting standards and the time and effort to become a Diplomate are indications that those pursuing this route are clearly committed to excellence. A greater number of orthodontists are now working towards Board certification, finding that it provides not only peer recognition and personal satisfaction, but also an additional means for the public to objectively evaluate the profession.

Communication, Convenience and Cooperation

Choosing an orthodontist is a subjective and difficult decision. The end results will include permanent changes to the teeth and face. Because there is no single definitive treatment plan, you must feel comfortable with the professionals who will be handling the care of your child as you enter into this long-term relationship. Ask about the orthodontist's background and philosophy. The orthodontist's approach will be a reflection of where and when he or she went to school, the continuing education courses taken and the familiarity with up-to-date reading about changes in the field.

Ask about what to expect when treatment is completed. Will there be a change in my child's facial appearance? Will she have a more or less prominent chin? Will there be a lot of teeth showing when he smiles? Feel free to discuss and question anything proposed by the orthodontist. It is important that both you and your child have a complete understanding of the long-range effects of any appliances, extractions and treatments and feel a part of the overall planning and decision-making.

Finding the right orthodontist also means feeling comfortable with the office facility and all who work there. Is the clerical and clinical staff friendly, professional, helpful, attentive and happy? Look at the ambiance of the physical facility to determine if this office is the place for you. It should be clean, modern, open and instill a feeling of warmth and confidence. Finally, be sure that the practice uses up-to-date sterilization techniques. The doctor and all clinical staff should wear latex gloves during all treatments and change them, with thorough hand washing, between each patient.

Inquire about convenience and promptness. Is there flexibility for your child's school and extracurricular schedule? Do you have to wait long once in the office for your appointment? Monthly visits are the most common and many appointments will be during school hours. Is the office located near home, school or work? Are there evening or Saturday appointments? How easy is it to get or change an appointment?

Once the orthodontist for your family has been chosen, understand that it is a relationship that will continue for many years. There should be a good, supportive attitude from your orthodontist and the staff. Positive reinforcement and good communication work best in achieving cooperation from youngsters.

What to Expect

Orthodontic treatment today need not be unpleasant. Regular visits are usually handled in an open-bay treatment area. Children often see their friends and socialize while waiting for appointments. Concerns about discomfort and appearance are reduced when they see their peers going through the same experiences. It is also a good time to see who's wearing the hot new-colored appliances, rainbow retainers and colored rubber bands.

Most active orthodontic treatment takes from one to three years. The actual time depends on the type of problem, at what age treatment is started, cooperation from the patient and the complexity of the case. Some courses of treatment may be handled in two separate phases of one or two years each with a rest period in between. Although treatment is seldom very painful, some discomfort is occasionally encountered and the doctor and staff should be sensitive to the patients' concerns, anxieties and comfort level.

The orthodontist will need to evaluate diagnostic records by studying models of your child's teeth, panoramic X-rays (to discern impacted or missing teeth), cephalometric head x-rays (a side view to determine if jaws are out of alignment) and facial photographs, to determine the appropriated treatment.

The question of the need to remove permanent teeth prior to active treatment is often a dilemma for parents. Ask the orthodontist if he or she does extractions or attempts to avoid extractions of permanent teeth. With the newer functional, expansion and growth modifying appliances and headgears it is now possible to handle the majority of malocclusions without the need to extract permanent teeth. Does the orthodontist provide early treatment with these appliances? These devices change the relationship between the upper and lower jaws, taking advantage of a child's natural growth forces.

The retention aspect of orthodontics is perhaps even more important than the active treatment. No matter how good the orthodontist, or how excellent the result, your child will have to wear a retainer of some sort for at least two years. Some malocclusions may even require retention for life to ensure that there will not be a relapse. Just as other parts of the body change with age, so does the mouth, and there may therefore be some shifting. The earlier a problem is corrected, before teeth are set in an improper position, the more likely that the results will be stable.

If you and your child want opinions on treatment from more than one orthodontist, ask for your records. Members of the AAO follow certain standards for diagnostic records, so that they should be transferable, making it unnecessary to incur additional expense for duplicates. Even though you may feel inclined toward selecting a particular orthodontist, if you are the least bit unsure of the proposed treatment plan seek a second opinion before beginning. In finalizing your decision, do not accept any treatment plan unless the doctor has a complete set of diagnostic records.

The actual cost of orthodontic treatment depends on the severity of the problem, the type of practice, and the care, skill and judgment that the orthodontist feels is required. The orthodontist should give you a total fee for the complete treatment and explain what, if any, additional charges you may incur. Convenient financing with an initial down payment and monthly installments can usually be arranged. Most offices also accept major credit cards as a convenience to parents. Although many insurance plans now include some orthodontic benefits, they usually have a lifetime maximum that is much less than the total agreed upon fee. Be sure to check with your insurance carrier and discuss any questions with the office staff or doctor.

Successful orthodontic treatment requires a cooperative effort between you, your son or daughter and your doctor. Each person must be comfortable with the other. The professionals in the practice, including the entire office staff, must be willing to communicate with you openly.

Orthodontics is for the health and benefit of some people. For others it's more cosmetic. If there is a problem and nothing is done, your child could be fine. But more than likely, a spacing, crowding or bite problem left untreated may lead to cavities and periodontal troubles because of difficulty cleaning, or headaches and face pains as a result of uneven stress on the jaw joints. If appearance is affected there may be self-image problems that could have a major negative effect on the quality of life. Orthodontists are keenly aware of how treatment will effect the dentition, the face, the smile and the whole demeanor of your child and will work with you to achieve healthy, beautiful results that will last a lifetime.

Questions to ask yourself

1. What is the orthodontist's professional reputation?
2. Where did he or she attend dental school and take advanced courses?
3. Is the orthodontist a Diplomate of the American Board of Orthodontics?
4. How many of my friends use this orthodontist?
5. How convenient is the office location and schedule for my family?

Questions to ask the orthodontist

1. When is an appropriate time to start?
2. Why is treatment necessary?
3. What kind of treatment? Extraction or non-extraction?
4. What happens if we decide not to treat?
5. What types of financial arrangements are available?
6. How is insurance handled?

Resources

American Association of Orthodontists
401 North Lindbergh Blvd.
St. Louis, MO 63141-7816
1-800-222-9969

American Board of Orthodontics
401 North Lindbergh Blvd.
St. Louis, MO 63141
314-432-6130

Special Needs

American Academy of Pedodontics
211 E. Chicago Ave., Suite 700
Chicago, IL 60611
312 337-2169

American Cleft Palate-Craniofacial Association
1218 Grandview Avenue
Pittsburgh, PA 15211
412-481-1376

Caring for Your Child's Eyes

by Blackwell S. Bruner, M.D.

Three-year-old Douglas sat within a foot of the screen, watching his favorite television show. His 8-year-old sister was frustrated with her piano practicing—the notes seemed to be jumping around the page. Their 13-year-old brother made paper airplanes instead of doing work in math class, because his teacher's small, neat numbers looked like bugs crawling across the blackboard.

All three children are exhibiting behavior which should be checked by an ophthalmologist. But they don't all necessarily need glasses. A parent, or even a technician screening a child, cannot be absolutely sure if there is a vision problem. It is very easy, though, for an eye doctor, using drops and instruments, to determine if there is nearsightedness (myopia). It is therefore important that any time you have a question about your child's vision, you should have it checked by an ophthalmologist.

Douglas, like other 3-year-olds, simply enjoyed sitting close to the TV. Able to clearly see the dog down the street and a plane in the sky, his vision was normal. The siblings were a different story. Their behavior, and a family history of nearsightedness, were additional indicators that his sister needed glasses for the first time and his brother needed a change in the glasses he'd been wearing for three years.

It is not difficult to monitor the vision of children who are old enough to communicate verbally and those who are screened in school. The situation is different, however, with preverbal children.

Does My Baby See?

Most parents will look at their newborn and immediately try to tell if the baby is responding to them visually. Babies can see at birth, but the visual system is not fully developed. During his first few weeks a normal, full-term infant may have some ability to look directly at you, but will also have uncoordinated eye movements. By three months, however, a baby should have straight eyes and be able to demonstrate sustained central fixation and smooth following movements.

Blackwell Smith Bruner, M.D., is a Washington native who attended the George Washington University (GWU) Medical School, and completed his ophthalmology residency training at the Washington Hospital Center. His pediatric ophthalomology training was at Children's Hospital National Medical Center. For more than 25 years he has been in private practice in Washington, and is licensed in Maryland and Virginia. Dr. Bruner has been an instructor at GWU and served on the academic staff of Children's Hospital National Medical Center.

In these early months, a pediatrician looks to see if an infant's eyes are anatomically normal and track properly and if the pupils are responding to light. By looking in the back of the eye, it is possible to determine the refraction, indicating whether the baby is nearsighted, farsighted or astigmatic. Even though a baby can't respond subjectively, if the eyes can fix on objects and follow them, and if their anatomy and refraction are normal, this usually corresponds to good vision.

When to Consult a Pediatric Ophthalmologist

If your pediatrician notices a problem or if there is a family history of visual disorders, it is important to consult an ophthalmologist. Case studies have shown that a person's vision, either good or bad, is established during the first decade of life. Only about 4 percent of children are born with congenitally maligned eyes (strabismus). It is also unusual for a baby to be born with a cataract problem. If left untreated this can result in irrevocable amblyopia, with a loss of central fixation and the ability to see anything other than large objects. Early surgery to realign the eyes in the case of strabismus and replace the lens in case of congenital cataracts will allow the brain to get equal input from both eyes and develop better binocular function.

Amblyopia (also known as lazy eye) is characterized by decreased vision as a result of strabismus, unequal refraction (where one eye is more or less nearsighted or farsighted than the other), cataracts, corneal disease or any other disorder that prevents the development of vision at a young age. Treatment performed before a child is 8 or 9 will generally be successful. Wearing glasses and using a patch over the good eye will stimulate the brain to use the eye that needs strengthening.

When all development has been normal during your child's regular pediatric checkups, a good time for a first visit to an ophthalmologist is between ages 3 and 4. At this point your son or daughter is old enough to give good responses regarding depth perception and color recognition and is still young enough to be treated successfully if a problem is found.

What Is a Pediatric Ophthalmologist?

If your pediatrician or primary care physician has made a referral, or if you feel it is time to see an ophthalmologist, one question you may have is whether or not to seek out a specialist.

All ophthalmologists are physicians who have spent three to four years after medical school doing intensive eye training in a hospital setting. Many then choose to train for one or two more years in subspecialties such as pediatric ophthalmology. In the Washington, D.C. area we are fortunate to have many pediatric ophthalmologists who were associated with Dr. Frank Costenbader, who developed the idea for the subspecialty during the 1940s and became internationally known for his work. In addition, the American Association for Pediatric Ophthalmology and Strabismus (AAPOS) was started here in 1974.

A specialist who limits his or her practice to children will tend to have a gentler approach and a wider range of experience with children of all ages. But if you already have a good relationship with a general ophthalmologist don't hesitate to schedule a visit for your child. You may want to start with a short appointment where your doctor can meet your son or daughter and discuss what to expect at the exam. This will give you an opportunity to decide if your ophthalmologist and your child would communicate well and be comfortable together.

Finding an Ophthalmologist

The best recommendations for finding an ophthalmologist for your child will probably come from your pediatrician. Ask your doctor how the ophthalmologists are thought of in the medical community. Have other families in the pediatric practice provided positive feedback about a particular doctor? Ask to get in touch with them if possible. Ask for your friends' recommendations. What are their impressions about an ophthalmologist and his/her practice in general? How long did it take to get an appointment? In a nonemergency situation you should not have to wait more than three weeks. How do they feel the ophthalmologist dealt with emergency or surgical situations as well as regular checkups?

Ophthalmologists do not have to be board certified to practice. But within five years after their medical residency, most have passed their board examinations. The American Academy of Ophthalmology and the AAPOS publish lists of board certified ophthalmologists and pediatric specialists. The District of Columbia and the Maryland and Virginia State Medical Societies also have lists of doctors in the area. In addition, these societies have information on any complaints or disciplinary procedures against the physicians. The Prevention of Blindness Society is a good local resource for information about ophthalmologists as well as for free educational pamphlets and vision screening.

Check your insurance policy to see if eye care is included. You may be required to use only certain eye doctors or you may need a referral from your primary care physician. Private practice fees for an initial examination will probably be in the $70 to $90 range. Feel free to inquire about fees and payment at the time you make your appointment.

Once you have the names of board-certified ophthalmologists, it is up to you to find someone with whom you are comfortable. Is the ophthalmologist accessible? Most have office hours from 8:30 to 5:00, but some may have evening or Saturday hours. Is the office conveniently located?

Schedule an informal visit with the ophthalmologist for your son or daughter. How does the ophthalmologist relate to your child? I have found that looking like the "guy next door," not wearing white or a jacket and tie, elicits a comfortable response in a child. A minimum of necessary low-key equipment and some gimmicks, such as toys or a television, will help relax a young child so that the medical examination itself might proceed almost unnoticed.

Does the ophthalmologist listen to you and answer your questions in direct understandable language? There is nothing so complex in medicine that cannot be explained. Does the doctor also talk to your son or daughter in a straightforward, engaging manner? Is the ophthalmologist associated with any hospital teaching programs? Those who are, often stay most up-to-date on new developments in the field.

After the ophthalmologist has examined your child's eyes, ask if everything is normal. Are there signs of disease or difficulties? Will your son or daughter need glasses? You should leave the office with the feeling that you understand the treatment plan and exactly what the ophthalmologist is trying to accomplish.

Optometrists and Opticians

Opticians only make eyeglasses. Optometrists deal primarily with diagnosis, refraction for glasses and contact lenses. In most states they are licensed to use dilating drops for diagnosis, but cannot prescribe medications to treat diseases. Academically, they have spent a prescribed number of years after college in the study of eyes at schools of optometry.

Unlike ophthalmologists, optometrists do not attend medical school, train in hospitals or study visual abnormalities. Some medical plans that include vision care will only cover services rendered by optometrists. While an optometrist may be very capable of providing exactly what your family needs, as a consumer you should be aware of the differences in educational background and experience and be prepared to ask questions about recommended treatments.

Continued monitoring should be provided through school screening and by parents. Once your preschooler has been seen by an ophthalmologist, and it has been established that development is healthy and normal, there is no exact time when a return visit is appropriate. Many doctors and parents prefer to schedule regular visits every two or three years.

School vision screening programs, which occur every two years in the Washington metropolitan area, as well as pediatrician and parental observation, can be sufficient to monitor your child's vision. Parents will usually know if their child is having trouble recognizing objects across a room. But it is also important to be aware of personality traits or behavioral changes that can have their roots in poor vision. For example, Denise was acting withdrawn and introverted. She was thought to have psychological problems until it was discovered that she was highly myopic. Denise was fine once she got her glasses. Many youngsters who have refraction problems have no idea that anything is wrong. They think they are seeing the world as it is supposed to be seen.

A school nurse or technician may contact you about taking your child for further vision testing. It will then be up to you, the parent, to help determine the need for glasses by discussing this with your ophthalmologist. Even though your 6-year-old is slightly myopic, you may decide to wait until your child is older and needs to see a blackboard across a classroom before getting glasses.

What happens if your child gets glasses but forgets or refuses to wear them? Nothing visually. Whether your child actually wears prescribed glasses will not affect his or her visual development as long as there are no other problems. But since there are benefits to good vision, parents should take an active role in getting their children to cooperate with any treatment plan.

Ocular Problems

A number of problems may warrant an emergency visit to your ophthalmologist. Some of these situations can also be handled by your pediatrician. Do not hesitate if there is ever any question about an injury: call a physician.

Many infants have problems with blocked nasolacrimal ducts, which cause increased tearing. This disorder is treated conservatively by local hygiene and antibiotic drops or ointment while waiting for the ducts to open. By the time a baby is 8 months old, 80 to 90 percent will open on their own. If the ducts do not open, they can be probed with a high degree of success. This is done with local or general anesthesia.

Toddlers especially, seem to get hit around the eyes. The bones of the face and the eyelids are very protective. Look in the eye for redness, bleeding or any foreign objects. The cornea may be scratched, giving a persistent foreign-body sensation. The doctor may prescribe local antibiotics and patch the eye for 24 to 48 hours. This usually takes care of these problems.

Children are frequently infected by bacteria causing conjunctivitis, producing a red eye and discharge. This infection responds well in most cases to a seven-day course of local antibiotic drops or ointment prescribed by your pediatrician or ophthalmologist. Older children commonly have problems with getting something—dirt, sand, chemicals—in their eye. If this happens the eye should be washed out with tap water only and you should immediately seek the care of your pediatrician, ophthalmologist or nearest emergency facility.

When ocular problems arise with very young children, it is likely that you would not yet have thought about choosing an ophthalmologist for your child. While emergency treatment can be handled by your family physician, this may be a good time to also begin looking toward the future. Talk to your pediatrician about specialists vs. general ophthalmologists. Observe whether your own eye doctor has young patients and how comfortable they seem in the office. Be ready to make an informed decision when the time is right for your child to see an ophthalmologist.

Questions to ask yourself

1. Would I prefer taking my child to a specialist (pediatric ophthalmologist)?
2. Is this person well thought of by my pediatrician or other physicians I know?

3. Is the ophthalmologist associated with a hospital teaching program?
4. How do my friends feel about the care given by the ophthalmologist?

? Questions to ask the doctor

1. Is my child's vision normal? If not, what can be done and what effect will it have on life and learning?
2. Is the anatomy of the eye normal?
3. Are there signs of disease or disorder?
4. What is likely to happen to my child's eyes in the future?
5. Are there any activities which should be avoided in my child's case?

Resources

American Academy of Ophthalmology
655 Beach Street
San Francisco, CA 94109
415-561-8500

American Association for Pediatric Ophthalmology & Strabismus (AAPOS) P.O. Box 193832
San Francisco, CA 94119
415-561-8575

Children's Hospital National Medical Center
111 Michigan Avenue, NW
Ophthalmology Department
Washington, DC 20010
202-884-3015

Medical Society of the District of Columbia
2215 M Street, NW
Washington, DC 20037
202-466-1800

Prevention of Blindness Society of Metropolitan Washington
1775 Church Street, NW
Washington, DC 20036
202-234-1010

Preparing Your Child for a Hospital Stay

by Amy E. Wheeler, B.S.

A trip to the hospital can be a frightening event for children. All the strange sights, sounds and smells conjure up vivid fears and misconceptions for most who enter. Some children worry about being left in the hospital without a loved one present. Others are concerned about the pain they may encounter and unpleasant procedures soon to be performed on them by strangers. Not knowing the facts, and what is *really* going to take place may be the greatest cause of stress for them. Although these fears are normal, children need to be prepared for hospital encounters in order to create as positive an experience as possible. Listed below are 10 tips that can help you achieve this.

• Gather as much information as you can about your hospital and the procedures your child will be undergoing. This will be beneficial when talking with your child and will help alleviate some of your own concerns. Children can quickly sense if you are nervous or uncomfortable with the surroundings and events.

• Ask questions of your child to assess what he/she may be thinking and to clear the air of misconceptions. Some questions you may wish to ask are: "Why are you going to the hospital?" and "What will happen while you are there?"

• Answer questions with honesty and in a manner your child can understand. Most children appreciate knowing the sequence in which events will occur and hearing descriptions which are sensory oriented.

• Be cautious with your wording. Words such as "shot," "stick" or "dye" can be easily misinterpreted or taken out of context thereby fostering painful thoughts. Maintain honesty, yet select softer, nonthreatening terms. For instance, "The doctor will prick your arm. It may sting a bit, but only for a short time."

• Be actively involved with the care of your child. Perhaps you can hold him/her during procedures. Your child will respond much more positively to restraint when in the hands of a loved one.

• Help provide ways for your child to cope during frightening procedures. You may wish to suggest counting out loud, singing or squeezing

Amy Wheeler, B.S. in Child Development, has worked in several children's hospitals helping parents and children adjust to hospital encounters. Currently she is a freelance writer on child development issues and the mother of two young children.

your hand. Mentioning that it's OK to cry will let your child express feelings she may have been fearful of doing. Also, allowing your child to make choices, no matter how small, will help put some control back into her hands. For example, your child may wish to pick which finger she wants blood taken from.

• Bring a favorite toy or security object from home that's comforting.

• Provide positive reassurance in all circumstances. Letting your child know how great he is doing works wonders.

• Be understanding of possible behavior changes following hospital experiences. Some children may be more teary-eyed or irritable or may regress in areas they once mastered. This is a normal response and should diminish with time. If these behavioral changes continue for more than a few weeks, you should speak to your family pediatrician.

• Give your child plenty of opportunities to play out the past events and talk openly about them. Playing "doctor" with dolls, or reading a children's book about hospital stays will provide a beneficial outlet.

Some hospitals have professionals known as Child Life Specialists who help children adjust to hospital experiences. They can provide play activities for your child and clearly explain procedures in an age-appropriate manner. Lastly, check to see if your hospital has any preadmission tours or orientations to enhance familiarity. Taking advantage of these resources and opportunities will aid in reducing any hospitalization anxieties your child may have.

Resources

Area Hospitals With Special Programs for Little Patients

Children's Hospital
111 Michigan Ave., NW
Washington, DC 20010   202-884-5000
Children can tour hospital before surgery. Parents can stay in room. Child Life program. Child Life specialists try to normalize hospital experience for children by helping them to work out feelings through games and activities. New Horizons program features a poet, visual artist, dancer and musician who come to work on projects with children. Artists and performers from such organizations as the Washington Ballet visit units where children are confined to their rooms, and perform in atrium. Hospital philosophy: treat the entire family when a child is ill or injured. Extensive social work program to help families connect to resources in community for continuing help, parents' support groups.

Georgetown University Hospital
3800 Reservoir Rd., NW
Washington, DC 20007   202-784-2000
Surgical tour, Child Life department, as well as three pediatric units. Parents can sleep in ward, but not in ICU. Hospital provides a cot in the parents lounge.

Howard University Hospital
2041 Georgia Ave., NW
Washington, DC 20060 202-865-1267
Tours. Parents can sleep in room, except for ICU; but hospital
provides space elsewhere in unit. General pediatric unit. 4-bed ICU.
Infants-adolescents.

Holy Cross Hospital
1500 Forest Glen Rd.
Silver Spring, MD 20910 301-905-0100
Preoperative class and tour for children coming in for surgery. Parents
can stay 24 hours and overnight, chair in room. No ICU. Child Life
program, special activities and play therapy. Philosophy: family
oriented, rather than just patient oriented.

Shady Grove Adventist Hospital
9901 Medical Center Dr.
Rockville, MD 20850 301-279-6000
Same-day pediatric tour. Parents can sleep in room with child. No ICU.
Playroom. Pediatric surgeon.

Montgomery General Hospital
18101 Prince Philip Dr.
Olney, MD 20832 301-774-8882
Tour. Parents can stay overnight with child. Beds and pediatric nurses
available as needed. No ICU.

Arlington Hospital
1701 N. George Mason Dr.
Arlington, VA 22205 703-558-5000
Tour. Parents can sleep in room with child. No ICU. Very small, self-
contained, able to be near children. Allow children to visit.

Alexandria Hospital
4320 Seminary Rd.
Alexandria, VA 22304 703-504-3000
Family-centered care for children from infancy to adolescence.
Special Saturday class to prepare children and their parents for
surgery. Parents can sleep in room with child. Neo-natal ICU but not
pediatric age. Certificates in bravery awarded to children. Special
menu selections for children. Playscape area with mural and fish tank.
21-bed unit with private rooms available

Fair Oaks Hospital
3600 Joseph Siewick Dr.
Fairfax, VA 22033 703-391-3124
Tour. Small, 7-bed pediatric unit. No ICU. In Emergency Department
one room decorated and equipped for children. Parents can stay
overnight with children. Playroom. Pediatric nurses present 24 hours.

Reston Hospital Center
1850 Town Center Parkway
Reston, VA 22090 703-689-9000
Tour. Parents can sleep in room. No ICU. Parents have food provided
for them when they stay or visit hospital.

Prince William Hospital
8700 Spring Valley Rd.
Manassas, VA 22110   703-369-8000
Tour. One parent can sleep in room with child. No pediatric ICU.
Brand new unit. 14 beds with 2 activity rooms for toddlers through
adolescents. Large kitchen where families can bring food from home.
Patio attached to unit.

★ Special Needs

Association for the Care of Children's Health (ACCH)
7910 Woodmont Ave., Suite 300
Bethesda, MD 20814
301-654-6549
Publications related to helping children and families cope with
hospitalization.

Coordination Center for Home and Community Care, Inc.
P.O. Box 613, Brightview Business Ctr.
Millersville, MD 21108
301-621-7830
Provides chronically ill children an alternative to lengthy hospital stays
through safe at-home treatment. Makes use of medical facilities in the
Baltimore/Washington area, organizes discharge, and helps set up and
monitor home care.

Pediatric Projects, Inc.
P.O. Box 571555
Tarzana, CA 91357
818-705-3660
Promotes the mental health of children undergoing health care.
Distributes medically oriented therapeutic toys and books for
children coping with illness, disability, medical treatment and
hospitalization.

Sick Kids Need Involved People (SKIP)
216 Newport Drive
Severna Park, MD 21146
301-261-2602
Offers information and education to families of children requiring
specialized medical care. Fosters home care for children dependent
on medical technology.

Parenting

At 10 a.m. Saturday, the Joneses' first baby was born in a nearby hospital.

By 10 a.m. Sunday, the newly expanded Jones family was back in their Washington home.

By 10 a.m. Monday, both parents were ready to return to the hospital. Their new son had been crying off and on for hours—mostly **on**, it seemed. They had tried all the suggestions in several childcare books: a diaper change, a feeding, a sip of water, rocking, walking, a lullaby. Still the baby howled.

"I want my mommy," sighed Mrs. Jones. Her husband laughed, but she wasn't really kidding.

Did the Jones need a grandmother, a doctor, or a live-in baby nurse? Or, did they simply need reassurance that some new babies cry a lot without having a serious problem?

Adding to a family can be a stressful time. Couples undergo great changes in their routines, in their lifestyles, in their emotions. First and foremost, they worry about the baby. Typically, they also worry about juggling careers and parenthood, finances, the altered nature of the marriage and lack of extended family nearby.

It's not unusual for one or both partners to feel overwhelmed. Some parents begin to suspect that they've lost their independence and freedom forever. Others may feel lonely, isolated, neglected or excluded.

Getting safely through the new-baby days is no guarantee that all is smooth sailing, either. Parents of older children often feel confounded and upset by behavior problems, squabbling and competition between their youngsters, and difficulties in school.

Parents will find guidance to deal with these challenges and others on the following pages.

Learning to Be a Parent
Area Programs for New Moms and Dads

By Erica Moltz, M.A., C.P.C.

A new parent experiences a profound transition that is at once joyful, exhilarating, confusing, demanding and physically exhausting. Support and education can supply invaluable assistance during this significant time of change. A group of peers going through a similar experience can help validate feelings and reactions and provide a new social network. This type of program can furnish information about infant development and temperament which will relieve some anxieties and help parents make competent decisions about their baby.

In the metropolitan area, many nonprofit organizations, hospitals, pediatric practices and local governments provide quality education and support to new families, offering the chance to participate in groups facilitated by trained leaders. Many of these groups continue even after the formal sessions end, providing an opportunity to develop lasting friendships and a sense of community.

The Challenges Facing New Moms

As a new mother grows into her role as a parent she faces many challenges: feeling competent with her baby, integrating motherhood into her identity and redefining her relationship to her partner, her family and friends. As she and her baby fall in love, her task is to develop her own style of mothering without relying on hard and fast rules about the "right" way to respond to her baby's needs. She also has to learn to decipher her infant's cues about eating, sleeping and crying. She must modify her expectations and images of both her baby and herself as a mother, and understand that her infant is not a blank slate on which to inscribe a personality, but is a separate being with a unique temperament.

One of the most challenging situations which goes to the heart of a new mother's identity is figuring out how to balance caring for her baby with career demands. Many mothers have found personal, creative solutions to balancing work and home either through job sharing, part-time work or putting their careers on hold. Other mothers return to work full time, either by choice or necessity, and often have to deal with guilt feelings and the challenging task of choosing an appropriate caregiver.

Erica Moltz, M.A., is a Certified Professional Counselor. In addition to being a PACE leader (see resource below), she works with individuals, couples and groups in her private counseling practice and is a consultant on Adoptions Together.

A new mother's relationship with her partner also goes through a major transition. Issues emerge about how to divide baby care responsibilities and on-going household obligations. If the mother is out of the work force for a significant time, financial strategies have to be renegotiated. The couple also has to create ways to clearly define themselves as a family while including extended family and friends in this new entity. Being exhausted and having considerably less time together may hinder a couple's ability to communicate about these changing concerns. And images of a "perfect" family may lead them to decide that something is wrong with them, a conclusion that will complicate what is actually a normal and inevitable developmental stage.

Many new mothers live far away from their extended family and don't have neighborhood friends to whom they can turn for support and advice. Fortunately, in the Washington area there is a plethora of support for new moms. Several organizations offer time-limited education and support groups to mothers of infants up to 6 months of age. Churches, hospitals, pediatric practices and county government adult education programs offer parenting classes and seminars. There are also support groups to meet specific needs and interests for adoptive moms, moms over 40, stay-at-home moms and moms suffering from postpartum depression.

The Challenges Facing New Dads

A new father also faces a myriad of challenges when he becomes a parent. He may feel the pressure of increased financial responsibility, especially if his partner's income has decreased or if she has chosen to step out of the paid work force to be at home with the baby. If he has chosen to be at home with the baby fulltime, his task will be to redefine both his role in the family and his future career path. Whether he is at home full time or comes home to his family at the end of the day, he may grieve over the fact that his relationship with his wife has changed so dramatically. At the same time, his task is to "fall in love" with his baby and learn to feel competent as a parent. It is for these reasons that fathers can also benefit greatly from being with other new fathers and their infants. Support groups can help fathers acquire self-confidence about their new roles and provide them with the parenting skills based on understanding their babies' behavior. Unfortunately, most new dads have few opportunities in their daily lives to talk with each other about reactions to their challenging new roles. The good news, however, is that some support and education groups are designed specifically for new fathers. These groups can also support fathers as they learn to balance their own needs with the needs of their wives and babies, in addition to career demands.

Questions to ask yourself

1. Are my expectations of myself realistic or do I feel as if I have to be a perfect mother, father?
2. Am I giving myself enough permission to feel ambivalent about being a parent?
3. How am I taking care of myself during this stressful time?
4. Do my partner and I have enough time alone together to refuel?
5. What kind of support from family and friends and/or employers do I need that I may not be asking for?

Question to ask the professionals

1. How long have you/your organization been providing parenting education?
2. How much preparation and experience have the instructors had specifically in parent education?
3. Who comes to these groups (proportion of fathers, single or step parents, care providers, average age, average education levels) and what is the attrition rate during a course?
4. What is the cost of this program? How is payment handled (deposit, sliding scale, financial assistance)? Are there membership or early registration discounts? A differential rate for a second parent or nanny from the same family?
5. Is there a maximum and minimum number of participants in a group? Ratio of leaders to group members?

 # Resources for New Parents

Arlington County Adult Education: Parenting classes. For mothers and their babies up to 6 mos. Six 90-minute sessions with ASPO/Lamaze trained leaders. Classes throughout VA and MD. 703-358-7200.

ASPO/LAMAZE New Mothers Group: For mothers and their babies up to 6 mos. Six 90-minute sessions with ASPO/Lamaze trained leaders. Classes throughout VA and MD. 703-644-4152.

Depression After Delivery: An 8-wk. support group for women experiencing severe postpartum depression. Provides telephone support and referrals to social services and physicians. 703-379-2494.

Fairfax County Parenting Education Center: Classes include "Baby and Me." 703-506-2221.

Family Education of Southern Maryland: Parenting workshops. 301-705-8527.

Family Education Network: Parenting classes, couple enrichment classes and workshops. 301-888-1020.

Frederick County Family Counseling Center: Mothers' group for mothers of infants to 5-year-olds. 301-694-9002.

Maternity Center: Class topics include Body-Shape, Parenting, Sibling, Nutrition and Postpartum Support. 301-530-3300.

Middle-Aged Moms Support Group: Monthly meetings for moms (age 40+) of infants and toddlers. Free. Commission for Women. 301-279-1800.

Moms' Club: Support group for stay-at-home mothers. Chapters throughout the Washington area. 410-750-9427.

Montgomery County Parenting Education and Family Support Programs: Parenting classes, play groups and support groups at five drop-in centers throughout Montgomery County. 301-929-2025.

Mothering Seminars: In Washington and Virginia: A 6-wk., 2-hr. support group/seminar for mothers of infants up to 6 mos. 703-450-0910. In Maryland: A 5-wk., 2-hr. support group/seminar for mothers of infants, birth to 3 mos. 410-381-5195.

Mothers' Access to Careers at Home (MATCH): Support group for mothers who operate a home-based business. 703-764-2320.

Mothers First: Support group for stay-at-home moms. Meets in Falls Church. Conducts play groups throughout Virginia and in Rockville. Conducts groups for fortyish moms of infants and young children. 703-827-5922.

Mothers at Home: Support group for stay-at-home mothers. Publishes *Welcome Home*, a monthly journal. 703-827-5903.

Mothers' Support Group: For mothers of infants up to 1 year. Babies invited. Meets in DC and Bethesda. Playgroups for toddlers. 202-244-8871.

Now That I'm a Mother, Who am I Really? Eight-wk. support group for mothers of babies 9 mos. and up. 301-585-7352.

PACE (Parents After Childbirth Education)
10600 Willowbrook Drive, Potomac, MD 20854 301-983-9133
MD, VA and DC locations, for parents with a new baby. Infant-5 1/2 months. Trained group leaders have a background in mental health or child development. Workshops for women in groups of 10 with two leaders in each group. Mother and child attend together in the a.m. Mothers develop a support system; also have a father's group.

Parent Care: Support and education group for parents with babies up to 6 mos. 703-642-2423.

Parent Education Network Support Group of Northern Virginia.
Informal meetings where speakers share their expertise on children
and parenthood. 703-548-8083 or 703-841-5188.

Parent Encouragement Program (PEP): An 8-wk. class for parents
of newborns to preschoolers. Located in Kensington, MD. 301-929-
8824.

Hospital Programs for New Parents

Almost all local hospitals in the area offer classes and/or support
groups for new parents. See Childbirth Classes page 40.

★ Special Needs

Council for Exceptional Children
1920 Association Dr.
Reston, VA 22091
703-620-3660
Clearinghouse for information about disabilities of all types, and
available resources.

National Parent Network on Disability
1600 Prince Street, Suite 115
Alexandria, VA 22314
703-684-6763 Voice/TDD   703-836-1232 fax
Information supplied to parents on disabilities of all types.

Parent Education Advocacy & Training Center
10343 Democracy Lane, Suite 206
Fairfax, VA 22030
703-691-7826
Assists parents in becoming effective advocates for their children
through training programs and consultation services.

Parent Place of Maryland (Parent Training & Info. Center)
7257 Parkway Drive, Suite 210
Hanover, MD 21076
410-712-0900 Voice/TDD   410-712-0902 fax

Parent to Parent Programs of DC - Easter Seal Society
2800 13th St., NW
Washington, DC 20009
202-232-2342
Links parents of newly diagnosed children with handicaps with
parents who have experienced similar situations.

Parents of Preemies
23020 Wild Hunt Drive
Gaithersburg, MD 20882
301-253-6534

National Maternal and Child Health Clearinghouse
8201 Greensboro Drive, Suite 600
McLean, VA 22102
703-821-8955
Publishes directory of over 400 voluntary, professional and self-help organizations.

Specialized Training of Military Parents (STOMP)
12208 Pacific Highway SW
Tacoma, WA 98499
1-206-588-1741
Provides information to military families on handicaps and available services.

Parenting Classes for Growing Families

How to Transform Hassles into Harmony

by Linda E. Jessup, M.P.H., F.N.P.

Your 8-year-old daughter insists she didn't eat any of the brownies you'd baked as a special dessert for dinner. Yet several brownies are missing and telltale smudges on her face suggest a different story. You:

> **A.** Tell her she's a liar and punish her by sending her to her room without dinner.
>
> **B.** Laugh it off, saying she has an overactive imagination.
>
> **C.** Say you're confused. Her words tell you one thing yet the chocolate ring round her mouth suggests another. Since in this family people have to be able to trust each other, you will each take a 10 minute cooling off period in a quiet place to think about the problem and then you can discuss the matter calmly and work out a solution together.

Or, 6-year-old Michael and his 4-year-old brother, Zeke, typically begin to fight and argue as soon as the older child gets home from school. Suddenly, as they tussle, Zeke bumps his head on the coffee table and begins to scream. You:

> **A.** Shout at the older child to stop being such a bully and tell him he may not watch his favorite TV show for being so mean.
>
> **B.** Rush to Zeke, cuddle him and give him a cookie.
>
> **C.** Check Zeke calmly and ask Michael to quickly wring out a wash cloth in cold water and bring it to put on his brother's bruised head.

Later in private, you talk with Mike, who complains that he's tired by the time he gets home from aftercare and Zeke starts bugging him the minute he walks in. You empathize but let him know that Zeke admires him tremendously and eagerly waits to see him all day. You ask if he would be willing to give Zeke a daily Special Time, a time the younger boy could count on, to do things Zeke initiates for half an hour. Then, at other times if Zeke starts to jump on him or bother him, the older boy can say,

Linda E. Jessup, M.P.H., F.N.P., is the Founder and Executive Director of the Parent Encouragement Program (PEP), Inc. The mother of seven (three biological and four foster children) has been a radio talk show host for nine years on WGTS-FM's program "Talk It Over."

"I'll wrestle with you in our Special Time if you want, Zeke, but right now I want my snack."

Important Parenting Challenges

Parents are faced many times a day with such dilemmas. Answer A suggests an authoritarian approach to discipline while B points to a permissive style of parenting. Selecting C indicates an approach which is neither autocratic nor permissive, but rather uses the democratic principles of developing the mutual respect, personal and social responsibility, cooperation and compassion for others which is promoted in most parent education programs today.

Obviously, raising and guiding children in this fast-paced world challenges the average adult in more ways than most of us could ever have anticipated B.C. (i.e., before children). Whether deterring a biting 2-year-old, dealing with a five-year-old who balks at going to bed or an 11-year-old who scatters dirty dishes all over the house and monopolizes the phone instead of studying, otherwise competent adults frequently find themselves feeling frustrated. They are bewildered and uncertain about how to respond in ways which fit with their personal values and long term goals for their children.

A New Era

It's no wonder parents feel so confused! The whole landscape of nuclear and extended families, neighborhoods, social networks, the media, and changing of community institutions such as schools, presents todays' parents with a multitude of dilemmas. Two-career parents, partners experiencing separation or divorce, issues of mobility, stress, and isolation all add new layers of complexity to today's tasks of parenthood.

Not surprisingly, thousands of parents are asking questions and seeking information about children's development and behavior that wasn't available during our parents' generation. Even where the traditional stores of knowledge do exist, such as within extended families, family-friendly neighborhoods and babysitting networks, today's better educated parents are still going outside to other, more authoritative sources for additional skills and answers.

These parents are finding that a family does not have to be in crisis to profit from parent education. Good parenting resources—from drop-in centers to support groups to classes—are fun, enriching and intellectually stimulating. New connections with others with same-aged children or with those experiencing similar life circumstances, can create child care trading partners and permanent friendships. These fathers and mothers are also discovering that concrete strategies which bring sanity to family life and improve relationships between family members can carry over into other arenas, such as the workplace, with friends or with aging parents.

Finding Help And Support

Many local hospitals, social service agencies, public school systems and private organizations have professional counselors or social workers who provide parenting courses and workshops at intervals or as part of an on-going program. Free-lance child development specialists also may provide parent workshops or classes. These professionals often use the commercial S.T.E.P. program (Systematic Training For Effective Parenting), Active Parenting, or a developmental or topical approach to parent education.

Also within the metropolitan area are organizations where leadership is provided exclusively by parents who have received extensive training, even certification, from the organization. This "peer empowerment" approach uses a skills-based curriculum, encouraging a high level of competence and self-sufficiency from group members. These groups are able to provide year-round, multilevel programs and personalized coaching. They generally offer classes in a variety of locations, but often have a drop-in center and a membership program with special benefits as well.

Some resources focus primarily on a specific life stage, such as infants, preschoolers or elementary-aged youngsters. Others deal with a designated issue, such as breastfeeding or communication skills, or with challenges such as hyperactivity or single parenting. Other groups provide a broad sampling of classes, seminars, workshops and even retreats, with groupings determined by children's ages.

There are so many opportunities to develop parenting skills in the metropolitan area that many "rough spots" can be avoided by finding and taking advantage of these resources.

 ## Questions to ask yourself

1. What is my parenting style? Is my approach and the approach of my spouse generally compatible or are we often in conflict over child rearing issues?
2. Who do I talk to at present when I have a parenting concern? Am I feeling isolated or do I have friends experiencing situations similar to my own?
3. What issues concern me the most with my child(ren)? Who in our family needs the most encouragement right now?
4. Would my spouse or some friends be interested in going to a workshop or taking a class with me?

 ## Questions for program administrators

1. How long have you/your organization been providing parenting education?
2. How much preparation and experience have the instructors had specifically in parent education?

3. Is a particular approach or commercial package used? Why do you recommend this approach?
4. Who comes to these groups (proportion of fathers, single or step parents, care providers, average age, average educational level) and what is the attrition rate during a course?
5. What is the cost of this program? How is payment handled (deposit, sliding scale, financial assistance)? Are there membership or early registration discounts? A discount for a second parent, grandparent or nanny, etc. from the same family?
6. What are the expectations of group participants (regular attendance vs. drop-in, reading, written or experiential home work)?
7. How are classes grouped (by children's ages—mixed or specific; beginning, intermediate, advanced levels; parents' marital status, etc.)?
8. Is there a maximum and minimum number of participants in a group? Ratio of leaders to group members?
9. What arrangements can be made for classes which are missed because of travel, illness, etc.?
10. Are children present during the group? Is on-site childcare available?
11. How often are courses offered? Would there be a variety of classes or a series of skill levels offered?
12. Does your organization offer:
    - workshops, talks or counseling demonstrations
    - a newsletter or other publications
    - membership (individual or family)
    - classes for children/summer camps
    - private consultations with a Parent Educator
    - support groups
    - social events
    - volunteer opportunities
    - a "warm line" for telephone coaching
    - "parents' morning/evening out" programs
    - a drop-in center/lending library/book store/toy exchange
    - professional counseling or referrals to counselors
    - workplace seminars
    - in-service programs for schools
    - referrals to other community services

Resources

The Child Center, Inc.
611 Rockville Pike/Suite 20
Rockville, MD 20852   301-279-5866
A private nonprofit mental health organization which operates with a
sliding scale fee structure. MSWs teach an 8-session STEP course
and other specialty classes on occasion.

Cooperative Extension Service
U.S. Department of Agriculture
University of the District of Columbia
901 Newton St., NE
Washington, D.C. 20017   202-282-3068
Offers family life education programs including parent education,
financial management, sound nutrition, diet and health.

Family Education Center of Southern Maryland
P.O. Box 537
Waldorf, MD 20604   301-705-8527
A nonprofit volunteer organization of lay people and professionals
providing a variety of educational programs based on the principles of
Alfred Adler. Parent study groups are STEP, Children The Challenge,
The Next Step, Changing Families (divorce, death, remarriage);
marriage enrichment courses; workshops and family counseling
demonstrations.

Family Education Network (FEN)
P.O. Box 318
Brandywine, MD 20613
301-888-1020
Offers parenting and marriage enrichment classes taught by trained
parents and professionals in more than 40 locations.

Georgetown University Medical Center
2233 Wisconsin Ave., NW Suite 317
Washington, DC 20007   202-342-2400
STEP classes in 6 sessions; parenting seminars such as
Understanding Healthy Families, Avoiding Holiday Stress, Bridging the
Gap Between Home, Childcare and School, Play Power, Taming the TV
and The Literate Home and Young Children.

HUG (Helping Understanding Grow)
8200 Gainsboro Ct.
Potomac, MD 20854 301-299-5513
A program for parents; lectures followed by discussion on a
variety of parenting topics.

Parent Care
6239 Executive Blvd.
Rockville, MD 20852   301-294-9338
A private, for-profit company which offers topical seminars and short,
sequential courses on Confident Parenting run by a husband-wife
team, Scott and Bonnie Buehler, who are Human Development
Specialists.

PACT (Parents and Children Together)
1657 Crofton Pkwy.
Crofton, MD 21114   410-721-7719
A nonprofit Family Resource Program comprised of parents and
helping professionals. Provides an integrated program of education,
resources and support to solve problems with confidence, feel less
isolated and increase parenting skills. Discussion groups for parents
of infants, older babies, preschoolers and early elementary children;
workplace seminars; STEP classes; workshops and talks.

Parent Encouragement Program (PEP), Inc.
1100 Connecticut Ave.
Kensington, MD 20895 301-929-8824
Year-round resource center/parenting programs based on the
principles of Adlerian Psychology. Classes for parents of babies-teens,
and marriage enrichment. Topics such as Handling Anger or
Decreasing Sibling Rivalry. Instructors are all experienced parents
themselves, highly trained and certified as Parent Educators.
Telephone coaching. Monthly Family Counseling demonstrations.
Morning classes have childcare available. Maximum class size is 20.
Members may form support groups. Community networks fostered.
Scholarships and payment plans.

Coping with Divorce
Getting Children Over the Rough Spots

by Carole L. Mandel, L.C.S.W.-C.

"**H**appy families are all alike; every unhappy family is unhappy in its own way." Thus Leo Tolstoy began *Anna Karenina* over 100 years ago. The words are truer today than ever before. The ensuing years have placed even greater demands on the family, with expectations of each member continually rising. We lead fast paced, demanding, competitive lives, and all too often our children get left behind. Separation and divorce add yet another challenge to the never-ending tasks of raising children. The breakup of a family causes indescribable pain to all involved, especially the children. A major change in their lives occurs over which they have no power or control. Just when their parents' lives are in turmoil, so are their own! As difficult as it is for adults to understand what went wrong in their relationship, it is even harder for their offspring. In response to this, the Washington area has many services, organizations and professionals who attempt to meet the needs of families in various stages of separation and divorce. Montgomery County mandates psychoeducation classes for parents going through this process which inform them of the impact of divorce on the development and adaptation of children. Strategies are offered to facilitate healthy adjustment and problem solving through communication skills. These classes can be followed by support groups for parents and children, or by family, couple or individual psychotherapy. Judges, attorneys and mediators are also available at these workshops to help parents mitigate the negative effects of separation and divorce on their children.

Impact on Children

Any trauma will have an impact on the development of a child. Parents and family are the most important factors in the lives of children of all ages. In general, the younger the child, the more dependent he is on the well-being of his primary caretakers. Stressed, angry, depressed, anxious parents are much less likely to be able to be adequately responsive to the needs of their child. This frequently interferes with or modifies the child's ability to successfully accomplish the developmental tasks at each stage in order to move unencumbered onto the next. Initially the child

Carole L. Mandel, L.C.S.W.-C, is in private practice in Potomac, Maryland, and is a senior staff member and supervisor for Community Psychiatric Clinic. She has presented conferences for professionals in the field of separation and divorce. She has an M.S.W. and is licensed in Maryland and Virginia.

may react to the breakup of the parental relationship with increased irritability or lethargy. A preschooler may exhibit regression to more infan-
tile behaviors, often wetting or soiling, or experience exaggerated separation anxiety, increased aggression or sadness. The school-aged child, 6 to
9 years old, may become angry or fearful due to feelings of betrayal. He
may feel deprived, which will manifest itself as an increase in possessive-
ness of material goods. Children this age often complain of torn loyalties,
feeling as if they have to choose one parent over the other. The 10 to 12
year old preadolescent may appear ashamed, resentful, rejected, lonely,
exhausted or angry. He may even try to assume more adult responsibilities. Tempting as this is to accept, resist this help, which you so sorely
need—your child has his own work to do. The adolescent may feel angry,
sad, ashamed, embarrassed, betrayed or guilty of contributing to the dis-
solution of the parents' relationship. This may make it difficult for him to
accomplish his task of separating himself from his family. These are but
a sampling of the predominant reactions children frequently experience.
If these or any other changes of behavior persist for more than two or
certainly three months, professional intervention should be sought, especially if you or your child find that feelings or behavior interfere with daily
activities. Loss is virtually universally experienced. While understanding
the difficulties the child is experiencing is certainly needed, so is discipline. Your children need to know they have two parents who will remain
their parents. The goal for all is to resolve the feelings that accompany
separation and divorce, to accept the reality of the new family and to use
these experiences to create a new beginning for the restructured family
entity.

New Families

Children need the reassurance that they will continue to be taken
care of by both parents. Therefore it is most helpful that certain basic
questions be answered as soon as possible; those dealing with custody
and accessibility. The most common custody arrangements are: sole
legal, joint legal, sole physical, joint physical, shared physical, and less
commonly, split legal custody. Physical refers to where the child resides,
while legal determines which parent is responsible for major decision
making, such as education or religion. The more equal the division of
responsibility, the more communication will be required of both parents.
When this can be accomplished with a high degree of cooperation, it is
usually most beneficial to all, as parents will feel valued in their roles and
children will indeed believe that they have two parents who continue to
care for them.

There is consensus in the research on children of divorce that the
degree of conflict before, during and after is a most important factor in
their adjustment. Thus when there is a great deal of conflict between
parents, areas of responsibility should be clearly defined so that negotia-
tion and opportunities for disagreement can be strictly limited. Access to
both parents, however, should be as consistent, reliable and frequent as

possible because children want and need two parents. It is helpful to remember that as youngsters grow so do their extra-familial needs, and parenting plans may need to be flexible or redesigned.

Immediately following the breakup, children usually find themselves in single parent families. The burdens on the newly single parent with whom the children primarily reside are overwhelming. Transitions in general are difficult and it falls on the shoulders of this parent to maintain discipline, give added reassurance, create new rituals and traditions, while retaining familiar routines; in short, to ensure that life continues on a predictable path. This can be accomplished most successfully when there are adequate support networks: relatives, friends, churches, schools and community organizations. The parent who no longer resides with the children often feels that it is an uncertain, ill-defined, devalued role to play. It is essential to overcome these feelings. It certainly does require thought and planning in order to remain familiar with the small things that are often taken for granted when we raise children on a daily basis. It takes work to learn the names of friends who change frequently, school subjects once difficult but recently mastered, accomplishments in extra-curricular activities, the names of teachers, doctors and heroes. Remembering these seemingly insignificant things lets your children know that they are still important to you.

Often just as parents manage to feel comfortable in these new roles, one of them remarries and this complicated process of adjusting begins anew. Blended families are people thrown together and expected to behave like "family" but with no shared history, no fond memories. In fact, they probably bring baggage from the lost original families. Childrens' accustomed positions, first born or baby, frequently change; allegiances are very confusing; roles and responsibilities require clarification. Patience, firmness and flexibility offer each one the opportunity to work out these new relationships. This is another chance to create the family you want, to broaden your circle of meaningful relationships. Remember, anything worthwhile requires effort.

Your children can't be protected from all pain, but must be shielded from some and certainly taught coping skills. One of the best coping mechanisms is having fun. Fun doesn't have to cost much money, but sometimes it does have to be a conscious decision you make. It is important to choose to play together and let other activities go by the wayside for the time being.

Where to Find Help

There are a multitude of mental health professionals trained and equipped to help you and your children find peace and even happiness in your new situation. A psychiatrist is a physician who specializes in the treatment of emotional or mental disturbances. After completing four years of medical school, he or she may have also completed at least a three-year residency in psychiatry. A clinical psychologist specializes in the treatment of emotional or mental disturbances. He or she will usually have completed four years of graduate education consisting of classroom instruction and supervised clinical experience treating those with emotional or mental illness culminating in a Ph.D, the Ed.D or the Psy.D degree. A clinical social worker specializes in treating those whose functioning is impaired or threatened by social or psychological stress or health problems. He or she will have completed two years of graduate education which includes supervised field instruction culminating in an M.S.W., an M.S.S.W. or an M.S.S. Each state and jurisdiction has its own requirements for licensure. Your family physician, family friends, school personnel and clergy are good sources of referral. There are many different health insurance plans today with their own requirements and it is necessary to check your policy first in choosing a mental health provider.

Questions to ask yourself

1. Is this mental health practitioner a person I can learn to trust?
2. Are we compatible? On the same wave-length?
3. Will my child feel comfortable with this practitioner?
4. Does this person show respect for my distress and for me?

Questions to ask the therapist

1. How long will the initial evaluation take and how much will it cost?
2. What credentials and experience have you, as a professional, had with issues of separation and divorce?
3. How long can you expect the therapy to take?
4. Will you work with one person, the child alone, the family, the couple?
5. How will you keep me informed of the progress?
6. What are your fees, sliding scale fee arrangements, method of payment and possibility of insurance coverage?

Resources

Referral Services

The American Association for Marriage & Family Therapy
301-279-8755
The American Psychiatric Association 202-682-6270
The American Psychological Association 202-336-5800
The Greater Washington Society for Clinical Social Workers
301-530-4765

Local Psycho-Education and Support Groups:

Center for Divorcing Families
640 East Diamond Ave., Suite A
Gaithersburg, MD 20877
301-840-2006
Information and workshops covering legal and emotional aspects of
divorce; offers educational booklets and a sliding-fee-scale legal
referral service.

Children of Separation & Divorce Center
2000 Century Plaza, Suite #121
Columbia, MD 21044
410-740-9553
Parenting Seminars (two sessions) give parents an opportunity to
understand how divorce affects children and how to continue to play a
vital parental role in their lives. Helping Stepfamilies Rebuild, for
couples that are remarried or thinking about it. Group sessions to
discuss managing the multiple relationships of extended families,
devising strategies for parenting and discovering new family rituals.

Community Psychiatric Clinic, Inc.
15944 Luanne Dr.
Gaithersburg, MD 20877 301-840-9636
Workshops and seminars for parents and children. Information
about effects of separation and divorce, how to strengthen coping and
problem solving skills; parenting seminars to help adults refocus on
the needs of their children.

New Beginnings, Inc.
13129 Clifton Road
Silver Spring, MD 20904 301-384-0111
Support group for recently separated and divorced men and women.
Chapters around the metro area meet for discussions, lectures and
social events.

Parents Without Partners
800-637-7974
This international organization has six chapters in the Washington
area which meet regularly and plan social events. To find the chapter
nearest you, contact the Chicago headquarters at this toll free number.

Single Parents Raising Kids - SPARK
P.O. Box 1631
Wheaton, MD 20915 301-598-6395
A diverse program of family, social and educational events are held
monthly for single parents with children under age 18. Support
groups, discussions, wine and cheese parties, field trips to museums
and other excursions are scheduled for families.

The Directory of Self Help Support Groups
7630 Little River Tpke., Suite 206
Annandale, VA 22003 703-941-5465
A listing of more than 1,200 support groups in the metropolitan area,
published by the Mental Health Assoc. of Northern Virginia.

Further Reading

Buger, Stuart, M.D. *Divorce Without Victims*. New York: Penguin Books, 1986.

Francke, Linda. *Growing Up Divorced*. Fawcett Publishing, 1985.

Kline, Kris & Stephen Pew, Ph.D.. *For the Sake of the Children: How to Share Your Children with your Ex-Spouse in Spite of Your Anger*. Rocklin, CA: Prima Publishing, 1992.

Ricci, Isolina. *Mom's House, Dad's House*. New York: MacMillan Publishing Co., 1980.

Trafford, A. *Crazy Times, Surviving Divorce*. New York: Harper & Row, 1982.

Wallerstein, Judith and Sandra Blakeslee. *Second Chances*. New York: Ticknor and Fields, 1989.

Education and Support For Adoptive Parents

by Ellen Singer, L.C.S.W.-C.

In the last 20 years, adoption has changed dramatically. While many families are still adopting infants of their own race, ethnic background and religion, there have been increases in transracial and cross-cultural adoptions and in the adoption of children with special needs. Another change is that after placement, more families are choosing to continue contact with their children's birth families through the exchange of letters, pictures or phone calls. In "open adoption," adoptive and birth families continue their relationship through visits. Whatever the situation, experts agree that adopted children face certain tasks and deal with specific issues that relate solely to their adoptive status. Thus, to parent effectively, adoptive parents need access to resources that relate specifically to adoption.

Support for Parents

Adoption is a life-long process, which means that issues related to adoption are likely to surface in different ways throughout a child's life. Adoptive parents who understand their child's feelings and experiences will most likely be able to provide the kind of support and guidance to help them resolve these issues.

Adoptive parents can find information for themselves and resources for their children through adoptive parent organizations which offer educational seminars for families, publish informative newsletters and sponsor social activities, such as play groups, holiday parties and other events. Some organizations invite all types of adoptive families to join, while others have been formed to meet the specific needs of families whose children come from other countries or religious backgrounds. Adoption agencies also offer seminars (often open to the public) and parents who have been clients of these agencies frequently form their own support groups for the purpose of exchanging information and socializing.

Many adoptive parents usually realize that they need education and support as they begin to consider when and how to talk with their children about being adopted. This task can be especially difficult for

Ellen C. Singer, a Licensed Clinical Social Worker, is the Clinical Director of Family Resource Center of Adoptions, Together, Inc. She is in private practice in Gaithersburg, Maryland. She is also a support group leader for RESOLVE.

transracial and cross-cultural adoptive families in which parents must grapple not only with questions relating to the adoption, but also with how to help their children deal with racism and prejudice.

Adoptive parents of children with special needs require information, resources and support to effectively address their child's "special need." The term "special needs" may refer to physical, emotional or learning disabilities or the fact that the child was older or part of a sibling group when adopted. Fortunately, there are organizations and support groups available for parents of these children. Public and private agencies as well as private counseling and mental health resources can also be invaluable for helping adoptive parents with their child's adjustment to the new family.

Questions to ask yourself

1. Do I understand what my child may be feeling about the adoption?
2. Do I know other adoptive families like my own that I can talk to about my experience and concerns?
3. Does my child know other children who are adopted, from the same race, country, etc.?
4. Do I feel comfortable answering questions and talking with family, friends and others about adoption?
5. If my child had an emotional or behavioral problem, would I know how to find a resource person knowledgeable about adoption?
6. How confident do I feel about my parenting skills with my child?

Questions to ask the professionals

1. When and how do I talk to my child about adoption? When and how do I share information about the birth history?
2. Exactly what happens in an open adoption, and what are the perceived advantages and challenges? How do you "open up" a closed adoption?
3. If my child is experiencing an emotional or behavioral problem, how would I determine if it was adoption-related or not, and how should I intervene?
4. How can I incorporate my child's cultural or ethnic heritage into our family life?
5. How can I help prepare my child to handle the questions and comments regarding his adoption, race or cultural status which is different from the rest of the family?

Resources

Associations and Organizations

Adoptive Family Network, Inc.
P.O. Box 7
Columbia, MD 21045-007
1-410-474-1040
Adoption classes, seminars, newsletter.

Adoptions Together, Inc.
Family Resource Center
3837 Farragut Ave.
Kensington, MD 20895 301-933-7333
Pre-and post-adoption services, support groups, workshops,
counseling.

Families Adopting Children Everywhere (FACE)
P.O. Box 28058
Northwood Station
Baltimore, MD 21239
301-488-2656
Family building through adoption class, newsletter.

Families Like Ours (FLO)
700 Seventh St., SW #827
Washington, DC 20024
Mary Blakeslee. 202-488-3967
Provides social activities and support for families with Korean
children.

Families for Private Adoption
P.O. Box 6375
Washington, DC 20015-0375
202-722-0338
Workshops, newsletter.

International Family Alliance (IFA)
P.O. Box 16248
Houston, TX 77222
713-454-5018
Provides information for biracial families, sponsors educational
programs and publishes a quarterly newsletter.

Latin American Parents Association (LAPA)
Maryland regional Chapter
P.O. Box 4403
Silver Spring, MD 20904
301-431-3407
Offers extensive materials on Latin American adoption. Publishes
newsletter, and holds educational and social functions.

National Adoption Center
1218 Chestnut St.
Philadelphia, PA 19107
215-925-0200
Has computerized national adoption exchange network which matches families with special needs children. Promotes the adoption of waiting children.

National Adoption Information Clearinghouse
11426 Rockville Pike/Suite 410
Rockville, MD 20852
Debbie Smith 301-231-6512
Free publications; referrals on infant, special needs and intercountry adoptions. Most comprehensive library of adoption materials in the country.

North American Council on Adoptable Children
1821 University Ave., Suite N498
St. Paul, MN 55104
612-644-3036
Serves as an umbrella for 500 local parent groups and coalitions that work on behalf of children awaiting adoption. Sponsors an annual conference for adoptive parents and professionals and coordinates Adoption Awareness Month.

RESOLVE of the Washington Metro Area, Inc.
P.O. Box 2038
Washington, DC 20013-2038
202-362-5555
Preadoption support groups, adoption info packet, monthly meetings, newsletters.

Adoption Support Groups

Adoptee-Birthparent Support Network: Help with search/reunions.
202-686-4611
Children in Common: Support group for families with children from Eastern Europe. 410-719-0939
Families for Russian and Ukrainian adoption: 703-560-6184
Families with Open Adoptions Support Group: 301-598-3690
Project Succeed, Adoptions Together, Inc.: Support group for special needs adoption. 301-933-7333
Social/Support group for Jewish Adoptive Families:
Ilene Gottfried 301-622-4757

Agencies Offering Continuing Education on Adoption

Family Resource Center, Adoptions Together: 301-933-7333
The Barker Foundation: 202-363-7751
Jewish Social Services Agency (Adoption Options): 301-881-3700

Further Reading

Books For Parents

Adopted Child (newsletter) P.O. Box 9362, Moscow, ID 83843. Louis Melina, Editor 208-882-1794.

Brodzinsky, David, Marshall Schecter, and Robin Henig. *Being Adopted*. New York: Doubleday, 1992.

Glazer, Ellen Sarasohn. *The Long Awaited Stork: A Guide to Parenting after Infertility*. Lexington MA: Lexington Books, 1990.

Kirk, H. David. *Shared Fate: Theory and Method of Adoptive Relationships*. Port Angeles, WA: Ben-Simon, 1984.

Johnston, Patricia Irwin. *Adoption After Infertility*. Indianapolis, Indiana: Perspectives Press, 1992.

Krementz, Jill. *How It Feels to Be Adopted*. New York: Knopf, 1982.

Lifton, Betty Jean. *Lost and Found: The Adoption Experience*. New York: Dial Press, 1989.

Melina, Lois. *Making Sense of Adoption: A Parent's Guide*. New York: Harper & Row, 1986.

Melina, Lois. *Raising Adopted Children: A Manual for Adoptive Parents* New York: Harper & Row, 1986.

Melina, Lois and Sharon Kaplan Roszia. *The Open Adoption Experience*. New York: Harper Perennial, 1993.

Rillera, Mary Jo and Sharon Kaplan. *Cooperative Adoption*. Westminster, California: Tri Adoption Publications, 1985.

Rosenberg, Elinor B. *The Adoption Life Cycle: The Children and Their Families Through the Years*. New York: MacMillan/Free Press, 1992.

Silber, Kathleen and Patricia Dorner. *Children of Open Adoption*. San Antonio: Corona, 1990.

Silber, Kathleen and Phyllis Speedlin. *Dear Birthmother*. San Antonio: Corona, 1983.

Van Gulden, Holly and Bartels-Rabb. *Real Parents, Real Children*. New York: Crossroad, 1993.

Books for Children

Preschool - Kindergarten
Brodzinsky, Anna B. *The Mulberry Bird: Story of Adoption.* Perspectives Press, 1986.

Freudberg, Judy and Geiss, Tony. *Susan and Gordon Adopt a Baby.* New York: Random House, 1986.

Lapsley, Susan. *I Am Adopted.* New York: Bodley Head, 1977.

Elementary
Bunin, Catherine and Bunin, Sherry. *Is That Your Sister?* New York: Pantheon Books, 1976.

Livingston, Carol. *Why Was I Adopted? The Facts of Adoption With Love and Illustrations.* New Jersey: Stuart, 1978.

Rosenberg, Maxine. *Being Adopted.* New York, Lothrop, 1984.

Schnitter, Jane. *William is my Brother.*

Adolescents
Nerlove, Evelyn. *Who is David? The Story of an Adopted Adolescent and his Friends.* Child Welfare League of America: 1985.

Special Needs

AASK (Aid to Adoption of Special Kids)
2201 Broadway, Suite 702
Oakland, CA 94612
415-543-2275   510-451-2023 fax

Children's Adoption Support Services
3824 Legation St., NW
Washington, DC 20015
202-362-3264

National Resource Center for Special Needs Adoption
Spaulding for Children
16250 Northland Dr., Suite 120
Southfield, MI 48075
810-443-7080
Advocates the adoption of special needs children and acts as a resource for agencies.

North American Council on Adoptable Children
970 Raymond Ave., Suite 106
St. Paul, MN 55114
612-644-3036
Coalition of adoptive parent groups advocating for rights of children with special needs who are awaiting adoption.

Childcare

Most Washington-area moms work. More than 70 percent of
mothers with children under 3 years of age have full-time
jobs. Working parents have a challenge that can sometimes seem
mind-boggling: they must arrange excellent care for their children while
they are away. How to find the right caregiver—one whom you can trust,
one with your values, good instincts and the ability to make your child
comfortable in your absence—is no small feat.

In the following pages you'll find the many types of childcare described in detail, from caregivers in the home such as nannies, au pairs
and baby sitters, to family daycare providers and comprehensive childcare
centers.

You'll find advice on how to interview a prospective caregiver, what
information to give the babysitter, and how to judge whether a specific
daycare center is right for your child. A listing of state approved childcare
centers is provided at the end of this chapter.

Finding Quality Care for Your Child

by Ann Byrne, M. Ed.
and Celia Boykin, M.A.

The status of childcare has changed dramatically over the past 20 years largely because the number of working women with young children has steadily increased. The kind of childcare available today is as varied as the kinds of families. As we understand more about how children learn, we try to place our toddlers in stimulating environments which will provide them with a variety of learning experiences. In the metropolitan area childcare ranges from nannies, educated in child development to caregivers who provide opportunities for several children to socialize two or three mornings a week, to full-time structured programs, academic in nature. Some programs are multicultural, while others emphasize technology, science, dance, religion, art, discipline, etc. Because of the Americans with Disabilities Act, families who have children with special needs are now also more likely to find childcare.

Parents choose specific childcare providers because of several factors including where they work or live, their income, the age of their child, and the number of children in the family, as well as the family's values. However, equally important to consider are those factors related to licensing standards.

As the need for childcare has increased, regulations for monitoring care have been established and/or revised to be more comprehensive. Increased scrutiny of childcare can also be attributed to media attention focused on several shocking child abuse cases which have surfaced in preschool programs.

Standards vary from state to state but most cover requirements for space, environment, health and safety, staff qualifications, ratios of adults to children served, curriculum, food and nutrition, parent involvement and recordkeeping. Parents seeking childcare should obtain a copy of

Celia Boykin, M.A. in Preschool Administration, has been involved in administration of early childhood programs for more than 20 years. She is an adjunct professor at Montgomery College and does extensive training of child care staff and boards of directors throughout the Washington area. She is coauthoring a book on child care administration. She is a partner in the Child Care Group, Inc.

Ann Byrne, M. Ed. in Human Development, has taught children, parents and early childhood students in the Washington area for more than 20 years. She is a regular contributor to the Washington Parent and is coauthoring a book on childcare administration with Celia Boykin. She is a partner in the Child Care Group, Inc.

their state childcare regulations to become familiar with the standards that must be met.

The first priority of childcare is to provide a safe and healthy environment for children. Centers are now designed to be easily maintained and to ensure that all the children can be observed by an adult at all times. The Center for Disease Control requires that state-regulated handwashing and diaper changing procedures be posted. These procedures must be followed by staff and parents because they contribute more than anything else to the prevention of illness in childcare programs. Regulations also require that childcare staff know First Aid and CPR.

One of the most significant changes in childcare is reflected in the efforts of organizations such as the National Association for the Education of Young Children. NAEYC has helped establish childcare as a profession by developing standards and professional ethics for childcare programs and staff which promote safe and healthy environments for young children and encourage developmentally appropriate activities and experiences. Adult to child ratios are recommended that ensure children can be properly supervised and their individual needs met.

The National Council of Early Childhood Programs oversees the accreditation—a voluntary self-study program evaluating childcare programs in four areas: classroom, staff, parent and administration. The National Association of Family Day Care Homes is an accrediting body for family childcare homes.

Choosing a center can be an overwhelming task because there is so much to consider. In addition to looking for criteria mentioned above, it is also important to consider your intuitions about the program and staff when visiting the center. You know your child better than anyone. If the center meets licensing standards and your other criteria, and if it "feels" right for your family, it probably is.

In-Home Care

Childcare provided in your own home, or what is known as "in-home childcare" ranges from the babysitter hired for an occasional afternoon or evening to full-time care so that parents can go to work or pursue other interests. For the purposes of this discussion, we will be referring to care provided on a consistent, regular basis by an adult over the age of 18.

There are a number of labels applied to in-home child care providers. Specifically, you may hear the terms: nanny, au pair and housekeeper.

A **nanny** is a person hired to provide childcare in your home, usually on a full-time basis. This person may live in or out. The length of employment is generally not limited; in other words, the person is employed until you or she terminates employment for any reason. Wages/salary are commensurate with the individual's educational background and experience.

An **au pair** is a childcare provider who lives in your home for a specific, limited period of time, in return for room, board and a limited stipend. Au pairs are often young women who wish to experience life in a foreign country or a different part of the United States. They are usually assigned by an agency which specializes specifically in au pair screening and placement. Fees, including travel expenses, are usually paid by the employer. Au pairs frequently work for a family on a one-year basis, returning to home after that time.

A **housekeeper** is generally hired to concentrate on the cleaning and maintenance of the home. Sometimes a housekeeper may be willing to provide childcare for the family as well. In these cases extra wages are often paid.

Licensing: Health and Safety

If an individual provides childcare only for your children in your own home, you may not be subject to local childcare licensing regulations. The childcare provider is your employee and your legal obligations are more defined by the Internal Revenue Service code regarding employer responsibilities than by childcare regulations.

However, if your provider cares for children other than your own in your home and receives payment for such services, there is a strong probability that local childcare licensing for family daycare homes applies to you. You should call the local childcare licensing office for your county to get a copy of the regulations for family daycare homes.

Standards set forth in childcare licensing regulations, whether for childcare homes or center-based care, are designed to provide a baseline for health and safety. You should understand what the regulations require so that you can guarantee at least that level of health and safety in your own home. For example, providers are required to have criminal background checks which may include fingerprinting. They must also have a pre-employment physical which includes a TB test. These standards may already be met if you hire your provider through a nanny or au pair agency—but it is incumbent upon you to find out. Licensing safety guidelines are also useful when preparing your home for in-home care. They are a "gatekeeping" mechanism to guarantee that the environment itself does not present a hazard for your child as he/she grows and develops.

Qualifications

A person who provides regular, in-home childcare services for your family needs to meet minimum staff qualifications as set forth in family daycare regulations. They must:

- Be at least 18 years of age
- Be in good health
- Have recent experience with children
- Have some formal education (courses, seminars, workshops) related to child health, safety and development
- Have adequate and acceptable references
- Have no police record related to child abuse or neglect.

You may choose to add qualifications dependent on your family's needs. For example, you may wish the individual to:

- Have a current, valid driver's license
- Know First Aid and CPR
- Have a sufficient command of English to communicate with the family and emergency personnel.

The Interview Process

Educating Yourself

Each interview with a childcare provider, whether an individual or agency, usually begins with a telephone call. It is always helpful to gather as much information in advance so as to make the most of the face-to-face interview. Steps in information gathering might include:

- Obtaining a copy of your county's local childcare licensing regulations for family day care homes;
- Asking for brochures and other informational materials from nanny and au pair agencies;
- Calling the IRS for information on requirements for employers;
- Reading books, pamphlets and articles regarding children/ family child care needs and appropriate resources;

- Using resources and support groups in your neighborhood, childbirth classes, church, synagogue or any other organization to "network" for families who have had successful in-home care or who may wish to share care with your family.

Preparing for the Interview

A primary element of successful interviewing is defining what it is your family needs and wants from the childcare provider.

Prepare a description which includes a list of "must haves," keeping in mind:

- Your child's needs (feeding, sleeping, play/stimulation, exercise);
- Your needs (work hours, sick/annual leave days, work travel, etc.), housekeeping duties if any;

Decide on the terms of employment.

- Amount of compensation that you can provide and if that will vary dependent on qualifications;
- Number of hours/days of leave provided including sick days;
- Any other benefits offered (Social Security payment, health, etc. Note that Social Security is not optional.)

Prepare questions that you wish to ask.

- Pre-screening questions for telephone responses to ads (if you are using a nanny or au pair agency, this step will usually be done by the organization);
- Questions for face-to-face interviewing.

The Interview

Standardize the interview.

- Introduce yourself and your child. Make the person comfortable by asking simple, nonintrusive questions or offering information about yourself.
- Begin by explaining the expectations for the job, including hours, days, compensation, benefits, etc. Ask if this is acceptable. If not, interview need not continue.
- Observe how the candidate interacts with your child.
  Does the candidate:
  speak to the child, not just to you;
  interact at the child's eye level;
  seem interested in the child;
  overwhelm or force the child to interact.
- Ask questions related to the position that do not require "yes" or "no" answers.

- Present some scenarios related to health and safety issues; what would happen on an average day with your child; person's viewpoint on TV/video exposure for children; person's concept of nutrition and feeding young children; attitude regarding appropriate discipline for children.
- Say when decision will be made and how person will be notified.
- Thank the person for coming and bid them goodbye.

Pros and Cons of In-Home Care

Pros: Depending on the age and health of your child, in-home care may be an excellent option for your family.

- Children who are under 2 years of age (technically considered infants in many licensing regulations) often do very well with an in-home care arrangement. They are not exposed to the myriad germs which are found in group settings and therefore, have fewer colds and childhood illnesses—especially children who have a tendency to upper respiratory or ear infections.
- With very young children, it is measurably easier to have the provider at the home since children do not need to accommodate parents' schedules. Hence, early morning and late day routines can be more flexible for the child and parent. Parents can dictate the child's feeding/sleeping schedule as opposed to the child adapting to a childcare center's schedule.

Cons: • The cost of an in-home provider may be significantly higher than family daycare or center-based care.

- Parents may not have an opportunity to directly monitor the care being given their child when they are a distance from the home.
- Children often need the advantage of a group experience on a regular basis as they begin to socialize. The home neighborhood may not provide such opportunities. Additional services such as a nursery school or classes to augment home care mean additional expenses.

Questions to ask yourself

1. How accommodating can I be to having someone working and/or living in our home?
2. What are my expectations regarding housekeeping or other tasks besides caring for our child?
3. What are the factors about which I cannot compromise in hiring a home provider?
4. Am I prepared to be an employer with all of the attendant paperwork and reporting responsibilities?
5. Am I prepared to find alternative care or stay home when my childcare provider takes a vacation or is ill?

❓ Questions to ask the provider

1. What is your primary reason for wanting to work as a home provider?
2. What work would you not be willing to do in a position as our home provider?
3. Are you willing to work late or early hours if necessary?
4. Would you be willing to stay overnight if work travel required me to be away?
5. Are you willing to take my child outdoors daily for fresh air and exercise?
6. Would you be willing to record the child's schedule and notes on his/her activities for me daily and meet with me as needed?
7. What is your view about TV?
8. What is your attitude regarding appropriate discipline for children?

 # Resources for Nannies

Association of DC Area Nannies
202-561-2922
Publishes a bimonthly newsletter, organizes member activities and lectures.

Fairfax County Office of Children
Division of Community Education and Provider Services
3701 Pender Drive/Fourth Floor
Fairfax, VA 22030 703-218-3700
Training for childcare providers, including nannies. Workshops for parents on how to choose childcare and interview the providers.

International Nanny Association - Member Services
125 S. Fourth Street
Norfolk, Nebraska 68701 402-691-9628
Nonprofit organization dedicated to the healthy development of children and their families by providing quality childcare. Gives information on hiring/placing/becoming a nanny.

Montgomery Child Care Association
2730 University Blvd. West/ Suite 616
Wheaton, MD 20902 301-946-1213
Workshops and courses on behavior management, child development, and activities with children in MD, VA and DC training sites. Nannies welcome.

The Child Care Group II
3015 Upton Dr.
Kensington, MD 20895 301-933-2291
Workshops and courses on all aspects of child development, child behavior, health and safety in childcare, and parent-staff communication. Available throughout the Washington area to anyone working with young children.

Publications

Keeping Kids, by Dr. Barbara Cunningham
703-527-8750
A $19.95 in-home training guide for nannies. Includes a model contract.

Nanny News - 1-800-634-6266
Bimonthly national newsletter for nannies and employers.

Resources for Parents

Locating Childcare

District of Columbia
Washington Child Development Council	202-387-0002
Department of Consumer & Regulatory	202-727-7225

Maryland
Frederick County
Child Care Licensing & Regulation	301-696-9766
Department of Social Services	301-694-2487
Frederick Child Care Consortium	301-662-4549

Montgomery County
Child Care Connection	301-217-1773
CONTACT Child Care	301-279-1260
Department of Social Services	301-468-4012
Child Care Licensing & Regulation	301-294-0344
Working Parents Assistance Program	301-217-1155

Prince George's County
Department of Social Services	301-341-3883
Child Care Licensing & Regulation	301-808-1685

Virginia
Alexandria
Child Care Office, D.H.S.	703-838-0750

Arlington County
Social Services Division	703-358-5108
Child Care Office	703-358-5101
Public Schools - Extended Day	703-358-6069

Fairfax County
Office for Children	703-246-5639

Falls Church
Dept. of Housing & Human Services	703-241-5005
Office of Community Education	703-241-7676

Loudoun County
Department of Social Services	703-777-0360

Prince William County
CONCEPTS in Child Care   703-335-7613

SHARE Care
5905 Namakagan Road
Bethesda, MD 20816 301-320-2321
Project SHARE is a computer-assisted data base to match families
whose childcare needs are compatible.

Family Childcare

Family childcare involves a licensed provider regularly caring for a small group of children in her home. Family childcare homes operate as "mini" childcare centers and have to meet requirements similar to those governing childcare centers. The children in family childcare programs usually vary in age and include infants through preschoolers, as well as older children, who need care before and after school.

Family childcare programs are small, home-based businesses and the providers are self-employed. There are specific hours of operation, written policies for parents, a planned program for the children, daily schedules and menus. The provider is responsible for meeting the requirements of an "employer" as defined by the Internal Revenue Service.

The maximum number of children a provider is allowed to care for in the home generally depends on space to be used for childcare. Within the number of children allowed, the number of infants a provider can care for is usually specified. These rules vary from jurisdiction to jurisdiction and are specified in state and local regulations.

Licensing: Health and Safety

Family childcare homes are licensed and monitored by the same state or local agency that licenses childcare centers. The license is valid for one year and must be displayed in the home. To become licensed, the areas of the home where children will be cared for must be inspected and meet certain standards. The family childcare provider as well as other adults in the home must have a yearly physical. They must be free of communicable diseases and tuberculosis. Providers are also required to have a valid First Aid or CPR certificate.

The Environment: Homes present some hazards for children which are not found in centers—and should be checked out before you place your child in one. There can be no loose paint, broken windows, splintered wood, exposed wiring or pipes, toxic plants or vermin. Toilets must function, there must be hot and cold running water and the refrigerator and stove must be operable. There must be unencumbered access to more than one exit, the phone must work and there must be adequate light and ventilation. A fire extinguisher, flashlight and first aid kit must be available. Bedding must be clean and cannot be shared, and toys must be safe. To prevent accidents, protective barriers must be placed around heating sources and at stairwells, and children must be protected from sharp utensils, poisons, medications and electrical hazards. In addition to the precautions taken outdoors at centers, see page 147. Tools and lawnmowers should be out of children's reach and should be off limits.

Illness: Licensing mandates that providers keep records of children who have health conditions which need monitoring or accommodating. If medication is to be administered, there must be procedures for documenting when it is given and it must be properly stored. Written procedures must specify when children must be excluded from the program because of illness and when they will be allowed to return after an illness.

Food and Nutrition: An important part of childcare is a good nutrition program. Children must have adequate, nutritious food whether provided at the family home or brought by the parents. All food and drink must be stored at the proper temperature.

Handwashing and Diaper Changing: Improper handwashing accounts for more illness in group care than anything. Specific procedures for washing hands and for diaper changing have been developed. Centers are required to post these procedures and they must be followed by staff and parents.

Qualifications

Before becoming licensed, a family provider must meet certain training requirements which usually include child development and curriculum planning. The training requirements to become licensed and to renew the license vary by jurisdiction. Having a current CPR and/or First Aid certificate and a fingerprint check are required by most states.

If the family day care provider becomes ill or has an emergency, someone must be designated to substitute. Families should know what arrangements have been made for care in these situations.

The Interview Process

Educating Yourself

Parents usually find family childcare providers and information about what to expect through referrals of other parents and from lists of licensed family homes provided by the local childcare office. The more you know, the more comfortable you will feel interviewing prospective providers.

Preparing to Interview

Contacting three to five providers is adequate to give you an idea of how services vary. The interview begins with a telephone call and this initial contact gives you your first impression of the provider. Providers can be screened with a few questions and then appointments made with those you feel are good prospects. Visit at least three homes even if you feel the first you see is a good match for your child. The interview will probably take place after the children have left because it will take some time. However, be sure to visit the home at another time when the children are there.

Pros and Cons of Family Childcare

Pros: • A setting with fewer children limits exposure to illness.

• Family childcare homes provide intimate home-like settings.

- Family providers are more likely to accommodate special circumstances such as late work hours, special diets.
- Family care may cost less than center-based care.
- Siblings remain together.

Cons: • Because family providers work in isolation, stress tolerance may be lower.

- Individual needs of mixed ages are difficult to meet.
- Older children are sometimes aggressive toward younger ones.
- There may be limited enrichment activities such as field trips.
- Observing your child without being seen is difficult.

Questions to ask yourself

1. Did the children get priority when I called or visited?
2. Were the children often told to "be quiet" or "go play"?
3. Was the provider clean and professional in demeanor?
4. Was there evidence of favoritism for girls or boys? For babies? For the provider's own children?
5. Were children referred to as "bad" or "good"?
6. Were children happy? Were they required to sit for long periods of time?
7. Was the house neat with everything in place? (A house that is too neat suggests children are not allowed to relax and play.)

Questions to ask the provider

1. How did you happen to become a family provider?
2. How do you ensure that each child's needs are met?
3. What kind of activities will you be initiating with my child?
4. What other family members will interact with my child?
5. How are children transported if going on trips or outings?
6. How do you see me being involved in your program?
7. How do you discipline children?
8. How will I be informed of what happens during the day?
9. Are there opportunities for all the parents to meet?
10. Will I be allowed to drop in during the day?
11. What are your policies regarding sick children, emergencies, safety, etc.

Resources

National Assoc. of Child Care Resources and Referral Agencies
1319 F Street, NW/Suite 810
Washington, DC 20004-1106
202-393-5501
This organization provides a local link between parents and care providers. They will answer questions for parents seeking childcare.

Center-Based Care

According to childcare licensing regulations, a childcare center means "an agency, institution or establishment that, for part of or all of the day, or on a 24-hour basis on a regular schedule, and at least twice a week, offers or provides childcare to children who do not have the same parent-age except as otherwise provided for in law or regulation." (COMAR 7.04.02, State of Maryland Code)

Criteria for center-based childcare revolve around several factors:

- There are *more than 12 children* receiving childcare;
- The site is usually not in the child's home, or that of a family daycare provider;
- There are multiple caregivers to accommodate the needs of the children.

Licensing: Health and Safety

There are specific health requirements for childcare centers, both for children and for adults providing care. In most licensed care situations, your physician must sign a form confirming that immunizations are current and that your child is in good health, before being admitted to the center. Adults must also have a health form filled out by a physician that indicates the absence of TB and other communicable diseases, as well as fitness to perform the work of childcare. Once a child is admitted, there are additional guidelines for excluding children who are ill with communicable diseases. Licensing authorities also define the procedure for administering medications to children while in the care of the center.

Health standards also apply to sanitary conditions in cleaning bathrooms, floors, kitchen and classroom surfaces; diapering procedures; handwashing for children and adults; conditions for storage of foods, cleaning supplies and medications.

Most licensing authorities also require that centers have at least one person on duty at all times with current certification in First Aid and infant/child CPR.

In addition, the Americans With Disabilities Act requires that programs which serve the general public must provide access to children with disabilities and make a reasonable effort to accommodate them.

Safety is an overriding concern in planning childcare center space and in the selection of equipment. Childcare regulations require a minimum amount of space per child (usually 35 square feet) to prevent overcrowding.

Fire regulations also require regular fire drills along preapproved routes; signs indicating exits; emergency lighting when the electrical system shuts down; a sprinkler or other suppression system in place. Fire extinguishers must also be regularly serviced.

Emergency safety numbers must be posted by each telephone so that staff or other adults can contact outside assistance when necessary.

When reviewing a center for initial licensing or renewal, licensing specialists follow a checklist of these requirements. Thus, if a center is licensed it means it provides at least minimal health and safety standards reviewed on a yearly basis.

Space requirements for children in centers usually reduce overcrowding and the resulting accidents which may occur. Sufficient equipment of appropriate size and in good repair also guarantees a safe environment for children. Centers must provide materials which are nontoxic and free of such hazards as lead paint. The Consumer Product Safety Commission guidelines on children's toys and equipment must be followed by centers.

Playground standards are also dictated by the local licensing organization. These should cover the type of ground surface covering used on the playground, especially under equipment; the height and type of equipment related to the age of children playing; the minimum square footage per child; and the variety of play areas (riding, climbing, sand, etc.) It is important to see if there are separate play areas for infants/toddlers, preschoolers, and school-age children. These groups do not mix safely together unless there is extra adult supervision.

All in all, parents should be prepared to check for health and safety provisions in any childcare center they visit. Seeing a current license in evidence is a first step. But parents must also observe and ask specific questions.

Qualifications

Staff qualifications are one of the most important elements in guaranteeing high-quality childcare services. Most states/counties have minimum standards of training which entitle a staff person to supervise a group of children. Aides or assistants usually are not required to have as much training. Research has shown that there is a direct correlation between *relevant* training and quality childcare. (Relevant training means training related specifically to the field of early childhood education: child development and curriculum as well as health and safety.)

Besides a degree in early childhood education, there are other credentialing programs which provide staff with good training. A group leader may have a certification as a Child Development Associate, having participated in an experience-based, supervised training program for those who are already working in early childhood settings. Staff can also take course work at community colleges or at local, approved training institutions to acquire senior staff certification upon completion of specific numbers of training hours (at least 64 hours, now 90 hours in many places).

It is important for parents to ask about staff credentials when they are touring or making inquiries about a center. While having a degree or certificate does not guarantee good childcare services, it does indicate a level of commitment and interest in young children.

The Interview Process

As already indicated, parents need to prepare themselves with some criteria for evaluating center-based childcare programs. Acquiring a copy of local childcare regulations is a good place to start. Call your local county government for this information. Another good resource is the list of accredited programs from the Academy of Early Childhood Professional Recognition division of the National Association for the Education of Young Children (NAEYC). Programs which are accredited comply with licensing standards as a baseline. Additional requirements for staff qualifications, program planning, administrative organization, parent input and health and safety indicate that the program is very high quality. NAEYC also has a list of publications, including pamphlets, which help parents evaluate programs. (Call 202-232-8777).

A tour and some opportunity to observe classroom operations is essential to gain a good understanding of how the program operates—and if it is a good fit for your family. In order to make that decision, the family must be clear on its needs. Hours of care needed, commuting time with your child, provision of meals and snacks and cost must be calculated in advance of a decision to select a center.

However, one of the most important criteria is not mentioned in licensing standards: the type of interaction between staff and child. NAEYC's accreditation criteria do mention speaking at the child's eye level, giving children age-appropriate choices and using positive discipline techniques. Parents need to look for these behaviors.

There is also a relative hierarchy of needs for each family. In other words, what's really important to you and what can you compromise on? Basic health and safety issues should never be compromised. However, you may be willing to pack lunch for your child if a center you really like doesn't provide it. Each family must determine whether center-based care is the best choice for the family, not just for the child as an individual.

Pros and Cons of Center-based Childcare:

Pros: • Center-based care provides children with excellent, supervised opportunities to learn *socially*, which is the primary way young children learn. The ability to interact in an age-appropriate fashion is a critical skill for children entering elementary school.

• Qualified staff can provide educationally stimulating programs in a planned setting.

• Children have the opportunity to interact with several adults as opposed to one or two, which increases the children's ability to adapt to adult personalities.

• Care is available whether a particular staff person is absent or not.

Cons: • Children are exposed to a wider variety of communicable diseases at relatively young ages. Those with tendencies to upper respiratory or ear infections may be repeatedly ill.

• Parents have to make alternative care arrangements or stay home when their child is ill.

• There is no flexibility in hours of care with most centers. Parents who have unusual work hours or work-related travel may find that they cannot adapt to a center's hours. When snow emergencies occur, a home provider or family daycare home may be able to accommodate late pickup more easily than a center.

• There is usually little flexibility on meals when a center serves lunch. Families whose children have special food needs may find more individualized meals in private care.

 ## Questions to ask yourself

1. What are my child's primary needs from a provider at his/her developmental stage? Is a childcare center best suited to my child? Are there any health considerations?
2. What does the family require from a childcare situation, taking into consideration: hours; days of week; vacation schedules; meals; location (including commuting distance)?
3. What can the family afford to pay for childcare services?
4. Are we willing to compromise on any of the above factors if we find a center which is outstanding for our child?

Questions to ask the administrators

1. What is the philosophy of your childcare center?
2. What role do parents play in the program?
3. Are parents free to visit the program at any time?
4. What are the qualifications of your staff? How are staff trained before hiring and after hiring?
5. Do parents have regular meetings and conferences with the staff?
6. How do staff communicate with parents on a daily basis?
7. Are there written policies and procedures that parents receive prior to enrollment?
8. Is the center licensed? Is it accredited by NAEYC?

★ Special Needs

Therapeutic Educational Day Care for Infants
Hospital for Sick Children
1731 Bunker Hill Rd., NW
Washington, DC 20017
202 832-4400
Serves children from birth through age 5 with multiple handicaps.
Other programs are available for children through age 21.

Tomorrow's Child - Daycare for Medically Dependent Children
Barklay Pavillion West, Suite 203 B
Cherry Hill, NJ 08034
609 354-9106
Information on nationally located centers. Skilled nursing care,
therapy services, educational development, infusion therapy.

Guide to Local Childcare Centers

For a listing of preschools (including Montessori schools) see the Preschool Guide on page 169.

District of Columbia

American University Child Development Center
4400 Massachussetts Ave., NW
Washington, DC 20016
202-885-3330

Bright Horizons
1000 Independence Avenue, SW
Washington, DC 20585
202-586-6737

Chevy Chase Plaza Children's Center
5310 43rd Street, NW
Washington, DC 20015
202-244-1402

The Child Care and Learning Center
Rt. 211 West, P.O. Box 520
Washington, DC 22747
703-675-3237

Creative Child Development Center
451 7th St., SW, Room 8278
Washington, DC 20410
202-708-1935

DC Dept. of Rec. & Parks ECE Branch-Atlantic, Etc.
1230 Taylor St., NW Room 204
Washington, DC 20011
202-576-7226

DOT Day Care, Inc.
800 Independence Ave., SW Suite 215
Washington, DC 20591
202-267-7672

Department of Recreation & Parks - Kenilworth
1230 Taylor Street, NW Room 200
Washington, DC 20011
202-576-7226

Early Environments
401 M Street, SW
Washington, DC 20460
202-260-7290

Foundry Child Development Center
1500 16th Street, NW
Washington, DC 20036
202-332-4010

Just Us Kids
625 Indiana Avenue, NW
Washington, DC 20004
202-219-3200

Lipton Corporate Child Care Centers Inc.
655 15th Street, NW
Washington, DC 20005
202-638-5222 and
202-842-1235

Natural Day Care, Inc.
2430 K Street, NW
Washington, DC 20037
202-338-6389

Rosemount Center
2000 Rosemount Avenue, NW
Washington, DC 20010
202-265-9885

Smithsonian Early Enrichment Center
14th and Constitution Ave.
Washington, DC 20560
202-786-2531

St. Alban's Day Care
3001 Wisconsin Avenue, NW
Washington, DC 20016
202-363-7380

U.S. Senate Employees' Child Care Center
190 D Street, NE
Washington, DC 20510-9022
202-224-1461

U.S. House of Representatives Child Care Center
501 First St., SE
Washington, DC 20003
202-225-9684

Maryland

The Arc/The Family and Infant Care Center
332 W. Edmonston Drive
Rockville, MD 20852
301-279-2165

Bel Pre Child Development Center
4001 Bel Pre Rd.
Silver Spring, MD 20906
301-598-4640

Beth Tikva Early Childhood Center
2200 Baltimore Road
Rockville, MD 20851
301-251-0455

Bethesda/Lynbrook Children's Center of MCCA
8001 Lynbrook Drive
Bethesda, MD 20814
301-656-4891

Beverly Farms Day Care
11614 Seven Locks Road
Rockville, MD 20854
301-299-6442

Brooke Grove Child Development Centr of MCCA
2702 Spartan Road
Olney, MD 20832
301-570-4525

Bureautots Child Care Center
3701 St. Barnabas Road
Suitland, MD 20746
301-899-0501

The Child Development Center
10011 Glen Road
Potomac, MD 20854
301-340-9139/301-299-8474

The Children in the Shoe, Inc.
3216 Coquelin Terrace
Rockville, MD 20815
301-654-6176

Crossway Child Development Center
Upton Road
Kensington, MD 20895
301-942-3247

Ft. Detrick Child Care & Development Center
Building #1776, Ft. Detrick
Frederick, MD 21702-5000
301-619-3300

Goddard Child Development Center
NASA/GSFC Code 200.9
Greenbelt, MD 20771
301-286-8588

Healthy Beginnings Child Development Center
5510 Fishers Lane
Rockville, MD 10952
301-443-0161

Kensington Day Care Center
9805 Dameron Drive
Silver Spring, MD 20902
301-593-9641

Kenwood Park Children's Center
7300 Whittier Boulevard
Bethesda, MD 20817
301-229-6687

Little Acorns Daycare Center
11315 Falls Road
Potomac, MD 20854
301-983-4372

Marriott Child Development Center
10400 Fernwood Road, Dept 874.62
Bethesda, MD 20817
301-380-1850

Montgomery College Child Care Services
7600 Takoma Avenue
Takoma Park, MD 20912
301-650-1516

National Naval Medical Center Child Development Center
8901 Wisconsin Avenue
Bethesda, MD 20814
301-295-0167

NIST Child Care Center
Building 308, Bowman House
Gaithersburg, MD 20899
301-975-2152

Park Street Children's Center
1010 Grandin Avenue
Rockville, MD 20851
301-424-8952

Peppertree Children's Centers
12900 Middlebrook Road
Germantown, MD 20874
301-540-1170

River Road Children's Center
6301 River Road
Bethesda, MD 20817
301-229-0474

Rockville Day Care
622 Hungerford Road
Montgomery County, MD 20850
301-762-7420

St. Camillus Childcare Center
1500 St. Camillus Drive
Silver Spring, MD 20903
301-439-1640

Virginia

ACCA Child Development Program
7200 Columbia Pike
Annandale, VA 22003
703-256-0100

Alive Child Development Center
2723 King Street
Alexandria, VA 22302
703-548-9255

Arlington Montessori House
3809 N. Washington Boulevard
Arlington, VA 22201
703-524-2511

Carousel Child Care Center
3408 Woodburn Road
Annandale, VA 22003
703-560-7676

Children's World-Franklin Farm Road
13220 Franklin Farm Road
Herndon, VA 22071
703-476-0400

Children's World-Locust
801 Locust Street
Herndon, VA 22070
703-471-1191

Children's World-Boundary Dr./ Pentagon CDC
200 Boundary Drive
Arlington, VA 22202
703-521-0223

Fairfax Hospital Child Care Center
3310 Gallows Road
Falls Church, VA 22046
703-207-2010

Falls Church-McLean Children's Center
2036 Westmoreland Street
Falls Church, VA 22043
703-534-4907

First Baptist Church of Clarendon Child Development Center
1210 N. Highland Street
Arlington, VA 22201
703-522-6477

Ft. Myer Child Development Center
Building 469 Room 308
Ft. Myer, VA 22211-5050
703-696-3095

Garrett Park School-Age Center
4806 Oxford Street
Garrett Park, MD 20896
301-946-6192

Gerard Majella Child Center
Marymount University
2807 No. Glebe Road
Arlington, VA 22207-4299
703-284-1638

George Mason University Child Development Center
4400 University Drive
Fairfax, VA 22030-4444
703-993-3750

Infant/Toddler Family Day Care of Northern Virginia
10560 Main Street
Suite 315
Fairfax, VA 22030
703-352-3449

Langley Children's Center
P.O. Box 9155
Rosslyn, VA 22209
703-482-0726

Little Acorn Patch, Ltd.
6226 Rolling Road
Springfield, VA 22152
703-451-7071

**Living Savior Lutheran Early
Childhood Enrichment Center**
5500 Ox Road
Fairfax Station, VA 22039
703-352-4208

Pals Early Learning Center
11480 Sunset Hills Road
Reston, VA 22090
703-435-0263

Reston Children's Center
11825 Olde Crafts Drive
Reston, VA 22091-2353
703-476-8150

Resurrection Children's Center
2280 North Beauregard Street
Alexandria, VA 22311
703-578-1314

Seven Corners Children's Center
6129 Willston Drive
Falls Church, VA 22044
703-352-4262

Teddy Bear Day Care
10689 Braddock Road
Fairfax, VA 22032
703-684-1172

UCM Bryant Early Learning Center
2709 Popkins Lane
Alexandria, VA 22306
703-765-0909

**University View Child Care Center/
Salvation Army**
4915 Ox Road
Fairfax, VA 22030
703-385-8702

Vienna Baptist Children's Center
541 Marshall Road, SW
Vienna, VA 22180
703-281-2021

Finding a Trustworthy Babysitter

by Donna Collins, B.S.

Doing your homework to interview and find a reliable babysitter who makes your child happy will provide the peace of mind you need to enjoy your night out. The very best way to find a good sitter is through a recommendation from a friend. If that is not possible then obtain character references from people not related to the sitter, and conduct a personal interview. In the interview go over all your expectations including fees, discipline, smoking, use of your home and the need for a notarized medical emergency care form.

If you like the person but are still not sure whether you trust her with your children, hire her to be a mother's helper while you are at home and can observe how things are going. By all means, talk to your children after the sitter is gone, to see how comfortable they were. Of course, bear in mind they may call a sitter "mean" who breaks up a fight or who stops a "fun" activity that she considers unsafe. Debrief the sitter as well and ask for a report of how things went. Insist that she tell you more than "everything was fine."

Families should leave certain information with their sitters. At a minimum this should include:

- Telephone numbers of a neighbor, a relative living close by, the doctor and 911
- The home address and telephone number
- Location of a fire extinguisher
- Children's names, ages and recent fears
- House rules including bedtime rituals
- Operation of any special equipment, such as a highchair or crib.
- Telephone number where you can be reached.

The more you use sitters the more adept you will become at finding good ones and at leaving them valuable written information. Some families place a wipe-off message board near the kitchen phone. A tape recorder can be used for messages for your child but is not recommended for emergency information, as tapes can be too readily erased.

Donna Fey Collins, B.S. Child Development and Family Life, is a preschool and Maryland certified music teacher. She teaches a spring babysitter training class for the Parent Connection, Inc.

If you have an infant you may be more comfortable using a neighbor-hood babysitting co-op, where parents take turns sitting for each other, or using local nursing students until your children are a little older. For older children a responsible teenager may be perfect. In any case try to introduce your children to a new sitter before you leave, because waking in the night to find a stranger in charge can be a scary experience.

Questions to ask yourself

1. What age sitter would be most appropriate? (A babysitter should be no younger than 12 or 13, older for infants.)
2. Would a male or a female be better?
3. Do I want someone with childcare training or can I be comfortable with an experienced sitter who has had no formal training?
4. Will we allow the sitter to have a friend over?
5. How do we feel about the sitter using a car?
6. How fluent should the sitter be in English and another language if it is used in the home? (The sitter should have the necessary skills to communicate in English in any case.)
7. Will we have the sitter on a trial basis first?

? Questions to ask the babysitter

1. What previous experience have you had caring for children the same ages as mine?
2. How late can you stay?
3. What are your fees?
4. How will you deal with my child if he refuses to go to bed, eat his dinner, turn off the TV, take a bath, or fights with his sibling?
5. How would you respond to an emergency situation?
6. How do you feel about our rules, i.e., no smoking, no visitors allowed, etc.?

Resources

Where to look for babysitters

- Friends' referrals
- Local high schools and colleges
- Youth groups at churches and synagogues
- Red Cross and hospitals where training classes are held
- Neighborhood newspapers and bulletin boards
- *Washington Parent* childcare section

 **Special Needs**

ARCH National Resource Center (respite care)
800 Eastowne Dr., Suite 105
Chapel Hill, NC 27514
919-490-5577   919-490-4905 fax
Guidelines for finding a babysitter.

Education

Only in Lake Wobegon are "all the children above average." As parents we know that some children are gifted, some average and some have a hard time keeping up—especially in school.

Assessing a school to determine if it is the appropriate setting to develop your child's potential is a difficult assignment. Finding a private school which will bring out the best in your child is a daunting task.

Even when things appear to be going well, parents wonder how to evaluate their schools or monitor their child's progress.

Families face many questions about the educational system and their child's place in it. How can they find the right preschool for their youngster? Is the local public school a solid one? When is a private school the better choice? Could an educational consultant help you sort out the possibilities? How can parents determine if their child shows signs of a learning disability? Will a tutor help?

The following pages offer advice about how to help your child get a good start in school, how to select a private school and how to get the right help at the critical times.

The Preschool Decision

by Janet Wintrol, M.A.

In the realm of parental responsibility, choosing a school for your child will head the list as one of the most significant, and perhaps confusing, decisions that you will ever confront. Selecting the "right" preschool program will be the first among several school decisions you will be making throughout your child's educational career.

The importance of this decision cannot be overestimated, as during the preschool years a child quickly develops cognitive, social, linguistic and motor skills. A good early childhood program enhances this developmental process, allowing your child to leave the security of home, with its unconditional love and acceptance, in order to explore a new environment. In preschool she or he will learn to negotiate social relationships with other children, accept routines and limits established by others, gain trust in adults and begin the process of becoming an independent, competent learner. It is an opportunity for you to share the joys and challenges of parenting with other moms and dads and to see your child through the more objective eyes of the educator.

Different Types of Preschool Programs

In seeking the preschool that best meets your family's needs and is the right "fit" for your child, you will discover different types of programs which vary in philosophy and design. Here are overviews of some of these programs.

Developmentally **play-based** programs provide a curriculum based on the principle that play is the means by which children learn and develop. Problem solving for predictable outcomes (i.e., block building or learning colors), as well as using knowledge for creative endeavors or for making valued friendships, is a key goal for children in a play-based program. **Montessori** programs provide a curriculum based on specifically designed materials which are used to develop different skills and abilities of the child. Fine motor skills, perceptual processing and music are stressed. Social skills, large motor activities and open-ended problem solving skills are built into the methods and materials. Many Montessori programs in the United States are modified to suit our cultural norms.

Janet Wintrol is Director of the National Child Research Center and has a B.A. in French/ Education, and an M.A. Special Education. She has 25 years of experience in the field of education, including teaching regular and special education, in-service training, program development and administration.

Programs with a serious **religious** affiliation may promote specific customs and celebrate the traditions and holidays of that faith.

Bilingually based programs place an emphasis on learning another language. The language of the culture may be the primary language spoken or a choice of languages may be available, as in the case of international school settings.

Parents should know that in all of these cases they can find both preschool programs that function solely as early childhood programs, and programs that may serve as the entry level to a school which continues through elementary and, perhaps, even high school.

Considerations in Choosing the Best Program for You and Your Child

Before investing too much time in the school search process, there are some general guidelines to help determine what is important to you. The following list will help you start the process. Check your preferences to obtain a profile of a school which will meet your needs.

Location

Near home ___
Near work ___
Near friends or family ___

Transportation

Walk ___
Drive ___
Public transportation ___
Carpool ___
School bus or van ___

Program Schedule

Hours

Half-day program ___
a.m. ___
p.m. ___
All day ___
Before school program ___
After school care ___
Optional lunch ___

Days

5 days a week ___
3 days a week ___
2 days a week ___
Optional ___
Summer program ___

Family Involvement

Cooperative program ___
  (Parents scheduled to work
  in classrooms on a regular basis)
Parent participation welcomed ___
  and encouraged
Volunteer opportunities available ___
Involvement at the Boardlevel ___
  is possible
Strong sibling admission policy ___

Diversity

Cultural ___
Racial ___
Economic ___
Religious ___

Tuition Costs

Tuition cost ___
How payments are structured
  Yearly ___
  Semester ___
  Monthly ___
Optional payment plan ___
Financial aid ___

Visiting the Schools

Having considered the above factors you can now determine which schools to pursue. At this point, you will need to visit and tour the programs which interest you. Ask both practical and philosophical questions and talk with other parents whose children attend. As you visit each school, keep in mind that the facilities (both indoor and outdoor), the program design and the curriculum opportunities all need to be carefully investigated.

When visiting the school, begin by observing the facilities. Look at the outdoor play opportunities for your child. There should be solid climbing equipment that promotes both upper and lower body development. There should be swings, slides and a good size sandbox with sand, toys and trucks. Various size trikes and wagons for riding and hauling should be available for the youngest to the oldest in the school. The play equipment should be appropriate for varying developmental ages (i.e., a small slide for the youngest children and a more challenging one for 4- and 5-year-olds). If a school has limited or no outdoor space, inquire if there is a park nearby where the children are regularly taken. If so, visit it. Ask how the children get there, and how often they go. If a park is not available, inquire how the program provides for large motor play.

Once inside the school, be sure to tour all of the classrooms, not only the one to which your child will be assigned. Observe whether the facility has self-contained classrooms or larger spaces that have to be organized for several classes. It is important to see the total picture and to determine the feel of the program because it is likely that your child will be there for more than one year. As you tour the rooms, look at the space arrangement. Is it organized and inviting? Is there ample space for a variety of activities, or does it seem cluttered and confusing? Observe the children. Are they engaged purposefully in the available activities? Listen to the noise level. Is it a busy, bustling hum or does it seem out of control? Where are the bathroom facilities and what are the policies concerning toilet training? Are the materials and equipment in the classrooms in good condition? Are the rooms bright and well lit? Does the facility meet the licensing codes for that state or jurisdiction? (A license should be displayed.) Does the school have a plan for exiting in case of emergencies?

Each school facility will have its own unique aspects. The building need not be a mansion, but it should meet basic health and local licensing standards. It should be clean and interesting and have a sense of organization. Whatever its size and space, it should be able to deliver a solid preschool program to your child.

Program Structure

You should next consider the program structure. You will want to know how many students are in the program, the various ages the school admits and how the school groups the children. For example, some schools mix ages (3 and 4) while others group only by a given age (3-3½ or 3-4).

As you examine the program structure, ask about the number of children in each group or classroom and the student/teacher ratio. What is the staffing pattern of the school (co-teachers, teachers and assistants)? Are there special teachers for music, art, movement, library, drama, etc.? Are there morning and afternoon classes? Is there an all-day program? Do the children eat lunch at school? Are snacks provided for the children? Is there a rest time included during the day? How much time is planned outdoors? What is a typical daily schedule for a given classroom?

Curriculum

Once satisfied with the program structure, parents should explore the program curriculum, which will vary somewhat at different schools depending on the school's philosophy. Regardless of philosophy, however, a preschool curriculum should in some way address all parts of the developing child: the social/emotional, language, motor and cognitive aspects. The materials should include big blocks, manipulative puzzles, easels, an area for dramatic play, books, many props, etc., to enhance play and imagination. Observe whether there is a balance between materials and activities being offered. Are children encouraged to create, negotiate, try out their ideas? Are children respected? Can the children make choices? Does the room seem child centered or teacher directed? What seems more important, the product or the process? In other words, does everything look like an adult completed the work or is the child's work valued? Is outdoor activity considered an important part of the curriculum and is it appropriately scheduled into the school day? Does the curriculum offer age-appropriate activities planned so that they contribute to the children's development in all areas and disciplines?

Staff

A school's staff is the critical ingredient in any program. Hiring practices, required credentials, in-service training, and support to classroom staff will vary, especially in early childhood programs. Here are some important questions: What is the experience and background of the program director? What are the requirements and credentials of the teaching staff? What is the level of training expected and what background do teachers have in early childhood education? Are the teachers from diverse backgrounds? If a program uses assistants or aides what are their required credentials? What is the staff turnover? Does the school provide in-service training opportunities for staff? What other resources are available to support staff? Are teachers for special subjects hired (music, art, drama, library, etc.)? It is important to know that the program you choose is staffed by a competent, well-selected staff who feel supported in their work. All this equals a happy, enriched environment for children.

Special Needs Program

If you have a child with special needs whom you want included in a preschool program, you should also ask: Will the school help make reasonable accommodations in the curriculum for the child's needs? Are the child's therapists able to work in the classroom if determined it is in the best interest of the child? Will the school integrate therapeutic goals into the classroom setting? Is there additional support built into the program for the child and the teachers? Have the teachers received any in-service training on a variety of special needs and how to address them? Does the school schedule allow the time needed for the child to receive the therapy? Does the school encourage parents to participate in programming for the child? Do parents feel supported by the school as they face the challenges of their child's needs?

The Application Process

The application process will vary from school to school, but there is one common theme that rings true in the Washington area—start early (the autumn before the school year that you want your child to enter!). Most programs take applications during the autumn and early winter and make a decision in February or March for the coming fall. More competitive schools require the child to have a "play visit" and in some cases to be tested for admission by a psychologist. Some programs have a "first-come, first-serve" arrangement and may fill quickly. It is very important to be aware of the deadlines and requirements of each program. If you have waited too long and your top choices are full, stay on the waiting list for these programs and continue to show your interest by calling occasionally.

Making the Decision

After all this hard work, you will be ready to make your final decision. In so doing, examine your feelings and ask yourself, "Could I see my child here? Will we, as a family, be happy here?" If you have reservations, try to define them for yourself to discover how crucial they are to accepting or rejecting a placement offer, keeping in mind no school is perfect. And finally, remember that no decision is written in stone. If, over time, you feel you and your child have ended up in the wrong program, you can always reevaluate and make a change.

Questions to ask yourself

1. Physical readiness—where does my child stand with regard to:
   - Napping
   - Toileting
   - Eating habits
   - Health
   - Endurance

2. Social/emotional readiness—how has my child progressed in the following areas:
   * Separation from home
   * Group experience
   * Place in family
   * Frustration level
   * Attention span
3. How involved do I want to be in the school program?

? Questions to ask the administrators

1. What is the basic philosophy of the school?
2. How long has the school been in existence?
3. What is the program design (half-day, 3-day, 5-day)?
4. Is the school licensed? Accredited?
5. What are the Director's credentials?
6. What are the credentials of the professional staff?
7. What is the longevity of staff members?
8. What is the application process?
9. What is the tuition cost?

★ Questions to ask if your child has special needs

1. What are the diagnostic recommendations for my child?
2. Will my child be able to make the most progress for his/her needs in a regular preschool or should my child be in a more intensive setting for children with special needs?

In a regular preschool setting
1. Are there other children with special needs in the school?
2. How long has the school been working with special needs children?
3. Does the staff have any special needs training or in-service work?
4. Do therapists ever meet with staff?
5. Do any therapists work at school?
6. Will the school set up communication with the therapists?
7. Will staff make curriculum accommodations as needed?
8. Will the local education agency pay for this program?

In a special needs preschool program
1. What is the overall philosophy of the program?
2. What are staff/student ratios?
3. What children are served in the program?

4. How are therapeutic services delivered?
5. What therapies are offered?
6. Is therapy included in the program cost or is it paid separately?
7. Do therapists and staff meet to discuss the children's progress? How often?
8. Are children pulled from class or are they seen in the class?
9. Is there any opportunity to be with peers who do not have special needs?
10. Will the local education agency pay for the private placement?

 # Resources

Associations

National Association for the Education of Young Children (NAEYC)
1834 Connecticut Avenue, N.W.
Washington, DC 20009 202-232-8777
Membership supported association with excellent resources for
written material and guidelines for quality early childhood education.

National Academy of Early Childhood Programs
1509 16th Street, N.W.
Washington, DC 20036
202-328-2601
Provides a list of accredited childcare centers and preschools.

Further Reading

> Bredekamp, Sue. *Developmentally Appropriate Practice*, Washington, DC: NAEYC, 1986.
>
> Bredekamp, Sue and Teresa Rosegrant, Editors. *Reading Potentials: Appropriate Curriculum and Assessment for Young Children*, Vol. 1, Washington, DC: NAEYC, 1992.
>
> Cavanaugh, Merry. *The Preschool Guide*, Washington, DC: 1993.
>
> Coerper, Lois H. and Shirley W. Mersereau. *The Independent School Guide* For *Washington, DC and Surrounding Area*, Chevy Chase, Md.: Independent School Guides, 1993.
>
> Lyons, Blythe and Missy Janes. *Choosing the Right School for Your Child*, Lanham, Maryland: Madison Books, 1990.

 # Special Needs

National Information Center for Children and Youth with Disabilities
A phone service which will research information and send you printout free of charge.
1-800-695-0285

Council for Exceptional Children (CEC)
A membership organization which is an excellent resource for information and literature on all disability areas and information having to do with the disabled.

Parent Information Training Center (PITC)
A resource to parents for gaining information about special needs programs and advocacy needs. There is one located in almost all area Local Education Agencies (LEA). Call each LEA for the number.

"Child Find"
A school system process for helping families with young children assess their child and determine if they need a special program. Referrals are made within the public school system to a specific program. Call your LEA and ask for the "Child Find" office.

Guide to Local Preschools

For a listing of childcare centers, see the Guide to Local Childcare Centers on page 151. Preschools offering classes beyond the 2nd grade level are listed in the Private School Guide starting on page 363.

District of Columbia

Amazing Life Games Preschool
1844 Mintwood Place, NW
Washington, DC 20009
202-265-0114

CCBC Children's Center
5671 Western Avenue, NW
Washington, DC 20015
202-966-3299

Chevy Chase Presbyterian School
One Chevy Chase Circle
Washington, DC 20015
202-363-2209

Children's House of Washington
3133 Dumbarton Street, NW
Washington, DC 20007
202-342-2551

Community Preschool of the Palisades
5200 Cathedral Avenue, NW
Washington, DC 20016
202-364-8424

DC Jewish Community Center Preschool
16th & Juniper Streets
Washington, DC 20012
202-775-1765

Family Montessori/Cathedral
3516 Garfield Street, NW
Washington, DC 20007
202-333-3133

Family Montessori Center
4115 16th Street, NW
Washington, DC 20011
202-723-2480

Gallaudet University Child Development Center
800 Florida Avenue, NE
Washington, DC 20007
202-651-5130

Gan Hayeled
2850 Quebee Street, NW
Washington, DC 20008
202-362-4491

Geneva Day School
11931 Seven Locks Road
Potomac, MD 20854
301-340-7704

Georgetown Montessori School
1301 35th Street, NW
Washington, DC 20007
202-337-8058

Midtown Montessori School
33 K Street, NW
Washington, DC 20001
202-789-0222

Montessori School of Chevy Chase
5312 Connecticut Avenue, NW
Washington, DC 20015
202-362-6212

Montessori School of Washington
1556 Wisconsin Avenue, NW
Washington, DC 20007
202-338-1557

National Child Research Center
3209 Highland Place, NW
Washington, DC 20008
202-363-8777

Owl School
1920 G Street, NW
Washington, DC 20005
202-462-4034

Randall Hyland Private School
2910 Pennsylvania Avenue, SE
Washington, DC 20020
202-582-2966

St. Columba's Nursery School
4201 Ablemarle Street, NW
Washington, DC 20016
202-363-4121

St. Patrick's Episcopal Day School
4700 Whitehaven Parkway, NW
Washington, DC 20007
202-342-2810

St. Paul's Weekday Nursery School
3600 Everett Street, NW
Washington, DC 20008
202-966-0214

School for Friends
2201 P Street NW
Washington, DC 20037
202-328-7237

Maryland

Abingdon Montessori School
5144 Massachusetts Avenue
Bethesda, MD 20816
301-320-3646

Agape Day School
13421 Georgia Avenue
Silver Spring, MD 20906
301-460-7744

All Saints All Day
3 Chevy Chase Circle
Chevy Chase, MD 20815
301-654-5339

Apple Montessori School
11815 Seven Locks Road
Potomac, MD 20854
301-340-2244

Aspen Hill Montessori School
3820 Aspen Hill Road
Wheaton, MD 20906
301-340-2244

Beth Sholom Learning Center
11825 Seven Locks Road
Potomac, MD 20854
301-279-7010

Beth Tikva Early Childhood Center
2200 Baltimore Road
Rockville, MD 20852
301-424-4399

Bethesda Country Day School
5615 Beech Avenue
Bethesda, MD 20814
301-530-6999

Bethesda Montessori School
7611 Clarendon Road
Bethesda, MD 20814
301-986-1260

B'nai Tzedek Nursery School
10615 South Glen Road
Potomac, MD
301-881-3028

Casa de Montessori
14015 New Hampshire Avenue
Silver Spring, MD 20904
301-384-8404

Chevy Chase United Methodist Preschool
7001 Connecticut Avenue, NW
Chevy Chase, MD 20815
301-652-7660

The Child Development Center
10011 Glen Road
Potomac, MD 20854
301-340-9139

The Child Development Center
8501 Postok Road
Potomac, MD 20854
301-299-8474

Circle School
15120 Turkey Foot Road
Darnestown, MD 20878
301-869-4607

Clara Barton Center for Children
7425 MacArthur Blvd.
Cabin John, MD 20818
301-320-4565

Concord - St. Andrew's Co-op
5910 Goldsboro Road
Bethesda, MD 20817
301-229-5225

Farrell Montessori School
8411 Harker Drive
Potomac, MD 20854
301-983-8181

Flower Hill Country Day
8507 Emory Grove Road
Gaithersburg, MD 20877
301-840-8448

Forest Glen Children's Place
1602 Brisbane Street
Silver Spring, MD 20902
301-681-5225

Franklin Schools
10500 Darnestown Road
Rockville, MD 20850
301-279-2799

Gaithersburg International Montessori
429 West Diamond Avenue
Gaithersburg, MD 20877
301-840-9335

Garrett Park Nursery School, Inc.
4812 Oxford Street
Garrett Park, MD 20896
301-933-5254

Julia Brown Montessori School
9650 Owen-Brown Road
Columbia, MD 21045
410-730-5056

Kensington Nursery School
3202 Decatur Avenue
Kensington, MD 20895
301-933-0041

Lexington Park Elementary School
400 Shangrila Drive
Lexington Park, MD 20653
301-862-2622

Lone Oak Montessori School
10100 Old Georgetown Road
Bethesda, MD 20814
301-469-4888

NIH Preschool
9000 Rockville Pike
Building 35 #1805
Bethesda, MD 20892
301-496-5144

Norbeck Montessori Center
4500 Muncaster Mill Road
Rockville, MD 20853
301-924-4233

St. Martin's In-The-Field Day School
375-A Benfield Road
Severna Park, MD 21108
410-647-7055

Silver Spring Learning Center
1401 Arcola Avenue
Silver Spring, MD 20902
301-649-1373

St. Thomas Parish School
14300 St. Thomas Church Road
Upper Marlboro, MD 20772
301-627-8475

Walden Montessori Academy
7730 Bradley Boulevard
Bethesda, MD 20817
301-469-8123

Wesley Nursery School
8300 Old Georgetown Road
Bethesda, MD 20814
301-654-5285

Westmoreland Children's Center
5110 Allan Terrace
Bethesda, MD 301-229-7161

Winchester School
3223 Bel Pre Road
Silver Spring, MD 20906
301-598-2266

Virginia

Accotink Academy Preschool
6215 Rolling Road
Springfield, VA 22152
703-451-5797

Alexandria Community Network Preschool
901 Wythe Street
Alexandria, VA 22314
703-836-0133

Arlington Montessori House
3809 N. Washington Boulevard
Arlington, VA 22201
703-524-2511

Annandale Preschool Association, Inc.
8410 Little River Turnpike
Annandale, VA 22003
703-978-6127

Annandale United Methodist Weekday Preschool
6935 Columbia Pike
Annandale, VA 22003
703-256-1100

Beverley Hills Church Preschool
3512 Old Dominion Boulevard
Alexandria, VA 22301
703-549-7441

Boyd School-Montessori Learning Center
1625 Wiehle Avenue
Reston, VA 22090
703-481-2999

Burke Country Day School
6215 Roberts Parkway
Burke, VA 22015
703-239-0875

Brooksfield School
1830 Kirby Road
McLean, VA 22101
703-356-5437

Chesterbrook Montessori School
3455 N. Glebe Road
Arlington, VA 22207
703-241-8271

Child Development Center
11508 N. Shore Drive
Reston, VA 22091
703-437-1127

A Child's Place
3100 Prosperity Avenue
Fairfax, VA 22031
703-698-8050

A Child's Place - Hollin Hall
1500 Shenandoah Road
Alexandria, VA 22308
703-765-8811

The Country Day School
6418 Georgetown Pike
McLean, VA 22101-2299
703-356-4282

Country Woodland School
7152 Woodland Drive
Springfield, VA 22151
703-256-9400

Corpus Christi Early Childhood Center
7506 St. Philip Court
Falls Church, VA 22042
703-573-4570

Creative Play School
845 N. Howard Street
Alexandria, VA 22304
703-751-3388

Creative Play School
8331 Washington Avenue
Alexandria, VA 22309
703-799-0335

Creative Play School
100 E. Windsor Avenue
Alexandria, VA 22301
703-836-7090

Elfland School
4511 Glenwood Drive
Alexandria, VA 22310
703-971-4337

Epiphany Preschool
1014 Country Club Drive
Vienna, VA 22180
703-938-2391

Embassy School
3013 W. Ox Road
Herndon, VA 22071
703-476-8667

Fairfax Academy of Learning
820 S. Carlin Springs Road
Arlington, VA 22204
703-671-5555

Fairfax UMC Preschool
10300 Stratford Avenue
Fairfax, VA 22030
703-591-3177

Falls Church Children's House of Montessori
3335 Annandale Road
Falls Church, VA 22042
703-573-7599

Frances Barton Meekins Preschool, Inc.
900 Maple Avenue East
Vienna, VA 22180
703-938-3588

Glebe Child Development Center
1714 N. Glebe Road
Arlington, VA 22207
703-522-6264

Glenbrook Cooperative Nursery School
10010 Fernwood Road
Bethesda, MD 20817
301-365-3190

Good Shepherd Lutheran School
1516 Moorings Drive
Reston, VA 22090
703-437-4511

Grace Episcopal School
3601 Russell Road
Alexandria, VA 22305-1799
703-549-5067

Great Falls Village Green Day School
790 Walker Road
Great Falls, VA 22066
703-759-4049

Heritage Academy of Greendale
6318 May Boulevard
Alexandria, VA 22310
703-922-6600

The Holden Montessori Day School
5450 Massachusetts Avenue
Bethesda, MD 20816
301-229-4024

Hope Montessori
4614 Ravensworth Road
Annandale, VA 22003
703-941-6836

Hunter Mill Country Day School
2021 Hunter Mill Road
Vienna, VA 22181
703-281-4422

Hunter Mill Montessori
2021 Hunter Mill Road
Oakton, VA 22124
703-938-7755

Keshet Child Development Center
3830 Seminary Road
Alexandria, VA 22304
703-370-9358

Lake Anne Nursery Kindergarten
12021 N. Shore Drive
Reston, VA 22090
703-437-0035

Meeting House Cooperative Pre-school
316 S. Royal Street
Alexandria, VA 22314-3716
703-549-8037

Montessori Country School
621 Alabama Drive
Herndon, VA 22070
703-437-8285

Montessori School of Cedar Lane
3035 Cedar Lane
Fairfax, VA 22031
703-560-4379

Montessori School of Herndon
940 Dranesville Road
Herndon, VA 22070
703-437-8229

Montessori School of Oakton
12113 Vale Road
Oakton, VA 22124
703-715-0611

Old Town Montessori School
115 S. Washington Street
Alexandria, VA 22314
703-684-7323

Parkwood School
601 Marshall Road, SW
Vienna, VA 22180
703-281-3707

Pixieland Preschool
4015 Annandale Road
Annandale, VA 22003
703-354-3446

Program for 4 Year-Olds/Mt. Vernon Elementary
2601 Commonwealth Avenue
Alexandria, VA 22305
703-824-6680

Reston Montessori School
1928 Isaac Newton Square, West
Reston, VA 22090
703-481-2922

Resurrection Children's Center
2280 N. Beauregard Street
Alexandria, VA 22311
703-578-1314

Ridgemont Montessori School
6519 Georgetown Pike
McLean, VA 22101
703-356-1970

Sleepy Hollow Preschool, Inc.
6800 Columbia Pike
Annandale, VA 22033
703-941-9791

St. Mark's Children's House
2425 N. Glebe Road
Arlington, VA 22207
703-276-1360

St. Mark's Montessori School
5800 Backlick Road
Springfield, VA 22150
703-451-4470

St. Matthew's Lutheran Day School
3200 Old Bridge Road
Woodbridge, VA 22192
703-494-3090

St. Paul's UMC Parents Day Out
1400 G Street
Woodbridge, VA 22191
703-494-7080

St. Timothy's Preschool
432 Van Buren Street
Herndon, VA 22070
703-437-4767

Springfield Academy
5236 Backlick Road
Springfield, VA 22151
703-256-3773

Sugarplum Day Nursery
1227 N. Scott Street
Arlington, VA 22209
703-527-1217

Sunset Hills Montessori
1980 Isaac Newton Square West
Reston, VA 22090-5001
703-481-8484

Sydenstricker School
7001 Sydenstricker Road
Springfield, VA 22152
703-451-4141

Tauxemont Cooperative Preschool, Inc.
7719 Ft. Hunt Road
Alexandria, VA 22308
703-765-9266

Trinity MOPS Preschool
2911 Cameron Mills Road
Alexandria, VA 22302
703-549-7422

Tyson's Corner Play and Learn Children's Center
7711 Old Springhouse Road
McLean, VA 22101
703-761-1151

Westfields Play and Learn Children's Center
14800 Conference Center Drive
Westfields, VA 22021
703-222-0898

How To Choose a Private School
Meeting Your Child's Needs

by Frances Turner, M.Ed.

There are many reasons parents decide to explore a private school education. They are as varied as the children themselves. As a parent, have you experienced anxiety about the fact that your child seems to be underachieving and losing self confidence? Do you feel that the class size is too large and lacks the individualization and nurturing that your child needs? Is there a possible learning disability or developmental lag that may require a more specialized learning environment? Do you have a bright child who is bored in school and has not developed the joy of learning? Does your child have a special talent or interest that is not being nurtured in the present school due to budget cuts and the elimination of extracurricular activities? Have you ever questioned whether your child is ready for kindergarten or should have an extra year before entering school? Is your child happy to go to school or does she look for excuses to stay home? Do you feel that your youngster is not working to full potential?

Private School Solutions

These and similar concerns have led parents to seek a more appropriate school setting that will meet the academic, social and emotional needs of their child. Faced with the prospect of having to select a private school, families often feel overwhelmed by the wide variety of choices in the Washington metropolitan area and the many differences in teaching styles and philosophies. As a parent you should view the private school selection process as an exciting opportunity, one that will encourage you to become more familiar with your child's unique qualities. This process may require a little "homework" on your part, but the end result will be well worth the time and effort. What you learn about your child and the schools will make you a wise consumer and will provide information that is invaluable for determining the types of programs that best meet your child's requirements.

The single most important goal to keep in mind when choosing a private school is that you are looking for a stimulating learning environ-

Frances Turner is an Educational Consultant providing services to PreK through secondary school students in the Washington metropolitan area. She is former Assistant Headmistress/Director of Admissions at McLean School, Potomac, MD, and is presently on the board of the Bender-Dosik Parenting Center, Rockville, MD.

ment that will enable your child to establish and maintain a positive self-image. When children feel good about themselves, they are eager to go to school and willing to take the academic risks necessary for real success. Keep in mind, as the process begins, that you are looking for a school that fits the needs of the individual child, and those needs may not be the same as your own or those of your other children. Although it is more convenient to have all the children in the family attending the same school, it is not always best for each individual's needs. One youngster may require structure while another may thrive in a more open, progressive environment. In some situations, siblings should attend different schools to eliminate competition. Every family's issues are different, and the outcome will vary according to the children's needs.

Three-Step Family Assessment

The actual search for a private school can be considered a three-phase family assessment process that begins before looking at a brochure or visiting a school. The first step consists of observing your child's capabilities and needs. Parents are very familiar with the unique ways in which their children behave and learn because they spend the most time with them. When observing your child, you will be evaluating developmental readiness, fine motor skills, attention span, language skills, learning style and personality. Always keep in mind that you are working towards these strengths as the building blocks to success. The second phase consists of assessing practical issues, that will, by necessity, eliminate some schools from your list. The third phase is consideration of the important personal family goals and values which will help you distinguish between different school philosophies. Once these areas have been determined and put into writing, they will serve as the criteria upon which each private school will be judged. Therefore take some time to commit your thoughts to paper.

The First Consideration: Your Child's Capabilities and Needs

It is important to keep in mind that younger children have different developmental rates and that certain readiness areas may develop before others, which may require a school which will allow them to work at an individual rate without pressure. Other children are stimulated by the challenge they receive in an academic program. Parents should also consider their child's birthday since it may have some influence on grade placement. The birthday cutoff for some public schools is in December while most private schools' cutoff is in September or October. There are some private schools that will even look more closely at summer birthdays. This policy stems from private school concern that children truly be "ready" for school. For the most part, private school students are older, particularly boys who mature a little later. Recent information indicates that with all things being equal, the older child will tend to assume leadership in the class rather than the younger child. The important element to consider, whether selecting a developmental program or an academic one, is that the expectations meet the readiness level of the child and that there are enough other children of the same chronological age with whom to socialize.

Fine Motor Skills

It is important to also consider your child's fine motor skills because these will affect his or her ability to learn and work in a classroom. These skills affect pencil control and the ability to complete handwriting tasks comfortably. Some private schools have more writing demands than others. Some children love to write and gain enjoyment when presented with these activities while other children find the pencil to be "the enemy" and may require extra time on tests or the opportunity to use a word processor.

Attention Span

A child's attention span and ability to stay on task and follow directions should be noted since it will impact on the decision to choose a structured or less traditional school, and will influence the size of the class in which the child will do well. Children who are easily distracted are more comfortable in small classes with less movement and noise, while youngsters who are inner-directed and well focused are stimulated by the cooperative learning in larger groups. Progressive schools tend to work better with youngsters who are able to work independently because they tend to be more informal. Traditional schools tend to provide more formal structure with expectations clearly defined. This type of learning environment is conducive to improved concentration.

Language Skills

Observing your child's ability to communicate and use language efficiently is another important area to assess. Is your child verbal and able to express ideas and feelings with ease? Can your child follow directions easily without much repetition? This information is important when looking at reading programs and writing expectations. Facility with language will also influence a parent's decision about the appropriate time to start a second language in the elementary grades, and for some children, it may be best to delay this until there is a firm foundation in English

Learning Style

Determining your child's learning style is an important key to help him achieve academic success. Some children learn best by using their auditory channel or by relying upon their hearing, while others are more visual. A few children require a more multisensory approach using tactile and hands-on, experiential learning for best results. Parents should think about how they learned in school. Auditory learners will thrive with lecture format, listening to tapes and handling a foreign language. Visual learners like to see information and thus retain it better in this form. An example is the student who asks for directions to be written down so that he can remember the information. Some private schools emphasize specific types of reading programs that stress a phonic or phonovisual approach, while other schools provide varied approaches to reading that will meet the needs of all learning styles.

Personality

Your child's personality will also affect the type of school you select. Is your child outgoing, inquisitive, independent and able to make friends easily? Or is your youngster shy, sensitive, often experiencing difficulty when separating from you or entering new situations? The answers to these questions will determine if the school environment should be more nurturing and individualized or one that encourages curiosity and independent decision making. What are the special talents that your child displays? Parents should find a school that will foster these interests because they will help to build self-esteem and make the school experience an enjoyable one. Some schools put particular emphasis on sports, while others are known for outstanding creativity and focus on the fine arts. A "future scientist" may need a strong science program, and many private schools offer separate science and computer classes in the elementary grades with specialists brought in to complement the program. When your list of observations is completed, it is important to have a conference with the current teacher to add any other pertinent information about your child's academics and social/emotional responses with peers.

The Second Consideration: Practical Issues

The second phase requires that you determine the practical issues that affect your family such as the distance you are willing to travel. This decision might influence your need for available bus transportation or carpool assistance. Another consideration is the cost of a private school and the question of need for financial assistance. Independent schools encourage families with a wide variety of backgrounds to apply and try to provide as much financial aid as possible, based on need. They will also provide information about loan programs and possible payment plans. In my opinion, if a family has limited income and can provide a private school for only a short time, I feel that the early years are the most important since that is the time when self-confidence is established and a firm foundation for reading, math and writing are developed. Parents may also want to question the amount of involvement they wish to have in the new school and the availability of extended day or daycare. The length of the school day, half day versus full day, will also be important to consider, particularly when selecting a kindergarten.

The Third Consideration: Personal Family Goals and Values

The third phase requires the consideration of personal family goals and values which may influence your decision about such issues as a nonsectarian school versus a church-affiliated school, the desire for a diversified student population, an interest in community service opportunities, the option of boarding school versus a day school and the question of a single sex school as opposed to a coed one. Recent studies have indicated that girls have gained some benefit in science and math and leadership skills in a single sex environment. Teenagers will often have strong feelings about the question of single sex schools versus coed, and their feelings need to be considered.

After all three phases have been completed, parents can create a mental picture of the "perfect school" that will incorporate all their child's needs. Where would it be, in the city or country? What would it look like? What special subjects should it have? What type of philosophy and teaching style? Children also enjoy participating in this activity and can truly describe their perfect school in detail. Youngsters are excellent diagnosticians when parents ask the right questions and truly "listen" to the answers. They know what areas are difficult for them, what hobbies and sports they enjoy and what subjects in school are most interesting. It is important to include your child in the private school search so that he/she can feel a sense of control about the future. It is all part of making the school match an enjoyable and positive experience.

School Visits

Now that you have done the "homework," you are ready to start to explore the private school options and learn more about the individual programs. Many private schools advertise their Open Houses in the local newspapers in the early fall. This is an excellent way to start visiting schools and accumulating brochures and videotape presentations, if available. In preparation for the school visit, parents should take along a copy of the checklist in this chapter, and include all of the questions that relate specifically to their child's needs. These will be the areas that you will take special note of on your tour and when meeting with administrators. In the Resources following this article are books found in the public libraries which list private schools in the area.

In addition, there are several directories available, including the Association of Independent Maryland Schools' (AIMS), *Private Independent Schools of Maryland*, the National Association of Independent Schools' (NAIS), *Boarding School Directory*, and the *Black Student Fund Independent School Directory*.

Washingtonian Magazine and the *Washington Parent* also publish a list of private schools in the fall and winter. Always include your local public school on the list for comparison at the end of the process.

First Reactions

During your visits, try to keep notes of your reactions and responses so that you can remember and compare them later. Use all your senses! Look for safety features first such as the condition of the physical plant and the variety and maintenance of playground equipment. Upon entering the school, is there someone to greet you at the door and to question your reason for being there? Or could you enter the school without anyone stopping to ask who you are? Once in the school, do you see any pictures on the walls or signs of learning or creativity? Do all the pictures look alike, or is there evidence of individuality and different levels of ability? What is your first impression of the school? Do the children appear happy? Are the teachers friendly? As you take your tour of the school is the atmosphere inviting and warm? Listen to the noise level. Is it too quiet or is there just the right amount of activity to let you know that there really are students in the building actively involved in learning?

Observing Classes

Take note of the facilities and special activity classes such as the gymnasium, library, science and computer rooms, art, music, drama and anything else particularly unique about the school. As you tour the classrooms determine the teacher-student ratio and general class size. Most private schools have classes that range from 12 to 16 children, and some become smaller with grouping for reading and math. Watch the interaction between the teachers and students. Is all the work being done by the teacher or are students encouraged to be actively involved? How do teachers respond to the children's answers? Are they positive and encouraging with praise or are they met with indifference?

Observe the classroom control and the disciplinary style of the teachers. Whenever possible, try to sit in on a class, although this may not always be permitted. Is the room well organized and the materials in good condition? If after watching a lesson for 10 minutes, you are not sure what concept is being taught, you can be sure that the students are also confused. Do the students look excited about what they are doing? Is every child included in the lesson or only the ones who seem to know the correct answers?

Meeting the Admissions Director

After the initial tour, arrange an interview with the Admissions Director to ask more specific questions. When you select a private school, you are really choosing a community. Determine the school philosophy and ask about the profile of a child who would feel most comfortable at the school. Discuss the credentials of the Head/Director and the number of years he/she has been at the school. The direction an institution assumes comes from the top. The Head is responsible for hiring teachers and setting the tone. Ask about the certification requirements of the teachers as well as teacher turnover. If too many faculty are leaving, this may be a sign of some instability or discontent. Question whether the school is nonprofit or privately owned. If there is a Board of Directors, who are its members? Are there parents on the Board? It is enlightening to find out what neighborhoods and schools the entering children have come from, and high schools and colleges where they have been accepted once they leave. This information will give parents some insight into the profile of the students and the level of their academic preparation. Parents of high school students are particularly interested in discussing college placement and preparation for this process.

When evaluating the curriculum, be sure to question the grading system and the opportunity for ability grouping in reading and math. How are these subjects taught? Does the school have the capability to enrich the gifted child and to support a youngster experiencing difficulty? What textbooks are used? Is there a particular approach to writing? When is foreign language introduced? How much homework can a student expect to have in each grade? How are discipline problems handled if they arise? What is the availability of resource specialists and tutors in the school?

The Admissions Process

Parents should start the admissions process in the early fall, around October and November, for entrance into a school for the following September. After attending Open Houses, studying brochures, reviewing your notes and recording comments on the parent checklist, it is time to set appointments for an interview for you and your youngster at the several schools you feel will match his or her needs. To eliminate stress try to keep the number to three or four schools with possibly a "stretch" school and one that appears to be a possible "safety." (In some cases, the public school will serve as an alternative, with some after school extra enrichment or remediation services added.) Try not to influence your child with your reactions. Assure your child that she is going to visit only to let you know if this is the kind of school where she is comfortable. The visitation day should be fun, and the child needs an opportunity to share the experience with you in an open, casual way. If your child did not enjoy the day, it is important to discuss this with the Director of Admissions in order to gain additional, helpful information about the visit and your child's reactions in that environment.

An application and fee will be required if you wish to apply to the school. Private schools are very helpful to families requiring financial aid and requests should also be made early in the fall for the following year.

There are certain natural entry points into private schools. PreK and Kindergarten, if offered, are good times to consider private school. However, parents should not take a child out of a positive school experience just to get into a new school at the "right time." That can be an example of moving a youngster into a school for the wrong reason. Third grade is the next entry point, because many primary schools end at second grade and feed into new schools that begin at third. A few schools have added extra classes for fourth grade, but most openings are by attrition. In recent years, sixth grade has become a popular time to consider private school because most of the public junior high schools now start in sixth grade. Seventh and ninth grade continue to be grades that offer more openings to students. Because this is a transient area, parents should inquire about an off year and hope for some attrition. Private schools tend to give some special consideration to siblings and children of alumni.

Many private schools will require admissions testing, usually administered by one of several area testing services. Parents can certainly have their children tested independently as well. It is important to ask if the test information will be available to you and explained if necessary. Children under 6 years of age may be given the McCarthy Scales of Children's Abilities and older youngsters will take the Wechsler Pre-School and Primary Scale of Intelligence(WPPSI) or a Wechsler Intelligence Scale for Children(WISC-III).

The following checklist (reprinted from *Choosing the Right School for Your Child*, by Blythe Lyons and Missy Janes, with the permission of the publisher Madison Books in Lanham, Maryland) should be very helpful when evaluating schools. See page 186 for citation.

School Evaluation Checklist

Grades and School Hours
- Is there a preK program? Is it full- or half-day?
- Is kindergarten full- or half-day? Is there a transition class available if your child turns out not to be ready to go to the next grade level?
- Which grades have the most openings?
- Do I want a school that includes Grade 3, 6, 8, or 12?
- When do most students leave to go on to the next school?
- What are the regular hours? Is there an early dismissal day?
- Is an extended-day program available? If so, is it also available on days off and during vacation periods?
- If the elementary school also has a middle and upper school, can you tour these as well?

Enrollment
- Is the school large or small? Does each grade have one or several sections?
- Are there expansion plans?
- What is the boy-girl ratio? How well is it maintained in upper grades?
- Where do students go next?
- What neighborhoods do students come from?
- Are the classes "old" or is there a wide range of January-December birthdays?

Philosophy and School Character
- What does the school say about its philosophy? What do other parents say about the school's focus?
- What is the school's religious orientation, if any? Will your child be required to attend religious services or classes?
- What is the racial, cultural, economic and religious diversity of the student body and teachers?
- Are students involved in community service activities?
- Is it an urban/suburban/rural school?
- What is the dress code?
- How do the students and teachers relate to each other? For example, are they addressed by first or last name?

- What is the age range of teachers? How many are male? How many female?
- What type of counseling is available?
- What is the school's atmosphere?
- What is the quality of discussion—noisy, busy chatter, silence?

Costs
- Application, testing, registration or tuition fees
- Payment plans, loan availability, financial aid (full- or partial tuition only)
- Extra fees: books, lunch, bus, extended day, extracurricular activities
- Expectations for further financial contributions
- PTA dues
- Is there an additional cost for tutoring, remedial work or extra time with a resource teacher?

Curriculum
- Does the catalogue describe the course of study? If not, ask the admissions staff or principal's office for more information.
- What is the reading curriculum, when does the formal program begin, what textbooks and teaching methods are used?
- What is the math curriculum? Are manipulatives and other materials available? How are workbooks used?
- What kind of social studies program is offered?
- Are there enrichment teachers, tutors, remedial teachers, etc. on staff?
- What is unique about the curriculum?
- Who teaches science? How often? Is the approach hands-on? Is there a lab?
- What is the level of music instruction? By whom is music taught? How often?
- Are computers available? What is taught? Are they integrated into the math, reading and science programs? How many students per computer in a class?
- What is the approach to the language arts program?
- How often is P.E. taught? Where, by whom and what is the focus?
- Are the arts programs integrated into the core subject areas?
- When does homework begin and how much time will it take?
- Is foreign language instruction available and when? Does the teacher speak only the language being taught while in the classroom? Are there language labs?
- Do teachers adapt to many learning styles (auditory, visual, tactile)?
- What is the grading and reporting system?
- How is the school day organized? How much time is allotted for free play?
- Is the academic program departmentalized or based on homeroom teaching?

Parental Involvement
- Can parents volunteer and, if so, what are the opportunities?
- Is there pressure to volunteer?
- What is parents' influence on school affairs?
- Who governs the school?
- Does the school rely on parent fundraising for operating costs, salaries, scholarships, teaching materials, equipment?

Facilities
- What does the campus look like?
- What do classrooms look like (organized, cluttered, interesting, colorful, comfortable, inviting)?
- Is there visual stimulation? Are classrooms sunny or dreary? What is the desk configuration? What is displayed on classroom and hallway walls?
- Is the play area large enough, safe, up-to-date?

Thoughts on Getting Ready
- Even if facilities are great, are they being used by the children?
- What does the library look like? Is it cozy, well stocked, used for other purposes, staffed by a librarian?
- Are computers available in classrooms and/or a special room?

Registration/Admissions
- Registration date or application deadline (Is early submission important?)
- What is the step-by-step process?
- What tests are required? Are tests from other schools accepted?
- What documents must be presented at time of registration?
- What are the procedures for applying to a public school that isn't within your home school's boundary?
- On what basis is an admissions decision made (age; prior educational exposure; religion; first-come, first-served; tie to the school; test results; teacher recommendation; other recommendation)?

Other Factors
- How far is the school from your home?
- How will your child get to and from school? How do most other students go back and forth?
- What after-school programs are available?

What Makes a School Unique
- Sectarian or nonsectarian and any corresponding implications for curriculum and school life
- A particular approach in the curriculum
- Facilities
- Diversity of teacher and student body
- Size of school and grades

- Unusual programs
- School spirit, ambiance
- Caliber of teachers
- School head
- Teaching styles
- Educational philosophy
- Degree of parent involvement

 # Resources

Association of Independent Maryland Schools (AIMS)
P.O. Box 813
Millersville, MD 21108
301-621-0787

National Association of Independent Schools (NAIS)
1620 L Street, NW
Washington, DC 20036
202-973-9700

Association of Independent Schools of Greater Washington (AISGW)
3609 Woodley Road, NW
Washington, DC 20016
202-537-1114

Independent Educational Consultants Association
4085 Chain Bridge Road Suite 401
Fairfax, VA 22030
703-591-1850

★ Special Needs

American Association of Children's Residential Centers
1021 Prince St.
Alexandria, VA 22314
703-838-7522

Directory for Exceptional Children
Porter Sargent Publishers, Inc.
11 Beacon St., Suite 1400
Boston, MA 02108
617-523-1670   617 523-1021 fax
Listing of more than 3,000 public and private schools, facilities and organizations serving children with the entire range of developmental, medical and emotional handicaps. Includes summer programs.

ERIC Clearinghouse on Elementary and Early Childhood Education
Access ERIC/ Dept. CCE
1600 Research Blvd.
Rockville, MD   20850
800-USE-ERIC
World's largest source of educational information available to the public. Includes public and private schools with special programs.

American Network of Community Options and Resources
4200 Evergreen Lane, Suite 315
Annandale, VA 22003
703 642-6614

National Association of Private Schools for Exceptional Children
1522 K Street, NW Suite 1032
Washington, DC 20005
202-408-3338

Maryland School for the Blind
3501 Taylor Ave.
Baltimore, MD 21236
410-444-5000

Maryland School for the Deaf
101 Clarke Place, P.O. Box 250
Frederick, MD 21701
301-662-5133

Further Reading

Blythe, Lyons, and Missy Janes. *Choosing the Right School for Your Child: A Guide to Selected Elementary Schools in the Washington Area.* Lanham, Md.: Madison Books, 1990.

Coerper, Lois and Shirley Merseraeu. *Independent School Guide for Washington D.C. and Surrounding Area.* Chevy Chase, Md.: Independent School Guides, 1993.

Peterson's Guide to Private Secondary Schools, 1994-95. 15th Edition, Princeton NJ: Peterson's Guides, 1994.

Weston, Susan Perkins. *Choosing a School for your Child.* Washington, D.C.: Office of Educational Research and Improvement, U.S. Department of Education, 1989.

WISER Directory of Educational Services in the Washington Area, Rockville, Md.: Washington Independent Services for Educational Resources, 11th Edition, 1995.

See Appendix I on page 363 for a comprehensive local Private School Guide.

Assessing Your Public Schools

by Kathleen Herman

It is important for you, as a parent, to become familiar with the philosophy, standards and characteristics of the public schools in your neighborhood (or in the area to which you are thinking of moving) because where you settle will have a tremendous impact on the quality of your child's education. You cannot easily transfer your child out of the neighborhood school because transfers are often difficult to obtain and are available only for significant reasons such as availability of childcare, or your child's health or specific academic needs. While some schools, notably magnet schools, welcome transfers, many schools have "closed enrollment" which means that the school is already overutilized and will not accept transfers.

School Profiles

If you are moving to the Washington area and are looking at the public school system, a phone call to the area offices might be the first step. Ask for the profiles, including standardized test scores, of the various schools within that system. This profile should include information such as size of the school; average classroom size; numbers of resource teachers; classroom aides; gender, racial and ethnic makeup of the students as well as the teachers; professional staff degree status, and years of experience of the faculty. Ask if there is a "master plan" that would outline plans for the future such as boundary changes or expected enrollment in future years. Ask if there are plans to open new schools or close old ones within the next few years. Once you have narrowed down the neighborhood where you wish to live, call the individual schools and arrange a visit. During that visit ask for the name and phone number of the PTA president and a copy of the most recent school newsletter.

School Visits

Now that you have chosen the school you would like your child to attend, there are several ways to assess that school.

Call the principal and make an appointment to visit. During that visit, observe the interaction between the students and teachers, among

Kathleen Herman is the mother of three children and sits on the executive boards of two PTAs. She is the copy editor of Washington Parent and an administrative assistant at CCBC Children's Center in Washington. For the past 17 years she has directed the Basic Skills summer school program at St. Albans School.

the students themselves, and, if possible, among the teachers. Are there parent volunteers in the school? How busy are they? Observe the physical plant of the school. Is it clean, are these facilities well utilized, is there broken equipment around? Take a quick peek into a student bathroom. A clean restroom is a pretty good indication of a clean school. Look at the school playground. Is the play equipment safe as well as challenging? Is there different equipment for the younger children than for the older children?

The bottom line, though, in any school, is the classroom teacher. Educator Haim Ginott talks about teachers being the decisive element in the classroom with the power to make a child's school-time hours miserable or joyous. Ideally the teacher should be an instrument of inspiration with the ability to create the emotional environment for learning. No multimillion dollar building, no state of the art equipment, can create this environment. This power is solely in the hands of the teacher.

 # Questions to ask yourself

1. Are the goals and objectives of the public school compatible with our own?
2. Does our child have any specific learning needs that can be met by any special program in the public schools? (If a child has slight to moderate learning disabilities, his learning needs can often be met in a public school. Many public schools have resource teachers whose jobs are specifically designed to work with students with learning disabilities.)
3. How do our own discipline policies mesh with those of the school?
4. What kind of transportation is needed to get our child to school?
5. Do we need before and after school care for our child? Does the school provide "inhouse" daycare?

? Questions for the school administrators

1. Is there a school nurse? (If your child has a health issue (diabetes, asthma, etc.), who handles it? Are parents notified if there is a contagious illness in a classroom (strep, chicken pox, head lice)?
2. Is there a counselor? What is the counselor's role in the school? Will that counselor help us to decide on an appropriate placement for our child upon graduation from elementary or middle school?
3. How are parent volunteers used in the school?
4. Does the school accept requests for specific teachers?

5. Are there extracurricular activities and proper facilities for these?
6. Can I, as a parent, give input about my child to help the school determine the best placement for him/her?
7. Can we obtain a profile of the school?

Other ways to learn about the school include:

Parent networking
PTA president
School newsletter
Feeder schools
Washington Checkbook magazine

 # Resources

Information on Profiles of Local Schools

District of Columbia
Your School Profile by the D.C. Committee on Public Education: 202-835-9011 (available in the Martin Luther King Jr. Public Library)

Maryland
Maryland School Performance Report: State and School Systems by the Maryland State Department of Education: 410-333-3865

Howard County
School Performance Program Report: 401-313-6682
Howard County Public School System: Test Results by School: 410-313-6682
Howard County High Schools: Scholastic Aptitude Test: 410-313-6682

Montgomery County
School Transfer Information Booklet: 301-279-3391 (should be obtained from the school)
Montgomery County Public Schools Performance Program Report: 301-279-3530 Available in the reference section of Montgomery County Public Libraries
Statistical Profiles: 301-279-3530
SAT, PSAT and College Board Achievement Test Results: 301-279-3530

Prince George's County
A School System of Choices: 301-952-6000
School Performance Program Report: 301-952-6000

Virginia
Virginia Summary Report: Outcome Accountability Project from the Virginia Department of Education: 804-225-2027
School Report: Outcome Accountability Project: 804-225-2027

Alexandria
School Membership By Ethnic Percentages: 703-824-6679
Test Score Information for Parents: 703-824-6638

Arlington County
Alternative Programs: 703-358-6000
Summary of Academic Performance Report: 703-358-6000

Fairfax County
School Profiles: 703-246-2991

Loudoun County
Report of Standardized Test Scores: 703-771-6440
Report of SAT Scores: 703-771-6440

Manassas City
Facts: 703-361-0166

Prince William County
Commonwealth of Virginia, State Assessment Program: Iowa Test of Basic Skills and Tests of Achievement and Proficiency: 703-791-7200
Summary of SAT Scores: 703-791-7200

★ Special Needs

Directory for Exceptional Children
Porter Sargent Publishers, Inc.
11 Beacon St., Suite 1400
Boston, MA 02108
617-523-1670   617-523-1021 fax
Listing of more than 3000 public and private schools, facilities, and organizations serving children with the entire range of developmental, medical, and emotional handicaps. Includes summer programs.

ERIC Clearinghouse on Elementary and Early Childhood Education
Access ERIC/Dept. CCE
1600 Research Blvd.
Rockville, MD   20850
800-USE-ERIC
World's largest source of educational information available to the public. Includes public and private schools with special programs.

The Role of an Educational Consultant in the School Search

by Frances Turner, M.Ed.

Parents often search for guidance when problems in school surface. Sometimes their child lacks confidence and is reticent to learn or unwilling to take the risks necessary for growth. Parents may be at a loss when their child comes home frustrated or in tears over difficult assignments. Many school-related problems are indicative of a simple mismatch between school and student. Yet the issues surrounding the choice of a new school seem anything but simple. This is when the services of an educational consultant can be extremely helpful. As a qualified professional who understands the family stress and the conflicts that can arise from school-related problems, the educational consultant simultaneously serves as a concerned listener for the parents, an advocate for the child and a valuable liaison between school admissions officers and the family. By evaluating the child's learning style, strengths, weaknesses and social/emotional needs, the consultant can help parents make informed decisions regarding schools and educational programs. Familiar with issues of school readiness, special needs programs and enrichment opportunities for gifted and talented students, the educational consultant provides sound advice in making choices geared towards the child's future success and self-esteem.

A Family and Child Assessment

Selecting a school is a team effort that traditionally takes several months. The process begins with a parent interview; the consultant takes background information, reviews the child's previous test results, and discusses family goals, values and any special concerns. A session with the child follows, which is valuable because as the child expresses school-related interests, concerns and expectations, the consultant gains a better picture of him, while allowing him to feel involved in the process. In order to assess basic academic skills, the consultant may administer informal testing at this time. If further testing is needed, the consultant refers the parents to the appropriate sources.

The consultant then prepares an evaluation and a carefully selected list of schools which she recommends that parents and child visit to-

Frances Turner is an Educational Consultant providing services to PreK through secondary school students in the Washington metropolitan area. She is former Assistant Headmistress/Director of Admissions at McLean School, Potomac, MD, and is presently on the board of the Bender-Dosik Parenting Center, Rockville, MD.

gether. She may offer some helpful suggestions about what to look for when visiting the schools, whether by appointment or during Open Houses. It is not uncommon for the consultant to contact the school's admissions officers and introduce the child from an objective point of view. (The goal here is not to present the child unrealistically but to solidify a good match between student and school.) As the search narrows, the consultant co-ordinates the necessary paperwork and teacher recommendations requested by the schools and offers assistance through final selection and acceptance.

Recommendations

The Washington metropolitan area is rich in its range of fine private and public schools, but parents are unaware of most of them, especially those which are lesser known, but may provide excellent programs extremely well suited to the child's needs. It is the consultant's job to provide information about these schools as well as those high-profile names with which the parents are already familiar.

Educational consultants usually work independently. They are trained professionals from various disciplines; former school administrators, admissions officers, counselors, psychologists, and educators who have extensive experience with a wide range of diagnostic tools and assessments appropriate for the elementary and secondary levels through the college and post-graduate phase. While consultant referrals from trusted friends are ideal, other good sources include private school admissions officers, the WISER Directory, which provides a listing of professionals and their backgrounds and the Independent Educational Consultants Association in Fairfax, Virginia.

Consultant service costs are based on the plan selected, and may be a flat fee, an hourly rate, or sliding fee scale. Fees in the Washington area range from $450 to $850 for day schools, higher for boarding schools.

As each student and situation is unique, parents should consider not only the consultant's background, reputation, and availability, but also her/his personal style, philosophy, and their own comfort level after the initial interview. Matching your child to the right school is a challenging experience. Choosing the right educational consultant can help you make the experience a successful one.

 **Questions to ask yourself**

1. Is my child happy in the school he attends?
2. Is he performing according to his potential?
3. Does my child have sufficient self-esteem when it comes to school performance?
4. Does my child's school provide an academic program commensurate with her abilities as well as social and emotional needs?

5. Does my child have special needs which are unattended in her current school placement?
6. Are there enrichment programs—academic, artistic, and athletic—offered in her school?

? Questions to ask a consultant

1. What are your credentials?
2. How will you assess my child's academic skills?
3. Do you specialize in placing children with ADHD, learning disabilities, or special needs ? Where have you placed them? What has been their success rate?
4. May I have the names of parents to call for references?
5. What is the procedure you use to evaluate my child's taste and talents to determine what school would be the best fit?
6. Can you contact the schools we select and introduce my child?
7. What are your fees? Do you charge a flat rate, hourly, or sliding fee scale?

Resources

Independent Educational Consultants Association
4085 Chain Bridge Road, Suite 401
Fairfax, VA 22030
703-591-4850
Publish free annual directory of area Educational Consultants.

WISER Directory of Educational Services in the Washington Area, Rockville, Md.: Washington Independent Services for Educational Resources, 11th Edition, 1995.

★ Special Needs

American Association on Mental Retardation
444 N. Capitol Street NW, Suite 846
Washington, DC 20001
202-387-1968
Promotes quality services for those with mental retardation.

National Information Center on Deafness
c/o Gallaudet College
7th St. & Florida Ave.
Washington, DC 20002
202-651-5051 Voice   202 651-5052 TDD

International Organization for the Education of the Hearing Impaired
c/o Alexander Graham Bell Association for the Deaf
3417 Volta Pl., NW
Washington, DC 20007
202 337-5220 (voice and TDD)

TRIPOD Grapevine
2901 N. Keystone St.
Burbank, CA 91504
800 352-8888
Information and referral service which can answer questions about educating and rearing a child with a hearing impairment.

Helping the Child with a Learning Disability

by Larry B. Silver, M.D.

A Learning Disability is a problem caused by how the brain processes information, resulting in difficulties with such basic skills as reading, writing or math, with understanding and expressing language, motor skills, and/or other skills such as organization or memory. A Learning Disability is not indicative of an intelligence deficit; children who have a Learning Disability possess at least average and often above-average intelligence.

It is important that the child with a Learning Disability be identified early and that necessary services be provided immediately, because with the proper help, this child can be successful in school and in life. However, without the necessary interventions, the child may fall behind academically, become frustrated in school, and probably become an underachiever.

The Individuals with Disabilities Education Act (IDEA) requires each public school system to seek out those students experiencing difficulties; to do the necessary studies to determine why the student is having learning problems and to provide the required services "in the least restrictive environment." Thus, some students will be helped within the regular classroom and some will receive help part-time or full time in a special classroom designed and staffed to address their special needs.

By Federal law, these evaluation and intervention services are available to all students, even those in private schools. If you suspect that your child might have a Learning Disability and your school has not initiated this screening process, you should request such an evaluation.

Clues Suggesting a Learning Disability

In about 40 percent of all cases of individuals with a Learning Disability there is a familial pattern. Parents, grandparents, aunts, uncles

Larry B. Silver, M.D., a Child and Adolescent Psychiatrist, is a Clinical Professor of Psychiatry and Director of Training in Child and Adolescent Psychiatry at Georgetown University School of Medicine. Prior to this position he was the Acting Director and Deputy Director of the National Institute of Mental Health. He has published extensively on issues relating to academic and school problems, including The Misunderstood Child, A Guide for Parents of Children with Learning Disabilities, *and* Dr. Larry Silver's Advice to Parents on Attention Deficit Hyperactivity Disorder.

and cousins may have had similar problems. Thus, if either parent has had or still has a Learning Disability or if a sibling has one, it is more likely that others in the family will, too. Therefore it is important to observe siblings for possible problems.

While learning disabilities are not officially diagnosed until a youngster enters first grade, evidence suggesting that the child is "at risk for a Learning Disability" will be apparent much earlier. This evidence might take the form of developmental delays in language, thinking (cognitive), and/or motor (muscle) functioning. Bear in mind that these delays may be normal and the difficulties might disappear over time. However, if they persist it is important to consider professional help.

With the preschooler the following experiences would suggest the need for professional exploration:

Language: The child is not using words to communicate by age 2½ to 3. By age 3 he is not speaking in long phrases or sentences. By age 4 to 5 parents and preschool teachers express concern that the child is having difficulty understanding what is heard or with finding the correct words to communicate.

Thinking: The child has difficulty understanding basic concepts relating to expected behaviors, games, toys or routines by age 3. He might have difficulty following more than one instruction at a time by age 4. Often the first clue is when the preschool teacher informs parents that their child is not performing at the level of the other children.

Motor: Running, jumping, climbing activities are not accomplished with ease and smoothness by age 3. Between 3 and 5 this child has difficulty with chores like dressing, buttoning, zipping, tying or handling a fork or spoon. The preschool teacher may comment that he is clumsy or awkward or has difficulty with coloring or cutting.

Kindergarten through Third Grade

The problems noted above often persist. With regard to language, the kindergarten teacher expresses concern about the child's ability to understand what is being said or to communicate. This child does not appear to learn the expected class behaviors or routines or to follow instructions as well as the other children. This child has more difficulty than others with tasks requiring eye-hand coordination or detailed hand activities such as required in arts and crafts projects or worksheets.

In first and second grade this child might have difficulty acquiring reading, writing or math skills. Reading problems might involve the first step, putting sounds to letters and sounding out words; or the next step, recognizing words by sight. Or the child might have difficulty holding a pencil or pen correctly to form letters and words. Some letters might still be written backward. She might have difficulty forming correct numbers and learning basic number concepts.

In third grade, students are expected to make a major leap. It is assumed that they know basic skills. The task now is to use these skills. The focus shifts from being able to read to understanding what you have read; from being able to write to being able to express a thought in writing; and from memorizing basic number facts and concepts to using this knowledge. The child who had trouble mastering the basic skills will have a difficult time in third grade. It is also possible that although the particular type of Learning Disability the child has did not interfere with learning the basic skills it now interferes with higher level thinking required to use these skills, resulting in difficulty with reading comprehension, written language and/or math.

Fourth - Sixth Grade

In fourth through sixth grades teachers build on the use of skills and expand from providing basic information to helping students acquire many areas of knowledge. Students with a Learning Disability may have difficulty doing the classwork and the homework. In addition to all of the possible problems noted earlier, the child might have a problem remembering information, organizing the materials or learning the specific sequence needed to do the work. It is at this point that he may become increasingly frustrated with school and school work.

What To Do if You Suspect a Learning Disability

First, discuss your concerns with your child's classroom teacher. If the teacher agrees, proceed with an evaluation. If the teacher says not to worry, your child will outgrow it, trust your intuition and don't wait. (Even if your family doctor says the same thing, don't wait.) Request that the appropriate professionals screen your child to determine if there is enough evidence to go forward with a more comprehensive evaluation.

What Is An Appropriate Evaluation?

The screening assessment should be conducted by professionals knowledgeable in Learning Disabilities who will observe the child in the classroom and review his class materials. In addition, a formal achievement test, or the equivalent, should be administered. With children under 6, the evaluation might focus more on the level of language, thinking and motor skills than on an achievement test.

A formal assessment for Learning Disabilities, consisting of three parts, is called a psycho-educational evaluation. This includes an intelligence test to determine intellectual potential and an achievement test (assessing levels of ability in reading, writing and math to determine if the child is above, at or below grade level). The third and final study is a specific test or a battery of tests that look at each aspect of learning in order to clarify areas of learning strengths as well as learning weaknesses or disabilities.

If these studies suggest that the primary difficulties are with language, a further assessment by a speech and language therapist might be needed. If the results suggest that the primary difficulties are with motor functions, an occupational therapist might do further studies.

The information obtained from these studies should clarify whether or not the child has a Learning Disability. If not, the results should suggest reasons for the academic difficulties. Public school systems use an additional factor in determining if a child is eligible for services. The Learning Disability must result in a significant discrepancy between potential and current performance. Each school system is allowed, by law, to define the level of discrepancy needed to qualify for services.

How to Get These Studies Done by the Public School

Your public school should provide the above evaluations, even if your child is in a private school. To start the process, speak to the principal of the school your child attends (or, if in a private school, with the principal of the public school your child would have attended). Submit this request that your child be seen **in writing.** Under federal guidelines, if the request is in writing, the principal must call a meeting of the appropriate school professionals within 30 working days. This meeting with you is called an Education Management Team (EMT) meeting. The school psychologist, Learning Disability specialist and others should have observed your child and reviewed any previous evaluations. At this meeting, these professionals might agree to do the formal studies or may say that they see no reason to do such studies at this time. If they decide not to do studies, you can appeal this decision. The principal will inform you of your right of appeal and the process involved.

If the evaluations are done, the professionals involved will meet with you again at an Admissions, Review or Dismissal (ARD) meeting (that is, the meeting where children are admitted into special education, or their progress is reviewed, or they have made such progress that they are ready to be dismissed from the special program). At this time the results are reviewed and recommendations made. These school professionals might agree to identify (code) your child as having a Learning Disability. If so, you will be informed of the types of services recommended and where these services are to be provided. Parents must agree to each recommendation before it can be implemented. If parents do not agree, they have the right to appeal. Once agreement is reached, these school professionals present a contract outlining what will be done. This contract is called an Individualized Education Plan (IEP).

Parents can have the above battery of psychological and educational testing as well as other studies done by private professionals. The results are then presented to the principal, who schedules an EMT meeting. The school professionals might accept the results from the private testing or might decide to do further testing before scheduling an ARD meeting.

What Should the School Provide?

It is important that this child receive remedial and compensatory help along with the necessary accommodations. These services might be provided as part of regular classroom activities; by taking the child out of the regular classroom for specific help, or by putting him in a special education classroom (called a resource room) for part or all of the day.

Children in private schools are entitled to receive these services at a convenient public school.

Someone trained in special education should be coordinating the total effort and should be providing much of the help. In addition, when needed, a speech and language therapist, occupational therapist or other professional might be involved.

Remedial efforts focus on helping the child to build on strengths while learning to compensate for weaknesses in order to maximize reading, writing and math skills. Compensatory efforts focus on using strengths and addressing weaknesses to help the child acquire effective learning strategies. The focus might be on using a word processor to compensate for written language difficulties, or books on tape for a reading problem, or on strategies for organizing materials or for memorizing information. The regular classroom teacher must understand how to accommodate the classroom and the curriculum to help this student succeed. The special education teacher is brought in to work with the classroom teacher to design the necessary program.

Sometimes budget limitations and lack of necessary professionals result in a child receiving less than the desired help. If parents can afford it, the services provided within the school might be supplemented by private specialists.

How Parents and Family Members Can Help

It is critical that parents fully understand the child's learning abilities and disabilities. The professionals conducting the assessments should explain this in a way parents can understand. The parents'job is to build on strengths while helping the child compensate for weaknesses. This effort is important when doing homework. It is equally important in understanding his behavior at home. The same memory problem that interferes with school work will result in the child forgetting to do things at home. The same language problem that makes it difficult for the child to follow what the teacher says will interfere with following parental instructions and advice.

A parent's knowledge of these strengths and weaknesses is essential in selecting chores, choosing activities or sports or finding appropriate camps. This knowledge is equally essential in helping the child to improve peer relationships and acquire social skills. Parents can learn these skills by reading books or by joining parent support groups.

Do You Need a Special School for Your Child?

Most children should be able to receive all necessary services within their public school system. If the services are not adequate, they can be supplemented by working with private professionals. If parents suspect that their child might need a private school specializing in students with Learning Disabilities, it is important to find a special education consultant to help with decision making.

It may be that the child can stay in public school if a greater effort is made by the school to provide appropriate help or if additional help is provided by private specialists. It may be that this child could be helped in a regular private school that has a special program or additional services for students with special needs. Or, it may be that the child needs to be in a school for students with a Learning Disability. This decision is difficult and working with a special education consultant is essential.

Remember, if your child has a Learning Disability, it is not the end of the world. With the right help, she will do well and will be successful. However, your tasks are onerous and, at times, may appear to be overwhelming. You must be informed so that you can be an assertive advocate, fighting to get the necessary help at each stage of your child's life.

You do not have to do this alone. There are good books that can help you. There are consultants and advocates available. And, there are parent support groups ready to share their knowledge with you.

Questions to ask yourself

1. Is my preschooler having difficulities with basic skills? Are language, thinking and motor skills up to the level of peers?
2. Can my child follow instructions and communicate at the level of classmates?
3. Has the classroom teacher told me that my child is having difficulty acquiring reading, writing or math skills between kindergarten and third grade or with utilizing these skills in fourth-sixth grades?
4. Is my fourth - sixth grader having trouble doing homework and class assignments, organizing materials or remembering information?
5. Does my intuition tell me that my child has a Learning Disability?
6. Do I need a special education consultant to help me work through all the possibilities?

Questions for the teacher and principal

1. Do you perceive of my child as having a Learning Disability?
2. When can the appropriate professionals screen my child to determine if there is enough evidence to go forward with a more comprehensive evaluation?
3. According to the diagnostic tests and ETM meeting, what is the diagnosis? If my child has a Learning Disability, what are the specific areas in which my child is deficient? What are her areas of strength? What therapy will be provided by the school?

4. If my child is admitted to special education, what type of remedial help is prescribed in his IEP Plan? Bear in mind that if you don't agree with the plan, you have the right to request an appeal.

❓ Questions to ask a private special education consultant

1. What are your credentials? Fees?
2. Do you specialize in helping children who have a Learning Disability and their families?
3. What type of plan would you devise for building my child's strengths and compensating for weaknesses at home and school?
4. What extra help do you suggest he needs which could be provided by private practitioners?
5. If you think my child needs a private school placement, which schools do you think are appropriate and what are the admissions policies?

Resources

Support Groups

The primary self-help group for parents with children who have Learning Disabilities is the **Learning Disabilities Association of America,** an organization of parents and professionals with a national office, state offices and local chapters. If you are looking for a private special education consultant, contact the local chapters listed below for recommendations from parent members.

National Office
Jean Petersen
4156 Library Road
Pittsburgh, PA 15234
412-341-1515

District of Columbia
Karen Brock
1848 Columbia Road, NW, #45
Washington, DC 20009
202-265-8869

Maryland
Irene Spencer
2314 Birch Dr
Baltimore, MD 21207
410-265-6193

Virginia
Kristen Otte
8007 Daffodil Court
Springfield, VA 22152
703-569-3710

Further Reading

Silver, Larry B. *The Misunderstood Child, A Guide for Parents of Children with Learning Disabilities.* Second Edition. New York: McGraw-Hill, 1994.

Smith, Sally L. *No Easy Answers. The Learning Disabled Child at Home and at School.* New York: Bantam Books, 1978.

★ Special Schools for Students with Learning Disabilities

District of Columbia

Kingsbury Day School - 30 S
2138 Bancroft Place, NW
Washington, DC 20008
202-232-1702
Ungraded, 5 - 11 years for children with LD.

Lab School of Washington - 250 S
4759 Reservoir Road, NW
Washington, DC 20007
202-965-6600
Ungraded elementary - 12th grade, 5 - 18 years for children with LD.

Lt. Joseph P. Kennedy Institute - 130 S
801 Buchanan Street, NE
Washington, DC 20007
202-965-6600
Ungraded, 6 months - 22 years, program for those with developmental disabilities.

Maryland

The Chelsea School - 125 S
711 Pershing Drive
Silver Spring, MD 20910
301-585-1430
1st - 12th grades, offers Orton-Gillingham techniques for LD students.

Foundation Intermediate School - 70 S
1835 Brightseat Road
Landover, MD 20785
301-772-1200
1st - 8th grade, for children with emotional/LD,

Foundation School of Montgomery County - 70 S
5320 Marinelli Road
Rockville, MD 20852
301-468-9700
7th - 12th grade for children with emotional/LD,

Foundation School of Prince George's County - 80 S
1845 Brightseat Road
Landover, MD 20785
301-773-3500
7th - 12th grade for children with emotional/LD,

Frost School - 35 S
4915 Aspen Hill Road
Rockville, MD 20853
301-933-3451
6th - 12th grade, emotionally troubled adolescents with LD.

Ivymount School - 200 S
11614 Seven Locks Road
Rockville, MD 20854
301-469-0223
Ungraded, infant - 15 years, children with LD, behavioral/emotional problems, or multiple handicaps.

McLean School of Maryland - 330 S
Lochinver Lane
Potomac, MD 20854
301-299-8277
K - 9th grade, mainstream program
and a specialized program for
children with a minimal LD.

St. Columba School - 270 S
7800 Livingston Road
Oxon Hill, MD 20745
301-567-6212
K - 8th grade, ungraded school for
children with LD.

**St. Vincent Pallotti High School -
445 S**
113 St. Mary's Place
Laurel, MD 20707
301-725-3228
9th - 12th grade, separate center for
children with minimal LD.

Summit School - 56 S
4205 S. Crain Highway
Upper Marlboro, MD 20772
301-952-0787
1st - 8th grade, ungraded school for
children with LD.

Thorton Friends School - 80 S
13925 New Hampshire Avenue
and
11612 New Hampshire Avenue
Silver Spring, MD 20904
301-384-0320
6th - 12th grade, for intelligent
underachievers.

Virginia

Different Drum - 24 S
7150 Telegraph Road
Alexandria, VA 22310
703-971-0778
14 - 19 years, for students with
learning, behavioral, or emotional
problems, trans.

Leary School - 136 S
6349 Lincolnia Road
Alexandria, VA 22312
703-941-8150
6 - 22 years for students with learning or emotional problems.

Oakland School - 75 S
Boyd Tavern
Keswick, VA 22947
804-293-9059
Ungraded, 1st - 9th grade, for
children with LD.

Oakwood School - 100 S
7210 Braddock Road
Annandale, VA 22003
703-941-5788
K - 9th grade; for children unable to
meet their potential.

St. Coletta School - 37 S
3130 Lee Highway
Arlington, VA 22201
703-525-4433
Ungraded school for children with
mental retardation and other disabilities, vocational training, ages 5-21 or
until employed.

**Timber Ridge School (Leary Educa-
tional Foundation) - 70 S**
P.O. Box 3160
Winchester, VA 22604
703-888-3456
11 - 17 years, 12-month residential
program for emotionally disturbed,
socially maladjusted, and/or LD
children.

Diagnosis and Treatment of Attention Deficit Hyperactivity Disorder

by Larry B. Silver, M.D.

Attention Deficit Hyperactivity Disorder (ADHD) is a neurologically based disorder manifested by one or more of the following three behaviors: hyperactivity, distractibility and impulsivity. These behaviors interfere with the child's availability for learning and participating in a structured class situation and with family, peer and other social interactions.

All children who are hyperactive, distractible and/or impulsive do not have ADHD. In fact, ADHD might be the least frequent cause for these behaviors. The most frequent are emotional problems, resulting in anxiety or depression, and Learning Disabilities, resulting in stress and difficulty attending to or completing academic tasks.

If your child has exhibited one or more of these three behaviors, it is important that you discuss the situation with teachers and other school professionals as well as with your family physician. You may need to see another specialist to establish whether or not your child has ADHD.

Clues Suggesting that a Child Might Have ADHD

There is a familial pattern with about 40 percent of children with ADHD. Thus, if either parent knows or suspects that he or she had or still has ADHD or if a sibling in the family has this disability, it is important to watch the other children for clues suggesting a possible problem.

As noted above, there are three types of behavior that would suggest the possibility that a child might have ADHD. The child with ADHD might have one, two or all three of these behaviors. Therefore it is not necessary that he be hyperactive to have ADHD. Each behavior might appear differently at different ages.

Hyperactivity: This child is not always running around the room

---

Larry B. Silver, M.D., a Child and Adolescent Psychiatrist, is a Clinical Professor of Psychiatry and Director of Training in Child and Adolescent Psychiatry at Georgetown University School of Medicine. Prior to this position he was the Acting Director and Deputy Director of the National Institute of Mental Health. He has published extensively on issues relating to academic and school problems, including The Misunderstood Child, A Guide for Parents of Children with Learning Disabilities, *and* Dr. Larry Silver's Advice to Parents on Attention Deficit Hyperactivity Disorder.

or "climbing the walls." More frequently, she will be fidgety, fingers or feet tapping, legs swinging, wiggling in the seat, up or down during meals or when doing homework. The very young child might be seen as more physically active whereas the older child is more likely to be fidgety.

Distractibility: Most of us allow all sensory inputs to enter our brain and then monitor these inputs, relaying only important information to the thinking part of our brain. Without this ability, our mind would be cluttered and unable to focus. With this ability to filter, we can be in a noisy place yet hear our own name perfectly well if it is called. Or, we can drive home and suddenly realize that we were daydreaming and do not know how we got home (our brain screens important information and sends it to the necessary areas for reaction).

But some people have difficulty filtering out unnecessary inputs. They are easily distracted and have a short attention span. Some have problems with visual inputs, being distracted by the movements of people or cloud formations or activity seen through a window. Others have difficulty with sound inputs, being distracted by people talking, the dog barking or telephones ringing.

Impulsivity: Some children seem not to think before they speak or act. They speak out in class without raising their hand or interrupt a parent who is on the phone. They say something and are sorry they said it before they finish. They might hit or yell before thinking or use poor judgment because they do not learn from experience since they do not pause long enough to reflect before they act. These children get into behavioral difficulties at home, with friends and at school.

If your child exhibits one or more of these behaviors, this doesn't necessarily mean he has ADHD. You must try to remember whether those behaviors have been exhibited from birth. Since ADHD is a neurologically based disorder that has been present since birth, the behaviors will have been *chronic* and *pervasive* in that they are persistent throughout the day, in school, at home, and with peers. A parent might recall that this child kicked more *in utero*, was active as an infant and started running as soon as he was able to walk. Or, this child could not stay focused during storytime as a preschooler and now cannot stay focused in elementary school. The parent hears everyone involved with the child expressing the same concerns—teachers, coaches, activity leaders.

However, if these behaviors are due to an emotional problem or a Learning Disability they will be noted to have started at a specific time or to occur at specific times or in specific situations. For example, he is hyperactive only in school. She is distractible only when asked to read. No one ever described this child as impulsive until fourth grade. It might be that the child has worries resulting in anxiety and depression. Look for signs of restlessness, irritability and inability to focus. Thus, if the behaviors began after a separation or divorce, death of a close relative, birth of a sibling or other emotional crisis, it is probable that the hyperactivity, distractibility and/or impulsivity are not due to ADHD.

What do you do if you suspect ADHD?

First, a parent should talk to classroom teachers and find out if they observe the same behaviors. After contacting the principal, it should be possible to have the school psychologist or other professionals observe in the classroom and report back to the parents. Sometimes the psychologist will have teachers fill out rating scales that attempt to measure hyperactivity, distractibility and impulsivity.

Second, parents should discuss their concerns with their family doctor who might be able to establish the diagnosis or refer them to a professional who works with children who have ADHD.

Parents should trust their intuition. If someone says, "Don't worry, he'll outgrow it," but the parent observes the behaviors and the impact these behaviors are having on their child and the family, the parent should request that ADHD be considered.

How is ADHD Diagnosed?

Although many professionals can observe or quantify the presence of these behaviors and conclude that a child has ADHD, only a physician can confirm this diagnosis. This physician might be a pediatrician, family practitioner or child and adolescent psychiatrist.

There are no formal psychological or medical tests that will establish the diagnosis, because while certain results on psychological tests might show that the child is hyperactive, distractible or impulsive, the results will not ascribe these behaviors to anxiety, depression, a learning disability or ADHD. There are no blood tests, physical findings or brain wave studies that will diagnose ADHD.

The diagnosis is made by clinical observations and history. First, it is important to establish that the child has one, two or all three of the key behaviors. Second, it must be documented that these existing behaviors are both chronic and pervasive.

How is ADHD Treated?

This disability is the result of a neurochemical deficiency in a specific area in the lower part of the brain (the Reticular Activating System). Thus, one of the primary approaches to treatment is the use of appropriate medications. These medications increase the amount of the deficient neurochemical in this area of the brain. Once the level is normal, the child becomes less active, better able to stay on task without being distracted and more reflective rather than impulsive. That is, these medications correct the neurochemical deficiency, allowing the child to function "normally." They do not tranquilize, sedate or drug the child.

Once the appropriate medication is started, it is important that other aspects of the disability be addressed. The child, his parents and siblings need to be educated about ADHD, its cause and the reasons for the academic and behavioral difficulties. The child might need psychological help, the family might need counseling or help establishing a behavioral program and the siblings might need help in changing family patterns of behavior. Parents might find help and understanding in a support group.

The school system must be informed of the diagnosis and the child's specific needs. Parents can ask that special programs and/or accommodations be provided at the school. Parents will need to read about ADHD or learn, from an advocate or a parent support group, how best to work with the school to develop the necessary individualized programs.

Medication alone is not enough. It is this total approach to the whole child and his family that works best.

Fifty percent of children with ADHD appear to mature out of these behaviors at puberty; 50 percent, however, continue the behaviors into adolescence. About half of these adolescents continue to experience ADHD as adults. We have no way of predicting which child will follow which pattern. Thus, the child might need help until high school, through high school or throughout life.

Remember, it is important that the child with ADHD be identified and helped as early as possible. If parents observe one or more of these three behaviors and know that they have been chronic and pervasive, they should persist in finding a professional to establish the diagnosis and to start treatment.

Between 50 and 70 percent of children with ADHD also have a Learning Disability. Thus, if a child is diagnosed as having ADHD and this child is also struggling in school, it is important to consider if he or she might have a Learning Disability (See page 195 for more on Learning Disabilities).

With the right treatment and help for the child, a supportive family and a cooperative school environment, this child will have a chance to do well, becoming successful academically and socially.

 Questions to ask yourself

1. Is my child hyperactive, easily distracted, and/or impulsive?
2. Does he/she exhibit these behaviors at certain times or in specific situations—or at all times?
3. Have I documented these behaviors?
4. Does ADHD run in our family?
5. What is my intuition telling me? Do I think my child has ADHD?

❓ Questions to ask the professionals

Teachers: Have you observed hyperactive, impulsive, unfocused behavior in my child?

The Principal: Can the school psychologist observe my child in class to provide an assessment? If my child has ADHD, what individualized special programs can the school offer us?

The Pediatrician: Can you make a diagnosis or refer us to a doctor or psychiatrist who can make a diagnosis?

The Psychiatrist: Does the family need counseling to establish a more productive pattern of behavior and response? Does my child need individual counseling? Do you specialize in ADHD cases? What type of medication would you prescribe? What are the effects of the medication?

 # Resources

Support Groups

In this area the primary support group is Children and Adults with Attention Deficit Disorder (CHADD).

CHADD National Office
499 NW 7th Avenue, Suite 308
Plantation, Florida 33372
305-587-3700

Local CHADD Chapters
Washington DC: Guy Hammer 301-493-4159

Maryland
Anne Arundel Co./Maryland: Kathryn Jacques 410-721-5376
Baltimore: John Selway 410-377-0249
Carroll Co./Owings Mills: Janice Borisevic 410-876-8615
Frederick, Maryland: Fred Balius 301-845-2801
Harford County: Susie Milburn 410-838-8534
Laurel: Mary Jo Dader 301-498-2162
Montgomery Co.: Marcie Fenster 301-869-2628
Southern Maryland: Cheryl Armbrester 301-884-7061

Virginia
Arlington/Alexandria: Eleanor Shannahan 703-525-1683
Fredericksburg: Phyllis O'Connor 703-720-5410
Northern Virginia: Maureen Gill 703-641-5451

Further Reading

Ingersoll, Barbara. *Your Hyperactive Child: A Parents' Guide to Coping with Attention Deficit Disorder*. New York: Doubleday, 1988.

Quinn, Patricia and Judith Stern. *Putting on the Brakes. Young People's Guide to Understanding Attention Deficit Hyperactivity Disorder*. Magination Press, 1991.

Silver, Larry B. *Larry Silver's Advice to Parents on Attention Deficit Hyperactivity Disorder*. Washington, DC: American Psychiatric Press, Inc., 1993.

Finding a Tutor for Your Child

by William R. Stewart, M.A.

The purpose of hiring a tutor is to make up for deficiencies aris-ing from your child's education, whether these stem from a less than ideal learning environment or from your child's own unique-ness. If a tutor is needed, it is important to provide one early in your child's educational development in order to minimize the gap which results from letting a problem go untreated. Students with special challenges may also benefit from the extra help a trained specialist can provide.

Recognizing the Problem

It is important to remember that we do not all learn in the same way or at the same pace. The fact that your child may not keep pace with the rest of his or her class in all subjects is not necessarily cause for concern. Not everyone needs a tutor; those who do may require such assistance only until they have mastered a particularly difficult or challenging aspect of a given course. Parents, nonetheless, need to be sufficiently involved with their child's education to be aware of any emerging problems. This means not only maintaining regular contact with the school and with your child's teacher(s), but also communicating with your child yourself. Al-ways review his or her day at school, and be sure to monitor homework (or the lack thereof) on a daily basis. Should areas surface where the child is not making progress, a competent tutor can help by focusing on the problem and by exploring ways of learning which the teacher may not always be able to apply in the classroom. Where special needs are present, expert support can make the difference between success and the frustra-tion which leads to failure.

Usually by the time a problem has surfaced so that your school must contact you to discuss it, your child faces a considerable learning gap. By monitoring your child's progress yourself, you should be able to stay ahead of such a situation. The first time a paper comes back with a lower grade than you would expect for your child's overall ability level should put you on alert, but wait to see if subsequent work indicates a growing under-standing and confidence; if not, intervention is necessary. Start with the

William R. Stewart is the Program Director of the Academic Preparation Center of Wash-ington Academy, a nonsectarian, private, coeducational college preparatory high school. He holds a B.A. in history, speech and theater, and German as well as an M.A. in German literature. Mr. Stewart has both taught and tutored students in a variety of subjects and test preparation for over 20 years.

school and your child's teachers. Do they feel the gap will be bridged in due course? Do they recommend a tutor? By all means discuss your concerns with the teachers if they have not already picked up on it. Ask if the school has support staff to diagnose learning disabilities, if you suspect this may be the problem. It is especially important to identify learning disabilities early, as they can seriously undermine your child's confidence that he or she can get the job done. If the school is defensive or unable to help, then outside assistance should be sought immediately.

The Types of Tutoring Available

Once the difficulty has been diagnosed, you will have an idea as to what type of tutoring your child needs. Is it a remedial concern (your child is behind because he or she has missed an important prerequisite or has an impediment to overcome) or a supportive one—the child grasps basic skills and understands most things but has difficulty with a particular subject or area? One last question to ask before engaging a tutor is: what approach is best suited to your child's personality, i.e., does he or she work best in a group or independently.

Armed with this knowledge, you are now ready to begin your search for the person best suited to help. Your child's school may be able to recommend someone, but avoid agreeing to having the child's teacher be the main source of outside help. In cases where your child is having difficulty understanding something, it is often no more than a question of that teacher's personality or approach to the subject which is not working for your child. Merely providing a different instructor often makes all the difference. With learning disabilities, it is a good idea to choose a center or practice with sufficient equipment and support staff to ensure adequate attention is given to the problem. A single individual may not be able to provide sufficient depth.

In cases where general academic support is needed, there are several advantages to turning to a center rather than hiring an individual. A center is usually in a better position to replace a tutor should the need arise because of illness, personality conflicts, scheduling problems or other factors, so that your child's needs are met without interruption. The requirements of maintaining an established business address may also assure greater reliability that the center will follow through on its commitment to you and your child. While an individual certainly must maintain his or her professional reputation in order to succeed, a center has even more at stake, as its entire reputation as an ongoing part of the community depends on the satisfactory performance of all aspects of its business.

Whether you choose an individual or a center, you will want to know what the tutor's qualifications, credentials, experience and approach are and how the tutor would establish the necessary rapport with your child. That the tutor is a certified teacher is no guarantee of excellence. You should try to find out the tutor's or the center's reputation among educators and other parents.

Finally, be sure your child is making progress, although it may take as many as three sessions, depending on the problem, for improvement to show. If you are concerned that progress is not being made, be sure to discuss this with the tutor or center director. It may be that a different individual should be assigned. In all cases, remember that the ultimate goal is for your child to be able to work independently; a good tutor will help your child to develop this very important skill.

Questions to ask yourself

1. Is my child usually eager to go to school?
2. Is my child not enjoying a given subject or activity?
3. Is my child finishing his assigned work? If so, is he completing the task successfully? (If the child thinks he or she is performing according to instructions, but still cannot achieve results, a learning disability may be present.)

Questions to ask tutors

1. What are your qualifications and experience?
2. What approaches to learning do you take?
3. How would you establish rapport with my child?
4. Can you provide me with references from satisfied parents?
5. What are your fees?
6. How much time do you spend on a lesson?
7. Are materials included in the fee?
8. Must I commit to an extensive contract?
9. Where will the instruction take place?
10. How flexible are you in scheduling and making up classes?

Resources

District of Columbia

Academic Preparation Center of Washington Academy
4301 Connecticut Avenue NW, Suite 147
Washington, DC 20008
202-362-7386
One-on-one and in-home tutoring by experienced teachers. SSAT, study skills and academic subjects from grade school. Over 20 years of service to the metropolitan area.

DC Tutors Inc
735 8th Street SE
Washington, DC 20003
202-543-7323
Academic tutoring, diagnostic testing, educational advocacy in all academic subjects for K-12. In-home tutoring by certified teachers.

Ideal Learning Center
1501 Gallatin Street NW
Washington, DC 20011
202-726-0313
Offers one-on-one tutoring for all ages on all subjects and courses. All tutors are certified teachers.

Kingsbury Center
2138 Bancroft Place, NW
Washington, DC 20008
202-232-5878
Complete diagnostic services and tutoring in all subjects for all ages. Tutors have completed a training course, they are specially trained to teach learning disabled students as well as subject matter tutoring.

Math Center
3311 Macomb Street NW
Washington DC 20016
202-244-6853
Diagnostic services and tutoring in math, geometry and algebra. An informal diagnostic test is required of every student. All tutors must complete training course by Persis Joan Herold, M.Ed., co-author of *Math Teaching Handbook*.

Maryland

Certified Learning Centers, Inc.
11309 Classical Lane
Silver Spring, MD 20901
301-774-3700
Remedial tutoring in most subjects; writing, speed reading, study skills and math workshops for preschoolers and older. Certified teachers with advanced degrees in areas of specialties.

Learning Dynamics Associates
15300 Basswood Court
Rockville, MD 20853
301-929-3232
Diagnostic testing and tutoring with emphasis on reading, writing, study skills and mathematics for children. One-on-one tutoring, seminars on study skills. Accelerated learning programs and remedial programs are offered. Every staff member has a Ph.D.

Potomac Tutors
10122 River Road
Potomac, MD 20854
301-299-6789
One-on-one tutoring for Grades K-12, both remedial and supportive. All academic subjects covered, including languages. Tutors have either a B.A. or M.A.

Specific Diagnostics
11600 Nebel St., Suite 130
Rockville, MD 20852
301-468-6616
Diagnostic testing, supportive and remedial one-on-one tutoring in all academic areas from age 3½. All tutors have teaching experience.

Sylvan Learning Center Headquarters
9135 Guilford Road
Columbia, MD 21046
1-800-338-2283
Tutoring in reading, writing, and math in 15 locations around the metro area. Remedial and supportive tutoring available. All tutors are certified teachers.

Tutoring Services
9913 Hall Road
Potomac, MD 20854
301-299-6920
One-on-one in home tutoring by qualified teachers. All academic subjects for elementary level. Study skills, SSAT, NPE, English as a second language, and special education. Remedial and supportive tutoring available.

Virginia

Back to Basics Reading Agency
740 N. Vermont Street
Arlington, VA 22203
703-528-3528
One-on-one tutoring in language and reading skills from age 5. Emphasizes application of skills to school texts and to books of appropriate interest and reading levels. Remedial and supportive tutoring available.

Creative Tutors
2414 Cavendish Drive
Alexandria, VA 22308
703-360-1277
In-home tutoring on any subject from preschool age. All tutors are certified teachers or are experts in technical fields for advanced students.

Huntington Learning Center
66371 Rolling Mill Place, Suite 103
Springfield, VA 22152
703-451-4466
One-on-one tutoring from grade K in basic skill areas such as reading, writing, math and study skills, remedial and enrichment tutoring. Nine metro area locations with state certified teachers.

Additional Resources from the *Washington Parent*

<u>**District of Columbia**</u>

Susan J. Kline, M.A.E.E.	202-537-1406
Traveling Tutors	301-585-0650

<u>**Maryland**</u>

T.L.C.	301-424-5200
T.D.D.	301-424-5203
Traveling Tutors	301-585-0650
Trust Tutoring	301-589-0733

<u>**Virginia**</u>

Creative Tutors	703-360-1277
Heritage Tutoring Service	703-780-5982
Traveling Tutors	703-893-9010
Tutoring for Success	703-242-8616
TutorFind	800-64-TUTOR

★ Special Needs

The Lab School of Washington
4759 Reservoir Road, NW
Washington, DC 20007
202-965-6600
One-to-one, in-home tutoring for all ages by well-trained teaching professionals with a background in tutoring learning disabled children.

Recommendations from teachers, other parents, local colleges and universities are also valuable sources of information on tutors.

 # Resource

Wiser Directory of Educational Services. Washington Independent Services for Educational Resources, 11th Edition, 1995.

Summertime

When 8-year-old Josh announced he wanted to go to camp in July, everyone in his family had a suggestion. His mom loved her swimming camp which she had faithfully attended year after year; his dad was partial to Scout camp which he claimed taught him to be self-reliant, and his grandpa reminisced about taking the family tenting and spelunking at the state parks. Each was convinced Josh would benefit from the very same summer experiences they had enjoyed as kids.

How do you figure out where to send your children nowadays, when there are literally hundreds of area summer camps and campsites, and a myriad of getaway spots offering all kinds of programs and activities?

Whichever you are looking for, shared family experience or a chance to let Junior become more independent, this chapter offers ideas and advice to help you create the perfect summer for you and your children.

Photo by Beverly Resneck Photography

Selecting the Right Summer Sleepaway Camp for Your Child

by Joanne Schuster Wilkenfeld, M.A.

This year more than 4 million children will spend at least part of their summer vacation at one of the 10,000 summer camp programs currently in operation in the United States. Camp can foster personal growth in a child in many ways. Summer camp is a place to meet new people, learn new skills, make lasting friendships, build self-confidence and create a lifetime of memories. Going to summer camp gives children a chance to get away from home, from school and from their own communities to develop a sense of independence, and establish their own identity. For today's working parents, summer camp provides the knowledge that their child's days are busy and filled with fun in a safe, secure environment.

A generation ago Washington area parents were able to ask their relatives or friends about summer camps in the area, as choices were fairly limited. But in the 1990s, there are so many choices available, and distances have been shortened because of the accessibility of affordable air and ground transportation, that parents really need to do their homework to find the right camp for their child.

Variety of Camps

The variety of camps in the United States is endless including day, residential, traditional, specialty, single sex, and coed camps, as well as religiously oriented and nonsectarian ones. They can be privately owned, owned and operated by local governments, run by nonprofit agencies such as Campfire or the Scouts, or be affiliated with a particular religious denomination. There are camps that cater to special needs populations, such as diabetics or learning disabled children, and others that will mainstream children with special needs into their general population.

Session length can vary too, from one week to a full eight weeks. Fees at camps vary widely also, depending primarily on the nature of camp ownership. Most sources agree that nonprofit camps charge between $15 to $55 per day, while those which are privately run can cost

Joanne Schuster Wilkenfeld, a business member of the American Camping Association, is a co-owner of Summer Solutions. A graduate of Skidmore College and George Washington University Graduate School, she has written articles on camping in national parenting publications. Summer Solutions has placed thousands of children in camp since 1984 and produces the area's largest camp fairs.

between $35 and $100 per day. In planning your camp budget, it is important to know that many offer discounts for early registration, early payment and two or more campers. A limited number of "camperships" are available at some privately owned camps; lower priced programs are often subsidized either by a church, local government or nonprofit agency.

In addition to traditional camps (offering a variety of sports and creative arts activities) that serve children ages 6 to 16, there are now a growing number of incredibly interesting offerings for teenagers such as teen travel or wilderness adventure programs. There are also many community service projects for teenagers, both in this country and overseas. And many college and prep school campuses now host academic programs during the summer, for both middle school and high school students.

Is Your Child Ready for Camp?

To begin the process of selecting the right summer camp you must gain insight into your child's personality and base your decision on his or her needs and preferences. Essentially this means that you do not choose a camp for your daughter because it was good for your niece or for your neighbor's child or even because you spent happy summers there. Focus on your own child. Your first decision will be whether he is ready for overnight camp, or whether he should attend a day camp. Child psychologists suggest that a child is ready to attend sleepaway camp if he has experienced being away from home by staying overnight with friends or relatives. Chronological age is not as important as the individual child's maturity level and willingness to go away to camp.

Most psychologists feel that a child should not go away to camp until age 7 or 8, but there are many success stories about children as young as 6. Others feel that a child should be able to read, since letters are an important part of the communication between parent and child. Very often it is the child who first comes to the parents with the announcement that he would like to go away to camp. This is your best indicator that he is ready.

The Right Environment

You need to look honestly at your child's personality. Different camps are better suited to certain children than others. Is your child shy or outgoing? Does she make friends easily? A smaller camp would probably be a wiser choice for the shy child. Does your child thrive on competition or is she burned out by the end of the school year. If the school year is filled with competitive activities and her basic personality is not so competitive, you may wish to place her in a summer camp environment where she will be less stressed than at school. You must take a good, honest look at your child's strengths and weaknesses and select a program that would provide a positive experience and would help your youngster grow as a person.

You also need to think about whether your child does better in a highly structured environment, where the day is prearranged, or whether he would prefer a freedom of choice, or elective program. Again a guideline is that the younger child will probably do better in a more structured program, whereas the older child, having been exposed to different activities, knows his likes and dislikes and prefers to have input into the day's schedule.

Next, you have to make the decision as to how far away from home you are willing to have your child go. Have you grown up in a different area of the country and would your child like to have the experience of living in that area? Do you have any reservations about putting your child on an airplane? Do you want to incur the additional expense of transportation? Is your child hesitant about being far away from home? In making your decisions about location, remember that in any emergency situation, the camp is acting as the parent in decision making. Therefore, you must have faith and confidence in the owners and directors, and your choice of location should not be based on your own proximity to the camp.

Assess your child's skills to determine whether you wish him or her to pursue a special interest in one area or whether exposure to a variety of lessons and programs would be better. For example, if your 10-year-old started playing soccer at age 6, plays on community-based teams and is moderately good, summer camp may be the time to seek out a specialty camp to further develop his soccer skills. Or you may decide that summer camp might be the perfect time for him to learn to play other sports and receive instruction in baseball, tennis, sailing, woodworking, ceramics and drama. In the former case, you would explore specialty camps or clinics for soccer instruction. In the latter, you would choose a traditional summer camp. This is when the parent needs to look at the child and determine what would be the best direction for his future growth. Most parents of younger children choose the traditional camp in order to expose the child to the broadest range of experiences.

Where to Begin the Search

Now that you have assessed your child's interests and capabilities, you are ready to begin your selection process. A good place to start is one of the directories of summer camp programs, such as *Peterson's Guide* or *The American Camping Association Directory of Accredited Camps*. These directories give you general information about the programs. However, since there are literally hundreds of quality programs for you to choose from, it is easy to get overwhelmed by these books.

Camp fairs are a wonderful opportunity to learn about a wide variety of programs in one afternoon. Presented during the winter months, these fairs bring together the owners and directors of the camps and the families interested in finding them. Exhibition booths are set up, videos or slides are displayed and applications and brochures can be picked up, all in one location during an afternoon.

Summer camp advisory services are a helpful source of information on sleepaway camps and teen programs. You can call for a free consultation with an experienced advisor, who in many cases has visited each of the camps and can give the family personalized information and advice on hundreds of programs. Camps pay commissions on placements from these referral services, enabling the service to remain free to parents.

The Selection Process

By now you should have made some fundamental decisions:
- Single sex or coed
- Full season or part season
- Large camper population or small camp
- Competitive or noncompetitive
- Traditional or specialty
- Geographic location
- Cost

Whatever route you chose, whether you do all the research on your own, or work with an advisory service, narrow your choices to five camps that fit most or all of your needs. Now your period of intense investigation begins.

Your first step is to contact the owner/director of the camp. He or she is the most critical person at the camp, responsible for choosing the staff and for the day to day operation of the camp. If at all possible have a personal meeting either at your home, the director's home, or at a camp fair. Ask about his personal philosophy and attitude toward the summer camp experience to get a feel for his or her personality and manner, as this will be reflected in staff and will set the tone for the summer. Ask the director such questions as how homesickness is handled. Watch the director interact with your child. Is he merely "selling" the program to you, or does he genuinely interact well with your child. If you do not feel comfortable with the camp director or the answers given to your questions, you should look at other programs—after all, the director will be your contact person for any concerns or special problems that arise; therefore your relationship with this key person is critical.

If at all possible, visit the camp while it is in operation. Many families look for sleepaway camps the summer before they plan to send their children just so they can visit the camps while they are in session. Sometimes this is not possible, and you may need to rely on a video or slide show to give you an idea about the facilities. Facilities at camps vary widely, from very rustic tents and outhouses, to fairly comfortable cabins with electricity and plumbing. This is a matter of personal preference for both you and your child. Also look at the facilities for sports, crafts, the dining hall and kitchen, the infirmary and medical facilities, and the waterfront. You should ask questions about health and safety procedures. For example, does the waterfront comply with Red Cross safety procedures? Is there a doctor or nurse at camp? How do children who are on medication receive it? What are the health and safety inspections like in the state where the camp is located? Is the camp accredited by the American Camping Association, the national organization that conducts inspections every three years for camps that seek ACA accreditation?

Ask questions about the staff. What is the camper/counselor ratio? In many camps it is 4:1 or 5:1. However, if your child has a special need, you may want a smaller ratio. What type of training does the camp provide for counselors? Most camps hold at least a week-long orientation prior to opening day. Ask what percentage of the staff is foreign. Many camps chose to staff with foreign counselors, and this is a matter of choice for you. Ask about the camp's policy toward smoking. Many camps today have no-smoking policies, even for staff. How does the camp handle major trouble situations—such as disruptive children, children who smoke or are caught with illegal substances. This is more of a problem at teenage programs, but the questions need to be asked because many of the staff at traditional camps are only 20 or 21 years old.

If you can't visit the camp in person, then look at the video which will often contain information specifically for families who are unable to visit personally. Here again, an advisory service may be very helpful, for they do visit their client camps while in operation, and can give parents the benefits of this first-hand observation. Advisors also have information about food service and preparation, accreditation, staff, facilities, philosophy, spirit and transportation.

Ask the camp for references and then call them. It is helpful to have a Washington area reference, so that you may ask specific questions such as those concerning transportation. Have a list of questions ready, so that you can find out about the camp from a previous camper and his family. Ask about the staff, the facilities, the kids, the food, the program. But do remember that not every reference will have had a positive experience at the camp. If you call a reference who did not have a good time and is not going back, make sure you find out if it was simply not a good match between that child and the particular camp.

Check to see if the camp has been recently inspected by its state board of health and safety or by the American Camping Association. To become accredited by the ACA, a camp must be visited every three years and evaluated on almost 300 different items related to health, safety, operation, facilities, programming, personnel and management practices. The American Camping Association will be pleased to provide parents with information on the mandatory standards.

Finally, it is important that you give your child an active role in the selection and decision-making process. Take him/her with you to the camp fairs. Read all the brochures and watch the videos together. If you visit the camp, take your child with you to interact with the director and staff. Ask for his or her input as you look at each program. By making your child feel part of the process, she or he will feel less apprehensive about leaving home and going away to camp—and more involvement means more excitement about the choice.

To review the research process:

1. Meet the director or at least talk at length on the phone.

2 Personally visit the camp, or at least see slides or a video.

3. Talk to references—other children who have recently attended that camp. Try to get at least one from the Washington area.

4. Check the accreditation of the camp, either from the American Camping Association or the state department of health.

5. Include your child in the decision-making process in an age-appropriate manner.

You have now reached the point where you are ready to make your selection. Remember, there is a camp for every child. Hopefully, the time you take to find the right summer camp for *your* child will result in a wonderful experience.

Resources

Associations

American Camping Association Inc.
5000 State Road 67 North
Martinsville, IN 46151-7902

Women's American Organization for Rehabilitation Through Training
451 Hungerford Drive
Rockville, MD
301-424-7541

Referral Services - Camp Advisors
Summer Solutions: Advisors on Camps and Trips
P.O. Box 2481
Springfield, VA 22152
703-255-2540; 703-569-2616; 1-800-729-7295

Student Summers
4066 Mansion Drive, NW
Washington, DC 20007
202-298-5929

Tips on Trips and Camps
P.O. Box 15068
Chevy Chase, MD 20825
301-670-1706

See Appendix II on page 373 for the Metropolitan Area Summer Camp Guide.

Furthur Reading

American Camping Association. *1994-95 Guide to Accredited Camps*.

Harbor School Parents Association. *Summer Fun! A Guide to Camps in Greater Washington*. Bethesda, MD: Harbor School 1992.

Peterson's Guides. *Summer Opportunities for Kids and Teens*. Princeton, NJ: Fetterwef, 1993.

★ Special Needs

American Camping Association
Bradford Woods
Martinsville, IN 46151
317-342-8456
Accredits camps throughout the country, and publishes a guide for parents.

Boy Scouts of America
Scouting for the Handicapped
2000 Cornwall Road
South Brunswick, NJ 08852
908-821-6500
Information on camps in the Eastern United States.

Camp Holiday Trails
P.O. Box 5806
Charlottesville, VA 22905
804-977-3781
Sleepaway camp in Charlottesville area; serves a broad range of children with medical management problems.

Girl Scouts of the USA
Scouting for Handicapped Girls
830 Third Avenue
New York, NY 10022
212-852-8000

Resources for Children with Special Needs
200 Park Avenue S, Suite 816
New York, NY 10003
212-677-4650
Publishes a national camp directory for children with special needs.

Family Camping

by Thomas J. Hillegass

Camping with your children provides a wonderful opportunity to have a great time, create wonderful memories and become closer as a family. Away from the distractions of home, only tasks that are immediate to "survival," like putting up tents and cooking meals, will demand your attention. The phone will not ring, the lawn will wait. When you're camping, basic chores require everyone to work together in a way that doesn't often happen at home and, amazingly, it turns out to be fun.

Younger children get to explore the flora and fauna and to test their independence in a natural environment. There are crawlies and critters to examine and lakes and other inviting places to swim in, accompanied by real fish and the occasional salamander. At night, there are campfires and marshmallows, plenty of darkness to pierce with the flashlight and a billion stars that don't come out in city skies. Even teens, if they grew up enjoying exciting family camping experiences, will not want to miss out, especially if they are allowed to take a friend along. The whole family will develop a new appreciation for the natural environment, its beauty and value.

Equipment

You don't need to go overboard on equipment to have a great camping trip, but some basics are essential. It is assumed that if you are a beginning camper you will start with a tent, not a $50,000 motor home. Some good ways to get camping equipment are:

1. Borrow from camping friends. They will be glad to help you with gear and advice and maybe go with you to get you acclimated.

2. Attend yard sales to buy beginning camping gear.

3. Shop at Play it Again Sports stores, which buy and sell used camping gear. There are several in the Maryland and Virginia suburbs; see your phone book.

- For low prices, try the Sports Authority, Herman's, Kmart or Wal-Mart.

Thomas Hillegass grew up in Philadelphia, with little experience of the country beyond the Schuylkill River. He discovered he harbors a lust for the natural world, and his wife and three children share his enthusiasm for the "togetherness" camping provides. He works as an Information Systems Manager with the U.S. Dept. of Transportation.

- For high quality, more pricey gear, try REI Cooperative or Eastern Mountain Sports (EMS).

- If you want to see more camping gear than you ever thought possible, go to H & H Camper Surplus in downtown Baltimore at Franklin & Eutaw Streets (a few blocks north of the Lexington Market). Drive a little—see a lot!

Equipment you need to start:

Tent: Dome tents are good, spacious, easy to set up, all around family tents. If the kids are old enough not to be frightened, get them a separate one. Note that a "three person" tent actually sleeps two people, a "five person tent" sleeps three. If the tent has sleeves that you push the poles through, avoid poles that have raised joints because they bind frustratingly in the sleeve.

Make sure the tent has plenty of netted ventilation under a large rain fly. Get a spray can of waterproofing (Camp Dry is one brand) and a tube of seam sealer and use both on the top of the rain fly and underside of the tent floor the first time you set it up and every spring thereafter. Cut a piece of plastic tarp and put it under the floor, making sure that it *does not* extend beyond the floor or it will channel the rain right under your tent.

Put the tent up in your yard before you go camping with young kids. It is a good safe environment in which to have the first experience. If they have slept in the tent in the backyard, they will sleep better when you are camping.

Stove: Don't figure on cooking meals over an open fire, romantic as this may seem. Get a two-burner stove. The propane are easiest for a beginner to use, the "white gas" kind (some use regular unleaded gas) make the most heat but can be temperamental.

Lantern: Take two good flashlights and a candle in a jar (like the citronella kind sold at drug stores) for your table.

Cooler: Get a good one if you don't have one. You'll need it for picnics/beach/etc. anyway. The new soft sided cooler bags take up less room but don't have the capacity and insulation of the solid ones.

Sleeping Bags: If you camp only in mild weather you can get by with very inexpensive sleeping bags. The parents may want a matching pair that can be zipped together. Any two matching bags that can be unzipped and laid out flat can also be rezipped together one on top of the other. Take pillows; you'd be surprised how hard it is to part with your pillow.

Mattresses: An air mattress or sleeping pad is a "must" for the parents and a good idea for the kids as well. Sleeping on the ground is a bummer.

One option is an air mattress (or "air bed"); a double is nice for adults. Get fairly good ones ($30-$40 for a double) but plan to replace them every couple of years anyway because they all get leaks with time.

Try not to get ones that are too "slick" on top; you want a little texture to keep the sleeping bags from going South while your head is pointing North.

Oh, and don't try to blow them up by mouth or even by manual pump. Get a pump that works from your car cigarette lighter, a high volume pump made specifically for inflatable toys. Some auto vacuums blow air out a round hole in the back and if it even approximately mates to your mattress it will work very well.

Another option is the self-inflating sleeping pad, but be aware that it tends to be thin and expensive. For the older folks, look for ones that are at least 2 inches thick (3 inches if you can find them) and get them inexpensively at Kmart or Wal-Mart.

Kitchen Gear: Get one of those all-in-one camping sets (includes pots, dishes and cups) at a yard sale. Most are aluminum but if you can get stainless steel it will keep you from exceeding your daily intake requirement of aluminum, which incidentally is zero.

Dining Fly: You can buy a reinforced polyethylene tarp to cover your table, complete with poles, cords and stakes, for $20 on sale. Do it! Rain, especially at mealtime, can be a real nuisance. The first time you put up your dining fly, enlist the whole gang and be patient, as you will feel like Lilliputians trying to stake down a squirming Gulliver.

Lawn chairs: Take one folding lawn or beach chair for each person. Sitting on picnic table benches or upended logs (especially after a rain) is not conducive to relaxing times and, near a fire, a stable seat is essential for all.

Keeping a list of stuff to take is an important part of happy family camping. Make yourself an initial list (on your word processor so you can update it), print it out *and take it with you camping*. As you find items you need but don't have, add them to the list right then and update your list when you get home.

Here is a "starter" list; you may want to delete some items and add others.

Camping List

Kitchen
- Kitchen pot kit (see above)
- Frying pan (the one in the kit won't be enough)
- Flatware
- Large, sharp knife
- Large spoon
- Spatula
- Can opener
- Potholders
- Ziploc bags
- Trash bags
- Paper cups and dishes

- Table cloth (plastic)
- Dish cloth (wash dishes in the big pot)
- Dish towels
- Dish detergent
- Scouring pad
- Salt and pepper
- Sugar
- Tea/coffee
- Matches
- Condiments (as your menu requires)
- Marshmallows

Gear

- Tents (including poles, stakes, ground tarp)
- Spray can of waterproofing and tube of seam sealer
- Sleeping bags
- Pillows
- Air mattress
- Pump
- Dining tarp (including poles, stakes, ropes)
- Plastic drop cloth (cheap, light, emergency rain protection)
- Rope and (spring, wooden) clothes pins
- Hammer or hatchet (for stakes)
- Work gloves (to protect hands while staking, fire tending, etc)
- Candle in a jar (like citronella)
- Stove
- Fuel for stove (funnel if needed)
- Cooler
- Water jug (2 gallons or more)
- Charcoal and starter (if you will grill)
- Saw (an inexpensive bow saw is safer than a hatchet)
- Folding chairs (one for each person; don't skimp on chairs)
- Flashlights (extra batteries)
- Newspaper (to start fire)
- Firewood (Coals to Newcastle, you say, but you will often *not* be able to take firewood from the woods!)

Personal

What you would take in your shaving kit or cosmetic bag for any trip but for camping be sure to add:

- Soap (in holder)
- Face cloth, hand towel, bath towel
- Tissues or toilet paper (emergency)
- Any emergency medications family members might need (consider bee stings, allergies, car sickness)
- First Aid kit
- Insect repellent
- Sun screen
- Calamine lotion
- Rain gear (ponchos are good)

Fun Stuff

- Hats
- Sunglasses
- Bathing suits
- River shoes (old sneakers or "reef runners," double as shower shoes)
- Beach umbrella
- Books
- Fishing gear
- Life jackets
- Innertubes
- Bird/flower ID books
- Roadside geology books (available for several states)
- Cameras
- Games
- Binoculars
- Family trip record (write down a record of your trip each day; you'll be glad you did years later, if not sooner)

 # Questions to ask yourself

1. Do I have the patience? You (and your spouse) must be able to adopt a "laid back in the outback" attitude to have a rewarding camping experience with children (or with anyone, for that matter). Be patient. Let the children help with *everything*. Don't rush them—let them make mistakes. This is not a military exercise, just fun in the woods. If you cannot keep cool, family camping is *not* for you.

2. Do I have a sense of adventure? One of the main attractions of camping is setting out on your own for an adventure. By camping, you can explore out-of-the-way places, away from

motels and restaurants, and you can experience nature in the night and morning, times when almost everyone else has retreated to a motel to watch TV or float in chlorine. While camping will bring the occasional nuisance and some discomfort, this is part of the adventure.

3. Do I enjoy planning and preparing? A major part of any hobby or sport has to do with the joy of anticipation, planning, procuring and tinkering with the "gear" involved. If you get to be a regular camping family, you will spend a lot of time on preparations and gear and at least one parent should enjoy each of these aspects.

Resources

Prime Camping Locations near DC

For an exhaustive list of private and public campgrounds and their features, be sure to get the Rand McNally or Woodalls camping guides at any bookstore. The campgrounds recommended below are all public (state or federal) and are a reasonable travel time from the Washington metropolitan area (3½ hours maximum; all distances and times are approximate) for a weekend trip. All have the following "basic" amenities:
- Wooded sites
- Bathrooms
- Usually clean
- Flush toilets (no pits)
- Sinks and mirrors
- Picnic tables
- Fireplaces
- Towns nearby

Maryland

Maryland State Parks - Cunningham Falls State Park
Lots of activities, lake swimming, waterfalls, camp store, hot showers, reservations 301-271-7574. Two areas; Manor and Houck (Houck is near the lake). Even has "camper ready" sites (with tent, dining canopy, stove and firewood) for $25-$30; good if you want to try camping with a minimal investment in equipment.
Directions: (70 miles; 1½ hours)
- To Manor area: From Frederick, MD take Rt 15 North for 15 mi. Manor area is on Rt. 15
- To Houck area: Pass Manor area on Rt 15, turn left at Rt 77, turn left on Catoctin Hollow Rd, follow signs to Houck area

Greenbriar State Park
Lots of activities, lake swimming, hot showers, reservations (301)791-4767
Directions: (60 miles, 1½ hours)
- I-70 to northwest of Frederick, take the exit to Rt 17 North (Meyersville exit)
- Rt 17 North, go short distance, turn left on Rt 40
- Rt 40 North to Greenbriar Park

Washington Monument State Park
A nice, small park, no showers, no swimming, no reservations. Near Greenbriar. Has "original" Washington Monument, not the big one but a smaller cousin.
Directions: (70 miles, 1½ hours)
- I-70 to northwest of Frederick, take the Braddock Heights exit to Alt Rt 40 west, go 9 miles to marked access road to park

Point Lookout State Park
Sandy, wooded area where the Potomac River and Chesapeake Bay converge, swimming in the river (jellyfish in midsummer), hot showers, reservations 301-872-5688.
Directions: (85 miles, 2 hours)
- Beltway (I-95/495) to Rt 5 South
- Rt 5 South, continue straight onto Rt 235 South
- Rt 235 South to Rt 5 South (again)
- Rt 5 South to park

Virginia

George Washington National Forest - Elizabeth Furnace
Beautiful valley in Massanutten Mountain; swimming in creek; showers, reservations 800-280-2267.
Directions: (85 miles, 1¾ hours)

- I-66 to Front Royal, take the exit for Rt 340/522 South
- Rt 340/522 South about 1½ mi, turn right on Rt 55
- Rt 55 West about 10 mi, turn left on Rt 678
- Rt 678 South about 4.8 mi (past Day Use Area) to Elizabeth Furnace family camping

Camp Roosevelt
Also in Massanutten Mountain; nice, small campground, not far from South Fork of the Shenandoah River (impromptu wading/swimming possible in river; nearby commercial tubing and canoeing trips), no showers, no reservations. Close to Elizabeth Furnace.
Directions: (100 miles, 2¼ hours)
From DC:
- I-66 to Rt 29/211 at Gainesville
- Rt 29/211 South to Rt 211 in Warrenton
- Rt 211 South through Sperryville to downtown Luray (don't take Rt 211 bypass around Luray)
- Rt 340 North a short distance, turn left on Rt 675 West
- Cross Shenandoah River on Rt 675, careful to stay on Rt 675 up the mountain (great view at the top)
- As you come down mountain, look for Camp Roosevelt sign
From Elizabeth Furnace:
- Continue on Rt 678 to its end at Kings Crossing
- Go left on Rt 675 to the sign for Camp Roosevelt

Todd Lake

Mountainous, very nice setting, lake swimming, no reservations, no showers. Complicated directions but worth getting a bit lost.
Directions: (140 miles, 3 hours)
- I-81 to just south of Harrisonburg, take the exit for R 257 West
- Rt 257 West to Bridgewater, turn left on Rt 42
- Rt 42 South about 2.7 mi and bear right onto Rt 809/Rt 747
- Rt 747 South through Mt. Solon about 6.5 miles and turn right on Rt 730
- Rt 730 North about 1.2 miles where it will run straight into Rt 718 (no turn required)
- Rt 718 North about 1 mi and turn left at the sign for Todd Lake onto Forest Route (FR) 95
- FR 95 about 5 miles to Todd Lake

Shenandoah National Park - Big Meadows

On Skyline Drive, no swimming, reservations required in summer and fall from Mistix 800-365-2267.
Directions: (100 miles, 2¼ hours)
- Same as Matthews Arm as far as national park entrance
- I-66 to Rt 29/211 at Gainesville
- Rt 29/211 South to Rt 211 in Warrenton
- Rt 211 South through Sperryville to National Park entrance
- South on Skyline Drive about 20 miles to campground

Loft Mountain

On Skyline Drive, no reservations, no swimming.
Directions: (120 miles, 2½ hours)
- I-66 to Rt 29/211 at Gainesville
- Rt 29/211 South to Rt 29 in Warrenton
- Rt 29 South to Rt 33 in Ruckersville
- Rt 33 to national park entrance
- South on Skyline Drive about 14 miles to campground

Virginia State Parks - Westmoreland State Park

Wooded Potomac riverside setting, swimming in the river or a pool, hot showers, restaurant, reservations 804-493-8821.
Directions: (95 miles, 1¾ hours)
- I-95 South to Fredericksburg, turn East on Rt 3
- Rt 3 East to signs to park

Additional Resources

Maryland: State Parks and State Forests
Info: 410-974-3771
Reservations: Call individual park

Virginia: State Parks
Info: 804-786-1712
Reservations: 800-933-PARK

Virginia: George Washington National Forest
Info: 703-564-8300
Reservations: 800-280-2267

West Virginia: State Parks and State Forests
Info & Reservations: 800-CALL-WVA

★ Special Needs

ACCESS National Parks - Guide
Superintendent of Documents, Washington, DC 20402
202-783-3238

Mobility International
P.O. Box 10767
Eugene, OR 97440
503-343-1284 Voice/TDD 503-343-6812 fax

Travel Information Service - Moss Rehabilitation Hospital
1200 W. Tabor Road
Philadelphia, PA 19141
215-456-9600 Voice 215 456-9602 TDD

Creative Arts

As local writer Sharon Cavaleer has so eloquently said, "The arts are the way we create ourselves, solve problems, express ourselves and our emotions, as well as bond with our civilization and its history." The importance of encouraging our children to appreciate and participate in music, dance, theater and visual arts cannot be overestimated. Witness the following children—does one of them sound familiar to you?

Four-year-old Susan doesn't care much for dolls. And she's only mildly enthusiastic about theme parks, hot-fudge sundaes and jumping rope. Susan would rather sketch, paint and color.

At age 9, Ned is already a budding actor. He has played the lead in every skit and play at school since he was old enough to speak and remember lines. For his last birthday, Ned asked for tickets to a play at the Kennedy Center.

Seven-year-old Carolyn wants to play the flute or French horn in the school band. Tooting happily in a group is her idea of Nirvana.

John enjoys more physically taxing activities. He loves football—but not as much as creative dance.

These children may not all be talented, but they are learning to love the arts and to see the world through a new and exciting medium. Their families want to encourage their creativity and provide the right type of private instruction for them. How do you find the best instruction for your child among the area's many teaching facilities?

As a parent you want to help your children develop their talents, deepen their skills and enrich their appreciation of the arts. The following pages offer the tools necessary to help them realize their creative potential.

Introducing Children to Classical Music

by Bonnie Ward Simon, M.A.

Introducing children to the world of sound is a challenging and complex task. The aural world is as varied and rich as the world of sight, and yet, the same parents who consider the reading of Shakespeare and Dickens and the viewing of Michelangelo and Rembrandt integral parts of an educated mind, will suddenly hesitate when asked about the importance of listening to a Beethoven symphony. Years of reading precede the enjoyment of Shakespeare, years of drawing and painting precede the first encounter with Rembrandt; similarly, years of listening to music must precede the appreciation of the great works of classical music.

Music for the Young Child

The parents of a newborn can begin building a child's musical vocabulary with the purchase of his or her first music box. Brahms' "Lullaby," excerpts from Mozart's "Eine Kleine Nachtmusik" and Flotow's "The Last Rose of Summer" are all available. More extensive selections exist, both in European gift shops and on recordings of antique music boxes. In addition, every baby's room should have either a small stereo system or a "boom box" radio-cassette player for listening to music. Music is soothing for nap time, cheerful for waking up time, excellent for rolling around and exercising.

From the ages of 1 to 3, your child should be actively singing. No car should be without a cassette player (many children's recordings still are not on CD); every child should have his or her own small cassette player. Begin collecting a music (and books on tape) library together. Always listen to them *together* the first time; this sends an important message to your child, namely, that you are also interested in listening. Be prepared for the tape that is pulled yard by yard out of its container; hopefully, this will be a one-time experience. Find a parent-child music group. You will learn songs that you and your child can share and take with you everywhere.

By the age of 3, your child may be ready to listen to several other kinds of music. Prokofiev's *Peter and the Wolf* with a book of pictures is

Bonnie Ward Simon, BA, MusEd, MA, MPhil, is Executive Director of the Washington Chamber Symphony and co-founder of the symphony's highly successful Concerts for Young People and Family Concert Series performed at the Kennedy Center.

appropriate. The American Ballet Theater's video of *The Nutcracker* is excellent for both girls and boys. Most 3-year-olds are still not socially ready to sit quietly in a concert hall. The concert hall experience demands a three-stage process, namely, that the child be able to (1) store up what he or she has heard, (2) recall it after the performance and (3) then be able to discuss it out of its time frame. Taking a 3-year-old to a concert is possible, but if the child is forced to behave in a situation-appropriate rather than age-appropriate manner, it will not be an enjoyable experience for either the parents or the child. Be grateful that we live in the age of excellent recorded sound and video, which can prepare your child for the grand moment.

The First Concert Experience

All children should be prepared for their first concert hall experience. If they are to attend *Peter and the Wolf*, they should have listened to it at least 25 times at home first; if they are going to *The Nutcracker*, you should have watched the video several times with them, stopping, explaining the story, talking about the dances, etc. If you are taking a child to a holiday sing-along concert, be certain the he knows the words to the first verse of at least half the songs listed on the program. Good preparation eliminates the need for disturbing and inadequate explanations during performances and allows the event to be an exhilarating, magical experience of something known on an intellectual level coming to life.

The ages of 6 to 12 are wonderful years for your child to attend live performances with you. The best young people's programming is entertaining and educational for both the parent and the child; even the musicians learn something at a fine concert for young people. The age to start is not fixed and depends on the child's level of interest, previous exposure, school-imparted listening skills, etc. If your child is not ready to sit quietly and listen for 20 to 35 minutes, wait until next year to take her.

Continue your listening at home and in the car with stories in music, such as *Peter and the Wolf* and *Mr. Bach Comes to Call* (the entire Classical Kids Series is excellent) and/or ballets with stories, such as *The Nutcracker, Sleeping Beauty, Swan Lake*. Continue to have tapes in the car and listen to The Beatles and Queen, music of their choice as well as yours. On stressful days, a good rule is that adults and children each have veto power.

In the final analysis, one must ask: Do I want my child to attend concerts and develop an appreciation of music? Do I want my child to play an instrument and develop performance skills? Do I want my child to intellectually be aware of music's place in our cultural history? Hopefully, a classical music-lover can be involved in all three aspects. We know that the best way to ensure that our children will be readers is to read ourselves. Unless we, as parents, have a genuine interest in classical music, our children will probably fail to go beyond a very rudimentary introduction to this art form. The good news, however, is that while some parents have musical backgrounds, most do not, and if this is the case, you and your child can begin to enjoy and learn about classical music together.

Questions to ask yourself

1. Do I like classical music?
2. Do I think that my child should like classical music because it (a) is socially correct, (b) will give him or her a lifetime of enjoyment, (c) will be a civilizing force on his or her personality, (d) is something that I have never learned to like but feel that I should?
3. Would I, as a parent, like to learn more about classical music?
4. Do I think that learning about a Beethoven symphony is as important as learning how to play baseball well or understanding a Shakespearean play?
5. Is this something that I would like to share with my child?
6. Is there time in my life to practice an instrument with my child every day?

Questions to ask the professional

1. What concerts are right for my child at this age? (The age requirement for concerts relates not to how musically gifted or interested the child is, but rather to his or her emotional and abstract conceptual development. Obey the guidelines for your sake, for the sake of the professionals running successful programs, and for your child's sake.)
2. What music will my child enjoy after Raffi and *Beethoven Lives Upstairs?*
3. Is my child enjoying his or her music lessons? (Not, is he doing as well as others his or her age?)
4. Should my child study an instrument at school and play in the band or orchestra?

Further Reading

Nichols, Barbara. *Beethoven Lives Upstairs.* New York: Orchard Books, 1993.

How to Find a Good Music Teacher

by Jan Childress

There is something of the artist in every child," said composer Carl Orff. "Let us help the child discover him." We need only observe a toddler at play to realize that Orff was right. Children are born with inherent musical instincts. But like all natural gifts, they must be developed with care.

When To Begin

There is no sacred rule about when to begin private lessons. Some youngsters are ready as early as 4, but many do better at age 6 or older. The choice of instrument is another decision you have to make. Although string instruments come in scaled-down sizes for little fingers, wind and brass instruments do not. Typically, children begin training on band instruments in fourth or fifth grade but it's possible to begin earlier, especially if the child is interested. Follow your child's lead if you can—what instrument is the most appealing to him or her?

Suzuki or Traditional Teaching?

Suzuki instruction is available to students of all ages, but the teaching methods developed by Shinichi Suzuki in Japan almost 50 years ago were meant to teach very young children, beginning at age 3, how to play a musical instrument. After studying the learning patterns of toddlers, Suzuki realized that their skills were slowly but inexorably developed by continuous practice, memorization, repetition, listening and mimicking. He put these concepts into his revolutionary teaching program.

Suzuki parents attend each lesson and help the child practice at home. Lessons are first learned by listening to tapes; the reading of notes is introduced only when the child grows older. With older beginning students, however, most American Suzuki teachers introduce music reading early on.

Because music reading is an integral part of their program, traditional teachers don't accept very young children into their studios. With their 6-to-8-year-old beginners, their studio activities will coincide with the child's reading development in school. Some traditional teachers want parents to attend a young student's lesson; others do not.

Jan Childress is a Washington-based writer and editor. She is updating her book, Tuning Up for Music Lessons, *which is based on interviews with dozens of local music educators, music education administrators, and arts presenters for publication in 1995.*

What Makes a Successful Studio

The lines between the two educational philosophies are blurring. Today's *best* music teachers—either Suzuki or traditional—are graduates of conservatories and universities, often with masters and even doctoral degrees. Trained in pedagogy and encouraged to keep their skills updated through seminars, they offer studio programs which are innovative and unique. No two studios are alike but they do share a few common principles:

• Regular performance classes or workshops where students meet and play for each other. This is particularly true of piano studios since these students don't have the benefit of an ensemble experience in school. In addition to the socialization, the frequent performance goals motivate the student to practice.

• Recitals and/or outside performance activities in a more formal setting than the studio. Most teachers (including band and orchestral instrument teachers) hold recitals at least once or twice a year, sometimes more often. In addition, many teachers participate in music festivals organized by the local professional music teacher associations.

• Theory instruction, either as part of the lesson or as a separate class. Because theory is the grammar of music, students learn to read music more quickly if the teacher provides specific instruction on scales, notation, key signatures, chords, etc.

Meeting the Teacher

Before signing up for lessons, request an interview (a reputable teacher should ask to meet you). What you're looking for is a good match between your child's personality and musical interest and a teacher's personality and professional qualifications. Your child will have the teacher's undivided attention for at least 30 minutes every week, probably a more intense relationship than with any other adult except you. If you've done careful research, you'll know when you've found just the right person.

Numerous music stores also offer lessons but you have to be careful. A music store is sales oriented; their education department is secondary and may not be well planned.

Many parents like the idea of a teacher coming to their home and you may be lucky enough to find a good one—usually a young person who is saving up to purchase a home and establish a permanent studio. If the teacher is professionally qualified, an itinerant teaching career is usually short-lived.

And ask your friends and neighbors. The best teacher may be right around the corner.

Questions to ask yourself

1. Is my child interested in music? Does my child:
   - Spontaneously sing or dance?
   - Enjoy listening to other family members play or sing?
   - Try to play the family's piano or other instruments?
   - Express an interest in a particular instrument?
   - Enjoy concerts, the ballet, musicals?
   - Watch performances on television? Listen to classical music on the radio, CD, record player?
2. Can my child sit still and concentrate on one subject for 15 minutes? 30 minutes?

Questions to ask a music teacher

1. Can you tell me what a typical lesson would be like?
2. I want my child to be able to read music easily. How do you teach music reading?
3. What styles of music do you teach? Classical only? A mixture of classical, jazz, contemporary, other styles?
4. Do your students ever bring their own selections of music to their lessons?
5. What are your requirements for practicing?
6. Do you hold performance classes, recitals? Are there other performance activities? Is there an upcoming performance class or recital that we could attend?
7. What is your fee? Do you wish to be paid weekly, monthly, by semester?
8. If we have to cancel a lesson, will my child be able to make up the lesson later?
9. What music school did you attend? Are you a member of a professional music teaching organization?
10. Are you currently performing? Will this affect my child's lesson schedule?

Resources for locating a music teacher

Maryland State Music Teachers Association (MSMTA)
A chapter of the Music Teachers National Association, its members are primarily piano teachers, with a smaller membership of voice, band and orchestra teachers. President, Ann Matteson: 301-441-2885.

Northern Virginia Music Teachers Association (same as MSMTA).
Teacher referral chairman, Janice Jansohn: 703-978-2662.

Washington Music Teachers Association (same as MSMTA)
President Margaret Frank: 301-654-6491.

Suzuki Association of the Greater Washington Area
A parent/student/teacher organization. Suzuki teachers offer
instruction in piano, flute and all string instruments.
Teacher referral service: 202-723-1237.

National Guild of Piano Teachers (Texas)
The Guild has several chapters, called centers, in the Washington
area. Call Texas headquarters for the center closest to you: 512-478-
5775.

School band and orchestra directors usually maintain a list of recommended teachers. Contact your neighborhood schools. In addition, Washington, D.C., is home to three music conservatories offering group classes
and individual instruction on most instruments by highly qualified teachers:

American University Preparatory Music Division: 202-885-3416
The Levine School of Music: 202-337-2227
The Washington Conservatory of Music: 301-320-2770

★ Special Needs

National Association for Music Therapy
8455 Colesville Rd., Suite 930
Silver Spring, MD 20910
301-589-3300
Provides packets of information for parents and schools on music
therapy. Current database of local music therapists.

Does Your Child Really Need Band?

by Bonnie Ward Simon, M.A.

By the time the "Band, Orchestra and Instrumental Music Lessons" form comes home from school (most school band programs begin in the third or fourth grades, orchestra programs in the fourth or fifth grades), you may feel that you and your child are already stretched beyond your limits. Most parents find themselves asking, "Does my child really *need* to join the band?" The surprising answer is: Yes, your child may need band!

This may come as an enormous surprise, but every child who begins an instrument will not continue. Trying it is a little like insisting that he try a new vegetable. Playing an instrument may even be good for one's health. Holding up a trumpet is like lifting arm weights. Marching and playing at the same time takes an incredible amount of coordination, as does tapping your foot and playing a complicated passage on the flute simultaneously. Playing an instrument requires that all parts of the body move in synchronous motion, with the brain at the helm.

But band offers something else. It is being part of a team. It builds instant friendships. It takes the young person beyond the common meeting grounds (same age, same class, same neighborhood, same brand of sneakers) and gives him or her an immediate new common bond. He or she shares a stand with another young person, shares a piece of music, discusses how to finger that high note or count that complicated rhythm. The star of the basketball team may play third trombone, and the one who has sat on the bench all season may play first trombone. Both will learn something from the experience. For some young people this is where they will be the star player; this will be their team sport. They will learn all the lessons of sportsmanship by listening to the coach (the conductor), being a team player (not playing faster than everybody else), helping to carry the equipment (stands, chairs, timpani), and being responsible (remembering the music and showing up on time for rehearsal). This may be the only team experience that some young people enjoy and, oddly enough, it is one of the very few team experiences which can stay with them and continue to be used throughout their lives. Few people are still playing basketball at 60, but many amateur musicians are still going strong at 85.

Bonnie Ward Simon, B.A., MusEd, M.A., MPhil, is Executive Director of the Washington Chamber Symphony and co-founder of the symphony's highly successful Concerts for Young People and Family Concert Series performed at the Kennedy Center.

Choosing an Instrument

But how do you choose which instrument? Do you allow your child to choose? How much influence should you exert? How do you increase chances for success, which I measure by how long he or she continues to play. Some children will have strong feelings. For instance, the saxophone or nothing! (The saxophone is probably the most popular instrument for boys at this time.) But often young people have little idea of the available possibilities. Most are familiar with the flute, trumpet and saxophone. Many will know what the trombone and tuba are. But what about baritone horns (they are like small tubas), glockenspiels (portable xylophones), oboes and bass clarinets? Those who play these instruments are often highly prized by their band directors and thought of as very special by their classmates. Perhaps your child would like to play one of these unusual instruments; if so, talk to your band director immediately and see what is possible. Go to the library or bookstore and find a book on musical instruments and thumb through it with your child to see if a particular one appeals. Here is a short list of recorded music for band instruments, which you might listen to together to see what sound appeals to your child:

Flute .... Mozart: Concerto in D
J.S. Bach: Brandenburg Concerto No. 4
Jazz: Bolling: Suite for Flute, Piano, Bass & Drums

Clarinet .... Gershwin: "Rhapsody in Blue" (beginning)
C.M.von Weber: Concerto for Clarinet & Orchestra
Jazz: recordings with Benny Goodman, Woody Herman,
Jimmy Giuffre

Trumpet .... Haydn: Trumpet Concerto
Jazz: recordings with Chet Baker, Wynton Marsalis,
Louis Armstrong, Dizzy Gillespie, Doc Severinsen

Saxophone ..... Ibert: Concert in da Camera
Jolivet: "Fantasie Impromptu"
Jazz: recordings with Stan Getz, Paul Desmond, Charlie
Parker, John Coltrane, Branford Marsalis

Oboe .... Handel: Oboe Concerti
R. Strauss: Oboe Concerto

Trombone ...... Solos by Arthur Pryor, Henry Filmore
Jazz: Tommy Dorsey

Tuba .... Vaughn-Williams: Tuba Concerto
Jazz: recordings with Stan Kenton
For young children: "Tubby, the Tuba"

Percussion ...... Chavez: Toccata for Percussion
      Bartok: Sonata for 2 Pianos and Percussion
      Sousa: Marches
      Jazz: recordings with Stan Kenton, various rock groups

Wind .... Mozart: Grand Serenade for 13 Winds
Ensemble Reicha: Trios, Quintets

Brass .... Gabrielli: Music for multiple brass choirs,
Ensemble   sometimes with chorus

Music for .... Hindemith: Symphony for Band
Concert   Holst: Suites for Band
Band   Grainger: "Lincolnshire Posey"
      Sousa: Marches

Investing Your Time and Money

Once you have selected an instrument, your band director can tell you where you can rent one. I suggest renting because your child may play for three months and announce that she has made a dreadful mistake; it really is the flute, not the trumpet which is the perfect instrument for her. Be flexible! Few professional musicians began on the instrument by which they are now making their living. If you have made a minor investment, it is much easier to change gracefully.

Be prepared! You will have to make an investment in your child's success. The cost: five minutes a day. Set a time when you both will always be together (five minutes before breakfast is the very best; or before or right after dinner, or directly after school, but always at the same time every day, because it is easier on everybody's nerves), your child will have a successful year. Do not expect your child to succeed if he practices alone for the first year. You will discover that you actually learn something and have fun. You will even discover that he will stop complaining about practicing if you always do it at the same time.

Probably the most important reason for adding band to your lives is that you are giving your child a tool for life. She will go off to a new school, take her instrument and immediately have a group of friends. Regardless of whether she is a fabulous player, or merely adequate, there will be a place for her and a welcome from the band director and the group. Your child may busk in a Paris railway station or march in the Yale Precision Marching Band, or just play throughout the high school years. Remember, this is not an attempt to create a professional musician, but a way to equip your child with new social skills, a new sense of responsibility towards a group, new tools for enjoying life, and a setting for having fun.

Resources

Area Music Stores for Rental/Purchase of Instruments

Ardis Music Center
1728 Connecticut Ave. NW
Washington, DC 20009
202-234-6537

Chuck Levin's Washington Music Center
11151 Veirs Mill Road
Wheaton, MD 20906
301-946-8808

Dale Music Company
8240 Georgia Avenue
Silver Spring, MD 20910
301-589-1459

Rolls Music Center
1065 W. Broad Street
Falls Church, VA 22046
703-533-9500

Veneman Music & Sound
8319 Amherst Avenue
Springfield, VA 22150
703-451-8970

Great Performances for Children in Washington

by Jan Childress

Taking your child to a concert or play—like reading a story—conveys a powerful message about how much you value the arts in your family's life. And today, more than ever before, parents must take a leading role in their child's artistic development as school districts across the nation continue to cut arts education and field trip budgets.

As with music lessons, your child's age is an important factor in deciding when to begin and what to see. By all means, take your baby to hear music! But the setting should be free-of-charge and completely informal so that you can walk around or leave if your child becomes restless. Outdoor performances are great choices, perhaps an event at a neighborhood nature center or a military band concert downtown. Since all the armed forces' bands are headquartered in Washington, DC, there are more opportunities to hear free, high-quality performances here than in any other city in the United States.

By age 3 or 4, most youngsters are ready for a short performance. Many local family concerts are free or value-priced. Choose a program that lasts 60-90 minutes, depending on your child's ability to sit still. Puppet shows, dramatized fairy-tales or nursery stories, dance programs and sing-alongs are appropriate for children of this age, and they'll stay involved longer if you have chosen seats close to the stage. Small theatrical spaces, such as the Kennedy Center's Theater Lab or the Smithsonian's Discovery Theater, are ideal. Large concert halls are more appropriate for older children and teens.

If an older sibling or your friends' children take part in a school band, orchestra or neighborhood dance studio, make sure to take your preschooler because of the personal interest aspect of the performances.

By the time children are old enough to sit through a school day, they're ready to attend a full-length concert or play. At this stage, their individual tastes should play a role in your entertainment plans. One 6-year-old may be transfixed by *Annie* while another prefers Chinese acrobats or the Boys' Choir of Harlem. Plan to introduce many performance styles and adjust your outings to their changing interests. And, as with many discerning theatregoers, don't expect them to like everything.

Jan Childress is a Washington-based writer and editor. She is updating her book, Tuning Up for Music Lessons, *which is based on interviews with dozens of local music educators, music education administrators and arts presenters for publication in 1995.*

Readiness and Etiquette Go Hand-in-Hand

Your child is ready for an indoor performance when he/she can sit **quietly** for a **minimum** of 30 minutes. Another sign of readiness is your youngster's ability to understand the concept of courtesy to others...the essence of good manners. These tips should be shared with your child:

- walk to your seat
- keep hands and feet to yourself
- do not talk or whisper when the performance is in progress
- enjoy your snacks in the lobby
- read your program but don't rattle it, tear it or throw it
- stay in your seat until intermission or until the performance is over (unless the conductor or actor tells you to stand).

Favorite Performances In & Around Washington

Of the hundreds of performances taking place around Washington, here are some favorites. You'll find these and many other family events advertised in local parenting publications such as *the Washington Parent*, as well as the Weekend Section in Friday editions of the *Washington Post* and Thursdays in *The Washington Times*.

Infants-Age 6

Armed Services Bands

Outdoor events: infants and up. Indoor events: ages 5-6 and up for these two-hour long concerts. Free.

Throughout the year, the four United States Armed Services bands perform at different sites in the Washington area. From early June to late August, they all present weekly concerts on a rotating basis on the East Terrace steps of the Capitol and the Sylvan Theater. Special pageants and concerts take place periodically during the summer, free but requiring reservations. For more information about all their programs, call:

The U.S. Air Force Band: 202/767-4310
The U.S. Army Band: 703/696-3718 or 703/696-3399 (Hotline)
The U.S. Marine Band: 202/433-5809
The U.S. Navy Band: 202/433-6090

The Kennedy Center
202/467-4600 (info. & Instant Charge)
TTD 202/416-8524 (hearing impaired)

The Kennedy Center's Education Department presents hundreds of performances for youngsters and their families, as well as school groups, each season. These include the National Symphony Orchestra's *KinderKonzerts* in the Theater Lab for 4-9 year olds and their *Family Concerts* in the Concert Hall for children, aged 5 and up. Programs for preschoolers and children in the early elementary school grades are usually in the Terrace Theater or Theater Lab, but older children and teens will also find plenty of events in the Eisenhower Theater and Concert

Hall. All performing genres are represented: theater, music, puppetry, dance, mime and story-telling. On all young people's series, at least one performance is signed for the deaf and hearing-impaired. For a complete listing of family events, call The Kennedy Center's Instant Charge or the hearing-impaired telephone numbers.

National Theater, Washington, DC 202/783-3372

Saturday Mornings at the National presents plays, magic shows and musical variety shows at 9:30 and 11:00 a.m. every Saturday from September through March. Ages 4 and up. Free.

National Zoo, Washington, DC 202/673-4989

Summer Serenades, featuring different professional performers each week, take place on Lion & Tiger Hill from late June to mid-August. Families can purchase box picnic dinners or bring their own. Concerts are 90-minutes long; free, no reservations necessary. All ages.

Smithsonian Institution, Arts and Industries Bldg. Washington, DC 202/357-1500

Discovery Theater presents plays and music events from September through July. The programming includes children's classics like *The Velveteen Rabbit* (pre-K through 2nd grade) as well as *Journey into Jazz*, for 4th-to-8th grade students, and much more. Ages: Pre-K to 8th grade.

Washington Chamber Symphony 202/452-1321

The WCS *Family Series*, in the Kennedy Center Concert Hall, includes *Holiday Spectacular Sing-Along*, a musical salute to Christmas and Chanukah (3 and up); *Stories in Music*, featuring works for orchestra and narrator such as *Peter and the Wolf* (4 & up); and *The Great Composers*, focusing on the life and music of one composer each year (6 & up).

Washington Performing Arts Society 202/833-9800, ext. 5

Although most of WPAS' programming takes place at The Kennedy Center, *Parade of the Arts* is held at George Washington University's Lisner Auditorium. The four-performance, culturally-diverse series is designed for children aged 4 and up. Their 1994-95 season includes South American and Asian dance ensembles as well as local artist Keter Betts and the Howard University Jazz Ensemble. Saturday afternoon performances last about one hour.

Wolf Trap Farm Park, Vienna, VA
Theatre-in-the-Woods: 703/255-1827
International Children's Festival: 703/642-0862
  The National Park Service directs Wolf Trap's *Theatre-in-the-Woods* program from early July to mid-August. The series includes puppet shows, storytelling, dance, mime and children's opera. Ages 4-12.
  Wolf Trap opens all its stages and lawns for the *International Children's Festival*, an outdoor event (rain or shine) which takes place over a two-day weekend every September. Hosts like Bob McGrath of "Sesame Street" emcee a variety of performances featuring artists from all over the world. Children can also participate in several hands-on workshops. Ages 3-12.

For Ages 6 and up

National Symphony Orchestra
202/467-4600, TDD 202/416-8524
Meet the Orchestra takes place on weekday evenings in January in the Kennedy Center Concert Hall. The NSO performs well-known orchestral classics in this performance/discussion program. Ages 9 & up.

Northern Virginia Youth Symphony Association, Annandale, VA: 703/642-0862
  One of the outstanding ensembles for Washington's young musicians (grades 3-12), the Northern Virginia Youth Symphony Association presents several concerts each season at sites in Northern Virginia. A wonderful opportunity for your youngster to hear other young people perform...beautifully. Maestro Luis Haza of the National Symphony Orchestra oversees an excellent staff of conductors and coaches and the results speak for themselves.

Washington Chamber Symphony 202/452-1321
  Under the direction of Stephen Simon, the chamber orchestra presents *Concerts for Young People* four weekends per season in the Kennedy Center Terrace Theater. Hour-long discussion/performances, narrated by "Magic Maestro" Simon, introduce children to classical music and great composers. Ages 6-12.

Washington Ballet, Washington, DC 202/362-3606
  This professional ballet company, founded in 1976, performs at The Kennedy Center every fall, winter and spring. Their annual *Nutcracker* production at the Warner Theater is a holiday tradition for many families. Their repertory consists of a mix of classical and contemporary ballets.

❓ Questions to ask the box office staff

1. Is there a suggested age level for this performance?
2. How long is the performance? Is there an intermission?
3. Can you briefly describe the performance? Are children invited to participate in the action on stage? (i.e., audience discussion, singing along? clapping? etc.)
4. How many seats are in the hall? Where are my seats located?
5. How much are the tickets?
6. We'd like to bring our baby, too. Are babies-in-arms admitted free of charge?
7. Are refreshments sold before the performance or during intermission? Can we bring our own snacks?

Further Reading

Childress, Jan. *Tuning Up for Music Lessons*, Second Edition. Washington, D.C.: 1995.

Getting to the Pointe: Selecting a Dance Program

by Marilyn Gaston
and Joanne Giza

What little girl doesn't dream of being a beautiful ballerina, twirling effortlessly on her toes in pink satin slippers, a crown poised gracefully on her head? Perhaps your son would be the perfect prince in a production of *Sleeping Beauty* or Mouse King in the classic *Nutcracker* ballet. A dance class can be a wonderful experience for a young child, and the number of youngsters enrolling in programs testifies to their popularity. But where to begin? And what to look for? These are the questions every parent must ask before buying that first pair of tights.

Getting Started

A child can start dance training at 4 if he or she has the concentration, but waiting until 5 or even 6 can be a better idea. Whether you call the classes for that age rhythmic dance, expressive dance or creative movement, the bottom line here is that there should be little or no technique (that is, no emphasis on the ballet positions of barre work). Little ones need to feel uninhibited; they need to be able to experience the music and have fun. This is a time for training the ear, a time to skip and play to the music. For after all, dance is a joyful art that needs to be taught joyfully. At age 7 or 8, children can begin "serious" dance classes that introduce technique slowly through classes that meet for 45 minutes to an hour once, or possibly twice, a week. If the student is taking any kind of athletic training, such as gymnastics, he or she may be able to move along faster because progress is determined by whether the body can take the stress the classes demand. A 9-year-old can expect to take class two or possibly three times a week for 90 minutes per class. As the child progresses, the number of classes per week can be increased.

Choosing a School

What type of school should you choose? Some parents might believe that since their child is very young or just a beginner, they need not be concerned with choosing the best possible school right away and that

Joanne Giza is the editor of Baltimore's Child.

Marilyn Gaston is the director of the Ballet Academy of Baltimore.

local recreation association classes will suffice until such time as the child exhibits a stronger interest or true talent. Although this might seem like a good option, many dance teachers find that children coming from these programs are at a disadvantage when they decide to enter a professional school with a more structured and demanding program, and they suggest that a better idea is to choose a school with an eye to the future. Whether or not the student becomes the world's next Baryshnikov or prima ballerina, your child will benefit from the lessons taught by a good school: an appreciation for the arts, a sense of self-esteem, and a form of physical activity that provides excellent posture and a strong, agile body for a lifetime. Most dance schools have ballet in the curriculum, and, in many cases, are geared primarily towards providing training only in classical dance. Some schools will teach ballet as part of a curriculum that includes other forms of dance, such as tap or jazz, as well. It is usually best for the beginner to enroll in ballet classes first. Because ballet is the foundation for other forms of dance, much of the vocabulary, the class structure, and even many of the steps appearing in other dance forms are derived from classical ballet technique. The best jazz, tap or modern dancers in the professional world have usually had strong background training in ballet before going on to develop careers in other fields of dance.

Looking for a Teacher

If there is one determining factor when considering a school it is the staff. Most instructors will cite either a professional performing career, a college degree in dance or certification in a major teaching syllabus such as Cecchetti Council, Royal Academy of Dancing or Vaganova or a combination of the above. While credentials are important, the teacher should possess other characteristics as well: the ability to communicate knowledge, a compassion for the "average" student as well as the aspiring professional and the patience to work within a teaching rather than a performing atmosphere. It is also important that the teacher be a good "demonstrator," possessing the strength and flexibility to execute steps and exercises correctly. This is an important factor especially for young children whose learning will be heavily dependent on the visual image set before them, as well as the desire to please someone they admire. Rapport with the students, especially the young ones, is crucial. Ballet can be repetitive, but a creative teacher can make it fun so that the difficult parts seem like play. Criticism, which is necessary, should always be constructive--never destructive.

Class Size

How large or small should the classes be? That's hard to say. The number of students in a class is partially dependent on the amount of physical space in the studio. What is important is that the teacher be able to give a certain amount of individualized attention to each student. Some teachers can do that with as many as 15 students or more. Others would do better with a smaller group of 10. It is important for the children to feel that the teacher is aware of each student's achievements and is helping each of them move to the next level.

The Studio

When exploring schools, it is important to look at the studio. This room should be equipped with a raised "floating" floor, i.e. a floor with an air space underneath, usually with a top surface of wood or wood subflooring, covered with stage flooring. This means the floor will have resiliency and will not eventually cause injuries to the knee, foot or back as a result of impact stress such as landing from jumps. Concrete or linoleum tile over concrete slab should be avoided at all costs and for all forms of dance. It is not only damaging to the body but may also be slippery, a double hazard for the dancer. Barres should be 42 inches high for adult/teen dancers or 32 inches high for children. Portable barres which adjust in height are also good. Fixed barres should be at least 8-10 inches from the wall to which they are attached so that there is no danger of children getting their heads caught accidentally between the wall and the barre and so that legs placed upon the barre will "clear" the wall. The studio should be equipped with adequate ventilation and/or air conditioning and should have large mirrors which allow the teacher to demonstrate in front of the students and still watch them. Later the students will use the mirrors to correct their own positions.

Recitals

Are recitals important? The recital should not be the determining factor for the parent looking at a program. In place of the recital, there should be parent and studio days when parents are welcome to come and observe. If the school you are interested in seems to devote most of the year to preparing only for the performance, or you are asked to spend a great deal of money on costumes each year, you should question the school's integrity. More important than a recital, there should be open communication between the parent and teacher. If a parent has a question, she deserves to have that question answered.

 # Questions to ask yourself

1. Is my child ready for a dance class? Does he/she like to dance?
2. What is appropriate for my child's age and ability?
3. How often do I want my child to have lessons?
4. What type of dance would be best for my child? What sort of music does my child respond to enthusiastically?

 # Questions to ask the instructors

1. What are the credentials of the dance teachers? How many teachers are there?

2. Is the equipment appropriate and safe, i.e., a "raised floor" and adequate ventilation?
3. What is the class size?
4. What are practice requirements?
5. Can I observe a class to determine the teacher-pupil rapport?
6. Are there recitals?
7. What are the fees and payment schedules?
8. If we have to cancel a lesson, can it be made up later?

Resources

Dance Centers

Academy of the Maryland Youth Ballet
7702 Woodmont Avenue
Bethesda, MD
301-652-2232
Ages 5-18. Preprofessional program with the Maryland Youth Ballet from the age of 8 and up. Classes more than once a week. Preballet, ballet, modern dance and jazz. Two studios with wood floors.

Arlington Center for Dance
3808 Wilson Blvd.
Arlington, VA
703-522-2414
Summer workshops and dance camps for children of all ages and abilities. Four studios. Sprung wood floors, three with Marley, two with hard wood for tap. Creative movement, ballet, modern, jazz and tap dance classes.

Ballet Academy of Northern Virginia
6905 Hickory Hill Road
Falls Church, VA
703-534-1528
Ages 3½ to 17. School has been in operation for 35 years. Russian Vaganova method used in technique ballet. Preballet and classical ballet classes. Wood floors.

Ballet Petite
5606 Knollwood Road
Bethesda, MD 20816
301-320-2321
Ages 2 - 5 years. Creative movement ages 2 - 4. Preballet, age 5. Class includes creative movement, music, costumes and props with a storybook dance for a magical ending.

Ballet Center of Washington, DC
2801 Connecticut Avenue, NW
Washington, DC
202-745-3533
Ages 4 - adult, students can get their P.E. credit by dancing here. Classes from preballet through Advanced. Suspended wood floor at this former home of the National Ballet. All students perform every year.

The Davis Center
6133 Georgia Avenue, NW
Washington, DC
202-726-7146
Ballet, pointe, modern, tap and jazz classes. Cecchetti method ballet, students tested by national examiners. Brand new wood sprung floors.

Interdance Ballet
5801 Devonshire Drive
Bethesda, MD
301-229-2771
Ages 3½ and up. Royal Academy of dancing method; play-ballet, preballet, ballet and advanced classes. Offer certificates and exams for the older children. Stage step, a special dance floor.

Joy of Motion Dance Center
1643 Connecticut Avenue, NW
Washington, DC 202-387-0911
5207 Wisconsin Avenue, NW
Washington, DC 202-362-3042
Summer Dance Camp for children (ages 3-7) (8-17). Floors, Marley, and wood. Creative movement, preballet, ballet, tap and jazz classes. Also a Teen Dance Company.

North Potomac Ballet Academy
10076 Darnestown Road, Suite 202
Rockville, MD 20850
301-762-1757
Classes for 4 yr.olds - adults. Two studios with wood sprung floors. Students perform with the Metropolitan Ballet Theater.

St. Mark's Dance Studio
3rd & A Streets, SE
Washington DC
202-543-0054
Floors: rosco, a linoleum on soft wood. Creative movement, ballet, pointe. A pre-professional company.

Washington School of Ballet, Inc.
3515 Wisconsin Avenue, NW
Washington, DC
202-362-1683
Ages 6 and up. Summer school for advanced students. Floors, Marley, sprung.

Dance Supply Stores

Artistic Dance Fashions
4915 Cordell Avenue
Bethesda, MD 301-652-2323
Dance shoes, ballet, tap, jazz. Fairy-tale dresses, dress-up costumes, hats, imaginative costumes. Also costume accessories, wands, wings, etc. Makeup.

The Dance Shop, Inc.
2427 18th Street, NW
Washington, DC 202-667-5045
Jazz shoes, leotards, unitards, ballet slippers, tap shoes, tights, pointe shoes, etc. Posts information about upcoming local dance center schedules and recitals. Caters to people in dance field.

Dancer
8010 Old Branch Avenue
Clinton, MD 301-856-2144
Leotards, tights, ballet shoes, tap shoes, jazz shoes. Sell fabrics and trims to make costumes. Wigs and makeup for face painting, recitals. Hats and accessories.

Dansant Boutique
6623 Old Dominion Drive
McLean, VA 703-847-0736
Specializing in ballet; leotards, tights, ballet slippers, toe shoes, jazz and tap shoes.

Gotta Dance Inc.
13659 Georgia Avenue
Silver Spring, MD 301-946-1110
Dance wear for children, ballet shoes, tap shoes, jazz shoes, leotards, tights. Everything a child would need to prepare for the first dance class. Wide variety of costumes at Halloween time for children.

Langley Bootery
7970 New Hampshire Avenue
Langley Park, MD 301-434-9297
Children's shoes and dance supplies. Tap shoes, jazz shoes, ballet shoes, leotards and tights.

Repeat Performance
5018 Nicholson Lane
Rockville, MD 301-881-0800
Leotards, leggings, jazz shoes, ballet shoes, tap shoes, bags, tights. High-quality costumes for sale. Nonallergenic theatrical makeup and gifts for the dancer. Skating, gymnastic and jazz apparel.

★ Special Needs

American Dance Therapy Association
2000 Century Plaza, Suite 230
Columbia, MD 21044
1-410-997-4040
Therapists use movement as a process to further the emotional, cognitive, physical and social integration of individuals. Referral of local dance therapists for interested parents. Provides techniques for healthy parent-child relationships.

To Be, or Not to Be
Your Child and the Dramatic Arts

by Janet Stanford

Mom: Fred, you know how much little Johnny was looking forward to
      trying out for the school play this year?
Dad: That and Nintendo are his only subjects of conversation.
Mom: Well, I'm just so disappointed for him.
Dad: Don't tell me, they put him in the Munchkin chorus.
Mom: No, Fred, he didn't get any part.
Dad: Come on, Edith, it's school. Everybody gets some kind of part.
Mom: No one did. Something about the budget—they cut the play.
Dad: They couldn't have!
Mom: Little Johnny is crushed.
Dad: Why, 20-some years ago, I played the Cowardly Lion at Central El-
      ementary—
Mom: —And *The Gazette* ran your picture on the front page, and the
      reviewer said—
Dad: —I had "promise." I still have that article.
Mom: What are we going to do for Johnny?
Dad: Heck, I don't know. Get him SuperNintendo?

Little Johnny's plight might apply to almost any child in the Washington metropolitan area today. And his mother is right to be concerned. With the tightness of most parents' schedules—torn between work and family and the proliferation of home entertainment devices for kids—it's convenient to simply trust that Johnny is getting all the education he really needs at school, and turn over the question of what to do with his leisure time to the electronic media. But even the most callus of us know in our hearts that a positive experience in the arts at an early age can make a lasting impression, and that to deny one's child this possibility is a mistake.

Why should conscientious parents ensure that their children participate in the dramatic arts? Over the last decade theater arts programs in

Janet Stanford is a theater artist and educator who is currently the Director of Theatre and Education for the Bethesda Academy of Performing Arts Imagination Stage. She has directed plays and taught theater courses at Goucher College, Mount Vernon College and Georgetown University. Several of her plays for adults and children have been produced by the Virginia Stage Company, Kennedy Center Programs for Children and Youth and the Source Theatre Company.

both public and private schools have been steadily eroding as budget cuts have forced educational systems to concentrate resources on the "three Rs."

However, the realm of dramatic art which includes the study and interpretation of human behavior, is often the key to helping youngsters integrate logical and sequential learning skills (represented in the "Three Rs" approach) with their powers of intuition, or what we might call feeling and creative skills.

How Acting Affects Learning

Cognitive Psychologist Dr. Howard Gardner has helped to legitimize the case for arts education with his theory of "multiple intelligences." His research along with other recent findings suggest that children learn in many different ways; that the logical/mathematical orientation of the traditional curriculum is directed at only one of seven intelligences which all people possess. Training in the art of acting can involve logical/mathematical reasoning as well as all of the other six: verbal/linguistic, visual/spatial, body/kinesthetic, musical/rhythmic, intrapersonal and interpersonal. Here's how:

Logical/Mathematical Intelligence: Acting out a simple nursery rhyme like "One, Two, Button My Shoe," or "Hickory, Dickory, Dock" can introduce young children to counting and the ideas of addition and time. "Musical Chairs" can become a hands-on lesson in subtraction. The concept of "cause and effect" is reinforced when students explore imaginary environments, touching a "hot stove," "feeling the rain," pretending to be a seed which when exposed to light and water grows into a flower. Stories and plays, from the simplest to the most sophisticated, show cause and effect in terms of human behavior. As such, archetypical characters from Pinocchio to Macbeth are valuable to enable us to consider the consequences of a deed before committing it.

Verbal/Linguistic Intelligence: Pulitzer prize-winning playwright Lanford Wilson has said that live theatre is the last remaining refuge for poetry in contemporary America. When participating in a drama program children are brought into contact with heightened and poetic language. They learn the pleasure of pronouncing new sounds and attempting new vocabulary. They experience the power of rhyme, alliteration and onomatopoeia. Eventually, they develop the muscular and breath control for good articulation and strong vocal projection. Above all, the love and appreciation of words which literature instills provides them with the tools they will need in order to communicate their ideas and feelings.

Body/Kinesthetic Intelligence: Acting training helps students to appreciate their bodies as performing instruments. In order to fulfil his potential as an actor, the student must treat his instrument with respect, feed it with healthy food, exercise regularly, and continually take on new physical challenges such as learning to dance or juggle. The would-be actor is encouraged and empowered to take risks, set personal goals and acquire the self-discipline to achieve them. In this way, he is "stretching" himself for any possible role—be it in film, stage or real life.

Visual/Spatial Intelligence: From an early age, children begin to form a critical appreciation of a play or movie by unconsciously distinguishing "good guys" from "bad guys" by the way in which they are visually presented.

Musical/Rhythmic Intelligence: The rhythm and timbre of speech is integral to spoken language and therefore to drama. Children begin by repeating simple lines of poetry or dialogue. They go on to memorize complete roles, complex stage directions, music and movement sequences. Often those who are not strong readers will memorize easily from a tape, or quickly pick up choreographed steps.

Intrapersonal and Interpersonal Intelligences: In the last two of Gardener's categories, we come to skill areas which, while clearly connected to dramatic training, are also of enormous value in life, whether the student's career turns out to be arts-related or not. By helping a child to acknowledge and express her emotions, by teaching her to understand and appreciate her physicality and by advancing her use of language, dramatic exercises lead to self-discovery and knowledge. The child who feels confident and comfortable with herself is also able to respect the needs of others, empathize with their situations and viewpoints and accept their differences. The lessons learned from putting on a school show go far beyond mere stagecraft. Hours of patience, give and take, listening, taking turns, practicing lines, songs, entrances and exits go into the collaborative effort before the curtain can rise on opening night. And when it finally falls, and the company joins hands to take a bow, everyone shares in the pride of accomplishment and recognizes, humbly, that it is only by uniting human energies that we create magic!

This, then, is why it is important for a conscientious parent to consider dramatic training for a child. The advantages are that dramatic arts training can:

- enhance your child's self-esteem, self-confidence and capability for critical thinking
- provide positive paths to channel youthful energies
- serve as a bridge to academic learning for those who do not respond to traditional educational methods
- provide students with a vehicle to learn about the world, their own and other cultures (past and present) and about themselves

How to Choose a Good Dramatic Arts Program

A variety of municipal and private organizations in the Washington area offer drama classes for children. Some professional theaters also have programs but usually cater to serious high school students. Casting agencies will also offer classes from time to time. Information about new classes which are forming as well as auditions for child actors are generally listed in "The Guide to the Lively Arts" in *The Washington Post*. Fridays and Sundays are the days when most organizations advertise. You may also want to check your local library or your local community "Recreation Department." The Cultural Alliance of Washington and your local Arts Council are additional resources. They should have the most current information on the many programs around the area.

It is important to know who sponsors any class you sign up for. Municipal and community centers—because they are publicly funded—offer reputable programs and, since they hold classes in schools or other public buildings, can be relied upon to meet reasonable standards of cleanliness and safety. When exploring a private organization try to confirm that it has been operating for at least three years and is incorporated either as a business or not-for-profit institution with a mission which includes education. You may request literature about any school or theater by telephone and ask for the credentials of the teaching staff. Beware of casting agencies which require you to pay for classes (or anything else) before accepting your child as a client. Generally speaking, even if you are interested in pursuing paid professional work for your child, you should begin by seeking out an educational program in theater arts which is creative rather than commercial in orientation. A talented child will blossom in the nurturing atmosphere of a legitimate drama program and will quickly adapt to the requirements of professional theater if and when the opportunity arises.

A visit to any drama school you are considering is recommended. Ask about class sizes, course goals and content, and whether or not the overall drama program provides a logical progression from one age and achievement level to the next. Up until Grade 3, children benefit most from creative drama classes which focus on storytelling, role playing, imaginative explorations in voice, movement and music and simple improvisational exercises. At the fourth grade level, children are developmentally ready to begin acquiring the techniques of voice and movement which relate specifically to performance. They should have physical and vocal warm-ups at each class, continue improvisational exercises and begin working on scripted material.

Since acting implies interacting, a minimum class size of 6 is preferred, 15 as the maximum. Classes above 15 make it difficult for the teacher to give the student much individual feedback and class exercises become dull if taking turns takes too long. Younger students (up to Grade 3) will probably respond best to a class period of about an hour while older students will enjoy a longer session of up to two hours. Prices of classes vary, depending on the sponsoring organization and the number of students per class. You will do well to call around and compare programs before selecting the right one for your child and budget. If you remain uncertain about whether or not a particular class will be right for your child, ask the school if you may audit the first class before deciding. Reputable organizations usually permit this, subject to enrollment. They should also agree to make a partial refund if you choose to drop a class before the third or fourth week.

Finally, the best gauge of any theater arts program is your child. If he looks forward to going, and is happy when he returns, the class is providing the proper kind of creative stimulation.

Questions to ask yourself

For children preschool through Grade 3

1. How does my child like to learn?
2. Does he like to sit and listen or move, play and experiment?
3. Is she highly suggestible, i.e., does she readily become involved in stories in an active way?
4. Does she like to imitate animals, people, sounds in the environment?
5. Is "Make-Believe" as real to him as real life?
6. Does he enjoy dressing up, singing, making faces and just being silly?

For children Grade 4 and up

1. Is my child's imagination a theatrical one?
2. Whether introverted or extroverted by nature, does she "come alive" in front of an audience?
3. Does he retain a strong sense of play?
4. Is he fascinated with stories, books and films?
5. Does he like to imitate characters, mimic friends, TV characters and teachers?
6. Does she invent characters and stories of her own?
7. Does she like to interact with other people?
8. Is her physical and vocal expression free, uninhibited?

Questions to ask the drama teacher

For drama teachers of preschool through Grade 3

1. What kind of activities do you offer in class?
2. What ideas or concepts are you teaching the children?
3. Do you incorporate literature into classwork?
4. Are there activities I can initiate to prepare for or follow-up on the class?
5. What experience do you have working with young children?
6. Do you have any open classes for parents to watch during or at the end of term?

For Teachers Grade 4 and up

1. What is your educational and professional background?
2. What is the orientation of your class—improvisational or scripted work?

3. Will my child be expected to memorize or do other homework between classes?
4. Will he have an opportunity to perform before an audience?
5. How large is the class?

Resources

Drama Classes

District of Columbia

Capitol Hill Arts Workshop, SE	202-547-6839
Fillmore Arts Workshop, NW	202-333-8340
Kennedy Center Ed. Program, NW	202-416-8803
Living Stage, NW	202-554-9066
Theatre Lab of Washington	202-265-3154

Maryland

Adventure Theatre, Glen Echo	301-320-5331
Bethesda Academy of Performing Arts	301-320-2550
Greenbelt Cultural Arts Center	301-441-8770
Harmony Hall Regional Center	301-292-8331
Jewish Community Center	301-881-0100
Round House Theatre, Silver Spring	301-933-9530
Summer Teen Theatre, Hyattsville	301-445-4500
Young Americans of Wash., Rockville	301-881-1139

Virginia

Children's Theatre of Arlington	703-548-1154
Fairfax Co. Community Services	703-324-4386
Herndon Community Center	703-435-6868
Little Theatre of Alexandria	703-683-5778
McLean Children's Theatre	703-790-0123
Mt. Vernon Comm. Children's Theatre	703-768-7689
Reston Community Center	703-860-1879

Costumes and Theater Supplies

Backstage, Inc.
2101 P Street, NW
Washington, DC 20037
202-775-1488
Playscripts, theater and film costumes and makeup

Libraries Specializing in Playscripts & Theater Arts

Martin Luther King Library
901 G Street, NW   202-727-1126
Washington, DC 20001

Gaithersburg Regional Library
18330 Montgomery Village Ave.   301-840-2515
Gaithersburg, MD

Arlington County Central Library
1015 N. Quincy Street   703-358-5990
Arlington, VA 22201

Associations

Alexandria Commission for the Arts	703-838-6348
Arlington County Cultural Affairs	703-358-6960
Arts Council of Fairfax County	703-642-0862
Arts Council of Montgomery County	301-530-6744
Cultural Alliance of Greater Washington	202-638-2406
Prince George's County Arts Council	301-454-1455

Encouraging the Artist Within
Your Child and the Visual Arts

by Marybeth Shea, M.P.A.

Every 4-year-old should be treated as an accomplished and celebrated artist. During the middle years, however, when reality sinks in many children find "art" discouraging, dissatisfied that their work does not reflect the world with photographic accuracy. At this point those who are talented begin to exhibit clear artistic aptitude—remarkable doodlings, exquisitely proportioned clay figures, refined color sense . . . which separates them from the masses. However, artistic ability does not belong only to the child able to render a perfect swan in soapstone or sketch a botanically accurate plant specimen. Many children with subtle or unusual creative insights can be overlooked if evaluated solely on sketching or modeling ability. Exposure to art helps all children, but is a boon for those with hidden talents.

Visual art, both the two and three dimensional kind, are really exercises in space, form, color and composition. Remembering these principles helps one to understand the effectiveness of Picasso's cubism, or marvel at the accuracy of a Rembrandt. To really appreciate art one must get involved in it oneself. For young children, the sensual pull of clay is hard to resist and such activity builds important fine motor skills. Tempura paints allow a child to commit the familiar forms of a dog, cat, sun, house and flower to newsprint.

Sometime in the middle years, the preferences and tendencies of your child may very well point to true artistic talent. You may want to foster the talent of the two-dimensional artist through painting, drawing, printmaking and photography. For the budding artist with tactile and spatial capability, three dimensional challenges like pottery, sculpture, weaving, woodcarving and sewing are good options. Equip your child with a range of materials, and make space in the basement, garage or attic for a studio. Adequate ventilation is a must. Natural light is best, but barring this, provide good overhead lighting (avoiding florescent bulbs) as well as desk lamps for spot illumination. Provide a small suitcase for carrying supplies to remote settings. A camp stool will make your nature

Marybeth Shea writes on family, literacy and arts issues for local and national publications, and teaches art and creative writing in schools through the Maryland State Arts-in-Education Program. She is a faculty member at the University of Maryland Family Arts Center, and is on the board of SCOP Publications, one of the oldest literary presses in the country.

or landscape artist comfortable in Rock Creek Park. Older children, serious about their work, can rent an easel for use in the National Gallery.

Art Supplies

Art supplies make great presents, appreciated long after the birthday or other occasion for which they were given. Begin with markers, colored pencils, potter's clay, Sculpey modeling compound, tempura, acrylics, etc. Real art supplies are nearly always better than the dime store variety. Older children will require an X-Acto knife set for cutting mats, collage work, balsa-wood carving and small architecture projects. For young children, be aware that solvents like acetone, spirits of turpentine, spray-mount and other supplies are toxic and must be used with caution. The hand washing rule applies at least as much to artists as it does to mechanics. Rubber gloves are a useful item for some projects. Provide Lava or Mechanix soap for cleanup. Some media, like clay, will dry the skin. Lotion and a manicure kit are useful post-studio session supplies.

Art Classes

Inspiration and support for the young artist comes in many forms. Trips to museums and galleries, craft fairs, hobby stores and art studios will stimulate new projects and allow your child to become acquainted with a variety of media.

Art classes for children vary in quality and cost. Look carefully and match your child's interest level and personality type with the facility's atmosphere. For example, one child delights in the Popsicle craft projects typical of community centers. Take heart, Frank Lloyd Wright played with sticks and blocks well into his teen years. Another child blossoms under the tutelage of a watercolor artist at a Saturday studio session at a local university. Handicrafts like quilting, embroidery, weaving, beadwork, jewelry making and stained glass are currently enjoying a renaissance in the art-crafts world. Many children with aptitude in this area are overlooked, because "true" artists only paint or sculpt. Applied arts like design, graphics, decoration, furniture-making, horticulture and architecture all have important visual and spatial elements. Encouraging your artistically inclined child to explore various media may very well lead him or her to a very satisfying career later in life.

Media Age Guide

These activities are arranged roughly by age. Most older children enjoy materials and projects listed for younger children, making for nice shared sibling projects. Be alert for safety, always supervising toddlers and preschoolers, and older children when using potentially dangerous equipment.

18 mo.-2 years: Thick, nontoxic crayons, sidewalk chalk, edible finger painting with Jell-O or instant pudding, homemade cornstarch Play-Doh, large color forms. A good space to experiment with those messy materials is in a large inflated plastic pool, brought inside, for the budding artist to use throughout the year.

2-3 years: Thick tempura paints and large brushes for floor and easel painting, Play-Doh, Silly Putty, crayons, markers, thick colored pencils, collage material.

4-5 years: Thinner colored pencils, tracing and stencil materials, Stockmar modeling beeswax, yarn for weaving and braiding, coloring books (in moderation!), clay (for hand-built projects), simple sewing, potato or sponge printing.

6-7 years: Oil pastels, watercolor pencils, acrylics, fabric paints, clay (handbuilt and thrown), paper-mache, cross-stitch on large count cloth.

8-9 years: Charcoal (variety of hardness), photography, watercolor paints, linoleum printmaking, fabric dyeing, grapevine wreath making.

10 years and older: batik and resist dyeing, oil paints, carving (soapstone, balsa-wood)

Atypical Art Activities:
- blueprinting and drafting
- doll house and bird house construction
- bead making
- origami
- spray-painting an abandoned spiderweb and pressing to cardboard
- flower and leaf pressing
- paper making
- pumpkin carving
- kite making
- topiary
- bonsai
- furniture refinishing
- flower arranging (Ikebana and American)

Outings Include:
- museums
- art galleries
- stone quarries
- marble and tile companies
- architecture firms
- plant nursery and landscaping firms

Resources

Family Arts Center
University of Maryland Stamp Student Union
College Park, MD 20742
301-314-ARTS

Smithsonian Museums
Hirshhorn Museum and Sculpture Garden 202-357-1300
National Gallery of Art 202-737-4215
Of note are special programs at the Hirschhorn and National Gallery of Art. Special tours can be arranged by contacting the docent coordinator. For example, both the Hirschhorn and NGA have a "Math and Art" tour. These and other customized tours are best arranged during the fall and winter months.

Pyramid Atlantic
6001 66th Avenue
Riverdale, MD
301-459-7154
This internationally recognized paper and book center offers classes on paper making, book binding, paper marbling, paper sculpture and graphics.

Local Arts Councils

District of Columbia
Capitol Hill Arts Workshop (CHAW)
202-547-6839
An array of visual arts programs and instruction for adults and children every afternoon and evening.

Maryland
Earth Arts Center
Adelphi, MD
301-937-1573
The Earth Arts Center specializes in art and nature projects. Classes and summer camp.

Maryland National Capital Park and Planning Commission
Arts Division
301-454-1450
Art and craft classes are held at numerous recreation and community centers in both Prince George's and Montgomery counties. MNCPPC also operates the acclaimed multidisciplinary arts centers of Montpelier Mansion and Harmony Hall, both offering arts classes to the community.

Virginia
Greater Reston Arts Center (GRACE)
703-471-9242
Youth Art Month and Summer Art Camp are two of the many activities held at GRACE.

McLean Project for the Arts
703-790-0123
Studio classes and workshops for adults and children, children's resource room for exploring art concepts using kits developed by artists.

Open Studios

Visit artists at work, but phone before visiting.

Montpelier Cultural Arts Studios
Laurel, MD
301-953-1993

Passageways, Inc.
Riverdale, MD
301-459-8038

Savage Mill Studios
Savage, MD
301-498-5751

Torpedo Factory
105 N. Union Street
Old Town Alexandria
703-838-4565

Further Reading

Younger children, especially the budding cartoonist or humorist, will enjoy any of the Ed Emberly Drawing Books. Step by step illustrations show how to "build" cars, monsters, spaceships, crocodiles, etc from simple shapes like circles, triangles, lines.

Blizzard, Gladys S. *Enjoying Art With Children, Exploring Landscape Art with Children, World of Play, Animals in Art* (four book series, each available separately). An art educator, Ms. Blizzard uses directed and open-ended questions to aid in the enjoyment of art. Biographical information about the artist is included. Ages 5-10.

Brooks, Mona. *Drawing with Children and Drawing For Older Children and Adults.* Creator of the Monart drawing method, Ms. Brooks presents an almost stand-alone art curriculum. The first book is appropriate from ages 3 through adult, and the second book can be used by artists as young as 8. These books are recommended for any family thinking seriously about art activity, and are a perfect starting point. Note: the Family Arts Center at the University of Maryland offers drawing courses based on the Monart method.

Hurd, Thatcher and John Casssidy. *Water Color for the Artistically Undiscovered.* Watercolor is a deceptively hard media, but Thatcher Hurd (son of Clement, illustrator of Good Night Moon) presents an easy and encouraging approach to watercolor techniques. Ages 9-adult.

McGraw, Shelia. *Papier Mache for Kids.* The best step-by-step guide to this three-dimensional form. Ages 5-11.

Micklethwait, Lucy. *I Spy: An Alphabet in Art.* New York: Greenbriar, 1992. Contains 26 paintings from the world's great museums, each containing objects from A to Z. Brief information about each painting and the artist is included. For all ages, but an especially nice artistic offering for the ABC set.

Solga, Kim. *Make Cards.*
Hershberger, Priscilla. *Make Costumes.*
These two books are a resource for practical applications of your child's talent. Ages 6-11.

Susskind, Shelia. *The Great Paintings Coloring Book: National Gallery of Art.* This is a serious coloring book for children over age 9. Your child can try to reproduce the colors of the original or try a completely different approach. Since this book is drawn from paintings in our very own National Gallery, make several visits in conjunction with this book. Highly recommended!

Wiseman, Ann. *MAKING THINGS: The Handbook of Creative Discovery.* Books on three-dimensional art are hard to come by for children. This collection is a welcome introduction to arts like scrimshaw, weaving, sand casting, tin can lanterns, etc. Highly recommended. Ages 4 through adult.

★ Special Needs

Art Therapy Association of Maryland
428 E. Preston Street
Baltimore, MD 21202
410-244-0836
Provides a list of local art therapists; works with families, children
and adolescents developing alternative coping skills and emotional
release through art.

Very Special Arts
125 Michigan Ave. NE
Washington, DC 20017
202-939-5008   202-939-5008 TDD
Offers visual arts programs for children with special needs.

Beauty is in the Eyes of the Beholder
Art Appreciation in Washington

by Karen Leggett

A 3-year-old looked at N.C. Wyeth's pirate painting, *Blind Pew*, and began chanting "yukky man, yukky socks, yukky shoes." The child returned to the picture several times during his museum visit to chant his opinion again. Milde Waterfall and Sarah Grusin, both of Northern Virginia, tell the story in their book *Where's the ME in Museum: Going to Museums with Children*. They note that the little boy was offering a genuine aesthetic response to the painting and they urge parents to allow and appreciate these uncensored natural reactions to art. Children experience "strong, open and unmasked responses to art," the authors write, and they need to know they can trust their reactions.

Washington abounds in ways for children to react to, and grow in, art appreciation. Virtually all the major museums and galleries offer tours or classes for schools, scout or religious groups or even small groups you organize yourself. You can often suggest your own topic or theme—and the education departments at each museum are usually eager to help. The Corcoran Gallery provides learning kits in advance of group workshop and visits. Topics include American art, sensory challenges, silkscreening, Greek myths and African and Latin American art.

Museum Programs for Children

The Hirshhorn offers monthly Young at Art programs, usually tied to a particular exhibit. "You have to start where the child is," says instructor Diane Kidd. Kidd always offers a "please touch basket" full of the artist's tools: paintbrushes, canvas, clay, clogs like the ones Willem de Kooning might once have worn. Once a choreographer created a dance in the Sculpture Garden so youngsters could use their bodies to learn about sculpture. "Art is very user-friendly," says Kidd, "use your imagination." And she expects parents to use their imaginations too—Young at Art is not a drop-off program!

The National Portrait Gallery offers an activity booklet for its exhibit "To the President: Folk Portraits by the People."

Karen Leggett worked for many years as a news broadcaster and program host at WMAL radio. She is currently reviewing children's books on "Radio Zone" and writing on educational and youth issues for The Washington Post, Washington Parent, ABC Radio and Voice of America. *She lives in Rockville with her husband and two children.*

Three family booklets from the National Gallery ask questions on many different levels to provoke a thoughtful response to famous works of art. Take Rubens' *Daniel in the Lions' Den*. Can you count all the lions in the den? Can you find two lions sleeping in the shadows? How do we know the lions are dangerous?

You can show your budding ballerina the on-stage world of Edgar Degas or try to balance a mobile of your own after seeing the huge Calder hanging in the East Wing of the National Gallery. Some youngsters might be lured to an art museum by a Teenage Mutant Ninja Turtle Tour. For the uninitiated, the four Ninja Turtles are named for four Renaissance painters—Leonardo, Donatello, Raphael and Michelangelo. The Smithsonian Resident Associate program is rich with opportunities to tour permanent or temporary exhibits and follow-up with a hands-on art experience.

The National Gallery has now taken a big step beyond its handsome and helpful booklets with a brand new *National Gallery of Art Activity Book: 25 Adventures with Art*, by Maura Clarkin. Each adventure addresses something special about visual art—exploring shade and tint, composition, mood, texture, shape and motion. In one painting by Gustave Caillebotte, *Skiffs*, children are asked to notice how the diagonal, zigzag pattern of the oars makes three small boats seem to be gliding quickly down a river. Youngsters are then encouraged to make their own patterns to decorate wrapping paper or notepaper. Or take another artist that makes some adults wonder what is art and what isn't—Jackson Pollock, who pours and drips and splatters paint all over huge canvases. The *National Gallery Activity Book* asks children to consider how Pollock reached the center without stepping on his canvas. "Imagine if you were able to step into this painting . . . what would it feel like? cobwebs? a dream? outer space?"

Books can be useful before or after a museum experience—to look at a work of art on a flat page, then find it on the museum wall; or learn about the artist and how he or she works. How would it feel to paint while lying on your back? How long do you think you could do that?

When you are sharing a visual art experience with your son or daughter, be open to the art and to your child. Make up stories about the work. Share your feelings and reactions. Enjoy the experience even if you don't enjoy a particular work of art. As Waterfall and Grusin write in *Where's the ME in Museum*, "a child's ability to renew an adult's sense of awe is one of the true wonders of the world."

 # Resources

National Gallery of Art
Self-guided tour booklets for families (West Building Highlights, Shapes and Patterns, Portraits and Personalities). Family programs on specific exhibits' after-hours programs for educators.

National Portrait Gallery
Children's Activity Guide for "To the President: Folk Portraits by the People."

National Museum of Women in the Arts
Family day once a month. All day family events in spring and fall. Periodic role model workshops with artists for teens.

Phillips Collection
Periodic family workshops. Special summer, holiday tours.

Museum of American Art
Periodic activities, family days.

Hirshhorn
Young at Art once a month program for families.

Corcoran
Family activity guides for different sections of the Gallery. Periodic workshops storytelling sessions, family days.

Smithsonian Resident Associate Program
Classes & single workshops for children alone or with an adult.

Further Reading

Clarkin, Maura. *National Gallery of Art Activity Book: 25 Adventures with Art.* Harry N. Abrams, Inc.: 1994

Greenberg, Jan and Sandra Jordan. *The Painter's Eye: Learning to Look at Contemporary American Art.* Delacorte Press: 1991.

Lyons, Mary E. *African-American Artists and Artisans* and *Deep Blues: Bill Traylor, Self Taught Artist; Master of Mahogany: Tom Day, Free Black Cabinetmaker.* Scribners: 1994.

Muhlberger, Richard, Metropolitan Museum of Art. *What Makes a Monet a Monet?* New York: Viking, 1993. (Also in this series: Brueghel, Degas, Raphael, Rembrandt, Van Gogh)

Waterfall, Milde and Sarah Grusin. *Where's the ME in Museum: Going to Museums with Children.* Arlington: Vandemere Press, 1989.

The Pen is Mightier . . .

How to Encourage Your Child's Creative Writing Ability

by Marybeth Shea, M.P.A.

Writing, once the primary means of culture exchange, is now unfortunately, an endangered art. Long distance telephone and fax lines have largely replaced letter writing. Children now think of writing as primarily a school task. Some excel in, some tolerate, others resist language assignments. Gifted teachers know that the key to developing competent writers is to provide them the opportunity to experiment with many forms of writing. Does your child's teacher assign a variety of writing tasks, including the personal and creative forms of essay, poetry, and storytelling, as well as functional forms of composition, research, and reporting? All too often, children think that writing begins with "What I Did on My Vacation" and ends with book reports.

Work with your school to ensure that writing occurs across the curriculum. "Whole language" programs are being implemented in some schools. This approach employs writing as a pedagogical tool in all subject areas. For example, science experiments are best understood through a written laboratory record. Math problems become clearer for some children if they are written out in longhand in addition to their numerical format. Word problems, long a measure of a child's ability to apply mathematical principles, also marry language to numbers.

Encouraging Your Child to Enjoy Writing

Perhaps the most innovative, but often poorly presented, writing option is keeping a journal or diary. Journals provide an opportunity for a child to note events and experiences, describe relationships and reflect on feelings. You can encourage your child to keep a diary by presenting her with any number of beautiful blank books in a variety of covers. Some children will record the day's events almost automatically, while others need a little encouragement. Here are some ideas to get your child started.

Make lists of favorite colors, animals, books, places, words, etc.. This technique is particularly appropriate for young writers or children who struggle with the mechanics of writing. Invite the writer to illustrate

Marybeth Shea writes on family, literacy, and arts issues for local and national publications, and teaches art and creative writing in schools through the Maryland State Arts-in-Education Program. She is a faculty member at the University of Maryland Family Arts Center, and is on the board of SCOP Publications, one of the oldest literary presses in the country.

entries: a picture is worth a thousand words. For the young child, you hope to nurture the impulse to make regular entries. Longer writing sessions will come with age and maturing hand-eye coordination.

Keep records of projects and hobbies. For example, model airplane builders can date their works and describe how long it took from start to finish. Collectors of rocks, pressed flowers, dinosaur figures, etc. can record acquisition dates, and keep a tally of desired future collectibles.

Interview the family and write their stories. Have your child transcribe an event from your own childhood which you have described in detail. Grandparents and other extended family members can also be interviewed for wonderful historical information about the family in the "olden days." Include a genealogy with this entry and you may find yourself making numerous visits to the National Archives in search of Great Aunt Ida's birthdate.

Keep trip notes while on vacation. Having your child record mileage, cities visited, tourist sites explored, etc. may be a springboard for greater reflection. Dedicate small spiral-bound notebooks to particular trips.

Write up family events. Invite your child to make entries about key family events and holidays. Religious rites of passage, graduations, births, arrival of pets, special meals and hospitality to visitors make happy entries. And, many counselors know the value of writing as therapy for children stressed by school struggles, social unhappiness, divorce and death. Writing can help your child weather life's many and often unexpected storms.

Keep a family calendar. Daily life at home presents other writing opportunities. Ask your child for assistance in keeping the family calendar. Use an oversized school calendar with generous date-squares, mount it in a central location with a marker attached by a string. Dictate grocery lists and car pool schedules to the young scribe. Children are surprisingly helpful when given meaningful, adult-like tasks.

Encourage letter writing. If you can resurrect the nearly lost art of letter writing, long-distance family and friends will bless you, and probably return the gesture. Nothing whets the letter-writing appetite more than a postcard or letter hidden among the bills and advertising circulars. In today's highly mobile society, families are spread across the country and sometimes around the world. The most satisfying pen pals are grandparents and cousins. Honor holidays and birthdays with a hand-written letter enclosed in a homemade card. My grandmother sent me a box of 50 years of our correspondence, including letters and postcards we had exchanged. Having this record is a delight, providing me with memories to share with my children.

Provide the right tools. Some balky writers respond to the beauty of a new medium like calligraphy or architectural lettering. One child blossomed when given a 79-cent erasable ink pen. Another enjoys the light feel of a mechanical pencil. Computers and software programs are a technological boon to all writers, but especially important to those who find the physical process of writing daunting.

Finally, nothing communicates "I Love You" or "I Am Sorry" more effectively than a note. Tuck a tender note in a lunchbox, stick a Post-It greeting on a mirror, put a poem under the pillow—make writing a part of your family traditions.

Supplies

- Post-It notes in many sizes and colors
- blank books
- notebooks or composition books
- scrap paper recycled into scratch pads by stapling together or storing loose sheets in an accessible box
- stationery—some commercial and some homemade with stickers and stamp-pad embellishments
- post cards
- stamps, address book
- year-planner calendar
- variety of writing implements including mechanical pencils and roller ball pens

 # Resources

Contests

The National Written and Illustrated by Children Awards
Landmark Editions
Box 4469
Kansas City, MO 64127
816-241-4919
Contest categories include ages 6-9, 10-13, and 14-19.

Fiction Contest—Highlights for Children
803 Church Street
Honesdale, PA 18431

Creative writing classes for children are held periodically at:

The Writer's Center
4508 Walsh Street
Bethesda, MD 20815 301-654-8664

The University of Maryland Family Art Center
College Park, MD 20742
301-314-ARTS

**Check with park division of local governments
Maryland National Capital Park and Planning Commission (Prince Georges and Montgomery Counties) holds such classes on an occasional basis.

Very Special Arts Young Playwrights Program
Kennedy Center for the Performing Arts
Washington, DC 20566
202-662-8899
Annual contest (February deadline) for playwrights between the ages
of 12 and 18 whose script treats some aspect of disability.

Further Reading

Beal, George and Martin Chatterton. *KingFisher First Thesaurus*.
New York: Kingfisher, 1993.

The Oxford Dictionary of Quotations (paperback) or Barlett's
quotations.

Kids Explore the Gifts of Children With Special Needs by the
Westridge Writers Workshop. John Muir Publications. This book
features profiles on inspiring exceptional people, all written by
students in grades 3-6.

Stone Soup, The Magazine by Children. this bimonthly publishes art-
work, poetry and fiction of children between the ages of 3 and 13.
The Children's Art Foundation, Box 83, Santa Cruz CA 95063
408-426-5557

Shopping

Many families know the frustration of a shopping trip that ends unhappily. Both parents and children feel tired and cross, with nothing to show for their efforts.

There's a remedy, though. Shopping can be much more than a necessary evil. It can even be a pleasant experience, filled with opportunities for children to learn.

All you need are some clear strategies for finding the best bargain or that perfect object, and the knowledge of how to keep your child happy in the pursuit of it.

These pages offer money-saving secrets, "family-friendly" stores and the best places to go find what you're looking for.

Photo by Shelley Shore Photography

No Time? No Money? Let's Go Shopping!

by Mindy Bailin

With a myriad of stores available in the metropolitan area and a limit to the amount of time and money you can spend, it is important to devise a strategy for shopping. Meet Tammy, Hope, Karen, Beth, . . . savvy shoppers with strategies to share.

Tammy shops with her 2-year-old at department stores like Hecht's and Macy's. She also frequents BabyGap and Gymboree stores for items on sale. Armed with a bag of gummy bears to keep her daughter happy, Tammy shops at the end of a season, saving 50 to 70 percent on items for next year.

Hope shops for her baby and 3-year-old at discount department stores. You need to know good quality merchandise when you see it , she reports. While it is time consuming culling through racks of children's clothes, if you know what you're looking for, you can do all your wardrobe shopping at discount stores. Why pay more when a $4 boy's bathing suit at discount will do?

Karen often orders clothes for her children through the mail by catalogue shopping. It's easier, especially in the dead of winter, to order by mail. Catalogue shopping is ideal for locating specialty items like certain craft supplies, kid's science kits, wooden toys and children's clothing out of season. Catalogues may offer swimsuits when local stores have long sold out. Catalogue shopping also offers more sizes in kids' clothing.

Beth is a savvy consignment and thrift store shopper. She prices merchandise at local thrift stores and contends it's possible not to buy any new clothing for children (except maybe underwear) if you know your stuff. Check for the clearance sales, usually twice a year at thrift and consignment stores. Right before they restock for the new season it's possible to bag some real buys. Even if it's not perfect, says Beth, if you didn't pay that much for it, you won't feel so bad if you toss it out.

Whether you're shopping at department stores, discount outlets, consignment and thrift shops or by mail, be a smart shopper. Know what you want and how much you want to spend. Buy next year's wardrobe at the end of this season when a sale can mean sizable savings. Know or carry a reminder with your children's clothing sizes. And when all else fails . . . go shopping.

Mindy Bailin is a public relations consultant, writer and teacher. For 10 years she produced and hosted a cable television talk show seen on 15 cable stations. She is the full-time mother of Michael, 8 and Jennifer, 6.

How to Make Shopping with Your Children a Positive Experience

You've timed your shopping spree to the exact minute. Your children are well rested, well fed and ready to go. You're equipped with snacks, changes of clothes, small toys and diversions, a stroller for young charges and a "to-do" list four pages long. What else could you possibly need?

The key to a successful shopping trip is often "family-friendly" stores and shopping malls. Once you have found them, you may never shop anywhere else. Family-friendly facilities make it easier for you to shop with children.

Look for malls and stores that provide shopping carts or free strollers. Store carts equipped with infant seats, strollers with double seats, and carts with seatbelt restraints can make your toddler travels safer and easier.

Frequent stores and malls with consistently clean restroom facilities equipped with changing areas. Some even offer limited baby supplies; others offer comfortable chairs with ottomans for nursing moms. Patronize these shops and let them know you appreciate their "family planning."

Some stores and malls feature child amusement facilities. Caldor has a free carousel in the center of the store. IKEA has free babysitting facilities with a ball room, video area, quiet coloring tables and a book nook staffed by store employees. Ramers Shoes has a toy piano for young virtuosos along with children's books for browsing, a glow room equipped with a black light for luminous sneakers and stickers for every young customer. Who wouldn't want to buy shoes there? Fair Oaks Mall has a stage area and stepped seating which makes a great picnic stop, a peaceful place for parents to rest and toddlers to climb, or a changing area in a pinch.

Youngsters old enough to play video games, skeeball and pinball may continue on an endless list of errands if promised a quick stop in the arcade. Check the yellow pages for lists of stores and services located in your neighborhood malls. Call the mall management office to inquire about family-friendly stores and facilities.

When planning a long excursion, a time-out in a toy store that has toys available for children to touch, explore and play with can be a welcome stop for your youngster. (That is, if you can leave the premises without having to make a major purchase.)

Vending machines and snack stops may also extend the fortitude of your 4-year-old. Many fast food chains, along with full service restaurants, offer child-size drinks and meal portions. If you are not planning a formal stop, be sure to pack drinks and snacks for your little ones.

After your foray through family-friendly malls and stores, know when to quit. Pushing the edge of the envelope may not be worth the disastrous results when dealing with a child in desperate need of a nap. The bad news may be that you did not quite accomplish what you planned. But the good news is..tomorrow is another day.

Resources

Children's Clothing

Artisans Kids
6830A Old Dominion Dr., McLean, VA, 703-506-0158
Store offers all handmade items made by local artisans. Unique
selection of clothes and even earrings. The displays are changed
frequently.

Beyda's Lad and Lassie
5444 Westbard Ave., Bethesda, MD, 301-656-2026
Neighborhood store that caters to the community and is very service
oriented. School uniforms available.

Caro's Fabrics and African Fashions
3018 Hamilton St., Hyattsville, MD, 301-853-3281
Only store in the area to sell handmade African clothes.

Children's Discount Mart
4003 Branch Ave., Marlow Heights, MD, 301-899-2121 and
5211 Indian Head Highway, Oxon Hill, MD, 301-839-2020
All clothes are sold at prices cheaper than at department stores.

Classics for Kids
10501 Metropolitan Ave., Kensington, MD, 301-949-3128
Unusual clothing store where all clothes are cotton and made from
natural fibers. Local artists contribute to store's stock. Not
commercialized. (5 doors down at Catch Can is their natural fiber
maternity wear store.)

Doodle Hoppers 4 Kids
7533 Huntsman Blvd.
Springfield, VA, 703-912-7200
Store carries Heartstrings, JG Hook and more, at prices lower than
department stores. Sports and dresswear ranges from newborn sizes
to 14 in both boys and girls. Half sizes and size 16 are also available
for girls. Special orders and free giftwrapping. Play area for children
as well as a selection of toys and jewelry.

Full of Beans—Stuff for Kids
5502 Connecticut Ave., Chevy Chase, DC, 202-362-8566
Own line of 100% cotton clothing. Natural fiber clothing is all
moderately priced. Some items in store are handmade.

Granny's Place
303 Cameron St., Alexandria, VA, 703-549-0119
Unique imported wooden toys and children's clothes from Europe and
Canada.

Hoohobbers-Tysons
1961 Chain Bridge Rd., McLean, VA, 703-893-1944
Specializes in "Innovations for Children." Safe, functional toys that
fold into small sizes. Rocking horses, directors chairs and easels are
examples of these brightly colored toys. Toys can be personalized.

Just Kids
5639 Stone Rd., Centreville, VA, 703-222-0815
Store has brand name clothing at discounted prices from infant to size 14.

Kids Closet
1226 Connecticut Ave, NW, Washington DC, 202-466-5589
Specialty shop in DC - convenient for the working mom.

Kids Gallery
Diamond Square Shopping Center, Gaithersburg, MD, 301-963-6449
Unique stock. Accessories and clothing for newborns to size 14.

Kramers
Montgomery Mall, 301-365-7988
One of the few stores specializing in boys and young men and offering a complete line of dress clothing including suits, blazers and tuxedos. (sizes 8-20 regular, slim, husky stout; sizes 36-41 short, long, regular) Also offers large selection of back-to-school and camp clothes. School uniforms available.

Les Enfants
5110 Ridgefield Rd. #207, Bethesda, MD, 301-656-4505
Quality clothing imported from Europe. Clothes are all cotton.

Little Sprout
3222 M St., NW, Washington, DC, 202-342-2273
Hand-painted, 100% cotton, affordable and often unique clothing.

Monday's Child
218 N Lee Street, Alexandria, VA, 703-548-3505
Traditional clothes, name brands. Handmade and handsmocked clothes. Christening outfits.

Name Droppers of McLean
1349 Chain Bridge Rd., McLean, VA, 703-847-8840
Mostly gifts which include personalized backpacks and umbrellas for children.

Once Upon A Child
Centreville, VA, 703-803-8849
Specializing in classical children's attire from the better manufacturers for preemies to size 10 girls and to size 14 boys. Clothes for holidays and birthdays.

Seventh Heaven
12288A Wilkins Ave., Rockville, MD, 301-231-4901
12125 Rockville Pike, Rockville, MD, 301-231-9077
6207 Oxon Hill Rd., Oxon Hill, MD, 301-567-9345
Large discount store specializing in infants and children's clothing where parents can find everything in one store.

Talbots Surplus Store
6815 Old Springfield Plaza
Springfield, VA, 703-644-5115
Quality kids clothes at a fraction of original cost.

Consignment Shops

Dani's Duds
P.O. Box 503, Merrifield, VA, 703-560-7722
A large-scale, weekend-long sale twice a year. People bring things in on consignment during the set-up period. Call for further information.

Jack and Jill
15934 Shady Grove Rd., Gaithersburg, MD, 301-926-3532
One of the largest consignment shops in area specializing in children's toys, equipment and furniture.

Kensington Caboose
10590 Metropolitan Ave., Kensington, MD, 301-929-0178
Clothing, cribs, toys, maternity.

Kids Again
2804 Sherwood Hall Lane, Alexandria, VA, 703-360-5854
Children's boutique; strollers, highchairs, etc.

The Whole Kaboodle
Crabbs Branch Way, Rockville, MD, 301-670-0766
Good-quality women's and children's clothing and maternity wear. Stuffed animals and baby equipment. Children's play area.

Kids' Stuff
5615 39th St., NW, Washington, DC, 202-244-2221
Superior quality children's clothing, shoes, furniture, toys and maternity wear.

Knee-High To A Grasshopper
7326 Carroll Ave., Takoma Park, MD, 301-891-3124
Children's clothes, toys, books, furniture and maternity wear.

Mama & Me Consignment
11033 Baltimore Ave., Beltsville, MD, 301-937-2523
PG County's only exclusively maternity and children's consignment shop.

Merry-Go-Round
36A Main St., Warrenton, VA, 703-349-2705
Quality children's and baby clothing, infants to teens, toys and crafts. Specializes in OshKosh and Baby Dior; also includes children's furniture, women's clothes and maternity wear.

Mother & Child
207 E. Holly Ave., Sterling, VA, 703-444-5042
7401 Annapolis Rd., Landover Hills, MD 301-330-8955
Quality furniture and clothes that are like new. Prices are 80% below retail.

Once Around Toys
17525 Redland Rd., Derwood, MD, 301-330-8955
Quality used toys like Fisher Price, Little Tykes, Playskool and Nintendo. One of the few stores in the area to sell used toys.

Paddington Station
448 Maple Avenue East, Vienna, VA, 703-938-0378
Toys, children's clothing, furniture, maternity and baby equipment.
Reasonably priced quality clothing.

Purple Goose
2206 Mt. Vernon Ave., Alexandria, VA, 703-683-2918
Up-to-date good-quality clothes all for children.

Secondhand Childhood
2647 N. Pershing Dr., Arlington, VA, 703-276-7740
Children's consignment shop from infant to 14 girls and 20 boys;
maternity wear. Enclosed play area for children. Clothing that doesn't
fit may be returned.

Shirley's Consignment Gallery
9561 Braddock Rd., Fairfax, VA, 703-250-6159
14834 Build America Dr., Woodbridge, VA, 703-491-6159
Children's apparel, maternity, baby furnishings and toys.
Carefully chosen items where quality comes before quantity.

Short Turnaround
12009 Nebel St., Rockville, MD, 301-770-2007
Larger than most consignment shops in the area. More accessories
and furniture including cribs and playpens. Extremely selective with
clothing.

Small Change
Lake Anne Center, Reston, VA, 703-437-7730
Clothes for infants to teens and mothers-to-be. Also a selection of
handmade crafts and clothes made especially for the store. Half-price
sale at the end of each season. Offers a playroom for children.

Treasured Child
9413-C (Old) Burke Lake Rd., Burke, VA, 703-978-4778
317 Sunset Park Dr., Herndon, VA, 703-437-9625
Equipment and furniture, maternity, toys, books and gifts. Quality
clothes at an affordable price.

★ Special Needs

Special Clothes
P.O. Box 4220
Alexandria, VA 22303, 703-683-7343
Free catalogue of adaptive clothing for boys and girls with disabilities
of all types. Sizes from 2 Toddler to 16-18 Teen.

Infant Furnishings

One stop shopping is key when you're shopping for infant equipment and supplies, especially with infants or young children in tow. If you can save time and money by making all your baby supply purchases in one place, why shop anywhere else?

When buying furniture, choose items from a company and a line that will be around in six months and in six years. While you may not be buying a desk for your 3-week-old, will the company be in business when you are in the market to buy a desk?

Take that stroller for a spin and test out any items that you have to assemble or learn to use. If you can't get the hang of that baby carrier right in the store, find another one. If you need two hands to put the crib side down and you're going to be carrying the baby in one arm, don't buy that crib.

Check the store's return policy. Do they have layaway? Do they deliver? Is gift wrapping free? Will they meet or beat advertised prices of identical items of competitors?

Because you do not have time to return defective baby gear, quality merchandise and dependable service are essential. When possible, buy equipment that will last for all the future needs of your family.

Infant Furnishings

A & B Furniture Inc.
11710 Baltimore Ave., Beltsville, MD 301 419-3500, 1-800-899-0690
This store is unique for the different manufacturers they carry, especially Vermont Precisions. Juvenile and baby furniture.

Baby Boomer
9534 Main St., Fairfax, VA, 703-425-1497
All shopping for a baby can be done in here: strollers, car seats, cribs, etc. Knowledgeable staff offering what's new and upcoming for baby.

Baby Planners, Inc.
301-570-9288
The company that comes to you. Allows expectant and bedrest women to shop at home at their convenience. Decorating services, furniture, murals and wallpaper. Birth announcements, too.

Baby Room at Burlington Coat Factory
Sterling Boulevard, Sterling, VA, 703-444-7044
Route 7, Bailey's Crossroads, VA, 703-379-7878
Sudley Rd., Manassas, VA, 703-368-6355
Pennmar Shopping Center, Forestville, MD 301-736-0085
Beltway Plaza Mall, Greenbelt, MD, 301-982-2386
Westridge Plaza, Frederick, MD, 301-698-0003
Everything for the child. Brand-name furniture, playpens, dressers, gifts and knick-knacks at good prices.

Baby-2-Teen Furniture
2731 Wilson Blvd., Arlington, VA, 703-525-2972
8612 Phoenix Dr., Manassas, VA, 703-631-2166
389 Main St., Laurel, MD, 301-953-9464
Largest selection of baby through teen accessories. Custom bedding and free layaway. Provides delivery and setup.

Bellini
12141 Rockville Pike, Rockville, MD, 301-770-3944
Upscale quality furniture from their own line. Custom designing for children's rooms is available at no extra charge.

Daisy Kingdom, Inc.
134 N.W. 8th Street, Portland, OR 97209, 1-503-222-9033
Readymade kits for the nursery.

Forever Young
5641 General Washington Dr., Alexandria, VA, 703-256-6937
Complete store for children. Help decorate and coordinate rooms. Personalization available. Cribs, furniture, equipment, bedding, gifts, accessories.

Lewis of London
7249 Arlington Blvd., Falls Church, VA, 703-876-9330
12248 Rockville Pike, Rockville, MD, 301-468-2070
High-fashion furniture with a European/Italian look, exceeding consumer safety regulations. The furniture grows with the children and can be added to.

My Room
Montgomery Mall, Bethesda, MD 20817 301-469-5058
Wood furniture for children coming out of the crib up to teens. Pieces can be added to, maximizing storage space as your child grows.

Paidi Infant and Juvenile Furniture Systems
14080 Sullyfield Circle, Chantilly, VA, 703-631-8050
Caters to the age group just beyond baby from 2 years to preteens. Free layout service that will set up the room for the child to match the decor of the house. Quality furniture that can grow with the children and adapt as they grow.

Precious Places
703-690-0854, 301-294-2295
Shop-at-home service. Specialty furniture, unique accessories, bedding, carpet, window treatments, wallpaper/borders, murals, stencils, complimentary design service.

Rooms by Design
6912 Arlington Road, Bethesda, MD, 301-654-2618
Unique gifts and accessories for children's rooms.

Catalog Shopping

Many mail-order resources offer a free catalog, while others charge a fee. Inquire whether the fee is deductible from your first order. It pays to ask whether the company is running a special promotion or discount. The following list offers a potpourri of mail-order outlets.

Catalog Shopping

Books and Tapes:
Butternut Books, 607-263-5620
Children's Book and Music Center, 800-443-1856
Music for Little People, 707-923-3991
Silver Burdett Press, 201-592-3424
Clothing: Infants
B2 Products, 800-695-7073
Baby Bunz & Co., 707-829-5347
Baby Clothes Wholesale, 201-572-9520
Brights Creek, 804-827-1850
Childcraft, 800-222-7725
Garnet Hill, 800-622-6216
Land's End School and Play Clothes, 800-856-4444
The Natural Baby Co., 800-388-BABY
Furniture:
A & B Furniture, 301-725-4994
Huddle Furniture for Kids, 213-836-8001
MaxiMoms, 619-278-8909
Stationery:
Current Inc., 800-525-7170
(also recently began offering children's clothing, children's home safety items and giftware)
Toys:
Discovery Toys, 800-426-4777
call for local demonstrations and catalog

Department Stores

While die-hard discount shoppers will regale anyone in earshot with the joys of buying off-price, savvy department store shoppers can often save the same amount of money and savor the selection of our area's major stores. To make the most of department store shopping, it pays to keep an eye on the sales in the newspaper, as well as special mailings that often are sent to credit card holders of individual store accounts.

Locate the children's department manager of your favorite department store (the store where you have the most luck buying the clothes both you *and* your children like) and ask questions. When do they offer their major markdowns? What days or weeks each month do they get new merchandise? Is there a special rack or section where clearance items or special buys are featured?

Pay attention to holiday and especially end-of-season sales. Buying wardrobe basics on sale at the end of the season in anticipated children's sizes for next season can save you time and money.

Here are most of the major department stores in our area featuring children's departments:

Bloomingdale's	Macy's	Saks Fifth Avenue
Hecht's	Montgomery Ward	Sears
JC Penney	Nordstrom	Woodward & Lothrop

Discount Clubs and Discount Chain Department Stores

Discount clubs and discount chain department stores offer one-stop shopping often at unbeatable prices. It is not unusual to find name brand children's furnishings, clothing, shoes, toys and books, sports equipment and art supplies under one roof.

To take advantage of unexpected bargains, always carry your children's shoe and clothing sizes with you. Be prepared with check or charge card to stock up when you stumble upon the ultimate birthday party gift. Buy a dozen and store them in a spare closet, saving future harried trips to the toy store with children in tow.

Baby gifts can be another staple of your secret stash. Just when you think you've got it covered, some distant cousin reports the birth of a newborn and you're making a mad dash to the store.

Discount clubs and discount chain department stores can increase your purchasing power and also save unnecessary shopping trips, if you plan ahead.

Ames	Kmart	Ross
Best Products	Kids R Us	TJ Maxx
B.J.'s Warehouse	Marshalls	Toys R Us
Burlington Coat Factory	PACE	Tuesday Morning
Caldor	Price Club	Wal-Mart
Evans		

Haircuts

While most hair salons today offer haircuts for children, do your homework before bringing your child into a salon for an actual haircut. Does the salon have an operator who specializes in children's hairstyling? Is there a separate area for children with diversions, videos, low sinks for children's shampoos? If possible, observe the stylist you've chosen while he/she cuts another child's hair. What is the stylist's approach and how does he/she handle a difficult, squirming or frightened child? And perhaps most important to your child, at the end of their hairy adventure is a peace offering (a lollipop or trinket) offered by the operator? These issues can make or break your child's next hair appointment. These hair salons specialize in children's haircuts or advertise their services for children as well as adults.

Cartoon Cuts
Congressional Plaza 301-816-3098
Fair Oaks Mall, 703-359-CUTS
Lakeforest Mall, 301-948-7020 and other locations
Supernintendo, Gameboy, videos, the circus wash, Sunday birthday parties.

Haircuttery and **Hair Pair** have numerous locations in the area. Check the Yellow Pages for their locations and numbers.

Photographers

When choosing a photographer to capture your family on film, it is important to plan ahead to prevent a photo fiasco. Interview the portrait photographer well in advance to discuss fees, studio or home location, and the services you wish the professional to provide. If possible, observe your photographer at work with other children/families. Ask to see their portfolio and call previous clients to gauge their satisfaction with the photo shoot, as well as the finished photos.

For package prices and, often, inexpensive photographs, check the Yellow Pages for photo studios in store chains like Sears or JC Penney. Plan to observe the photographer in action before booking an appointment. Ask for the package prices and options in advance. Also find out if appointments are scheduled, or first-come, first-served. Observe the atmosphere: is it friendly with relatively happy clients and staff, or is the scene frenzied and stressful?

Examples of the following photographers' work appears throughout this book:

Glogau Studio
5110 Ridgefield Road
Bethesda, MD 301-652-9577
B/W and color children's portraits; individuals or groups
see Parenting, page 102

Kids by Kim - Kim Nye Zeiss
3609 38th Street, NW
Washington, DC 202-362-3027
B/W and color casual portraits; children and families in their favorite places
see Medical, page 14, and Childcare, page 130

Nancy Jamieson-McGuire
5902 Gloster Road
Bethesda, MD 301-229-4845
B/W and hand-tinted portraits of children
see Education, page 158

Shelley Shore Photography
4800 Chevy Chase Drive
Chevy Chase, MD 301-656-2299
B/W and hand-colored portraits of children and families
see Shopping, page 288

Beverly Resneck Photography
2852 Albemarle Street, NW
Washington, DC 20008 202-244-1738
Specializes in B/W and color photography in studio or on location
see Summertime, page 218

Barry Stelzer Photography
6116 Smith Avenue
Baltimore, MD 301-881-9193
B/W and color portraits of children and families taken in your home
see Creative Arts, page 238

Other photographers whose work frequently appears in *Washington Parent:*

Leslie Cashen Photography
3242 Ellicott Street, NW
Washington, DC 202-363-5682

Michael Kress Photography
7847 Old Georgetown Road
Bethesda, MD 301-654-0909

Cindy DeVore
6925 Kerry Dale Road
Springfield, VA 703-569-8905

Bill Owen
4014 Bird Road
Kensington, MD 301-946-1967

The Yellow Pages include information for photographers at the following stores:

Expressly Portraits
JC Penney
Kmart

Olan Mills
Sears
Snap Shops

School and Art Supplies

Toy stores, discount department stores, area drug store chains, supermarkets, office supply stores and discount buying clubs all carry school and art supplies. A new contender in the retailing mix, the "everything's a dollar" stores can also be an inexpensive source of art materials.

These area school and art supply specialty stores also offer an extensive selection of materials for your budding artist and your child prodigy:

Crown Education and Teaching Aids
14215 N. Centreville Square, Centreville, VA 703-631-8066
15914 Shady Grove Rd., Gaithersburg, MD, 301-948-5710
304 Riggs Rd., NE, Washington, DC, 202-529-3470
Everything that an elementary or nursery school teacher would need. Educational games, and toys, manipulatives, transparencies, social studies, math, English, reading and phonics books.

J.L. Hammett
Oakton Shopping Center, VA, 703-938-0047
Springfield Tower Mall, VA, 703-569-2303
Weis Festival at Muddy Branch, Gaithersburg, MD, 301-330-7680
Educational supplies, reference books, work books, supplies for children and teachers.

Kaybee Montessori
615-A Lofstrand Lane, Rockville, MD, 301-251-6319
Supplies and teaching materials for Montessori teachers. They carry glass beads for math. Covers all didactic areas, botany, math and language.

School Box
7112 Columbia Pike, Annandale, VA, 703-914-0656
All teacher resource books, educational posters, workbooks,
textbooks, classroom decorations.

Teachers' Mart
5765-M Burke Center Parkway, Burke, VA 703-250-6777. Wide
selection of resource books and workbooks for elementary school
teachers and parents.

Shoe Shopping Tips

As we all know, the fit and feel of your shoes are important. The job
of fitting your child for shoes should not be left to holiday or summer help
with no experience selling children's shoes. Look for experienced sales-
people who know how to relate to children. Look for full lines of quality
shoes rather than fad or trendy shoes that will soon go out of style and
out of favor with your young fashionplate.

Does the store keep a record of your purchases and child's sizes?
Does the salesperson tell you when it's not necessary to buy new shoes
because there's still room and wear left in your child's current pair?

Ask to be put on the mailing list for sales. Inquire about discounts
or promotions or discounts for multiple purchases.

Nothing beats a comfortable pair of shoes . . . except maybe a pair of
your child's comfortable shoes, properly fit, with plenty of wear left.

Stores specializing in children's footwear:

Buster Brown Shoe Stores
Throughout the area.
Strictly a children's shoe store, orthopedic work, excellent selection of
sizes and widths; they take time to fit the shoes.

Stride Rite Shoe Stores
Throughout the area.
Stride Rite, Capezio, Nike, L.A. Gear, dress shoes, Willis, Peaks and
other brands

Jeanne's
Westwood II Center
5110 Ridgefield Road
Bethesda, MD 301-654-3877
Infants, children's, teenagers

Just Shoes
3301 Mexico Ave., NW
Washington, DC, 202-244-2224
Domestic and imported children's shoes

Lazarus Shoes
4852 Bethesda Ave.
Bethesda, MD, 301-656-6722.
Large selection of leading brands in quality school and athletic shoes,
boots, dance, ballet and soccer shoes.

Ramer's Shoes
3810 Northhampton St., NW
Washington, DC, 202-244-2288
Stride Rite, Sebago, Keds, Little Capezio, very narrow to extra wide.

Shoe Train Ltd.
1075 Seven Locks Rd.
Rockville, MD, 301-279-5515
Sneakers, dress shoes, everyday shoes, sizes start at 2 (young) through size 12 (young adult). All widths.

Tanzman's Shoes for Children Thru Adults
5212 N. Wilson Blvd.
Arlington, VA, 703-522-2235
Carry shoes for infants, prewalkers and some sneakers. Dress shoes, casual and parochial school shoes. Winter boots, sandals, pool shoes for infant-15 years.

For discount shoes try the Payless for Kids chain, listed in the Yellow Pages.

★ Special Needs

M.J. Markell Shoe Co., Inc.
504 Saw Mill River Road
P.O. Box 246
Yonkers, NY 10702
Orthopedic sneakers sized to accommodate braces.

Starlight Footwear
21537 Kapok Circle
Boca Raton, FL 33433
Free catalogue of easy-on, easy-off footwear in all widths.

Sporting Goods

Sporting goods can be found in many major toy store chains and also discount department stores and catalog showrooms. The following listing is an area sampling of multisport stores. For a particular sport such as soccer, skiing, gymnastics, etc., there are multiple listings in the Yellow Pages devoted to single sport enthusiasts. Check your phone books for locations of the following leading area sports stores:

Herman's World of Sporting Goods
REI
The Sports Authority

For used equipment try:

Play It Again Sports
18707-C N. Frederick Rd., Gaithersburg, MD, 301-840-1122
4888 Bolling Brook Parkway, Rockville, MD, 301-231-9064
1112 Lee Highway, Fairfax, VA, 703-352-8284
1094 Elden St., Herndon, VA, 703-471-5215
6125-A Backlick Rd., Springfield, VA, 703-569-5595
10354 Portsmouth Rd., Manassas, VA, 703-257-1649
Used and new skates, baseball, lacrosse, exercise, soccer, hockey,
sports equipment, used—but not used up.

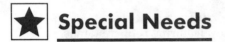

★ Special Needs

ABLEDATA
8455 Colesville Rd., Suite 935
Silver Spring, MD 20910-3319
301-588-9284   800-227-0216
Maintains an up-to-date database listing more than 15,000
commercially available products designed for people with disabilities.

Flaghouse
150 No. MacQuesten Pkwy, Suite 95083
Mt. Vernon, NY 10550
800-793-7900
Adaptive products such as sports equipment, furniture, toys, games.

Tips on Toys

• When searching for a particular toy, especially a popular one, call ahead
to see if that item is in stock and save yourself an unnecessary trip to
the toy store.

• Choose durable toys made of quality materials. When possible examine
your purchase, checking for safety features and no small detachable
parts. Pick toys that will be around for years to come.

• Choose age and skill appropriate toys for your child. While *you* may
want that train set, will your toddler or your 10-year-old?

• Ask if they gift wrap toys for free or for a fee. Will they special order an
item? Do they offer rainchecks for a sale item that is out of stock?

• Remember that many toy stores also stock books, videos and sports
equipment.

Toys and Books
Arlington Hobby Crafters
6176 Arlington Blvd., Falls Church, VA, 703-532-2224
Store for children 8 and up that sells model planes, trains and cars.
Many models are on display.

Barston's Child's Play
5536 Connecticut Ave., NW, Washington DC, 202-244-3602
Excellent service with a varied assortment of toys for all ages. For
older children there are strategy games and computer software.

Book Nook
9933 Rhode Island Ave., College Park, MD, 301-474-4060
Large selection of used books in good condition.

The Bookstall
10144 River Rd., Potomac, MD, 301-469-7800
Large selection of children's books.

Counterpane Gallery of Toys
2900 Clarendon Blvd., Arlington, VA, 703-525-4551
Emphasis on real things like cars and trucks.

Earth Toys
322 S. Washington St., Alexandria, VA, 703-684-1407
An out-of-the-ordinary toy company, featuring rubber stamps, puzzles, toys, etc. made in America. Educational kits and crafts, fine arts supplies. Classes for adults and kids.

FAO Schwartz
Tysons Corner, VA, 703-917-9600
Upscale toy store. Original New York store is where the editor's father bought her dollhouse furniture long ago.

Games for Less
7065 Brookfield Plaza, Springfield, VA, 703-644-4950
Specialty store selling video games at reduced prices. Some new, some used.

Georgetown Zoo
3222 M St., NW, Washington, DC, 202-338-4182
Specialty store; stuffed animals from $11-$600, all in plush, some talk; brands include Dakin and Gund. Wide variety of travel toys, activity sets and coloring books.

Kiddlywinks
13300 Franklin Farm Rd., Herndon, VA, 703-478-9272
One of the few toy stores that sells classical and educational toys as well as the more popular toys of today.

Learningsmith
3222 M St. NW, Washington DC, 202-337-0800
WETA-Public television's learning store for children of all ages. Fun, educational books, videos, games and software covering every topic from architecture to astronomy.

Once Upon A Time
120 Church St., NE, Vienna, VA, 703-255-3285
Dollhouses, Gund, Steiff, dolls, books, Brio, Playmobil, Breyer, Lundby, Erector sets.

One Two Kangaroo
4238 Wilson Blvd., Arlington, VA, 703-522-4422
Children's learning store for newborns-teens. Numbers, letters, creative mind games, science projects, stuffed animals, books. A unique selection.

Play N'Learn
12217 Nebel St., Rockville, MD, 301-816-3227
A "kid friendly" atmosphere! Store features Rainbow Play Systems and a full line of Little Tikes. Specialty toy store with many play systems on display that kids can try.

Sullivan's Toy Store
3412 Wisconsin Avenue, NW, Washington, DC, 202-362-1343.
Since 1954. Quality toys, competitive prices. Arts, craft, hobby supplies. Parking.

Toy Company
36A Catoctin Circle, Leesburg, VA, 703-777-6633
Educational toy store with lots of books, toys and art supplies from Europe.

Toys . . . Etc.
12948 Middlebrook Road, Germantown, MD, 301-540-5777
Only full line dealer of Little Tykes, also Step 2. Playmobil, Brio, Lego and Creativity for Kids. 800 feet of play area for children to try out the toys.

Tree Top Toys & Books
3301 New Mexico Avenue, NW, Foxhall Square, Washington, DC, 202-244-3500
Knowledgeable staff helps you choose the best toy from wide selection of specialty toys. Also has free story times and book parties. Call for a schedule of events.

Turtle Park Toys
4115 Wisconsin Avenue NW, Washington, DC, 202-362-8697
Staff helps select from educational toys and extensive book section.

*See page 343 for children's book stores that offer regularly scheduled story times and literary events.

★ Special Needs

Toy Guide for Differently-Abled Kids
National Parent Network on Disabilities
1600 Prince Street, Suite 115
Alexandria, VA 22314 703-684-6763
Free consumer guide to help adults choose toys, games and sporting goods that are fun and enhance language or motor skill development for children with special needs.

Food Shopping Made Fun

While many parents quiver at the thought of grocery shopping with their children, a little planning can prevent the hassle and headache and a "teachable moment" may even transpire. Here are some helpful hints to make grocery shopping a positive experience for parent and child.

Whether attempting this feat with one child or more, it is imperative that all participants make a potty stop or have a diaper changed before embarking on this family adventure. Grocery shoppers must be well fed before entering the produce portals. Energy levels must also be at peak, thus making before meal-time and two minutes to nap-time definite no-nos in terms of timing. The Hell hours, 5 to 7 p.m. are also not recommended for a shop-till-you-drop soiree.

For infants and young children, packing a bottle, juice box, teething pretzel or series of healthy snacks is advisable. (The operative word here is "series." You do not want to be reduced to crawling around the floor of the fish department searching for the gooey cookie dropped by your one 1-year-old, who is now wailing at the top of her lungs.)

Snack packing will also avert your arrest as you madly tear open an array of candybar wrappers in a feeble attempt to quiet your toddler. Wet washcloths are key for sticky fingers following your en-route snack service.

While food shopping can be a mundane task for you, think of it as a learning experience for your youngster. Grocery shopping is a lesson in nutrition, and in math, as well as preparation for later life-skills. It can be viewed as a new adventure every time you bring your child along.

Ask your non-readers to search for colors in the supermarket. Parents who plan ahead can make a scavenger "shopping list" of color squares on a sheet of paper. No time to plan ahead? Shout out a color as you walk the aisles and ask your youngster to identify an item that matches that color. The fruit and vegetable aisle is a natural for colors. Or search for numbers. What food is sold in ones? twos? sixes? a dozen?

Plan-ahead parents can also cut out logos or pictures from food packages or magazines and paste them on paper for a pictorial shopping list. Reading readiness activities could include an alphabet list. Find a food item that begins with B and so on. Beginning readers can have a "words only" list.

Use these lists again and again or make new ones for each visit. No time for lists? No problem. Keep your child guessing through the supermarket as you ask questions that relate to the five senses. Name a fruit that is sweet. Name a fruit that is sour. What food is squishy? What food has a hard shell? What foods are round? Rectangular? Flat?

Youngsters can practice simple math and money matters while supermarket shopping. A small calculator can keep an elementary school youngster interested in the price of potatoes. Weights and measurement comparisons can also be made during your excursion. Let your child participate in counting fruit, selecting the cookies, loading or unloading the cart or matching the coupons to the products purchased. A little planning can go a long way in making your trip to the supermarket fun for you and your child.

Family Togetherness

The other chapters in this book address the many practical aspects of raising a child. In this chapter, we focus on the "one for all and all for one" mentality so prevalent in happy families and how to develop it through daily activities and special events.

In the '90s, it seems everyone is running faster and faster to achieve financial security or career satisfaction, putting a tremendous strain on family life. Countering the negative effects which this places on children doesn't necessarily require a big change in lifestyle. It *does* mean that we as parents need to adopt the right approach to ensure that all members of the family connect with one another in meaningful and lasting ways.

The daily activities shared in your home will provide the necessary stability for you and your children. Through these shared activities, ranging from bedtime stories to birthday parties, you can create the threads of experience to weave into a precious fabric of family life. These traditions will instill the sense of security and belonging that sustain a family many years after the children have become adults.

Today busy parents are asking "What is quality time? How can I spend it with my family?" "Quality time" really is taking the time to show the respect and love which every member of the family deserves, no matter how young or how old, from the youngest toddler to great grandma. There are many ways to make this time special for each member of the family and, in so doing, make it very meaningful for all.

How to Make Birthday Celebrations Truly Happy

by Ann Byrne, M.Ed.

Scene I: A mob of raucous children, ages 4 to 6, runs amok in your living room (a la "Mrs. Doubtfire,") spilling punch and squashing chocolate cake under foot. You try to settle them down for the magician who is attempting to perform in the midst of the chaos, but they won't listen. You retreat to the bathroom for a large bottle of aspirin, eschewing the liquor cabinet. You vow that never again will you allow more than one extra child into your home or host a children's birthday party. What's wrong with this picture?

Scene II: A lively group of the selfsame 4-to-6-year-olds arrives at your home at 4 p.m. After playing penny pitch, they help themselves to fruit punch with dinosaur ice cubes and settle down for the magician's 45-minute show. You put the last minute touches on the birthday table as the pizza is delivered. Children move to the table for pizza and birthday cake. After eating, your child accepts a gift from each guest and gives them a wrapped favor in return. Children depart between 6 and 6:15 p.m., thanking you and smiling. You must be dreaming, right? Is it possible to turn Scene I into Scene II? Can families enjoy each child's special day without the headaches of chaotic parties or disappointed children? Read on!

Family Birthday Rituals

The birth of a child into a family is a justifiable reason to celebrate. Sharing the joy with family and friends at a party has become a cultural ritual which children anticipate with great relish. Unfortunately, sponsoring a child's birthday party can be stressful for the family unless parents think and plan carefully. After discussing options, the family may decide on an alternative plan to a children's party—a special dinner menu, birthday treats at school, planting flowers or a tree, or a family activity or trip which includes everyone. One child I know has lunch "out" with his father each year. Another parent writes a letter to her child each year on her birthday. Some childcare centers or schools welcome donations of books or toys in a child's name on his/her birthday. Books can be marked with a special bookplate noting the child's name on the donated item. If the family opts for a children's party, however, there are many factors to consider.

Ann Byrne, cofounder and past director of The Parent Connection, is currently a partner in the Child Care Group and Director of Family Services of Crossway Community.

What's the Point of Kids' Parties?

Believe it or not, parties are excellent opportunities for modeling and coaching social skills. Good manners and graciousness are most easily acquired through social exchange rather than through lectures and rules. Beginning with how invitations are distributed (by mail or dropped off at the home unless everyone at school is invited), each phase of a party is an opportunity for learning. Children pick up clues at birthday parties about appropriate social responses by observing their parents, other important adults and older children. With appropriate coaching, the birthday child's friends will be seen less as bearers of gifts and more as honored guests. The birthday child can practice social graces as he greets the guests, introduces newcomers to a group, receives gifts graciously and makes sure guests have refreshments and favors. And how many of us learned the lost art of the post-party thank you note?

If the entire family plans a birthday celebration, the birthday child can develop thinking and problem-solving skills by participating in this "grown up" activity. Selection of a theme, deciding on entertainment, food and favors, and working within a reasonable number of guests for her age are planning skills which a child can begin exercising as young as the preschool years. In addition, siblings may have fewer pangs of jealousy when they are included in the plans and have specific ways to participate. A sibling can answer the door, put away coats, assist with games, serve food and distribute favors and will do so more joyfully if she is included in the planning.

The Party's in the Planning

Like a researcher or detective, the more carefully parents establish the who, what, when and where of a party, the more successful and less stressful the event will be. Caution: Surprise parties are discouraged for young children under age 10 since the suspense may actually traumatize a child.

Your child's temprament: If a child is quiet and slow to warm up, a large number of guests or boisterous entertainment may be overwhelming and promote a negative response. A small, select group of friends at home where the child feels comfortable and in control, or a single guest on a family outing may be a better choice. Just as adults have individual tastes on how they wish to spend their birthdays, children are entitled to have a party that they will enjoy.

Who to invite: Children should suggest the names of guests; parents should set the number. The much-quoted rule of thumb for numbers of guests, "the child's age plus one," may be advisable for children under 5—especially if the child is quiet. Don't forget that parents of children under 3 must also be included in the group, requiring adult space and a separate menu.

Hugh Turley who presents magic shows for children ages 4 and up says that he performs for an average of 15 to 20 children at a party. As long as parents prepare children in advance for a live performance, says

Turley, and there are sufficient adults present to monitor the party, the size of the group can be greater than the child's age. An added note: If parents of guests attend the party, they also need to be primed not to compete with any entertainment that is provided for the children. Several entertainers mentioned being distracted by adult voices when they were trying to hold the children's attention.

When to have a party: When planning for little ones, remember that children under 3 function best mid-morning since many still nap. If parents are working and children have napped, an early evening event combining party and dinner may prove successful. An hour to an hour and a half is ample time for a party in this age group. When a meal is to be served, young children may need to be fed first to avoid hunger tantrums!

School-age children can comfortably deal with a party two to two and a half hours in length. If lunch or dinner is included, be sure to inform parents. A reasonable division of time according to *The Penny Whistle Party Planner* by Brokaw and Gilbar is:

- Arrival: Plan for multiple guests with an activity;
- Middle: Extra games or planned entertainment;
- Food followed by quiet table games;
- Videotape of the party;
- Departure: Favors given as guests leave.

In her popular book, *The Parent's Almanac*, Marguerite Kelley advises parents to drive guests home to avoid late pickups!

Where to have a party: Obviously, most parties for the youngest children will be held at home, where children feel most comfortable. A recreation or family room, even a garage or patio, offers more "kid-proof" space and less likelihood of damaging breakables. Toys not needed for the party should be put away since there may be disagreements about sharing. Refreshments should be served in the kitchen or other hard-surface floor area, or out of doors. Outdoor sites such as parks are ideal if the weather holds and there are extra adults present. (Always have a "rainy day" plan!) Caution: Any outdoor site should be inspected ahead of time at child's eye level for safety and supervisory needs.

For children over age 4 or 5, out-of-home sites can be wonderful for a party. The traditional favorites, bowling or sports events, have been enhanced by game rooms such as Discovery Zone or Fun and Games. Specialized programs for animal lovers are available through a number of individuals and groups including FONZ (Friends of the National Zoo) or Reston Animal Park. If your child is a budding dancer, Germantown Studio of Dance offers a ballerina birthday package.

What to plan: The family budget must be a realistic part of any planning. Parents often get caught up in keeping up with their child's friends. Costs for in-home performances of clowns, magicians or other shows vary from $125-$250 for a 45 to 60 minute program. The price may include invitations, favors for a specific number of guests and a special item for the birthday child. When refreshments and decorations are added, plus the family's gifts for the birthday child, a birthday party can be a significant investment. It helps parents to remember that the goal is not to outdo friends but to personalize the event with your child's special stamp. Spending a great deal of money may send the wrong message to your child. The question to keep asking is, "Who is the party for?"

Parties With a Theme

A novel approach to planning is offered by Parties in a Bag. For a cost of $50-$75, the family may select from over 30 themes a kit that includes invitations, decorations, favors, favor bags and a party planner which details games and suggestions for appropriate menus. The kit is sent directly to your home within three days of ordering via UPS. While the kit is set up for eight children, more may be added. You may also tailor your order by selecting only parts of the kit.

There are substantial advantages to having a performer or show at a party. One is that there is an instant theme. Discovering Science provides a range of science themes including astronauts, dinosaurs, bubbles, "slimey chemistry" and flying machines, according to owner Theresa Kurz. The most popular for children over age 8 is the "crime lab." Catriona's Castle will bring props and costumes based on specific stories for children to act out. Children are entertained and learn at the same time. If your family has the appropriate space and your child particularly enjoys animals, Zoo Shows will bring an environmental program involving live animals to your home. Cabaret Carol has, among many other acts, clowns, a selection of 20 popular cartoon/fictional characters or a petting farm with a pony for rides, rabbits, lambs and chicks.

(See Birthday Guide, page 319, for information on how to contact these and other birthday party providers.)

Children can still help prepare some of the decorations: placemats can be decorated with stickers matching the theme, placecards can be printed for each guest's seat (prevents jockeying at the table,) paper chains can be made to string around doors or windows, and edible treats such as dips or punch can have a child's touch. Preparing something with your child before the party gives you a chance to chat and slow down.

Plan for the Unexpected: What really matters is that thought, care and planning go into the event. Several entertainers cautioned that parents should not expect them to be babysitters. Adults need to be nearby to step in if needed to handle an unruly child. If a child is separated from the group for a few minutes and has the rules re-explained, usually he will settle down. First aid supplies need to be handy for the occasional small accident. Extra food and favors also cover a particularly hungry horde or a lost gift.

And a Peaceful Good Night: The most practiced hands in my neighborhood say to do minimal cleanup and collapse with your family. Go over the fun, laugh at the chaos and share your child's special moments over the Polaroid pictures that a friend or relative took. Despite your vow to the contrary, in your heart of hearts, you know you'll do it all again next year!

Creative Ideas
for Extra Special Birthdays

by Karen Leggett

O nce upon a time, birthdays were always held at home and children always came in party clothes. Now boys and girls come in everything and go everywhere—but there can still be a lot of charm, memories and good fun built into birthday parties at home.

Summer Parties

Do you have a summer birthday on the calendar this year? Recreate the Olympics in your backyard around whatever sport tantalizes your child. My son designed his own obstacle course, using bushes, balls, swings and slides. Everyone was timed with a stopwatch but we also made sure everyone received a gold medal (chocolate covered, of course!). Perhaps you remember the signature music of the Olympics when ABC was covering them — the big bass drum and the trumpet fanfare. With the help of the deep, legendary tones of my former colleague at WMAL, Bud Steele, we recorded the names of the young guests over that music and let it boom throughout the neighborhood as each child walked up for a medal: their grins were wider than the backyard! (When the real Olympics followed a few weeks later, one of the younger siblings asked her mother if the winners' medals were also filled with chocolate!)

Another summer birthday success was a backyard carnival—half a dozen simple games that could be run by a few older children; youngsters won tickets and exchanged them for small prizes. The birthday child helped choose and even make the games and everyone enjoyed the freedom of a real carnival—playing the same favorite game over and over again. There was enough activity to keep everyone busy for quite a long time.

My brother and sister-in-law sent a party of 3-year-olds on a backyard safari: stuffed animals and photographs of animals peeked out of trees and bushes and each child was equipped with binoculars made of two cardboard tubes. Green ribbon transformed the deck into a jungle. Lunch of "peanut butter and elephant" sandwiches, made with elephant cookie cutters, was served in zoo cages made of shoe boxes.

Karen Leggett worked for many years as a news broadcaster and program host at WMAL radio. She is currently reviewing children's books on the Radio Zone and writing on educational/youth issues for The Washington Post, Washington Parent, *ABC Radio, and* Voice of America. *She lives in Rockville with her husband and two children.*

Washington Parent editor Deborah Benke also used the birthday menu to complement her young son's love of trucks—the cake was cut into squares and shaped into a truck with cookie wheels; a miniature road construction vehicle decorated each child's piece.

Pirate parties are a perennial favorite. My mother and I used McCall's *Giant Golden Make-it Book* to throw a pirate party for my brother and many of the same ideas worked three decades later for my son. We used large white poster board as sails to turn the picnic table into a pirate ship; invitations were treasure maps and if you are so inclined, you can even use big pretzel sticks to let the kids have a sword fight.

Winter Parties

Now these wild affairs are all well and good outside; but what about the birthdays that fall in November or February? Not to worry. My brother, who has never allowed the child within him to die, fashioned a submarine facade in his basement and took a position behind one of the open port-holes, allowing himself to be the target for a barrage of wet sponges.

Susan Miller, now a Rockville mother throwing clever parties for her own children, remembers being a winter child who wished for a summer birthday.

She still recalls the time her mother turned her party into a picnic, with beach towels and sand toys all over the floor. Then there was the Hawaiian luau when her father drilled holes in coconuts to hold everyone's fruit punch. Now Susan paints flowers on plastic tea cups to make them look like porcelain for her own daughter's tea party. Everyone made a floppy paper garden hat; there was lump sugar for the tea and lemonade —one lump or two? Everyone decorated a flower pot and took home a tiny watering can with a packet of seeds.

My daughter just celebrated her eighth birthday with an Aladdin theme—and you (or the kids) really can make more of the party para-phernalia than you can buy even for these Disney parties. My son helped design the magic lamp invitations and every child used sequins and rib-bon to decorate a miniature flying carpet, cut from brightly colored rem-nants of material. We had 10 little girls standing in dreamy fantasy around our kitchen table, busily producing their own glittery masterpiece. Chil-dren also enjoy decorating their own goody bags—a fine way to keep occu-pied between early and late arrivals.

We borrowed a game from a British friend called "Pass the Parcel." Fill a box with a candy or small treat for each child; wrap the box as many times as there are youngsters at the party and under each wrapping, write down an action or task. The parcel is passed around the group while music is played; the child holding the parcel when the music stops un-wraps one layer and does whatever the note says—"sing like Jasmine," "hop on one foot," etc. Treats all around when the last layer is unwrapped!

Even the hitches in a homemade birthday party become the stuff of memories. I watched a bouquet of helium balloons sneak out of my car into the highest tree while I carried in the cake—and my husband forever captured me on the birthday videotape in a futile attempt to rescue them! Long after the party and umpteen snowstorms later, the balloons were still stuck in that tree.

But how on earth are you going to squeeze all this partying into your already crazy week? All the planning and preparation together won't take as long as you probably waited in line to sign up your youngster for swimming lessons in Montgomery County this spring! I put tassels on all those little flying carpets during one hockey practice and you can plan a lot of the details with your child while you're running all those interminable errands together. There are lots of books full of party suggestions and your children's interests will give you some clues. You tend to find the time and the ideas once you have the state of mind—let the child in you come alive again; rejoice that there is still a time when people look forward to birthdays and celebrate! The day after our Aladdin adventure my daughter asked with all sincerity, "Let's do it again tomorrow! I'll be 9!"

 # Resources

Birthday Guide

Amazing Events and Fabulous Parties-Santa Claus Productions: Emphasizing magical interaction-humor-variety (games, movement, magic, pranks, finger painting, crafts). Experienced with preschool to adult. Super heroes, Princesses, Genies, Dinosaurs, Madhatters, "Murders," Ponies. 301-946-3471.

Archaeology for Kids: Children dig an archaeological site with professional archaeologists. They excavate authentic prehistoric and historic artifacts and bones. 301-270-0575.

Bethesda Academy of Performing Arts Children's Theatre: Children enjoy a quality children's theater birthday party. Three options: tickets only, tickets and party room, or tickets, party room and arts workshop. 301-320-2550.

Bethesda Theatre Cafe: Family movies on most Saturdays, rated G or PG. Parties for 10 or more, including food, beverage and film. 301-656-3337.

Biggo Productions: Entertainment for birthday parties. Clowns, magicians, costumed characters and more.

Bingo & Buddies: Clowning and magical entertainment. Jugglers, face painters, stilt walkers, caricaturists and "balloonatics." 301-422-9367.

Cabaret Carol: Character performances for children's birthday entertainment. Barbie, Cinderella, Princess Jasmine, etc. 301-422-9367.

Catriona's Castle: Hands-on children's theater for one or two hours. Children act out story in costumes. 301-972-7549.

Charlotte Russell's Musical Experience: You provide food, decorations and space; Charlotte provides games and simple paper crafts. 703-356-5195.

Chesapeake Recreation Rentals: Party Amusement Attractions In Your Own Backyard! Space walk or play in hundreds of colorful balls, ride the gyro or try the carousel. 410-893-9323 and 800-954-0140.

Children's Parties with Barbara Sontz: Program includes Raffi and Disney songs, puppets, circle games, rhythm instruments and the child's favorites. 703-323-5917.

Christian & Company: "One-stop shopping" for birthday entertainment and the exclusive source for "Christian the Magician" and "A Clown Company." 703-425-6663.

Circus Day Productions: Original birthday parties, featuring traditional and clown magicians. Educational assemblies for daycares, schools, libraries and community events. 410-730-3572.

Connie's Confectionary: Chocolate birthday parties. Cake, ice cream, punch and the fun of molding and then eating chocolate candy. 301-428-1400.

Corky and Co: Ages 4-10. A blend of music, puppets, magic, ventriloquism and comedy. 301-681-8757.

Discovering Science: Young scientists can explore dinosaurs, space bubbles, slime, aerodynamics. Challenging science experiments. 301-718-6208.

Discovery Zone Fun Center: Funbelievable Fitness is the name of the game with slides, tubes, tunnels, mazes, obstacle courses and mountains to climb, plus a private party room and host/hostess. 301-231-0505.

Ellen's Entertainment: Birthday party and audience participation specialists. Clowns, magicians, princesses, Purple Dinosaur, Bunny, Big Song Bird, Ninja Turtle and your child's favorite characters. 301-596-6443.

Friends of the National Zoo: FONZ family members can enjoy birthday parties at the National Zoo. 202-673-4961.

Kaydee Puppets: Will come to your home or party location and share familiar fairytales. Shows are geared for ages 3-6. 703-560-2108.

Kids Moving Company: Participatory entertainment with movement, music and imagination. 301-656-1543.

Magic with a Comic Touch: Comedy magic with lots of participation. 301-589-3021.

Music Alive: "Participatory" music party for children ages 3-6. Music with movement, stories, rhythm instruments and nursery rhymes. 301-951-6289.

The Music Man: provides musical entertainment for your child's party, incorporating singing, movement, games and instruments in a 45-minute session. 301-946-8863.

O.B. the Clown: Magic and entertainment by one of their own: 11-year-old clown does magic tricks for kids 2-6-years-old. Props disappear, silly stuff happens and cookies bake by magic. 301-963-3129.

Olney Theatre: Presents 4 professional productions for families and numerous special events yearly. Have a unique Birthday/Theatre party before or after a show in the rustic Actors Residence next door! 301-924-5269.

Party Central: Party Central runs the show providing entertainers, animals, moon bounces, ball crawls, etc. 301-977-0010.

Party Gym: Comes to you with a 50-minute playtime of Tot gym or Music gym designed for ages 1-10. Games and activities with a parachute, tumble ball, innertubes, tunnel, teeter totter, balance beam, musical instruments, music, songs, balloons, hoops, bean bags and pinata 703-281-7754.

Party Ponies Co: Operating for the past 10 years, providing pony rides, a petting farm, face painting, balloon sculpted animals and sleigh rides (Dec.- March, no snow required). Bring entertainment to your school or house. Insured, licensed. 703-690-2880.

Potomac Horse Center: Party at the horse farm. Hay rides, pony rides, candy in the haystack hunts, apple bobbing, stable tours and a special party room. 301-208-0200.

Reston Animal Park: Celebrate your birthday with some real party animals. Reston brings the animals to you, or you can have the party at the park. 703-759-6761.

Sportland America: Activities include: kiddie rides and play area, adventure challenge, roller skating/blading, miniature golf, arcade games, pizza, prizes and much more. Party hotline 301-840-8404.

Zoo Show: Bringing fascinating animal programs to your home, featuring: starfish, monkeys, alligators, hawks and owls (depending on availability and season). 410-265-8009.

Birthday Supplies

Tuesday Morning: See Yellow Pages for locations around the Beltway. Close-out retail, everything is 60-90 percent off. Cutlery, paper goods.

The Party Store: 1803 Wisconsin Ave., NW, Washington, D.C. 202-333-3200. Party favors for kids of all ages.

Marjacks: 1352 Holten Ln., Langley Park, MD, 301-434-8500. Basic party supplies, noisemakers, balloons, wide range of color selection, bulk foods, fruit cocktails, sodas, catering supplies.

Party Mart Discount: 174 Halpine Rd., Rockville, MD 301-770-7110. All party supplies, discount store.

The Paper Store: 7712 Woodmont Ave. Bethesda, MD, 301-657-2100. 11 locations in the metro area. Everything for children's parties.

Creative Kids Party Planners: Everything from cakes and favors to decorations and entertainment. Power Rangers, Purple Dinosaurs, tea parties, theme packages and more. Complete party packages delivered. 703-968-4411.

MJDesigns: A complete assortment of traditional party items including balloon bouquets, party favors, cards, gift wrap, novelties, confetti, cake decorating and candy making supplies, gifts at great prices. Locations in Maryland and Virginia.

Now & Then: Takoma Park store with good assortment of small items. Party invitations, decorations, favor bags, gift wrap and stickers. 301-270-2210.

Party In A Bag: offers children's themed party bags. Your Party Bag includes customized invitations, thank yous, decorations, paper products, games, supplies, favors, a party planner and extra surprises! Packages are ordered by phone and shipped within 3 days. 301-776-5395.

Toys . . . Etc.: Everything for a special party; unique favors, party bags, balloons, old-time candy, games and even a how-to party book. 301-229-8300.

Whirligigs & Whimsies: Special party favors, unusual party bags, balloons and an extraordinary selection of goodies. 301-897-4940.

Economy Party Supplies: One of the area's largest discount supply stores. Over 40 different children's party patterns in stock. Balloon delivery available. 703-237-2789.

Special Cakes

Custom Cake Design, Rockville, MD, 301-216-1100.
Custom-made work, specializes in sculpture-figure piping, three-dimensional, life-like look.

Heidelberg Pastry Shoppe, Arlington, VA, 703-527-8394.
Cake decorating computer. Bring a photo of children's faces or animals to be reproduced on a cake.

Connie's Confectionary, Inc., Germantown Commons Shopping Center, 13020 Middlebrook Rd., Germantown, MD 301-428-1400. Storybook cakes, doll cakes, copyrighted characters, etc.

Further Reading

Atyeo, Marilyn. *Birthdays: A Celebration*. Atlanta, Humanics Limited, 1984.

Brokaw, Meredith and Annie Gilbar. *The Penny Whistle Party Planner*. St. Louis: Fireside Books, 1992.

Ellison, Virginia. *The Pooh Party Book*. New York: Dell, 1991.

Guarniccia, Steven. *The Birthday Party Book*. New York: Crown Publishers, 1987.

Levine, Shar and Allison Grafton. *The Science Party Book: Simple Instructions for Spy Parties, Bubble Parties and Much, Much More*. New York, NY: Wiley, 1990.

Marzollo, Jean. *Birthday Parties for Children-How to Give Them, How to Survive Them*. New York, NY: Harper, 1993.

Thornberry, Milo Shannon. *The Alternate Celebrations Catalogue*. From Alternatives 404-961-0102.

Warner, Penny. *Happy Birthday Parties*. New York, NY: St. Martin, 1985.

Cooking is More than a PB&J

by Roberta Gottesman

Learning about food and cooking can be a wonderful way for you and your children to spend "quality" time together. You can introduce them to a world of cuisines and teach them the pleasure of creating a meal that will be appreciated by the entire family. Many favorite recipes are handed down through the generations to create a family identity. The holidays are often the times when these recipes are shared and great grandma's favorite dishes are brought to the table with pride. Children can join in the rituals and preparation of these meals feeling they have played an important role. This gives children a special sense of their own tradition and culture.

And, if cooking is the window to a culture, then through different ethnic cuisines children can explore the world. We are lucky in the Washington metropolitan area that there is such a diversity of cultures and their cuisines. There are specialty markets from Indian to Thai to Northern Italian featuring ingredients and foods from these lands. Exploring these markets to prepare an exotic meal is a marvelous way to give children an international adventure . . . and then you can explore the often inexpensive ethnic restaurants around town with your children, who have developed sophisticated palates through the cooking and tasting experience.

There are also many international fairs held throughout the year at churches and in a diversity of ethnic neighborhoods where children can sample specialties. It's great fun to expose children to new tastes (and eating utensils!) once their interest has been piqued.

 **Resources**

Ethnic Markets to Explore with Your Children

Aphrodite - Middle Eastern and Greek
5886 Leesburg Pike
Falls Church, VA 703-931-5055
A large assortment of olives, cheeses, pickles, nuts, olive oil, fresh meats and several types of breads; prepared dishes include hummus, spinach triangles or stuffed grape leaves.

Roberta Gottesman, President of Piccolo Press and editor of this book, is a lawyer who has written numerous books, including The Child and the Law, The Music Lover's Guide to Europe, *and* Finding Fun and Friends in Washington.

Eko Food Store - Sub-Saharan Africa
6507 Annapolis Rd.
Landover Hills, MD 301-341-5050
African and West Indian foods, herbs and spices. Two kinds of
Ghanian breads, one Jamaican. Also long-grain rice, gari and black-
eyed peas. Fresh vegetables and frozen foods.

Merkato Market - Ethiopian
2116 18th St., NW
Washington, DC 202-483-9499
A large array of spices, as well as spice blends, fresh meats, Ethiopian
coffee, breads; also Egyptian fava beans, rice, barley, bulgur,
chickpeas and dals. Recipes available.

Caribbean Market II- East Indies
7505 New Hampshire Avenue
Langley Park, MD 301-439-5288
A plethora of West Indian products such as spices, Irish moss,
vanillas, meats, vegetables, canned products and fish.

Casa Lebrato - Salvadoran
1733 Columbia Rd., NW
Washington, DC 202-234-0099
Products from Latin and Central America.

Da Hua Market - Chinese
632 H St., NW
Washington, DC 202-789-4020
A large frozen-food section, fresh produce, many spices, condiments,
Chinese snacks, and spices. They also have fresh meat, fish and fowl,
utensils, woks and cookbooks.

The Deli - Italian
480 Elden St.
Herndon, VA, 703-435-9085
Many different kinds of pasta, fresh mozzarella, prosciutto, smoked
and fresh sausage, bel paese, and other Italian specialties; wines.

Duangrat Oriental Food Mart - Thai
5888 Leesburg Pike
Falls Church, VA 703-578-0622
Huge selection of Thai products. Fresh produce, fish and fruit. The
owners operate a well known restaurant behind the market.

Gira International Persian Grocery and Cafe
3250 Duke St.
Alexandria, VA 703-370-3632
A combination cafe/grocery where you can order prepared Persian
dishes, buy cookbooks and ingredients such as spices, dried legumes,
herbs, phyllo dough and more.

India Spices and Appliances
3901 Wilson Blvd.
Arlington, VA 703-522-0149
Indian teas, cookbooks, spices, rices and locally made desserts. They
also have some fresh produce.

Indian Super Market - Indian & Ethiopian
8107 Fenton St.
Silver Spring, MD 301-589-8423
Indian spices, chutneys, canned foods, breads and frozen dishes. A large selection of spices for Ethiopian foods and Ethiopian breads.
La Cuscatleca Grocery Store - Latin American
14412 Jefferson Davis Highway
Woodbridge, VA 703-490-4907
Products from many Latin American countries, fresh meat and produce, chorizos, and Andean herbs and spices.

Lebanese Butcher - Middle Eastern
113 East Annandale Rd.
Falls Church, VA 703-533-2903
Halal meat such as veal, lamb, beef, chicken and spiced lamb sausages; they also have Lebanese prepared dishes: hummous, labneh, baba ghanouj. Fresh produce, spices and other Lebanese items.

Mikado - Japanese
4709 Wisconsin Ave., NW
Washington, DC 202-362-7700
Fresh fish for sushi and sashimi, as well as ready-made sushi. Wide selection of fresh produce used in Japanese cooking.

Nipa House Emporium - Philippine
5509 Leesburg Pike
Falls Church, VA 703-379-0595
Coconut products and other items from the Philippines, including ice cream.

The Next Step: Restaurant Readiness

Ready to compare that great dish your family cooked last week with restaurant cuisine? Here are some questions to ask yourself about restaurant readiness.

 # Questions to ask yourself

1. How much patience does your child have—can he or she sit through a meal in a restaurant?
2. Are you up to entertaining your young child in the restaurant? (If you're not, you may suffer the consequences—a fidgety or unhappy child.)
3. What books or toys can you bring to entertain your child?

 # Questions to ask the restaurant staff

1. Does the restaurant welcome children?
2. How crowded is the restaurant—is there a long wait?
3. Do you have booster seats?
4. Do you have baby changing facilities in the restroom?

 **Resources**

Further Reading

Koralek, Derry. Editor 13th Edition, *Going Places With Children*. Rockville, Md.: Green Acres School, 1992.

Lawson, Jim C. *The Washington Ethnic Food Store Guide*. Washington, DC: Ardmore Publications, 1992.

Washingtonian Magazine, "Cheap Eats" section each month.

Washington Post Weekend section, September 9, 1994. "Bring the Family."

Exercising Body and Mind Together

by Roberta Gottesman

S taying fit and healthy as a family goes hand-in-hand with eating nutritious meals and providing the best medical care for your children. And, by sharing an interest in participatory sports parents and children form a lifelong bond that offers them a chance to enjoy the activity as a family.

Children who begin taking ski, golf, or tennis lessons when they are 5 or 6 years old progress quickly and can soon join their parents on the slopes or golf course for outings and family vacations. Family hikes and bike rides offer a chance to exercise and have fun together, close to home or further afield.

Every neighborhood has a community center where families can enjoy a variety of classes to get everyone up to speed. In addition to offering special courses, the local department of recreation is a place for all family members to exercise year-round, both indoors and out. The following should help interested families find a convenient source of fun in their communities.

Resources

District Of Columbia

Department of Recreation and Parks
3149 16th Street, NW
Washington, DC 20010
202-673-7671 (Recreation Info.), 202-673-7671 (Dial-An-Event)
The District maintains 104 community centers and recreation facilities. Free biannual catalogues and monthly calendars available in local libraries.

Maryland

Gaithersburg Department of Parks and Recreation
502 South Frederick Avenue
Gaithersburg, MD 20877
301-258-6350
The *City of Gaithersburg Recreation Guide* is printed quarterly and is available at the Montgomery Village Library, all city schools and all City of Gaithersburg facilities. There is information on courses and special events, on the activities of the Casey Community Center, the Gaithersburg Aquatic Center and the Summit Hall Farm Park Pool.

Maryland-National Capital Park and Planning Commission
& Montgomery County Parks Department (MNCPPC)
9500 Brunett Avenue
Silver Spring, MD 20901
301-495-2525
Park It! A Guide to Parks in Montgomery and Prince George's County
includes maps of many of the 700 parks and facilities owned by the
Commission in both Montgomery and Prince George's counties. The
publication includes information on campsites, stables, tennis courts,
swimming pools, boating and fishing, ice skating, historic sites, arts
facilities, gardens, nature centers and special facilities. *Park It!* is
free, and Montgomery County's *Guide to Parks* is available at the
regional parks for $2.

Montgomery County Department of Recreation
12210 Bushey Drive
Silver Spring, MD 20902-1099
301/217-6820
The Guide to Recreation and Leisure Services is mailed to all county
residents and is available at libraries or by calling the above number.
Call 301-217-6880 for information on Arts and Leisure classes.

Prince George's County Department of Parks and Recreation
6600 Kenilworth Avenue
Riverdale, MD 20737
301-699-2407
The *Seasonal Guide*, mailed to all Prince George's County residents,
lists the classes and activities in the County's more than 35
community centers and nature centers. Although information on the
County as a whole is available at the number above, more details are
available at the regional offices:
Northern Area: 301-445-4500; Central Area: 301-249-9220; Southern
Area: 301-292-9006

Rockville Department of Recreation and Parks
111 Maryland Avenue
Rockville, MD 20850
301-309-3340
The City of Rockville Recreation and Parks Guide, available at
Rockville City Hall, the Rockville Library, and the Twinbrook Library,
details several hundred offerings in aquatics, arts, sports, fitness,
crafts, family events and senior programs.

Takoma Park Recreation Department
7500 Maple Avenue
Takoma Park, MD 20912
301-270-4048
The *Recreation Guide* is available at the Takoma Park Recreation
Department and its next door neighbor, the City Library.

Virginia

Alexandria Department of Recreation, Parks & Cultural Activities
1108 Jefferson Street
Alexandria, VA 22314
703-838-4831
In Your Neighborhood, mailed to all residents and available in libraries, recreation centers, and the Torpedo Art Factory, details the classes and programs offered at 7 pools, 11 recreation centers and numerous parks and ball fields in Alexandria.

Arlington County Department of Parks, Recreation and Community Resources
2100 Clarendon Boulevard
Arlington, VA 22201
703-358-3313
Information on Arlington County's 10 community centers and park and recreation activities is published in *Education and Recreation in Arlington*, available at all county libraries and recreation centers.

Fairfax County Department of Recreation and Community Services
12011 Government Center Parkway, Suite 1050
Fairfax, VA 22035-1115
703-324-5500
703-324-4FUN (4386)
Sponsors a wide curriculum of classes and other activities at Fairfax County's seven community centers and other locales. Profiles of these programs are found in *Leisure Pursuits and Classes, Etc.*, mailed to all residents and available at county libraries.

Fairfax County Park Authority
3701 Pender Drive
Fairfax, VA 22030
703-246-5574
Fairfax County Park Authority manages 8 recreation centers, 6 nature centers, 3 lakefront parks and various historic sites. *PARKtakes*, the agency's quarterly listing of classes, events, services and facilities, is mailed free to subscribers. For a free subscription, call 703-246-5588.

Falls Church Department of Recreation and Parks
Falls Church Community Center
223 Little Falls Street
Falls Church, VA 22046
703/241-5077
Schedule of Classes and Community Programs is available at the Falls Church Community Center and library.

Herndon Parks and Recreation Department
Herndon Community Center
814 Ferndale Avenue
Herndon, VA 22070
703-435-6868
Quarterly brochure with details on classes and facilities is mailed to all residents and is available at the Herndon Community Center. Over 1,000 class offerings and activities include sports, arts, festivals and fairs, theater trips and health and fitness. From water babies to seniors, the Herndon Community Center has something for everyone.

McLean Community Center
1234 North Ingleside Avenue
McLean, VA 22101
703-790-0123
Classes, fitness programs, a teen center, the highly acclaimed Alden
Theatre and much more are sponsored by the McLean Community
Center. The *Quidnunk*, published three times a year, has all the details
and is available at the Center.

Reston Community Center
Hunters Woods Center
2310 Colts Neck Road
Reston, VA 22091
703-476-4500
National touring productions join with local companies in the
performing arts program at this center, which also offers an aquatics
program, classes to please all interests and special events for adults
and young people. The monthly newsletter, *CenterStage*, is delivered
to area homes, and a complete schedule of classes and activities is
published three times a year.

Vienna Parks and Recreation Department
Vienna Community Center
120 Cherry Street, SE
Vienna, VA 22180
703-255-6360
Quarterly brochure detailing all department activities available on
request.

★ Special Needs

Adapted Sports Association, Inc.
6832 Marlette, Marlette, MI 48453

American Athletic Association for the Deaf
3916 Lantern Dr., Silver Spring, MD 20902

Blind Outdoor Leisure Development
533 E. Main St., Aspen, CO 81611

National Association of Sports for Cerebral Palsy
P.O. Box 3874 Amity Station, New Haven, CT 06511

National Foundation for Wheelchair Tennis
3055 Birch St., Newport Beach, CA 92660

National Handicapped Sports and Recreation Association
1341 G St., NW, Washington, DC 20005
Farragut Station, P.O. Box 33141, Washington, DC 20033

North American Riding for the Handicapped Association, Inc.
P.O. Box 100, Ashburn, VA 22011

Special Olympics, International
1325 G St., NW, Suite 500, Washington, DC 20005-4709

Planting a Garden With Your Child

by Diana Rubin, J.D.
and Beth Werhle, A.S.L.A.

Worried that your children are watching too much television or playing Nintendo all day long? Tired of arts and crafts projects that leave glue, sequins and feathers all over the house? Concerned that your kids aren't eating enough fruits and vegetables? If you answered yes to even one of these questions, it's time to think about planting a garden with your kids.

If you do, your harvest will include a child with greater respect for the environment, a sense of how to nurture living things, an increased willingness to eat the fruits (and vegetables) of his own labor and a realization that food doesn't grow on grocery shelves or in restaurants.

Planting a garden, indoors or out, is relatively inexpensive and easy. It gets you and the kids outdoors together. And it's fun! With a little parental help, gardening can be enjoyed by all but the youngest child. All you need is a small plot of land, a balcony or a sunny windowsill. Add a few gardening tools, soil nutrients, mulch and seeds. Your kids will supply the only other necessary ingredient—a willingness to get dirty!

For an outdoor garden, plant anytime after the last frost date—April 15 in Washington and April 30 in the suburbs. But you can start your seeds indoors four to six weeks before the last frost date. And you can plant all the way up to June 15, provided you use seedlings after mid-May.

Step One: Picking a Plot

Giving kids their own yard space to cultivate instills a sense of pride in their garden and creates a feeling of ownership. Those feelings will motivate them when it comes to taking care of the garden.

The smallest plot that's workable is three feet by three feet, but a somewhat larger area is preferable. The spot should receive at least six hours of direct sunlight daily, and be near a water source. One good choice is an area set aside within an adult's garden where the soil is already prepared for planting.

Diana Rubin, J.D., is currently a freelance writer and lobbyist representing the Obsessive-Compulsive Disorder Foundation on Capitol Hill. She is the founder and Executive Director of the Trichotillomania Support Network of Greater D.C., a nonprofit dedicated to helping compulsive hairpullers.

Beth Wehrle, A.S.L.A., is a landscape architect who works in the Washington area. She teaches landscape design at George Washington University when not gardening with her children.

There are several factors to consider in deciding how large to make your child's garden. On the one hand, the larger the space, the more varieties of plants you can grow. Children like variety, and it increases the chance of success. But it's easy to plant more in May than a child can take care of in August. A good rule of thumb is the younger the child, the smaller the garden.

Step Two: Getting Ready

After you've picked your child's plot, it's time to visit the garden center. Take the kids with you. They'll relish choosing what to grow by looking at pictures on the seed envelopes, touching the vats of flowers and thinking of fruits and vegetables they like to eat.

You'll need to stock up on the following essentials: one adult shovel, enough soil nutrients (leaf compost, peat moss or composted manure) to cover your garden two inches thick, enough mulch to cover the ground two to three inches thick, an organic basic fertilizer and seeds or seedlings. For each child, you'll also need a rake, a trowel and a watering can or hose, both with a spray attachment. Most gardening supply stores carry child-size implements. It's worth paying more for the metal tools, because the plastic ones don't last.

If you are feeling thrifty, you can procure free leaf compost from a number of local municipalities whose phone numbers we've listed below. Or, pick up "Zoo Doo" at the National Zoo. Children get a kick out of learning that manure can fertilize gardens, and they'll get a subtle message about recycling.

A few general principles should guide you as you help your children make their selections. Kids like to see a quick response to the attention they've lavished on their piece of land. Their sense of time is limited, and a few weeks can seem like an eternity when they're waiting for results. So steer them toward plants that grow quickly. The fastest-growing vegetable is a radish, which takes a month to appear.

And since nothing grows a gardener faster than success, choose plants that are easy to grow. Carrots, leaf lettuce, sugar snap peas, tomatoes, cherry tomatoes and strawberries are all good choices. For a larger garden, consider pumpkins, squash, peppers or cucumbers. Foolproof flowers include marigolds, zinnias, snapdragons, black-eyed susans and sunflowers.

Kids also like to grow plants that have personality, fragrance, texture and color. They'll be tickled by faces in a pansy or sunflower; by the fragrance of pinks or lemon verbena; by the texture of a wooly lamb's ear, and by the vibrant color of snapdragons or cosmos. If you're growing vegetables, choose a mixture of vegetables that produce food above ground, like squash, tomatoes and pumpkins, and below, like carrots and radishes.

These suggestions are just guidelines, though. The ultimate choice should rest with the children. Letting children choose what to grow is the key to keeping them involved and interested in their garden.

Step Three: Preparing to Plant

You'll need to work on the soil before you plant. Plain old dirt is never adequate for growing healthy plants. Kids will love this task, as it gives them license to mess around in the dirt.

Be sure they wear clothes you don't care about, and let them go. There's nothing like the sensual pleasure of digging in the dirt, making holes and discovering what lives in the ground to turn children on to gardening.

First, remove all the weeds in the plot by the roots. Next, use the shovel to dig and loosen the dirt. It's best to dig about a foot deep, breaking up all the clumps. Depending on your children's ages and strength, they may need help with this step. If the soil is too hard to dig, water the ground and wait a day. Breaking up the soil is an important step in starting a healthy garden.

Spread the soil nutrients—either compost, peat moss or Zoo Doo—about two inches thick over the loosened soil. Mix it into the soil by digging and turning the soil with your shovel. Then, smooth out the bed with your rake, leveling all the bumps. Use your hands to raise the seed rows into mounds or hills. Be sure to make a path around the outside of the garden, and in between the rows, if space permits. Paths help the child avoid pressing down the newly turned soil or stepping on the plants.

Next, spread about two inches of mulch over the entire garden and rake smooth. Tell your kids that mulch is like a blanket for your plants that keeps the soil moist and keeps the weeds out.

Step Four: Planting Your Garden

Soak your seeds overnight to speed sprouting. But remember wet seeds must be planted the next day or they are useless.

Pull the mulch away from the row where you will be planting. The seed package directions will tell you how deep and far apart to plant the seeds. But the concept of spacing is difficult for small children; they have no idea how large a plant will actually grow. Don't worry if they plant too many seeds in one place. You can help them thin out the seriously overcrowded seedlings later, if necessary. And as a general rule, resist the urge to oversupervise your child's gardening. Let the kids have fun and see for themselves what results.

After the seed is in the earth, press down the soil gently and water carefully. Don't water so much that it puddles around the plant, or the seeds will wash away. Explain to your children that the plants are thirsty and need to drink, but too much water can drown them. Until the seeds sprout, the children should check the soil with their fingers daily to make sure it has not dried out. If it has, water it. Once seedlings have sprouted, spread the mulch in a thin cover around the plants to keep the moisture in the ground and reduce weeds.

If your children are planting seedlings, make sure they water the soil first. Pull the mulch back and dig a hole deep and wide enough to fit the roots. Put the seedling in the hole, covering the roots and the lower part of the stem with soil. Water gently, and then spread the mulch around it. Check the seedlings every day to make sure they don't dry out. They require extra watering in the beginning.

It's a good idea to mark the rows you've planted by writing the names of the plants and the child on the backs of popsicle sticks.

Step Five: Tending Your Garden

Tending the garden is essential, and can be one of the most enjoyable parts of gardening with your child.

Working in the garden allows kids to explore the world of the earth and its creatures. They can dig, hide toys, play hide and seek and pretend to be all sorts of things. And they are fascinated with what they find in the dirt. An ordinary rock to you is a shiny treasure to a 4-year-old. Caterpillars, earthworms, ladybugs, butterflies and spiders are a source of endless fascination. They also serve a useful function by pollinating plants, preying on undesirable insects, and conditioning the soil. Get out the bug jar and take a moment to marvel over the infinite variety of mother nature's offspring.

Regular watering is a must and a task children love. There's nothing like an excuse to get wet to whet their interest. When there is little or no rain, water the garden twice a week, until the soil feels as damp as a wrung-out sponge. When there has been rain, and you're not sure whether your garden needs water, just check the soil. If it feels dry, get out the watering can. Don't use too much water, or too forceful a spray, or the plant will drown, and the seeds will wash away.

While watering, your child should be on the lookout for insect damage or disease. If there are holes in the leaves, look for caterpillars, snails or slugs. Some can be picked out by hand and thrown in the garbage.

Many bugs are too small to catch by hand, but don't use chemical pesticides or insecticides in a child's garden. A strong squirt of soapy water will usually get rid of small bugs, and give the kids a thrill. Natural methods of pest control can also help your child appreciate that a pesticide-free vegetable tastes great, though it may look less than perfect. Remind your kids that not all bugs are harmful.

One task no gardener can afford to shirk is weeding. Try to get the entire root of the weed, or it will grow back.

Another job is to fertilize your garden regularly with a basic organic fertilizer. Fertilize the first week after planting and then every three or four weeks, following the directions on the package. Remember to water thoroughly after fertilizing.

Although tending a garden is a lot of work, it needn't be tedious. Hold your child's interest by making a game of garden tasks. See who can pull the largest weed, or the biggest root. Pretend you're a detective, hunting for helpful or harmful insects inhabiting your garden. Make believe you are a gentle rain shower while watering the garden.

It's hard for the supervising adult to judge how long a child can garden at a given time. A good rule of thumb is to limit each work session to

20 minutes. It's critical not to force a child to garden after his patience, endurance or interest is exhausted. There's no surer way to turn gardening into a dreaded chore. In fact, assume you will do some of the work yourself, at first. As the years go by, if you have instilled a love of gardening in your child, this initial investment will more than pay off.

Step Six: Waiting

Waiting must be mentioned because a child's concept of time is much less developed than an adult's, and a week can seem like an eternity. Since it takes a month for even the fastest growing vegetable to grow, it's easy to see why waiting is the hardest part of gardening for children.

To make the wait easier, mark a calendar with the date you planted your seeds or seedlings. Note the days you water and the days you weed. For young children who don't read, use stickers to mark the calendar, or let them draw pictures of what they did in the garden. Show them how long they can expect to wait for their crops.

Step 7: The Harvest

The harvest is one of the best parts of gardening. It's a time to sit back, smell the flowers and count the pea pods. Chomp on a baby carrot you've just pulled out of the earth. Help your child make a bouquet for the dinner table, and hear the pride as he tells a friend he grew the flowers himself. Make nature bracelets by taping scotch tape, sticky side out, around your child's wrist, and pasting petals from her garden onto the bracelet.

And, don't forget to eat what you've grown. Make your own dip and have a dipping party with the freshly harvested vegetables. You'll be amazed at how your children relish eating vegetables they previously scorned simply because they grew them in their own garden.

If Your Garden Is Shady

You can grow all sorts of vegetables and flowers with only four hours of direct sunlight a day. When growing in the shade, start your garden with seedlings, not seeds. Good vegetable choices include radishes, carrots, leaf lettuce, strawberries, raspberries and blueberries. Begonias, impatiens, coleus, browallia and pansies will also do well in the shady garden. If your yard gets less than four hours of direct sunlight, consider planting Virginia bluebells, trillum, crested iris, bleeding hearts, chelones or ferns, all woodland flowers native to the Washington area.

If You Don't Have A Yard

You don't need a yard to have a garden. If you have a balcony or patio, plant a whiskey half-barrel with a cherry tomato plant and add a few petunias around the edges for color. Smaller vegetables, such as radishes and leaf lettuce, can be grown in a barrel garden or a window box.

Make a potting mixture that is two-thirds soil and one-third composted manure, leaf mold or peat moss. You'll need to water more often, because the soil in containers dries out more quickly than the ground. Test your container by sticking your finger in the pot. If the top inch is completely dry, it's time to water.

Just for the Fun of It

Once you get the basics down, there are literally hundreds of ways to make gardening come alive for your children. Try growing a pizza garden by planting tomatoes, peppers, oregano and basil. Carve the child's name into a growing pumpkin with a ballpoint pen, just breaking the skin. As the pumpkin grows, the name will grow too.

Or, make a tepee with easy to grow runner beans and morning glory vines. Tie together six bamboo poles approximately six feet long in the shape of a tepee and plant three or four seedlings or seeds at the base of each pole. Attach trellis netting to the poles to give the tepee more of an enclosed feeling from the start. Trellis netting can be bought anywhere seeds are sold. Morning glories grow very quickly and should begin to cover the tepee within a month.

There's no end to the ways you and your children can enjoy gardening together, if you just use your imagination. But don't overlook the simple pleasures of gardening with your children. Seeing whose fingernails are dirtier, or sharing a glass of cool lemonade when you're hot and sweaty, admiring the colors in your first marigold, or biting into a tomato right there in the garden—these are the small moments that gardening memories are made of. Once you open the garden gate to your children, they may never turn on the television or play Nintendo again!

Resources

Local Gardens to Enjoy with Children

Aztec Garden, OAS Building
17th St. & Constitution Ave., NW
Washington, DC 202-458-3000.
(M-F 9:30 a.m.-5 p.m.)
In addition to seasonal plants and gardens are the banana, coffee, palm and rubber trees.

Brookside Gardens
1500 Glenallan Ave.
Wheaton, MD, 301-949-8230.
(Conservatories open M-F 10 a.m.-5 p.m. Sat, Sun and holidays 10:30-4. Grounds open daily 9 a.m.-sunset.) Partially handicapped accessible. 50 acre public display garden. Free. The grounds feature conservatories and 11 types of gardens. Children like the Japanese teahouse and lake with its ducks, geese and fish. The Horticultural Library has some children's books.

Constitution Gardens
West Potomac Park
17-23rd Streets and Constitution Ave., NW
Washington, DC 202-485-9880.
(Open daily dawn-dusk)
Strollers permitted. Includes a six-acre lake with a cultivated island.

Dumbarton Oaks Gardens
1703 32nd St., NW
Washington DC, 202-342-3200.
(2 p.m.-5 p.m.; April-October 2-6 p.m.) Strollers permitted. 10 acres
of gardens located in Georgetown. Winding paths through an expertly
manicured garden makes for an enchanting experience.

East Potomac Park
Haines Point
Ohio Drive, SW
Washington, DC
202-426-6765. 619-7222, public affairs.
(Open daily dawn-dusk)
Picnic tables. Over 100 acres of park, including Victorian garden,
which is maintained by local residents.

Glover Archbold Park
202-426-6833.
(Open daily dawn-dusk)
100 acres with picnic facilities.

Green Spring Gardens Park
4601 Green Spring Rd.
Alexandria, VA, 703-642-5173.
(Grounds open daily dawn-dusk)
Strollers permitted. Picnicking permitted. Gardens include fruit
orchard, vegetable gardens, a greenhouse, two lakes and natural
woods.

Hillwood Gardens
4155 Linnean Ave. NW
Washington, DC 202-686-5807.
(Tuesday-Saturday 11 a.m.-3 p.m.)
They have a Japanese garden, a rose garden, a French garden and a
greenhouse.

Kenilworth Aquatic Gardens
Kenilworth Ave. & Douglas St. NE
Washington, DC 202-426-6905.
(7 a.m.-5 p.m.)
Strollers permitted. Over 100,000 water plants on 11 acres of ponds,
as well as frogs, turtles, etc.

National Arboretum
3501 New York Ave. NE
Washington, DC 202-475-4815.
(Weekdays 8 a.m.-5 p.m., Sundays 10 a.m.-5 p.m.) Strollers
permitted. Japanese garden, 10 a.m.-2 p.m. daily. Picnicking
permitted. This 444-acre garden contains an aquatic garden, a
Japanese garden and a dwarf conifer area.

U.S. Botanical Garden
1st St. & Maryland Ave., SW
Washington D.C. 202-225-8333
(9 a.m.-5 p.m., June-August 9 a.m.-9 p.m.)
These gardens contain a jungle, a waterfall and a cacti garden. They also have special activities.

Where to call for free or inexpensive composted leaf mold:

In Virginia as a Fairfax County resident, you can pick up free composted leaf mold at one of two transfer stations: 4418 West Ox Road, or 850 Furnace Road in Lorton. Call 703-631-1179 for more information.

In Vienna, call 703-255-6300 to have it delivered free.

In Arlington, you can have cheap composted leaf mold delivered by calling 703-358-3636.

In the District call 202-727-4825 for free delivery of composted leaf mold.

Maryland no longer provides free delivery.

Further Reading

Bjork, Christina and Lena Anderson. *Linnea's Windowsill Garden*. New York: Random House, 1992. Questions, facts, care, recipes, how to plant seeds.

Handelsman, Judith F. *Garden from Garbage, How to Grow Indoor Plants from Recycled Kitchen Scraps*. R & S Books, 1989.

Oechsli, Helen and Kelly. *In My Garden: A Children's Gardening Book*. New York: MacMillin Publishers Company, 1985. "Solid, step-by-step advice to the beginning gardener about 7 popular vegetables."

Selsan, Millicent E. and Jerome Wexler. *Eat the Fruit, Plant the Seed*. Brookfield, CT: The Millbrook Press, 1993. Step-by-step planting of different seeds that come from edible fruits, such as papaya and kiwi.

Wilkes, Angela. *My First Garden Book, A Life Size Guide to Growing Things at Home*. New York: Knopf Books, 1992. Potting, window plants, gardens, herbs, general care.

How to Encourage Your Child to Love Books

by Kevin Dohmen, M.Ed.

Reading remains the single most important skill necessary for success in school. Recent studies on reading indicate that more than 85 percent of students who read for 30 minutes or more each day become fluent readers.

One way to encourage your child to read is to make reading a family activity, by setting aside a daily family reading time. It is often difficult for kids to read if their friends in the neighborhood are outside playing, so arrange evening reading times and take advantage of rainy days.

Reserve 30 minutes or so each day (or every other day) when everyone in the family reads, preferably in the same room so that parents can provide a role model. Having everyone involved tends to make staying with the task much easier for the reluctant or non-fluent reader, and even for the too-busy mom or dad.

Be sure the entire family is consulted about convenient reading times. Try to accommodate everyone's needs. If a proposed time conflicts with someone's favorite TV show, discuss alternative times. If you have a VCR, you can tape a program that airs during reading time. You may want to point out that watching a taped program is more fun because you can fast-forward through the commercials. If you have younger children who want to read aloud with a parent or older sibling, they can read and be read to in another room during family reading time. As they become more adept at silent reading, they can begin reading with the rest of the family. If you can't be there to read with your child because of work or a school schedule that doesn't give you a lot of time together, then read a few pages a day into a tape recorder. When your youngster has listened to your reading, have him/her read several pages into the recorder for you to listen to while you are driving to work or relaxing at lunch. Everyone should be allowed to choose his or her own book, regardless of whether some reading seems too difficult or too easy; and no one should have to report on the reading unless he or she wishes to do so. No one need finish every (or any) book. This is pleasure reading, pure and simple.

Kevin D. Dohmen, M.Ed., is a learning consultant working with parents, teachers, children and adult learners on a wide array of subject areas and educational issues. He specializes in developing techniques to enable each learner to maximize his or her unique way of learning.

The key is to make reading fun and interesting. Make sure reading is not just an exercise. Also look for storytelling times at local libraries or children's museums, and check the newspaper for local events that would interest your child.

Children's Bookstores: More Than Just a Place to Buy Books

by Mindy Bailin

Make friends with the proprietor of a children's bookshop and a wealth of information and magic can unfold. Need a book for a special child about a special subject for a special occasion? Ask your children's librarian or head to the nearest children's bookstore.

Many children's bookstores plan special events, book signings, book character visits, book talks and bedtime stories for little ones who are invited to come in their pajamas. Most often these events are free and scheduled at convenient times for parents and children. Ask to be put on their mailing list or ask for a calendar of special events.

Often quality videos, as well as records and audio cassettes, are stocked in your local children's book nook. Inquire about special orders and gift wrapping. Make it a point to bring your child along when browsing for books. It's a habit that shouldn't be broken and may encourage a lifelong passion for reading.

 ## Resources

Children's Bookstores

A Likely Story
1555 King Street
Alexandria, VA 703-836-2498
Story times on Tuesdays for ages 18 months-3 years. Story time and craft project Saturdays for ages 2 and up; reservations, free.

Aladdin's Lamp
126 W. Broad Street
Falls Church, VA 703-241-8281
Story times on Wednesday and Saturday mornings at 11 a.m. Ages 2 1/2-6 years; reservations, free.

Bookoo Books for Kids
4923 Elm Street
Bethesda, MD
301-652-2794
Weekly story time Thursdays at 11 a.m.

Mindy Bailin is a public relations consultant, writer and teacher. For 10 years she produced and hosted a cable television talk show seen on 15 cable stations. She is the full-time mother of Michael, 8 and Jennifer, 6.

The Children's Book Shop
5730 Union Mill Road
Clifton, VA 703-818-7270
Call for story times.

Cheshire Cat Children's Books
5512 Connecticut Avenue NW
Washington, DC 20015 202-244-3965
Authors and illustrators discuss their books.

Color Book Gallery
8309 Richmond Highway
Alexandria, VA 703-360-0501
Multicultural children's books, games, toys, puzzles.

Cricket Book Shop
17800 New Hampshire Avenue
Ashton, MD 301-774-4242
Storytime during the summer months.

Fairy Godmother
319 7th Street SE
Washington, DC 202-547-5474
Periodic storytimes and workshops.

Politics and Prose
5015 Connecticut Avenue, NW
Washington, DC 20008 202-364-1919
Fiction reading group for girls in grades 6-7.

*See page 305 in the Shopping chapter for toy stores that have extensive book departments. Some also have book parties/events.

Children's Magazines

Fun for them to receive in the mail! Makes a great gift.

Boys Life
1325 W. Walnut Hill Ln.
P.O. Box 152079
Irving, TX 75015-2079
The Boy Scout magazine for Grade 3 and up.

Cobblestone
The History Magazine for Young People
7 School St.
Peterborough, NH 03458
History. Grade 4 and up.

The Cricket Magazine Group
Box 593
Mt. Morris, Il 61054-7666
Ladybug (ages 2-6), Spider (ages 6-9), Cricket (ages 9-14)
Children's literature—poems, stories and folktales.

Kid City—Publication of Children's Television Workshop
P.O. Box 53349
Boulder, CO 80322-3349
Science, nature and technology for ages 6-9.

Odyssey
7 School St.
Peterborough, NH 03458
Deep space articles for bright kids. Grade 5 and up.

Ranger Rick
8925 Leesburg Pike
Vienna, VA 22184-0001
Published by Natural Wildlife Federation
Adventures and stories dealing with wildlife. Ages 6-12.

Sesame Street
P.O. Box 52000
Boulder, CO 80322-2000
Ages 2-6.

Sports Illustrated for Kids
P.O. Box 830609
Birmingham, AL 35283-0604
800-992-0196
Sports. Grade 3 and up.

321-Contact
$E=MC$ Square
P.O. Box 51177
Boulder, CO 80322-1177
Magazine about science, nature and technology. Ages 8-12.

National Geographic World
P.O. Box 2174
Washington, DC 20013
Geography, the natural world. Ages 8-12.

Your Big Baby Guard
8925 Leesburg Pike
Vienna, VA 22184-0001
Published by National Wildlife Federation; nature for very young
children. Ages 3-5.

Zillians—Consumer Reports for Kids
P.O. Box 54861
Boulder, CA 00322-4861
Taste tests, pencil tests; teaches kids to manage money. Grades 5-6.

Special Friends: Pets and the Family

by Robert M. Mueller, D.V.M.

One of life's great joys can be the pleasure, companionship and fascination provided by a wonderful pet. There is nothing more idyllic than gazing at a child running through a field with his dog bounding alongside. Horse owners know the thrill of galloping along woodland trails and bird and fish lovers enjoy the elegant plumage and beautiful colors of their favorite species.

Often, as parents, we have embraced the animal kingdom and welcomed its members into our home—and not just dogs and cats. Other pets include certain kinds of rodents, lagomorphs (rabbits), and invertebrates (insects and hermit crabs).

However, there are some important things to consider before bringing a new family member home. As simple as this may sound, the single most important question to ask yourself is, "Do we really want a pet?" Impulse buying of a living creature usually ends in disappointment, if not disaster.

As a practicing veterinarian, I can assure you that if you carefully consider what you want to get out of owning a pet and compare the benefits to the family's capability to meet the animal's needs, you will have already gone a long way toward insuring a long and happy relationship.

Pets afford children the opportunity to nurture, observe, interact with, and feel responsible for, another living creature. And, due to the compressed lifespan of animals, the children will observe the natural order of life. They are witness to the stages of the helpless young, the exuberant adolescents, followed by contented middle age with the gradually developing infirmities of old age, and finally, the death of a beloved family member.

The ritual of providing food, water, grooming, exercise, quality time and love are very helpful in teaching children the discipline needed in daily life. Pet ownership will greatly enhance the child's self-worth, and the feeling he or she has toward other family members, as well as toward people in general. Even on a bad day, when a child turns to his beloved pet, he can draw and give comfort and solace through interaction with the animal.

This holds true for adults as well. After a grueling day on the job,

Robert Mueller, D.V.M., is a Washington native and owner of the Hampden Lane Veterinary Office in Bethesda, Maryland. He married a cat-loving client and together with their two children they share a home with various animal friends.

it is hard to beat a brisk walk with your dog or a game of cat and mouse with your favorite feline. For all family members, healthful, vigorous play with a pet surpasses the alternative of vegging out in front of the television set.

How to Choose the Right Pet

A trip to the library is great for starting your search. Try checking out a few books on dog care, cat care (i.e., general husbandry of the animal in which you are interested).

Next, comes a trip to a quality local pet store. (Leave your wallet at home so you are not tempted to buy.) At the store you can discuss more aspects of pet-care maintenance and get an overview of the choices available.

For those desiring to adopt a dog or cat, try going to some of the local dog and cat shows to talk to the owners concerning their breeds' pros and cons.

Of course, after "adopting" your pet, have its health checked by your local veterinarian. Most reputable breeders and pet stores will give you a grace period in which to have this done. Hopefully, this will spare you the heartbreak of adopting an unhealthy animal. Don't neglect animal shelters as places to find a pet.

In addition, try to schedule your adoption during a relatively quiet time for your family. Bringing a pet home just before vacations or Christmas tends not to be the best idea.

In most cases, when an animal is treated with kindness, respect, gentleness, and love, it will respond threefold. Indeed, the love engendered by a healthy, well-trained pet can truly enrich your life.

Questions to ask yourself

1. What are the ages and maturity of my children?
2. What are the work/activity schedules of the children and adults in the family?
3. Who really will be the primary caregiver? (90% of the time, that's Mom.)
4. How much upkeep does the pet require?
5. Who will take care of the pet during vacations?
6. Does any family member have any known medical problems with animals, such as allergies?
7. Is there any special training required for this particular animal?
8. Is the breed's temperament suited to our lifestyle?
9. Are we planning a home renovation or move soon?

Resources

Animal Shelters Where Pets are Waiting to be Adopted

District of Columbia Animal Shelter
1201 New York Avenue, NE
Washington, DC 20002
202-576-6664

Washington Animal Rescue League
71 Oglethorpe Street, NW
Washington, DC 20012
201-726-2556

Washington Humane Society
7319 Georgia Avenue, NW
Washington, DC 20012
202-333-4010

Montgomery County Animal Shelter
14645 Rothgeb Drive
Rockville, MD 20850
301-279-1823

Prince Georges County Animal Control
8311 D'Arcy Road
Forestville, MD 20747
301-499-8300

Animal Welfare League of Alexandria
910 South Payne Street
Alexandria, VA 22314
703-838-4775

Fairfax County Animal Shelter
4500 West Ox Road
Fairfax, VA 22030
703-830-1100

Teaching Your Children to Help Others

Volunteering with your Kids

by Karen Leggett

A parent named Miriam Stein once wrote poetically and profoundly of her "mother's paradox":

I bought my 9-year-old daughter roller skates today
They cost 20 dollars
Two miles away children eat cereal for dinner
It's all their family can afford....
    I want so desperately to teach my daughter
To be sensitive to inequities
To reach out to help others
    but I also want her to enjoy the roller skates.

Offering your child opportunities to volunteer in the community can be one way to resolve the paradox. Children can do everything from weeding a garden or baking cookies to becoming a short-term brother or sister to a foster child—the intensity of the volunteer experience is up to you. Children under 12 are often introduced to volunteering in groups—through Scouting, religious organizations and schools; there are a few places for individual volunteers under 12 and more and more chances for *family* volunteering.

Where to Volunteer

The simplest way to find a place whose needs mesh with your skills and schedule is to call places where you would like to serve as an adult and see what jobs they have that children could do. At shelters and soup kitchens, families are encouraged to serve a meal or join with another family to prepare a meal.

At Bailey's Crossroads Community Shelter, one family arrived for planting day with two older sons who ended up helping two shelter residents erect a basketball hoop. At Shepherd's Table in Silver Spring, one young boy discovered the variety of people who need free meals when he

---

Karen Leggett worked for many years as a news broadcaster and program host at WMAL radio. She is currently reviewing children's books on the Radio Zone and writing on educational/youth issues for The Washington Post, Washington Parent, ABC Radio and Voice of America. She lives in Rockville with her husband and two children.

was assigned to log in each new arrival. "You're welcome anytime!" said the chef, eager to encourage a burgeoning spirit of giving and caring.

Nature centers are perfect for family volunteering. Meadowside Nature Center in Montgomery County has bluebird boxes to be tended and all of the centers need help with gardening and trail maintenance. With Garden Resources in the District of Columbia, families can help clear vacant lots to be turned into urban gardens. The Potomac Appalachian Trail Club and the Anacostia Watershed Project organize regular weekend trash pickup sessions in Rock Creek Park and along Washington's "other river." The volunteer network organizes many of these environmental volunteer projects.

Families can dip into history with the Fairfax County Heritage Resources Branch where there is always an archaeological excavation in the summer. Winter volunteers can process artifacts in laboratories. The Claude Moore Colonial Farm in McLean is one of the few places where younger children can volunteer individually or as families. In fact, the youngest volunteer was only 7 weeks old. Director Anna Eberly says young people want to do something that "needs to be done, not something to make them go away. Don't underestimate what they can do!" They can weed or pick potatoes, shuck corn and act out costumed living history events.

One of the most intense volunteer experiences comes from Volunteer Emergency Families for Children. Families are thoroughly screened to take in abused, neglected or runaway children for 1 to 21 days—children who are waiting for a foster home or need a break from their own homes. One volunteer mother finds the younger "emergency children" become playmates for her only child; the older ones treat her the way they would like to have been treated—watching videos with her, braiding her hair.

Each county or city has a volunteer clearinghouse with lists of specific jobs and staff who know which ones are "family-friendly" volunteer opportunities. Doingsomething is a volunteer network that publishes a monthly newsletter of weekend and weekday projects, many accessible to families—like taking children on outings from Carpenter's Shelter for families in Alexandria, sorting food at the Capital Area Community Food Bank or distributing sandwiches to homeless people on the streets ("grate patrol"). Community Ministry branches in several jurisdictions know where the greatest needs are in particular communities. Interages in Montgomery County organizes projects to bring groups of children into contact with senior citizens.

Volunteering is a satisfying, growing experience to share with children. "Every volunteer is a leader by example," says a doingsomething newsletter. "We are engaged in the issues before us, discovering, learning, searching for answers, helping others."

Resources

Volunteer Clearinghouses

Alexandria Volunteer Bureau	703-836-2176
Arlington Volunteer Services	703-358-3222
Interages	301-949-3551
Montgomery Co. Volunteer & Community Service Center	301-217-4949
Prince George's Volunteer Action Center	301-779-9444
Prince William Volunteer Action	703-369-5292
Volunteer Center of Fairfax County	703-246-3460
Volunteer Clearinghouse of D.C. (D.C. Cares)	202-663-9207
Volunteer Emergency Families for Children	703-494-6956

Volunteer Opportunities for Children and Adults

American Hiking Society
P.O. Box 20160
Washington, DC 20041
Published directory of outdoor opportunities nationwide; $7.

Anacostia Water Shed Society
5110 Roanoke Place/Suite 101
College Park, MD 301-513-0316
Accept families as volunteers. Children may begin volunteering (with adult) at age 5.

Bread for the City
1606 7th St, NW
Washington, DC 202-332-0440
Accept children as volunteers beginning at age 12.

Capital Area Community Food Bank
645 Taylor Street, NE
Washington, DC 202-526-5344
Accept children as volunteers, aged 14 and up.

Chevy Chase Audubon Society
8940 Jones Mill Rd.
Chevy Chase, MD 301-652-9188.
Accept volunteers of any age with their families to come help with grounds work.

doingsomething
1500 Massachusetts Ave, NW
Washington, DC 202-393-5051

Fairfax County Heritage Resources Branch
Fairfax, Virginia 703-237-4881

Friends of the Earth
1025 Vermont Ave, NW/Third Floor
Washington, DC 202-783-7400
Accept families and children over 9 years as volunteers.

Food and Friends
P.O. Box 70601
Washington, DC 202-488-8278
Accept children of driving age, or any age child with parent to
volunteer to work in the kitchen.

Greater DC Cares
2300 N St. NW, Fifth Floor
Washington, DC 202-663-9207,
Families and children may volunteer, but children under 18 are not
covered by their insurance.

Nature Conservancy
Maryland Chapter, 301-656-8673
Children of any age with their families are welcome as volunteers for
weekend and day activities.

People-Animals-Love (PAL)
4832 MacArthur Blvd., NW
Washington, DC 202-337-0120
Bring animals to visit children in hospitals and animals to nursing
homes.

Potomac Appalachian Trail Club
703-242-0693
Accept children beginning age 14 to work on trails.

So Others Might Eat (SOME)
71 O St., NW
Washington, DC 202-797-8806
Accept families with children as volunteers.

Tree Action
Herndon, VA 703-471-4337
Like to have children as volunteers especially for gardening projects.
Usually the parents are involved with their children. Gardening,
restoration, tree-planning, in a localized area.

Wonderful Washington
Daytrips and Outings

by Kathryn McKay

It's not hard to plan an exciting day in and around Washington—one that raises the whole family's spirits and fills the children with a sense of wonder. It goes without saying that everyone in the family can enjoy an outing to explore our exceptional zoo or the city's vast array of outstanding museums.

But have you ever considered a trip to a local farm at berry-picking time or a behind-the-scenes look at a local firehouse or newspaper or the F.B.I.?

The next time your child says, "There's nothing to do," think about a change of scenery and take advantage of the area's nearly inexhaustible resources for the three E's: "Exhilarating, Educational Excursions."

Many books and resources providing detailed information on day trips and outings for children are included at the end of this article. Here are a few types of outings you won't want to miss!

Remember, wherever you choose to go on your excursions and outings, plan ahead and when you reach your destination, be as spontaneous as your children!

Fun at the Farm

Visiting a local farm offers your family the chance to leave the hustle and bustle of the city—or the frantic routine of your home—for more bucolic surroundings.

Maryland and Virginia showcase many kinds of farms. For a colonial experience, step back in time at the Claude Moore Farm at Turkey Run in McLean, Virginia, or the National Colonial Farm in Accokeek, Maryland. To see a certified organic farm at work, check out the Potomac Vegetable Farm in Vienna, Virginia.

If the farm you are visiting has animals, remind your children to move slowly near the animals and not to make any loud noises or sudden motions that will startle them. At several farms, with supervision, children may try daily farm chores like milking cows, collecting eggs warm from a nest or feeding ducks.

Kathryn McKay is a freelance writer and editor. She writes a column called In Our Own Backyard for Washington Parent. A Washington area resident since 1967, she lives in Bethesda, Maryland with her husband and two young sons.

Some farms offer "pick your own" patches that can cover anything from apples to pumpkins. The Washington area has an eight-month growing season that starts in May with strawberries and ends in December with Christmas trees.

Throughout the year, many farms have special activities including sheep sheering, hay rides and even scarecrow workshops. Call ahead to find out what's happening.

There's something for everyone down on the farm!

Behind the Scenes

In *The Wizard of Oz*, when Dorothy's dog Toto pulls back the curtain, Dorothy finds herself face to face with the Wizard of Oz and a behind-the-scene look at the Emerald City.

This type of insider's view of Washington can provide a whole new perspective on what makes our town tick. You can take your children behind the scenes to learn about everything from the F.B.I. to a small bakery in the suburbs.

If your preschooler is a future firefighter, there's sure to be a fire station nearby where they'll be glad to put your child in the driver's seat of a big fire truck. For children interested in other types of service work, post offices, gas stations and police headquarters will open their doors to children if you call ahead to make an appointment. And if your child is interested in the military service, the Pentagon and U.S. Naval Academy have tours.

For the future Connie Chung or Bob Woodward in your family, opportunities exist to learn how the news really lands on our doorstep and appears on television. Area television stations, newspapers and even radio stations will gear tours to students. Call your favorite newspaper or station for details. For most media tours, children must be at least 10 years old.

A behind-the-scene look at grocery stores and restaurants can help satisfy your child's hunger for more food facts. Many of these tours also include a bite to eat along with lots of information. Check with the store or restaurant's headquarters for more information.

For the future entrepreneur in your family, a trip to the Bureau of Printing and Engraving is in order. Here, your child will see millions of dollars being manufactured. Children who are environmentalists will be glad to know trees aren't cut down to make bills: they are made of cloth —75% cotton and 25% linen. The Bureau is a popular tourist attraction so call ahead and be prepared for a wait.

When it comes to planning a behind-the-scene outing, be creative and look to your kids for clues. Many businesses and organizations would be delighted to show off for your children.

American History Comes to Life

No matter what page in American history your child is studying, it can be brought to life here in the Washington area.

To begin, take your child to the Old Stone House in Georgetown, which is believed to be the oldest building in Washington. People dressed in colonial garb demonstrate homemaking tasks such as spinning and quilting. Along the way, you can learn about every decade of American history through the many memorials, museums and monuments that make Washington a top tourist attraction. You can end with a glimpse of the future as American history is made almost every day by our legislators and justices at the U.S. Capitol and the Supreme Court.

Outside of Washington, from Frederick, Maryland, to Fredericksburg, Virginia, there are dozens of places to explore Civil War attractions and battlefields run by the National Park Service.

Museums in the Maryland suburbs that interest children include the historic Surratt House in Clinton, the College Park Airport and Museum, the Clara Barton National Historic Site at Glen Echo, the Montpelier Mansion in Laurel, the Beall-Dawson House in Rockville and the National Capital Trolley Museum in Wheaton.

Virginia's varied attractions include the Boyhood Home of Robert E. Lee in Alexandria, Arlington National Cemetery, the Sully Historic Site in Chantilly, the Colvin Run Mill in Great Falls, Morven Park in Leesburg, Gunston Hall in Lorton and, of course, Mount Vernon, George Washington's home.

Living in Washington offers countless opportunities to gain a historical perspective of events past, present and future.

Off to the Zoo!

Washington is full of political animals. But if you really want some bipartisan fun with animals, head for the National Zoo.

It's free and it's fun! From antelopes to zebras, children of all ages are entertained at the National Zoo, where 5,000 animals from all over the world strut their stuff, fan their feathers or just doze in their dens.

One of the world's best zoos, the National Zoological Park, as it's officially named, has many outstanding features including a tropical rain forest exhibit, a reptile discovery center and a zoo lab with hands-on activities for children 3 to 7 years old. For in-depth information, you can take the Family or the Naturalist audio tours.

However you decide to tour the zoo, wear comfortable shoes and clothing. There are several miles of trails at the zoo, some of them quite steep. If your children become too tired to walk, baby carriers and single and double strollers can all be rented.

Be sure to keep an eye on your children. The biggest safety problem at the zoo is not from the animals; it's from children wandering off.

For a healthful and inexpensive meal, pack your own food. There are plenty of benches and picnic tables available. The zoo's food for people is fast-food style.

The zoo is located on 163 acres along Rock Creek Park, near the heart of Washington and on Metro's Red Line. There are entrances at Adams Mill Road, Beach Drive and the 3000 block of Connecticut Avenue, NW. You may find a parking space on the street and save yourself a few dollars. On beautiful weekend days and holidays, you may have to wait for a parking spot in the zoo lot.

To find out what's new at the zoo, stop at any information Kiosk for a list of the day's events. There's always lots to do at the zoo!

Tips for Successful Outings

* Call for information before you set out. Hours, directions and fees are subject to change.
* When you arrive, stop for maps and information.
* Review safety rules with your children.
* Bring a camera for lasting memories.

Questions to ask yourself

1. What type of trip is appropriate for the ages of my children?
2. When is the best time to take my children out for an excursion?
3. What do I need to pack? (sunscreen, camera, umbrella, diaper bag, etc.)
4. Are there any books that can help prepare my children for the trip?
5. Are there any steps that I can take to ensure my children's safety?

? Questions to ask when planning a trip

1. Hours of operation: Which times of day are the least crowded? Are there long lines?
2. Directions to the site—Is it near Metro? What are the parking options (availability and cost)?
3. Cost—How much does the site charge for admission, events, programs, etc.? Are there group discounts?
4. Food facts— Is there food available? If so, is it nutritious and how much does it cost? Is there a picnic area?
5. How much of the site is accessible by stroller or wheelchair?
6. Are there special programs that might interest my children?
7. Are there materials that can be sent in advance to prepare for the visit?
8. What are the safety rules for children?

Resources for Parents

Publications:

For great ideas for fun family outings, check the following back issues of *The Washington Post* Weekend section at your local library:

Amusement Parks Around Washington
Astronomy Programs for Kids
Bike Trails for Families
Children's Workshops on Recycling
Cross-Country Skiing
Fish Hatcheries
Hands-On Exhibits @ Air & Space Museum
Historic Prisons Around Washington
Hockey-Watching the Capitals Practice
Ice Skating
In-Line Skating
Nature Centers w/ Children's Programs
Newspaper Tours
Parks with Swamps Around Washington
Produce Pick-Me-Ups
Taking Children to Sporting Events
Wing-Watching at Area Airports

Other publications:

Washington Parent, "In Our Own Backyard" column

The Washington Post, Weekend Section (Fridays), "Saturday's Child" column

The Washington Times, Thursday Weekend section

Local recreation department newsletters. See page 329 for their telephone numbers.

Further Reading

Churchman, Deborah and Anne H. Oman. *Saturday's Child*. Arlington, Va.: Washington Book Trading Company, 1987.

Colbert, Judy. *Places to Go With Children in Washington, D.C.* San Francisco, Ca.: Chronicle Books, 1991.

Koralek, Derry. Editor 13th Edition, *Going Places With Children in Washington, D.C.* Rockville, Md.: Green Acres School, 1992.

Pescatore, John. *Family Bicycling in the Washington-Baltimore Area*. Washington, D.C.: EPM Publications, 1993.

Rubin, Beth. *Frommer's Family Travel Guide: Washington, D.C. With Kids*. New York, NY: Prentice Hall Travel, 1994.

Resources for children

Gulliver's Travels. *A Kid's Guide to Washington, D.C.* San Diego, Ca.: Harcourt Brace & Co., 1989.

Krementz, Jill. *A Visit to Washington, D.C.* New York, N.Y.: Scholastic, 1987.

Pedersen, Anne. *Kidding Around Washington, D.C., A Young Person's Guide.* Santa Fe, N.M.: John Muir Publications, 1993.

Weston, Marti and Florri Decell. *Washington! Adventures for Kids.* Vandemere Press, Arlington, Va.: 1990.

Appendix I

Area Private School Guide

⚚= Preschool   **(= extended day care**   **⚘ = Boys**   **K = Kindergarten**

N = Nursery   **🚌 = transportation**   **⚘ = Girls**   **🛏= boarding**

★ = Special Needs Program   See Page 202 for a guide to special needs schools.

District of Columbia

Aidan Montessori School - 130 S
3100 Military Road, NW
Washington, DC 20015
202-966-0360
Pre - 6th grade, ⚚ (

Annunciation School - 200 S
3825 Klingle Place, NW at
39th Street & Mass. Avenue
Washington, DC 20016
202-362-1408
K - 8th grade, (

Beauvoir, National Cathedral Elementary - 357 S
3500 Woodley Road, NW
Washington, DC 20016
202-537-6492
Pre - 3rd grade, ⚚ (

Blessed Sacrament - 367 S
5841 Chevy Chase Parkway, NW
Washington, DC 20015
202-966-6682
Pre - 3rd grade, ⚚ (

Capitol Hill Day School - 230 S
210 South Carolina Avenue, SE
Washington, DC 20003
202-966-6682
K - 8th grade, (

Children's Studio School - 300 S
8th & T Streets, NW
Washington, DC 20005
202-387-5880
Pre - 4th Grade, Arts only

Edmond Burke School - 254 S
2955 Upton Street, NW
Washington, DC 20008
202-362-8882
6th - 12th grade

Georgetown Day School - 575 S
4530 MacArthur Boulevard, NW
Washington, DC 20007
202-333-7727
Pre-K - 8th grade, ⚚ (

Holy Trinity School - 340 S
1325 36th Street, NW
Washington, DC 20007
Pre-K - 8th grade, ⚚ (

Jewish Primary Day School of Adas Israel Congregation - 85 S
2850 Quebec Street, NW
Washington, DC 20008
K - 6th grade, (

Lowell School - 199 S
4715 16th Street, NW
Washington, DC 20011
202-726-9153
Pre-K - 3rd grade, ⚚ (

Maret School - 513 S
3000 Cathedral Avenue, NW
Washington, DC 20008
202-939-8800
K - 12th grade, (

Mater Amoris Montessori School - 50 S
36th and Ellicott Streets, NW
Washington, DC 20008
202-362-3729
Pre - 6th grade, ⚚

National Cathedral School - 550 S
Mount St. Alban, NW
Washington, DC 20016
202-537-6374
4th - 12th grade, (🏃

National Presbyterian School - 214 S
4121 Nebraska Avenue, NW
Washington, DC 20016
202-537-7500
Pre - 6th grade, 🖐 (

Nativity Catholic Academy - 250 S
6008 Georgia Avenue, NW
Washington, DC 20011
202-723-3322
Pre - 8th grade, 🖐 (

Our Lady of Victory School - 125 S
4755 Whitehaven Parkway, NW
Washington, DC 20007
202-337-1421
Pre - 8th grade, 🖐 (

Parkmont School - 62 S
4842 16th Street at Blagdon St, NW
Washington, DC 20011
202-582-2966
6th - 12th grade

Rock Creek Int'l School - 130 S
2200 California Street, NW
Washington, DC 20008
202-387-0387
Pre - 4th grade, 🖐

St. Albans School - 560 S
Mount St. Alban, NW
Washington, DC 20016
202-537-6440
4th - 8th grade, 🏃

St. Ann's Academy - 231 S
4404 Wisconsin Avenue, NW
Washington, DC 20016
202-363-4460
Pre - 8th grade, 🖐 (

St. Anselm's Abbey School - 198 S
4501 S. Dakota Avenue, NE
Washington, DC 20017
202-269-2350
6th - 12 grade, 🚌

St. Patrick's Episcopal Day School - 415 S
4700 Whitehaven Parkway, NW
Washington, DC 20007
202-342-2805
Pre - 6th grade, 🖐 (

Sheridan School - 213 S
4400 36th Street, NW
Washington, DC 20008
202-362-7900
K - 8th grade, (

Sidwell Friends School - 1,053 S
3825 Wisconsin Avenue, NW
Washington, DC 20016
202-537-8100
5 - 12th grade, (🚌

Washington Int'l School - 250 S
2735 Olive Street
Washington, DC 20007
202-364-1825
Pre - 3rd grade, 🖐 (🚌

Washington Int'l School - 450 S
3100 Macombe Street, NW
Washington, DC 20008
202-364-1800
4th - 12th grade, 🚌

Maryland

Ascension Lutheran School - 195 S
7420 Ardmore Road
Landover Hills, MD 20784
301-577-0500
Pre - 8th grade, 🖐 (

Barnesville School - 170 S
21830 Peachtree Road
PO Box 404
Barnesville, MD 20838
301-972-0341
Pre - 7th grade, 🖐 (

The Barrie School - 488 S
13500 Layhill Road
Silver Spring, MD 20906
301-871-6200
Pre - 12th grade

Berwyn Baptist School - 140 S
4720 Cherokee Street
College Park, MD 20740
301-474-1561
Pre - 6th grade, ✋

Bullis School - 512 S
10601 Falls Road
Potomac, MD 20854
301-299-8500
3rd - 12th grade

Calvary Lutheran School - 123 S
9545 Georgia Avenue
Silver Spring, MD 20910
301-589-4001
K - 6th grade, (

Capitol Christian Academy - 469 S
620 Largo Road
Upper Marlboro, MD 20772
301-336-2200
K - 12th grade, (

Charles E. Smith Jewish Day School - 1,051 S
1901 E. Jefferson Street
Rockville, MD 20852
301-881-1400
K - 12th grade

Chesapeake Academy - 235 S
1185 Baltimore/Anapolis Boulevard
Arnold, MD 21012
410-647-9612
Pre - 5th grade, ✋ (

Christ Episcopal School - 192 S
109 S. Washington St.
Rockville, MD 20850
301-424-6550
Pre - 8th grade, ✋ (

Christian Family Montessori School - 75 S
3628 Rhode Island Avenue
Mt. Rainier, MD 20712
301-927-7122
Pre - 5th grade, ✋

Clinton Christian School - 617 S
6707 Woodyard Road
Upper Marlboro, MD 20772
301-599-9600
Pre - 12th grade, ✋ (

Concordia Lutheran School - 274 S
3799 East-West Highway
Hyattsville, MD 20782
301-927-0266
Pre - 8th grade, ✋ (

Connelly School of the Holy Child - 270 S
9029 Bradley Boulevard
Potomac, MD 20854
301-365-0955
6th - 12th grade, 🧍

Evergreen School - 110 S
10101 Connecticut Avenue
Kensington, MD 20895
301-942-5979
Pre - 6th grade, ✋ (

French International School -1,124 S
(Lycee Rochambeau)
9600 Forest Road
Bethesda, MD 20814
301-530-8260
Pre - 12th grade,
French baccalaureate, ✋ (🚐

German School of Washington, D.C. - 545 S
8617 Chateau Drive
Potomac, MD 20854
301-365-4400
Pre - 13th grade, German required to enter

Gibson Island Country School -106 S
5191 Mountain Road
Pasadena, MD 21122
410-255-5370
Pre - 5th grade, ✋ (

Glenelg Country School - 415 S
5191 Mountain Road
Glenelg, MD 21737
410-531-5880
Pre - 12th grade, (🚐

Grace Brethren Christian School - 640 S
6502 Surratts Road
Clinton, MD 20735
301-868-1600
Pre - 12th grade, ✋

Grace Episcopal Day School - 246 S
9411 Connecticut Avenue
Kensington, MD 20895
301-949-5860
1st - 6th grade, (

Green Acres School - 307 S
11701 Danville Drive
Rockville, MD 20852
301-881-4100
Pre - 8th grade, ✋

Harbor School - 160 S
7701 Bradley Boulevard
Bethesda, MD 20817
301-365-1100
Pre - 2nd grade, ✋ (

Hebrew Academy of Greater Washington - 640 S
2020 Linden Lane
Silver Spring, MD 20910
301-587-4100
Pre - 12th grade, ✋ 🚌

Hebrew Day Institute - 200 S
11710 Hunters Lane
Rockville, MD 20852
301-984-2111
Pre - 6th grade, ✋ (

Hebrew Day School of Mont. Co. - 100 S
1401 Arcola Avenue
Silver Spring, MD 20902
301-649-5400
K - 6th grade, (

Heights School - 260 S
10400 Seven Locks Road
Potomac, MD 20854
301-365-4300
3rd-12th grade, 🧍 🚌

Hellenic American Academy - 85 S
10701 S. Glen Road
Potomac, MD 20854
301-299-1566
Pre - 5th grade, Greek ✋ (

Henson Valley Montessori Day School - 65 S
7007 Allentown Road
Temple Hills, MD 20748
301-449-4442
Pre - 6th grade, ✋ (

Holton-Arms School - 663 S
7303 River Road
Bethesda, MD 20817
301-365-5300
3rd - 12th grade, 🧍 (🚌

Holy Cross Elementary School - 45 S
4900 Strathmore Avenue
Garrett Park, MD 20896
301-949-0053
K - 8th grade

Holy Redeemer School - 350 S
9715 Summit Avenue
Kensington, MD 20895
301-942-3701
K - 8th grade, (

Holy Trinity Episcopal Day School - 285 S
13106 Annapolis Road
Bowie, MD 20720
301-262-5355
K - 8th grade, (

Indian Creek School - 421 S
Evergreen Road
Crownsville, MD 21032
202-621-7167
Pre - 8th grade, ✋ (

John Nevins Andrews School - 340 S
117 Elm Avenue
Takoma Park, MD 20912
301-270-1400
Pre - 8th grade, ✋ (🚌

Julia Brown Montessori School - 110 S
1300 Milestone Drive
Silver Spring, MD 20904
301-622-7808
Pre - 3rd grade, ✋ (

Julia Brown Montessori School - 110 S
9450 Madison Avenue
Laurel, MD 20707
301-498-0604
Pre - 3rd grade, ✋ (

Landon School - 620 S
6101 Wilson Lane
Bethesda, MD 20817
301-320-3200
3rd - 12th grade, 🧍

Little Flower School - 260 S
5601 Massachusetts Avenue
Bethesda, MD 20816
301-320-3273
Pre - 8th grade, ✋

Lone Oak Montessori School - 110 S
7108 Bradley Boulevard
Bethesda, MD 20817
301-469-4888
Pre - 4th grade, ✋ (

Maharishi School of the Age of Enlightenment - 60 S
12210 Georgia Avenue
Wheaton, MD 20902
301-949-8530
Pre - 6th grade, ✋ (

Manor Montessori School - 182 S
10500 Oaklyn Drive
Potomac, MD 20854
301-299-7400
Pre - 3rd grade, ✋ (

Manor Montessori School -
11200 Old Georgetown Road
Rockville, MD 20852
301-299-7400
Pre - 3rd grade, ✋ (

Mater Amoris Montessori School - 125 S
18501 Mink Hollow Road
Ashton, MD 20861
301-774-7468
Pre - 6th grade, ✋

Mater Dei School - 223 S
9600 Seven Locks Road
Bethesda, MD 20817
301-365-2700
1st - 8th grade, 🏃

McLean School of Maryland - 330 S
Lochinver Lane
Potomac, MD 20854
301-299-8277
K - 9th grade, mainstream program;
specialized program for children
with a minimal learning disability,
★ 🚌

Montessori Children's House - 160 S
5004 Randon Stone Lane
Bowie, MD 20715
301-262-3566
Pre - 8th grade, ✋ (

New City Montessori - 60 S
3120 Nicholson Street
Hyattsville, MD 20782
301-559-8488
Pre - 12th grade, ✋ (

Newport School - 280 S
11311 Newport Mill Road
Kensington, MD 20895
301-942-4550
Pre - 12th grade, ✋ (

Norwood School - 325 S
8821 River Road
Bethesda, MD 20817
301-365-2595
K - 6th grade, (

Oneness Family School - 52 S
6701 Wisconsin Avenue
Chevy Chase, MD 20815
301-652-7751
3rd - 6th grade, (🚌

Our Lady of Lourdes School - 165 S
7500 Pearl Street
Bethesda, MD 20814
301-654-5376
K - 8th grade, (

Paint Branch Montessori School - 105 S
3215 Powder Mill Road
Adelphi, MD 20783
301-937-2244
Pre - 6th grade, ✋ (

Primary Day School - 175 S
7300 River Road
Bethesda, MD 20817
301-365-4355
Pre - 2nd grade, ✋

Queen Anne School - 240 S
14111 Oak Grove Road
Upper Marlboro, MD 20772
301-249-5000
6th - 12th grade, (🚌

Riverdale Baptist School - 808 S
1133 Largo Road
Upper Marlboro, MD 20772
301-249-7000
K - 12th grade,

**St. Andrew's Elementary School -
125 S**
4 Wallace Manor Road
Edgewater, MD 21037
410-266-0952
3rd - 5th grade,

**St. Andrew's Episcopal School -
360 S**
8935 Bradmoor Drive
Bethesda, MD 20817
301-530-4900
6th - 12th grade,

St. Bartholomew's School - 223 S
6900 River Road
Bethesda, MD 20817
301-229-5586
K - 8th grade,

St. Camillus School - 280 S
1500 St. Camillus Drive
Silver Spring, MD 20903
301-434-2344
K - 8th grade,

St. Catherine Laboure School - 506 S
11811 Claridge Road
Wheaton, MD
301-946-1717
Pre - 8th grade,

St. Elizabeth School - 400 S
917 Montrose Road
Rockville, MD 20852
301-881-1824
K - 8th grade

**St. Francis Episcopal Day School -
209 S**
10033 River Road
Potomac, MD 20854
301-365-2641
Pre - 3rd grade,

St. John's Episcopal School - 158 S
3427 Olney-Laytonsville Road
Olney, MD 20832
301-774-6804
K - 8th grade,

St. Mark's School - 525 S
7501 Adelphi Road
Hyattsville, MD 20783
301-442-7440
Pre - 8th grade

St. Peter's Catholic School - 300 S
2900 Sandy Spring Road
Olney, MD 20832
301-774-9112
K - 8th grade,

Sandy Spring Friends School - 400 S
16923 Norwood Road
Sandy Spring, MD 20860
301-774-7455
PreK - 12th grade,

Severn School - 502 S
201 Water Street
Severna Park, MD 21146
410-647-7700
6th - 12th grade,

Sidwell Friends Lower School - 280 S
5100 Edgemoor Lane
Bethesda, MD 20814
301-656-4081
Pre - 4th grade,

Sligo Adventist School - 381 S
8300 Carroll Avenue
Takoma Park, MD 20912
301-434-1417
Pre - 8th grade,

Spring Bilingual Montessori Academy - 60 S
2010 Linden Lane
Silver Spring, MD 20910
301-587-3511
Pre - 1st grade, Italian, French, &
Spanish,

**Stone Ridge School of the Sacred
Heart - 630 S**
9101 Rockville Pike
Bethesda, MD 20814
301-657-4322
Coed Pre-K, 1st-12th grade,

Thorton Friends School - 80 S
13925 New Hampshire Avenue and
11612 New Hampshire Avenue
Silver Spring, MD 20904
301-384-0320
6th - 12th grade, for intelligent
underachievers, ★

Trinity School - 382 S
4985 Ilchester Road
Ellicott City, MD 21041
410-744-1524
K - 8th grade, (🚌

Village Montessori School - 150 S
20301 Fulks Farm Road
Gaithersburg, MD 20879
301-977-5766
Pre- 3rd grade, ✋ (

Washington Christian School - 285 S
1820 Franwall Avenue
Silver Spring, MD 20902
301-649-1070
Pre - 8th grade, ✋ (

Washington Episcopal School - 245 S
5161 River Road
Bethesda, MD 20816
301-652-7878
Pre - 6th grade, (🚌

Washington Waldorf School - 317 S
4800 Sangamore Road
Bethesda, MD 20816
301-229-6107
Principles of Rudolf Steiner,
Pre - 12th grade, ✋

Woods Academy - 225 S
6801 Greentree Road
Bethesda, MD 20817
301-365-3080
Pre (Montessori) - 8th grade,
✋ (🚌

Virginia

**Alexandria Country Day School -
225 S**
2400 Russell Road
Alexandria, VA 22301
703-548-4804
K - 8th grade, (

Aquinas Montessori School - 175 S
8334 Mt. Vernon Highway
Alexandria, VA 22309
703-780-8484
Pre - 6th Grade, ✋ 🚌

**Blessed Sacrament Grade School -
364 S**
1417 W. Braddock Road
Alexandria, VA 22302
703-998-4170
Pre - 8th grade, ✋

Brooksfield School - 90 S
1830 Kirby Road
McLean, VA 22101
703-356-5437
Pre - 2nd grade, ✋

Browne Academy - 260 S
5917 Telegraph Road
Alexandria, VA 22310
703-960-3000
Pre - 8th grade, ✋ (

**Burgundy Farm Country Day School
- 260 S**
3700 Burgundy Road
Alexandria, VA 22303
703-960-3431
Pre - 8th grade, ✋ (🚌

Cardinal Montessori School - 50 S
1424 G Street
Woodbridge, VVA 22191
703-491-3810
Pre - 3rd grade, ✋ (

**Cloverlawn Academy International -
50 S**
3455 N, Glebe Road
Arlington, VA 22207
703-538-4022
Pre - 7th grade, ✋ (

**Congressional Schools of Virginia -
375 S**
3229 Sleepy Hollow Road
Falls Church, VA 22042
703-533-9711
N - 8th grade, ✋ (🚌

Corpus Christi Elementary School - 405 S
3301 Glen Carlyl Road
Falls Church, VA 22041
703-820-7450
1st - 8th grade,

Edlin School - 60 S
10922 Vale Road
Oakton, VA 22124
703-758-1855
K - 8th grade, p.m. sports program,

Embassy School - 50 S
1701 N. Bryan Street
Arlington, VA 22201
703-525-7728
Pre - 3rd grade,

Fairfax Baptist Temple Academy - 260 S
9524 Braddock Road
Fairfax, VA 22032
703-323-8100
Pre - 12th grade

Fairfax Brewster School - 200 S
5860 Glen Forest Drive
Baileys Crossroads, VA 22041
703-820-2680
Pre - 6th grade,

Gesher Jewish Day School - 137 S
8900 Little River Turnpike
Fairfax, VA 22031
703-978-9789
K - 6th grade,

Grace Episcopal School - 95 S
3601 Russell Road
Alexandria, VA 22305
703-549-5067
Pre - 5th grade,

Grasshopper Green/Kenwood Schools - 180 S
4955 Sunset Lane
Annandale, VA 22003
703-256-4711
Pre - 6th grade,

Green Hedges School - 180 S
415 Windover Avenue
Vienna, VA 22180
703-938-8323
Pre - 8th grade,

Highland School - 230 S
597 Broadview Avenue
Warrenton, VA 22186
1-703-347-1221
Pre - 8th grade,

Hill School - 195 S
Box 65
Middleburg, VA 22117
703-687-5897
K - 8th grade

Immanuel Lutheran School - 100 S
109 Bellair Road
Alexandria, VA 22301
703-549-7323
K - 6th grade,

Juniper Lane School - 45 S
3106 Juniper Lane
Falls Church, VA 22044
703-533-8890
N - 3rd grade,

Langley School - 450 S
1411 Balls Hill Road
McLean, VA 22101
703-356-1920
Pre - 8th grade,

Leesburg Christian School - 160 S
Route 1, Box 252B
Leesburg, VA 22075
703-777-4220
Pre - 12th grade,

Loudon County Day School - 170 S
237 Fairview Street, NW
Leesburg, VA 22075
703-777-3841
K - 8th grade,

Montessori School of Alexandria - 100 S
6300 Florence Lane
Alexandria, VA 22310
703-960-3498
Pre - 6th grade,

Montessori School of Holmes Run - 75 S
3527 Gallows Road
Falls Church, VA 22042
703-573-4652
Pre - 6th grade,

Montessori School of McLean - 165 S
1711 Kirby Road
Mclean, VA 22101
703-790-1049
Pre - 6th grade,

Montessori School of No. Virginia - 130 S
6820 Pacific Lane
Annandale, VA 22003
703-256-9577
Pre - 4th grade,

New School of No. Virginia - 65 S
9431 Silver King Court
Fairfax, VA 22031
703-691-3040
K - 12th grade

NysCare - 130 S
12345-G Sunrise Valley Drive
Reston, VA 22091
703-476-6795
Pre - 6th grade,

Nysmith School for the Gifted - 400 S
13525 Dulles Technology Drive
Herndon, VA 22071
703-713-3332
Pre - 7th grade,

Oakwood School - 100 S
7210 Braddock Road
Annandale, VA 22003
703-941-5788
K - 9th grade; specializes in children
unable to meet their potential.

Our Savior Lutheran School - 150 S
825 S. Taylor Street
Arlington, VA 22204
703-892-4846
K - 8th grade,

Pinecrest School - 90 S
4015 Annandale Road
Annandale, VA 22003
703-354-3446
Pre - 4th grade,

Potomac School - 876 S
1301 Potomac School Road
McLean, VA 22101
703-356-4101
Pre - 12th grade,

Queen of Apostles School - 300 S
4409 Sano Street
Alexandria, VA 22312
703-354-0714
K - 8th grade,

Randolph-Macon Academy - 418 S
201 W. 3rd Street
Front Royal, VA 22630
703-636-5200
6th - 12th grade

Sacred Heart Academy - 230 S
1713 Amherst Street
Winchester, VA 22601
703-662-7177
K - 8th grade,

St. Anne's-Belfield School - 823 S
2132 Ivy Road
Charlottesville, VA 22903
804-296-5106
Pre - 12th grade,

St. Bernadette School - 500 S
7602 Old Keene Mill Road
Springfield, VA 22152
K - 8th grade

St. Columba School - 270 S
7800 Livingston Road
Oxon Hill, MD 20745
K- 8th grade, parochial
school;program for children with
learning disabilities.

St. Leo's School - 650 S
3704 Old Lee Highway
Fairfax, VA 22030
703-273-1211
Pre - 8th grade, Seton Center for L.D.,

St. Luke Catholic School - 244 S
7005 Georgetown Pike
McLean, VA 22101
703-356-1508
K - 8th grade, Seton Center for L. D.,

St. Rita School - 210 S
3801 Russell Road
Alexandria, VA 22305
703-548-1888
K - 8th grade,

St. Stephan's & St. Agnes School
400 Fontaine Street
Alexandria, VA 22302
703-549-3542
K - 8th grade, ☾

Springfield Academy - 200 S
5236 Backlick Road
Springfield, VA 22151
703-256-3773
Infant - 3rd grade, ✋ ☾

Stuart Hall School - 105 S
P.O. Box 210
Staunton, VA 24402-0210
703-885-0356
6th - 8th grade

Talent House Private School - 330 S
9211 Arlington Blvd.
Fairfax, VA 22031
703-273-8000
6 weeks - 7th grade, ✋ ☾

Tara-Reston Christian School - 250 S
10742 Sunset Hills Road
Reston, VA 22090
703-438-8444
K - 8th grade

Town and Country School of Vienna - 150 S
9525 Leesburg Pike
Vienna, VA 22182
703-759-3000
Pre - 3rd grade, ☾

Vienna Junior Academy - 117 S
340 Courthouse Road
Vienna, VA 22180
703-938-6200
Pre - 10th grade, ✋

Wakefield School - 250 S
P.O. Box 869
Marshall, VA 22115
703-364-4111
Pre - 12th grade, ✋ 🛏

Westminster School - 280 S
3819 Gallows Road
Annandale, VA 22003
703-256-3620
K - 8th grade

Schools Offering Day and Boarding Programs

Maryland

Garrison Forest School - 502 S
300 Garrison Forest Road
Owings Mills, MD 21117
410-363-1500
1st-12th grade

McDonogh School - 180 S
8600 McDonogh Road
Pikesville, MD 21117
410-363-0600
K - 12th grade, 9th - 12th grade,
🛏

Sandy Spring Friends School - 400 S
16923 Norwood Road
Sandy Spring, MD 20860
301-774-7455
Pre - 12th grade, ✋ ☾ 🛏

Virginia

Flint Hill School - 561 S
10409 Academic Drive
Oakton, VA 22124
703-242-0705
Pre - 12th grade, ✋ ☾ 🛏

Fork Union Military academy - 650 S
P.O. Box 278
Fork Union, VA 23055
804-842-3212
6th - 12th grade, 🧍 🛏

St. Catherine's School - 750 S
6001 Grove Avenue
Richmond, VA 23226
804-288-2804
Pre - 12th grade,
for 9-12th grade, 🛏
K-7th grade, ☾ 🧍

Special Needs

See page 202 for a list of schools with programs for children with special needs.

Appendix II

Metropolitan Area Summer Camp Guide

The following is a list of local day and sleepaway camps, summer programs, lessons and workshops. Many are very popular and fill quickly. Call early for specific dates and fees. (Those with 🛏 offer sleepaway programs. Those with ★ offer programs for children with special needs as well as programs for the general public.)

District of Columbia

Aidan Artsummer DC 202-966-0360; Ages 3-10. Art, Theater, Music and Dance.

American Juku August Morning Math Camp DC 202-362-2657; Grades 1-7. Accelerated math program.

American Soccer Camp at American University DC 202-885-3014. Ages 6-18. Coed, Ages 6-16, skills camp. Boys, Ages, 12-18, advanced camp.

Beauvoir Summer Programs DC 202-537-6482; Ages 3-10. General, Academic, CIT, Sports, Computers in Outdoor life, Spanish through art and Junior camp. Extended day.

Boy Scouts of America National Capital Area Council MD 301-530-9360; Grades 1-5 and up. Day camp for those who have completed grades 1-4. General, Science, Sailing, Aquatics, grades 5 and up.

Camp Keetov—Washington Hebrew Congregation DC & MD 301-279-7505 & 202-362-2517; Ages 2½-6. Outdoor play, Water play, Sports, Nature, Arts and crafts, Drama, Music and Special events.

Capitol Hill Arts Workshop DC 202-547-6839; Ages 4-12. Arts and recreation. Five 2-week sessions, each with a different arts theme.

Capitol Hill Day School DC 202-547-2244; Ages 4-14. General, Swimming and Field trips.

Capitol Hill Montessori DC 202-543-3727; Ages 4-9. General.

Chevy Chase Baptist Church Children's Center DC 202-966-3299; PreK. General. P/T programs for 2 and 3-year-olds.

Corcoran School/Gallery of Art DC 202-628-9484 & 202-628-3186; Ages 6-18. Studio art.

District of Columbia Jewish Community Center DC 202-775-1765; Ages 3-13. Science, Sports, Arts, Tennis, Daily swimming, Camp Adventure. Transportation.

Edmund Burke School DC 202-362-8882; Summer Studies Grades 6-12 and Sports Camps Grades 8-12.

Emerson Preparatory School DC 202-785-2877; Ages 14-18. 6-week summer session. Academic Classes. Opportunity to earn High School credits.

Friends of the National Zoo "Summer Safari" DC 202-673-4961; Entering K-Grade 7. Discover the wonder of animals in hands-on adventures for kids.

Fun Da Mentals DC 202-686-0151; Ages 8-18. Basketball, Soccer, Softball and Computers.

George Washington University Summer Sports Camps DC 202-994-7546; Ages 7-12. Four sessions.

Georgetown Montessori DC 202-337-8058; Ages 2-6. Art, Swimming, Music and French.

Georgetown University Summer Camps DC 202-687-2400. Boy's lacrosse, Boy's baseball, Football, Tennis, Girl's lacrosse, Girl's volleyball and Summer day camp.

Heat, Inc.-H. Edwards DC 202-885-3017 or 885-3000; Ages 6-17. Junior Tennis Camps/Lessons at the American University.

Joy of Motion Dance Center DC 202-387-0911; Ages 3-18. Creative movement, Jazz, Tap, Pre-ballet and Ballet.

Kingsbury Day School DC 202-232-1702; Ages 5-11. Morning academics and Afternoon camp.

The Learning Center DC 202-842-2790; Ages 3-12. Sports, Academic Enrichment, Arts and crafts.

Levine School of Music Summer Camp DC; 202-337-2227; Ages 3-12. Features Music, Dance and Stories from Latin America, Strings camp, ages 6-16. Two 3-week sessions.

Little Folks Summer Camp DC 202-333-6571 Ages 3-7. A recreational day camp combining Arts and crafts with lots of other Activities.

Lowell School Camp DC 202-726-9153; Ages 3-10. General.

Maret School DC 202-939-8848; Ages 3 years-Grade 12. Day camp, ages 3-8. Math, Humanities, Foreign language, Art, Study skills, P.E., Sports, grades 5-8. Math, Humanities, Foreign language, Photography, Study skills, grades 9-12. 🛌

Nation's Capital Girl Scout Council DC, MD, VA 202-337-4300; Ages 5-18. General. Two Residential camps in VA. Summer programs in all areas. 🛌

National Child Research Center (NCRC) DC; 202-363-8777; Ages 2½-6. General, Movement, Drama, Ceramics, Music, Arts and crafts. Six 1-week sessions.

National Presbyterian School Summer Camp DC 202-537-7500; Ages 3-11. General, Arts and crafts, Swimming, Sports, Creative dramatics, Computers and Science/Technology.

Rock Creek International School "Merry-Go-Round-The-World Summer Camp" DC 202-387-0387; Ages 3-10. Multicultural, Multilingual, Sports, Swimming, Music, Visual and Performing Arts and Overnight camping trip.

Rock Creek Park Horse Center DC 202-362-0117. Horseback riding.

St. Albans Summer Program DC 202-537-6450; Ages 7-18. Day Camp, Ages 7-12. General, Sports, CIT and Summer school, Ages 7-18.

St. Anselm's Abbey School DC 202-269-2350; "Abbey's Adventures." Entering Grades 5-8 and high school. Enrichment program, Day camp. Study skills, Princeton SAT review.

St. Columba's Summer Day Camp DC 202-363-4119; Ages 3-8. Play oriented.

St. Patrick's Episcopal Day School DC 202-342-2813; Ages 3-12. General, Swimming, Outdoor adventure, Sleep away camp. Extended hours. 🛌

School For Friends DC 202-328-7237; Ages 2-4. General, Arts and crafts, Swimming and Conflict resolution.

Sheridan School DC 202-895-0250, ext. 113; Creative Arts & Summer Adventure, ages 3-13, Day camp, One and 2-week sessions, Music, Drama, Dance, Puppetry, Canoeing, Swimming, Sports and Field trips. Shanandoah Discovery Camp, ages 8-13, Sleepaway camp, Six one-week sessions, Horseback riding, Rocketry, Soccer, Crafts, Canoeing, Field trips. Grades 6-8, Outdoor Living Skills Program. [=]

Sidwell Friends School DC 202-537-8133; Ages 3-18. Day camp, ages 3-10. Residential Camp on Eastern Shore, Ages 8-16. Summer studies, Ages 8-18. Arts, Drama, Basketball and Tennis. [=]

Smithsonian Associates Summer Camp DC 202-357-3030; Ages 4-13. Nature, Animals, Theater, Video, Magic, Mystery, Art, etc.

Summer Discovery Nature Camp DC 202-364-311; Ages 3-12. At Discovery Creek Children's Museum of Washington. Outdoor nature camp, Art projects, Science experiments and Live wildlife.

Theater Lab of Washington DC 202-265-3154; Ages 12-16. Voice, Movement, and Scene Study plus a Final Presentation. Taught by prominent members of Washington's professional theater community. 2 sessions, 4 weeks each.

TIC Summer Camp DC and VA 703-241 5542; Ages 7-16. Half-day Computer or Video, half-day Sports. Drama. Two campuses: Georgetown Visitation or Episcopal High School.

Washington International School DC 202-364-1827; Ages 3-18. Language, Sports, Arts and General activities.

YMCA of Metropolitan Washington DC, MD, VA 1-800-473-YMCA; Ages 3-16. 1 and 2-week sessions. Arts and crafts, Field trips, Music, Nature, Sports and Swimming. Specialty Camps: Dance, Drama, Gymnastics, Horseback riding, Sailing and more.

Yates Field House DC 202-687-2400. General day camp, Ages 5-11. Tennis camp, Ages 9-14. Half-day Tennis, Ages 6-8. Boys Lacrosse; Girls Lacrosse; Girls Volleyball; Boys Football; Boys Baseball, Ages 8-12. Pitching camp, Grades 9-12.

Maryland

Adventure Theatre MD 301-320-5331. Performance workshops for Grades 1-7, and 7 and up. Music, Theater games, Makeup, Technical skills and more.

All Saints' All Day Child Care Center MD 301-654-5339; Ages 5-9. Swimming, Field trips, Activity clubs, Camping skills, Free swim and Sports; Professional staff.

Audubon Naturalist Society MD 301-652-9188 x3006; Ages 4-12. Nature camp with outdoor explorations.

August About The Town MD 301-229-6798; Ages 5-12. A day camp on the move! Every day a new field trip to nearby museums, parks and roller rinks. Also, Swimming, Sports and Arts.

Bar T Ranch MD 301-948-3172; Ages 5-13. General, Academic. Also, Bar T Travel Camp: 4 1-week trips for Ages 11-15. 1 1-week trip for Ages 9-15. 3 1-week trips for Ages 11-17. Five locations. [=]

Barnsville School MD 301-972-0341; Ages 4-12. Camp Pow Wow, Riding, Swimming, Arts and crafts, Computer, Team games, Outdoor adventure, Theme camps: Colonial days, Zoo animals, Nature.

Barrie Day Camp MD 301-871-6200; Ages 3½ yrs-Grade 8. Montessori, General, Computer, Theater and Equestrian. Transportation and Extended day.

Battle Creek Cypress Swamp Sanctuary MD 410-535-5327; Ages 6-9 and 10-14. Nature-related themes. |🛏|

Bel Pre Children's Center MD 301-598-4640; Ages 3-12. Soccer, Swimming, Field trips, Arts and crafts. NAEYC accredited.

Beth Tikva MD 301-251-0455; Ages 2-5. General.

Bethesda Academy of Performing Arts DC, MD and VA 301-320-2550; Grades 1-12. Grades 1-6, Arts Express/Arts Express Plus. Grades 4-8, Summer Theatre Campus. Grades 9-12, Summer Repertory Theatre. Theater and Dance performance.

Bethesda Country Day Camp MD 301-530-6999; Ages 2½ to 8. General.

Bethesda-Lynbrook Summer Camp MD 301-656-4891; Ages 2-12. Sports, Swimming, Field trips, Music, Arts and crafts. NAEYC accredited.

Beverly Farms Summer Camp MD 301-299-6442; Ages 3-12. Soccer, Sports, Cooking, Computers, Arts and crafts, Field trips and Swimming. NAEYC accredited.

B'nai Shalom of Olney Summer Program MD 301-570-0699; Ages 2-5. Arts and crafts, Theme weeks, Drama, Puppet Shows, Music and Movement activity.

Boy Scouts of America National Capital Area Council MD 301-530-9360; Grades 1-5 and up. Day camp for those who have completed grades 1-4. General, Science, Sailing, Aquatics, grades 5 and up. |🛏|

Brooke Grove Children's Center MD 301-946-1213 & 301-570-4525; Ages 2-12. Soccer, Swimming, Swim instruction, Arts and crafts. NAEYC accredited.

Brookside Nature Center MD 301-946-9071; Ages 5-14. Nature, Environment, Ecology, Crafts, Field trips and more.

Bullis Boys Basketball Camp MD 301-299-0003 or 301-540-6166; Boys, Ages 6-16. Games, Fundamentals, Guest speakers, Contests, Tournaments and Giveaways.

Bullis School MD; Academic, Grades 3-11, 301-299-0003. Discovery day camp, Ages 5-12, 301-949-4642. Baseball/Softball, Ages 6-13, 301-299-0003. Soccer, Ages 6-16, 301-299-0003. Basketball, Ages 9-14, 301-299-0003. Tennis, Ages 5-18, 301-299-8000. Also, Beginner and Intermediate Lacrosse, 301-299-0003. Wrestling for beginners and advanced, 301-299-0003.

Butler School Summer Camp MD 301-977-6600; Ages 3-13. General, Equestrian, Fishing, Canoeing, Tennis and Art.

Camp CLC MD 301-871-6600; Ages 2-5. Day, General.

Camp Keetov—Washington Hebrew Congregation DC & MD 301-279-7505 & 202-362-2517; Ages 2½-6. Outdoor play, Water play, Sports, Nature, Arts and crafts, Drama, Music and Special events.

Camp Letts MD 301-261-4286; Ages 7-16. Overnight, YMCA. Sailing, Horsemanship, Waterskiing, and more. Emphasis on friendships and building self-esteem. |🛏|

Camp Moshava MD 800-454-2205 & 301-593-4944; Grades 4-10. Kibbutz/Zionist atmosphere, Israeli culture and Hebrew. Non-competitive. 11th grade Israel program. 12th grade junior camp. |🛏|

Camp Olympic MD 301-926-9281. Ages 3-14. General, Horseback Riding, Tennis, Swimming and Gymnastics. Also pre-school program.

Camp Outer Quest MD 301-469-2298; Ages 10-17. Rock climbing, Kayaking, Canoeing and Swimming. 3, and 9-week programs. Day trips in outdoor adventure.

Camp Potomac Woods MD 301-299-1566; Ages 3-12. Swimming, Horseback riding, Outdoor sports, Arts and crafts, Drama, Adventure and fun. Extended care. Preschool program. Full and half day options.

Camp Ruach (at Shaare Tefila) MD 301-681-8694; Ages 2-5. Two 3-week sessions. Summer fun in a loving environment.

Camp Tall Timbers MD 301-649-5577 or 1-800-944-0663; Ages 7-16. Residential. Located in the Blue Ridge Mountains. Swimming, Riding, Tennis and more. |▭|

Camp Techno-Kids VA & MD 301-718-6208; Ages 5-10. Science, Computer, Sports, Games, Art and more.

Camp Wabanna MD 301-262-3304; Ages 7-16. Christian. Aquatic activities.

Camp Waredaca MD 301-570-4191; Ages 7-15. Day camp. Horseback riding and Swimming.

Capitol Camps MD 301-468-2267; Grades 3-12. Judaic programming, Team sports, Performing arts, Water sports in lake and pool, Fine arts, Outdoor education and Ropes course. Entering Grade 11, CIT program. Grades 11 and 12, Summer in Israel. |▭|

Children Specialteas MD 301-320-2517; Girls, Ages 4-8. One week program. Etiquette, Craft, and Teaparties

Childway MD 301-384-5753, Ages 9 wks-toddler. 301-474-3355 and 301-937-7988; Ages 2-12. General.

Compuquest MD 301-384-ABCD; Ages 3½-grade 5. 3½-K, half days. Grades 1-6, "Weird Science and Summer Fun." Grades 2-5, "Simple Machinery Concepts with LEGO Dacta TM." Computer and non-computer activities. Indoor and outdoor activities. Theme: Animal Adventure.

Computertots & Computer Explorers MD 301-365-8687; Ages 3-11. Week-long morning computer camps at various Montgomery County sites.

Create Arts Camp in the City MD 301-652-ARTS; Ages 3-12. Movement, Music, Art, Drama, Stitchery, Stone carving, Photography and Video.

Crossway Camp for Peace MD 301-942-3247; Ages 5-12. Unique camp promoting Leadership skills, Conflict resolution, Creative thinking, Appreciation of cultural diversity, Community building, Peace studies and more. Swimming, Sports skills, Music, Drama, Creative arts and Field trips.

Early Childhood Center MD 301-424-8065; Ages 2-4. General.

Echo Hill Camp MD 410-348-5303; Ages 7-16. Sailing, Skiing, Windsurfing, Ropes course, Fishing, Crabbing, Sports, Crafts and more.

Evergreen Camp 95 MD 301-942-5979; Ages 2.3-12. General. |▭|

Farrell Montessori School MD 301-983-8181; Ages 18 Mo.-5 Years. General.

Feet First Summer Dance Camp MD 301-656-9076; Ages 6-16. 2-week summer sessions. Also Music Video camp.

Flower Hill Country Day MD 301-840-8448; "Summer Days USA". Ages 2-6. Arts, Crafts, Music, Indoor and outdoor play.

Forest Glen Children's Place MD 301-681-5225; Ages 2-5. Waldorf inspired program. Creative play experience, Outdoor exploration activities along Sligo Creek. Half or full day.

Franklin Summer Days Rockville, MD 301-279-2799; Ages 2-6. Montessori or traditional.

French International School MD 301-907-3265; Ages 4-12. General, Sports, Computers, Crafts, Cooking, Swimming and French classes. All actitivies conducted in French, no knowledge of French required.

Friendship Summer Camp MD 301-384-6914; Grades K-8. Christian program integrates Activities, Trips, Music and Sports.

FutureKids Computer Camps and Classes MD & VA. Ages 3-16. Bethesda, 301-718-4777. Rockville, 301-424-6168. Columbia, 410-997-1400. Gaithersburg, 301-924-1858. Potomac, 301-299-8775. McLean, 703-821-0847. Arlington, 703-534-4282. Annandale, 703-750-9820. Herndon, 703-707-0619. Woodbridge, 703-491-3122. Desktop Publishing, Simulation, Keyboarding, Animatin, DataBase Management, Mystery Puzzle, Robotics, Sports Fever, Computer Assisted Design, Cartoon, Dinosaur, Space Adventure, Megabyte Zoo and Music Makers. 1 and 2-week camps.

G Street Fabrics MD 301-231-8982 x226; Ages 8-19. Sewing Classes.

Garrett Park MD 301-946-6192; Ages 4-12. Outdoor program, Soccer, Arts and crafts, Sports, Computers and Swimming. NAEYC accredited.

Geneva Camp MD 301-340-7704; Ages 2-6. General, Arts and crafts, Field trips, Science and Creative movement.

Georgetown Hill Child Care Center MD 301-299-7360, 301-299-2350; Ages 2-8. Swimming, Sports, Ecology and the Arts. New Air-conditioned building.

Georgetown Preparatory School MD 301-493-5000; Ages 6-13. General, Tennis, Basketball, Touch football and other Sports.

Gifts Summer Camp Art Classes MD 301-365-7907; Ages 18 Mos.-4 Yrs. Four, 6, 8 or 12-week sessions. Outdoor play, Creative movement, Drama, Music, Arts and crafts and storytelling.

Nation's Capital Girl Scout Council DC, MD, VA 202-337-4300; Ages 5-18. General. Two Residential camps in VA. Summer programs in all areas. |=|

Glen Echo Park MD 301-492-6229. Call for information on children's art classes and camps.

Grace Episcopal Day School Summer Programs MD 301-585-3513, 301-949-5860; Ages 3-10. Special themes, Natural science, Environmental studes and Creative arts.

Green Acres Summer Day Camp MD 301-913-9569; Ages 4-12. General, Camping.

Hands On Science MD 301-881-1142; Ages 4-Grade 6. Science.

Harkaway Farm Riding School MD 301-972-8217; Ages 6-18. Horseback riding.

The Heights School MD 301-365-4300; Boys, Grades 3-8. Natural History Camp for Boys, Grades 3-5; Sports and Exploration Camp for Boys, Grades 6-8.

Holden Montessori MD 301-229-4024 or 202-265-0885; Ages Toddler-6. General.

Holton-Arms School Creative Summer MD 301-365-6003; Ages 6-13. General camp with an emphasis on the Arts. |🛏|

Holy Child Summer Camp "Express Yourself" MD 301-365-0955; Girls, Grades 8-9. Focus: Decision-making, Problem-solving, Cooperation and Self-expression.

Jewish Community Center of Greater Washington, Rockville MD 301-881-0100; Ages 3-teens. General, Tennis, Multi-arts, Performing arts, Travel for teens and CIT. Programs for children with disabilities. ★

Kehilat Shalom Summer Camp MD 301-869-7699 or 301-869-8887; Ages 2-5. Two 3-week sessions. Five days a week, Ages 3-5. Three days a week, Age 2.

Kensington/Forest Glen Children's Center MD 301-593-9641; Ages 2-12. 2-week theme camps. Field Trips, Soccer, Swimming, Arts and crafts. NAEYC accredited.

Kenwood Park Children's Center MD 301-229-6687; Ages 5-12 (must have completed kindergarten). Swimming, Field Trips and more.

Kid Ship Sailing School MD 410-267-0610; 1-800-638-9192; Ages 5-15. Sailing instruction for kids in 2, 3, 5, and 10 day courses. |🛏|

Kids Moving Company MD 301-656-1543; Ages 3-5. 10 1-week sessions. Movement, Music, Creative arts, Trampoline, Obstacle courses. Climbing and Balancing equipment.

La Petite Childcare MD 301-428-1709, 301-963-0986; Ages 2-12. General summer activities including Swimming and Field trips.

Landon Summer Program MD 301-657-0072; Ages 3-Adult. General, Sports, Arts, Day camps and Academics.

Little Acorns Summer Programs MD 301-983-4372; Ages 2-6. General, Arts and crafts, Water play, Games and Special events. Accredited program, Small camp, Creative arts program and Enrichment program.

The Manor Montessori School MD 301-299-7400; Ages 18 Mos.-8. Montessori Program with Swimming, Computer, Soccer, PE, Music, Art and Field trips.

Marvatots & Teens Gymnastics Summer Camp MD 301-942-0088; Ages 3½-5 and 6-15. Gymnatics.

Maryland College of Art and Design MD 301-649-4454; Ages 4-adult. Summer art camp.

Maryland-National Capital Park and Planning Commission/Prince George's County Department of Parks and Recreation MD Northern Area: 301-445-4500, TTY 301-445-4512. Central Area: 249-9220. Southern Area: 292-9006. Ages Preschool-17 years. General, Theater arts, Basketball, Teen trips, Arts, Sports, Computer, Swimming, Living history, Judo, Nature, Tennis, Dance, Drama. Field trips and Drill team.

Merrymount Equestrian Center MD 301-868-2109; Ages 8-16. Horseback riding.

Montgomery Child Care Association, Inc. MD; Infant-12 years. 8 locations. Bel Pre/Strathmore 301-598-4640. Bethesda 301-656-4891. Bethesda/River Road 301-229-0474. Garrett Park 301-946-6192. Olney 301-570-4525. Potomac 301-299-6442. Rockville 301-424-8952. Silver Spring 301-593-9641. General.

Montgomery County Department of Recreation MD; 301-217-6930; Ages 5-14. General, Therapeutic recreation, Sports, Special interests, Creative theater, Tennis, Science and Technology. ★

Montpelier Cultural Arts Center MD 301-953-1993; Ages 6-13. Art and wildlife camp and Visual arts classes.

Musical Theater Summer Day Camp MD 301-881-1139; Ages 7-17. Three stimulating sessions. Voice, Dance, Acting, Performance and Final showcase. Sponsored by Young Americans of Washington, Inc.

National Video Players (NVP) MD and VA 703-734-3280. Computer and video game clubs featuring Educational Games, Keyboarding, Computer literacy and Video Game Tournaments.

Norwood School MD 301-365-1211, Ages 4-12 and PreK. Art, Computers, Music, Science, Keyboarding, Math enrichment and Sports. PreK program. Adventure Program.

Olympic Gymnastics MD 301-680-2547; Ages 4 and up. Tumbling, Trampoline, Parachute, Arts and crafts.

Oneness Family Peace School MD 301-652-7751; Ages 3-12. Unique summer programs. Swimming, Field trips, Arts and crafts and Instrumental music.

Park Street Children's Center MD 301-424-8952; Ages 2 Months-12 years. Special events, Swimming, Arts and crafts and Field trips. NAEYC accredited.

Potomac Dance Center MD 301-299-7504; Ages 8-11 and Teens. Ballet, Jazz, Tap, Choreography, Dance history, Vocabulary and more.

Potomac Glen Riding School MD 301-299-8810; Ages 7 and up. Full day and extended day program. Beginning to advanced.

Potomac Horse Center MD 301-208-0200. Riding, Arts and crafts, Trail rides, Stable management and more.

Potomac Nursery School Summer Camp MD 301-340-8444; Ages 3-6. General. Two-week sessions. Part and full time.

Potomac Village School MD 301-299-5779 & 301-294-7551; Ages 2-6. Swimming, Basketball, T-ball, Outdoor sports, Music and Arts and crafts.

Prince George's Gymnastics Club MD 301-937-7583; Ages 6 and up. Gymnastics.

River Road Children's Center MD 301-229-0474; Ages 2-5. Field Trips, Arts and crafts, Special events, Swimming and Theme weeks. NAEYC accredited.

Riverdale Baptist School Camp MD 301-249-7000; Grades 1-6. General, Religious, Roller skating, Swimming, Bowling, Field trips and Gym activities.

The Rockville Day Care Association, Inc. MD 301-762-7420; Ages 2-12. Locations throughout Montgomery County. Theme weeks, Arts and crafts, Swimming, Sports, Cooking, Language arts, Nature study, Field trips, Music, Science and more.

The Rockville Nursery School/ Kindergarten MD 301-762-2678; Ages 2½-6. General.

Round House Theatre MD 301-933-9530; Grades 1-12. Grades 1-5, Drama, Visual arts and crafts, Storytelling and more. Summer Institute, Grades 6-12, beginning and advanced, actors and technicians; work with directors and designers from Washington DC Theatre Community.

Rustic Woods Summer Day Camp MD 301-262-3566; Ages 3-12. General, Swimming and Horseback riding.

Sandy Spring Friends School Summer Day Camp MD 301-774-7455; Ages K-16 years. General, Sports, Science, Nature, Crafts and Trips.

St. Camillus Child Care Center MD 301-439-1640; Ages 2-12. Weekly field trips, Arts and crafts, Swimming and General.

Science Encounters MD 301-718-6208; Ages 5-10. At the National Wildlife Federation (Vienna, VA). Science, Computers, Art, Sports and Games. Miles of nature trails.

Seven Locks Baptist Preschool MD 301-424-0039; Ages 3-4. Preschool.

Sportstar Camp MD 301-588-7767; Ages 5-13. Basketball, Soccer, Kickball, Softball, Tennis and more.

Spring Bilingual Montessori Academy MD 301-587-3511; Ages 2½-6 and up. Arts and crafts, Italian, French, Spanish, Swimming and Field trips.

The Summer Programs at the Washington Conservatory of Music MD 301-320-2770. Includes Private. Instruction on all instruments and Voice, Orchestra and Chamber groups, as well as the very popular Early Childhood Music classes.

Tartan Farms MD 301-972-8567; Children and Adults. Equestrian.

Tennistar Camps MD 301-588-7767; Ages 6-16. Tennis for Beginners, Intermediates and Advanced. (Also introducing Tots Program). Located at Stone Ridge School in Bethesda.

Timber Ridge Camps MD 90 miles west of DC 410-484-2233. Traditional camp with free choice scheduling in Circus, Horseback riding, Performing arts, Creative arts, Athletics and more. |☪|

Town & Country Day Camp (at the Newport School) MD 301-942-4550; Ages 3-16. General, Computer, Gymnastics, Science, Academics, Tennis, Drama, Chess and Railway speedway.

Washington Episcopal School MD 301-652-7878; Ages 4-15. Swimming, Sports, Overnight trips, Theatre videos, Theme programs, Computers, Sleep camps and residential camps. Extended day. Small groups with adult counselors. |☪|

Watkins Regional Park MD 301-249-9220 or 6202; Ages 6-12. General, Nature.

Westmoreland Children's Center MD 301-229-7161; Ages 3-11. 5 1-3-week sessions. Arts and crafts, Field trips, Theme projects, Outdoor exploration, Water play and more.

The Writer's Center MD 301-654-8664; Ages 8-17. Writing.

Young Discoverer MD 301-229-3466; Ages 21/2-31/2. Arts and crafts, Music and Creative movement.

YMCA of Metropolitan Washington DC, MD, VA 1-800-473-YMCA; Ages 3-16. 1 and 2-week sessions. Arts and crafts, Field trips, Music, Nature, Sports and Swimming. Specialty Camps: Dance, Drama, Gymnastics, Horseback riding, Sailing and more.

Virginia

Appalachia VA 301-585-8109; Girls ages 7-16. Overnight; Traditional program with 16 activities including many sports and arts. |☪|

Aquinis Montessori Summer Day Camp VA 703-780-8484 or 703-780-1001; Ages PreK-6. General, Swimming and Arts and crafts

Bayberry Riding Camp Spotsylvania, VA 703-972-2605; Girls Ages 7-15. Riding Camp: beginner through advanced. |≥|

Blue Fox Farm Equestrian Summer Camp VA 703-690-7922; Ages 9-adult. Day camp; Strictly English riding and Horsemanship. Two lessons per day, plus 3 hours of practical horse subjects.

Boy Scouts of America National Capital Area Council MD 301-530-9360; Grades 1-5 and up. Day camp for those who have completed grades 1-4. General, Science, Sailing, Aquatics, grades 5 and up. |≥|

Brooksfield School VA 703-356-5437; Ages 2½-4. Swimming, Tennis, Field trips, Pony rides, Nature studies, and Dance.

Browne Summer Camp VA 703-960-3000; Ages 3-15. General, Recreational, Academic and Specialty day camps. CIT.

Burgundy Farms Summer Day Camp VA 703-329-9495 and 703-960-3431; Ages 3-15. General, Swimming pool, Performing and Visual arts, Science/computers and Sports. Barnyard and pond on premises.

Burke Country Day School VA 703-239-0875; Ages 2-12. Weekly themes, Art, Nature, Water activities, Visitors and Field trips.

Camp Carysbrook VA 703-836-7548; Girls, Ages 6-16. Residential traditional camp. |≥|

Camp Discovery VA 1-800-222-2672; Girls, Ages 6-15. Residential with General and Equestrian programs. |≥|

Camp Friendship VA 1-800-873-3223; Ages 6-16. General with specialized equestrian program and teen challenge trips. |≥|

Camp Greenway at the Madeira School VA 703-556-8213; Ages 6-15. Swimming, Archery, Canoeing, Inner quest, Riding camps and CIT. Extended day.

Camp Hanover Mechanicsville, VA 804-779-2811; Ages 7-17. Adventures in Christian Community. Canoeing, Hiking and General programs. |≥|

Camp Horizons Harrisonburg, VA 1-800-729-9230; Ages 7-18. Traditional Camp 2 week sessions, Teen Adventures 1 and 2 week sessions. |≥|

Camp McLean VA; 703-790-0123; Ages 3-12 and Grades 4-9. Ages 3-12. Nature, Arts, Sports and Recreational swim. Grades 4-5 and 6-9 Summer theater workshops. ACA accredited.

Camp Rim Rock Winchester, VA 1-800-662-4650; Girls, Ages 7-17. General, strong in Horseback riding. |≥|

Camp Techno-Kids VA & MD 301-718-6208; Ages 5-10. Science, Computer, Sports, Games, Art and more.

Carousel Child Care Center VA 703-560-7676; Ages, Infant-8 yrs. General.

Children's Theater of Arlington VA 703-548-1154; Ages 5-14. Pantomime, Improvisation, Movement, Staging, Acting and Music. Final presentation for family.

Congressional Day Camp VA 703-533-9711; Ages 3-14. General. ACA accredited.

The Fairfax Academy of Early Learning VA 703-671-5555; Ages 2-6. General, Arts, Crafts, Swimming and Field trips.

Fairfax-Brewster School VA 703-820-2680; Ages 4-13. General, Sports, Swimming, Arts, Crafts, CIT and Junior counselor program.

Fairfax County Park Authority VA 703-246-5574; Ages 3-17. General, Drama, Basketball, Tennis, Sports, Outdoor nature, CIT, Excursion Camp and Preschooler camps.

Flint Hill School Creative Arts Camp & Sports Academy VA 703-281-1006; Sports Academy. Ages 6-17. Creative arts thematic camp sessions for ages 4-12. Academic Enrichment sessions for grades 4-12.

Four Star Tennis Academy VA 703-573-0890 or 800-334-7827. Overnight Adult and Junior Tennis Camps at UVA in Charlottesville; Junior Camp Ages 9-17. Junior tennis day camps. Ages 8-16 in MD and VA. |🛏|

FutureKids Computer Camps and Classes MD & VA. Ages 3-16. Bethesda, 301-718-4777. Rockville, 301-424-6168. Columbia, 410-997-1400. Gaithersburg, 301-924-1858. Potomac, 301-299-8775. McLean, 703-821-0847. Arlington, 703-534-4282. Annandale, 703-750-9820. Herndon, 703-707-0619. Woodbridge, 703-491-3122. Desktop Publishing, Simulation, Keyboarding, Animatin, DataBase Management, Mystery Puzzle, Robotics, Sports Fever, Computer Assisted Design, Cartoon, Dinosaur, Space Adventure, Megabyte Zoo and Music Makers. 1 and 2-week camps.

Nation's Capital Girl Scout Council DC, MD, VA 202-337-4300; Ages 5-18. General. Two Residential camps in VA. Summer programs in all areas.

Grasshopper Green and Kenwood Day Camp VA 703-256-4711; Grades K-6. General.

Greendale Summer Camp VA 703-971-0200; Ages 4-12. General.

Hank Harris Tennis Academy VA 703-379-6530, ext. 453 or 703-683-5183. Ages 10-18. Sessions weekly. Learn tennis skills in a positive atmosphere. Episcopal High School campus. |🛏|

Harmony Children's Center VA 703-471-9400; Ages 2½-12. General, Field trips, Swimming, Arts and crafts.

Langley School Summer Adventure VA 703-356-1920; Ages 3-17. General, Enrichment and SAT prep.

Massanutten Military Academy's Summer Cadet Program VA 703-459-2167; Coed, Completed Grades 6-11. Boarding and day. Academic credit, Leadership training, Swimming, Camping, Horseback riding, Sports and Field trips. |🛏|

Montessori School of Northern Virginia VA 703-256-9577; Ages 3-7. Montessori activities with a Science focus.

Mount Vernon Community Children's Theater VA 703-768-0703; Ages 5-16. Drama performance workshops. Three 2-week sessions. Two locations.

Nation's Capital Girl Scout Council DC, MD, VA 202-337-4300; Ages 5-18. General. Two Residential camps in VA. Summer programs in all areas. |🛏|

National Video Players (NVP) MD and VA 703-734-3280. Computer and video game clubs featuring Educational Games, Keyboarding, Computer literacy and Video Game Tournaments.

The New School of Northern Virginia VA 703-691-3040; Ages 7-17. Computer Camp. Video, Fine arts and Desktop publishing.

Northern Virginia Developmental Preschool VA 703-356-2833; Ages 2-6. Language enrichment, Drama, Cooking, Outdoor play, Music and Art.

Northern Virginia Gymnastics Academy Summer Camps VA 703-430-5434; Ages 3-18. Ages 3-5 and 6-13, Tumbling, Arts and crafts, Pit/Trampoline, Obstacle course. Ages 6-18, Tumbling, Pit/Trampoline, Gymnastics, Strength/Flexibility, Arts and crafts. Ages 8-18, Cheerleading camp.

Northern Virginia Regional Parks VA 703-528-5406. Programs for children and families.

The Pied Piper Theater Camp The Center for the Arts VA 703-330-ARTS; Ages 8-13; Apprentices, Ages 14-16. Acting, Dance, Music, Voice and Technical theater. Shakespeare workshop theater for teens. Several 2 and 3-week camps.

Potomac School Summer Programs VA 703-749-6317; Ages 3-17. General, Soccer, Summer theater, Outdoor science, Outdoor skills, Academic enrichment and Arts. August programs.

Prince William County Park Authority VA Day Camps; Ages 6-13; 703-792-7060. Outdoor Adventure Day Camp; Ages 11-15; 703-494-5288. Sports Challenge Day Camp; Ages 8-13; 703-791-2338. Youth Fitness Camp; Ages 10-15; 703-791-2338. Dance Camp; Ages 3-12; 703-361-7126. Tennis Camp; Ages 8-17; 703-361-7126. Racquetball Camp; Ages 8-13 ; 703-791-2338.

Ravel Dance Camp VA 703-759-1516; Ages 6-13. Dance and Musical performance at Great Falls.

Reston Montessori VA 703-481-2922; Ages 2½-10. General, Swimming and Field trips.

Soccer Academy VA 703-385-0150; Ages 5-14. Soccer. Day camp programs that provide instruction to children in the development of techniques, individual tactics and soccer tournaments. 🛏

The Springs Montessori VA 703-941-1411; Ages 2½-6. Event oriented summer camp.

St. Anne's-Belfield Summer Programs VA 804-296-5106; PreK-Grade 12. Summer camps, ages 3-12. Sports camps, Grades 3-12. Adventure camp, Grades 1-8. Theater camp, Ages 8-15. Summer school, Grades 9-12.

Summer Excitement Camps VA 703-636-2008; Ages 10-18. Computer game programming, SAT prep, Journalism and Politics, Band and Drum major, Martial arts, Singing and Golf. 🛏

Summer at St. Stephen's and St. Agnes VA 703-823-0609; Day camp in 2 week sessions; Swimming, Sports, Arts and Crafts, Science, Computer; Extended hours available; Sports camps in 1 week sessions; Baseball, Basketball, Lacrosse, Soccer, Tennis, and Softball. Academic summer classes.

Summer Theatre Workshop VA 703-790-0123; Grades 4-5 and 6-9. Voice, Movement and Acting with guest artists. Students rehearse and present a performance in Alden Theatre.

Sunset Hills Montessori Children's House VA 703-481-8484; Ages 2½-6. Montessori based camp with emphasis on Art and Nature.

The Talent House Private School/Camp VA 703-273-8000; Ages 6 Weeks-Grade 6. General.

TASC for Teens VA 800-296-TASC or 703-YES-TASC; Ages 11-17. Two-week Canadian Wilderness Adventure Camps to North Ontario: Canoe expedition, Fishing outpost camp and Fishing camp. 🛏

Tennis USA VA 703-379-4455; Ages 5-16. Tennis located on the campus of St. Stephen's and St. Agnes School. One and 2-week sessions.

TIC Summer Camp DC and VA 703-241-5542; Ages 7-16. Half-day Computer or Video, half-day Sports. Drama. Two campuses: Georgetown Visitation or Episcopal High School.

The Town and Country Day Camp of Vienna VA 703-79-3000; Ages 2½-11. Sports, Swimming, Arts and crafts and Field trips.

YMCA of Metropolitan Washington DC, MD, VA 1-800-473-YMCA; Ages 3-16. 1 and 2-week sessions. Arts and crafts, Field trips, Music, Nature, Sports and Swimming. Specialty Camps: Dance, Drama, Gymnastics, Horseback riding, Sailing and more.

★ Local Special Needs Camps

District of Columbia

Gallaudet University DC 202-651-5130; Ages 2-9. For both Hearing and Deaf; General. All day.

Jewels of Ann School Summer Camp DC 202-529-5446; Ages 2-12. General, Remedial.

Lab School of Washington DC 202-965-6600; Ages 5-18. Academic and recreational program for bright children with learning disabilities.

Maryland

Camp Greentop Catoctin Mountain National Park, MD 410-323-0500; Preteens-adults. Summer residential camp for children and adults with physical and multiple disabilities. ACA and MD Youth Camp certified. adults. 🛏

Camp Littlefoot MD 301-424-5200; Ages 2-6. Therapeutic speech/language and language enrichment programs. Treatment and Learning Center.

Capitol Camps MD 301-468-2207, Grades 3-12. Judaic programming, Team sports, Performing arts, Water sports in lake and pool, Fine arts, Outdoor education and Ropes course. Entering Grade 11, CIT program. Grades 11 and 12, Summer in Israel. 🛏

Chelsea School MD 301-585-1430; Grades 1-12. Learning disabled.

Frost Summer Program MD 301-933-3451; Ages 6-10 for children with mild-moderate learning disabilities including ADD. Sports, Field trips, Confidence course, Academics, Drama, Arts and crafts, Speech and language therapy, Computers and Special projects.

Jewish Community Center of Greater Washington, Rockville MD 301-881-0100; Ages 3-teens. General, Tennis, Multi-arts, Performing arts, Travel for teens and CIT. Programs for children with disabilities.

Montgomery County Public Schools Creative Communications MD 301-279-3163; Grades 3-8. Gifted, Underachieving or Handicapped students focus on improving their communications abilities and organizational skills through their strengths and interests.

Montgomery College Summer Youth Program MD 301-251-7914; Grades 8-11. Writing classes for Gifted and Talented. Jazz, Theater, College prep. Kids College, grades 5 and 6; 301-251-7939. Summer Challenge, grades 3-6 for gifted students. Summer Student Writing Institute, grades 3-8.

Montgomery County Therapeutic Recreation Summer Camps MD 301-217-6890, TDD: 217-6891; Ages 5-21. Special and Mainstream camps for youths with developmental delays, learning, emotional and physical disabilities. Teens with mental retardation and disabilities, ages 5-18. Creative afternoons, ages 5-21.

Prince George's Community College MD; 301-322-0875 or 322-0878. Creative Learning Experience Camp, Grades 3-6, for TAG-identified children. Keyboarding for the Microcomputer for TAG identified children. The Reading, Writing and Math Clinics, Grades 5-8, for diagnosis of areas of difficulty; A French is Fun course for Grades 3-6. Basketball camp for Grades 6-12. Daycare before and after sessions.

Reginald S. Lourie Center for Infants and Young Children MD 301-984-4444; Ages 3-5. Therapeutic Summer Camp.

Virginia

Camp Superkids VA 703-591-4134; For children with asthma, Ages 7-10. Children learn to control and manage their asthma while enjoying summer camp. American Lung Association of Northern Virginia.

Index